CORPORATE CRIME
UNDER ATTACK

The Fight to Criminalize Business Violence

Francis T. Cullen University of Cincinnati

Gray Cavender Arizona State University

William J. Maakestad Western Illinois University

Michael L. Benson University of Cincinnati

second edition

 LexisNexis®

 anderson publishing
A member of the LexisNexis Group

Corporate Crime Under Attack: The Fight to Criminalize Business Violence, Second Edition

Copyright © 1987, 2006

Matthew Bender & Company, Inc., a member of the LexisNexis Group

Phone 877-374-2919
Web Site www.lexisnexis.com/anderson/criminaljustice

Library of Congress Cataloging-in-Publication Data

Corporate crime under attack : the fight to criminalize business violence / by Francis T. Cullen . . . [et al.] -- 2nd ed.
    p. cm.
    Rev. ed. of: Corporate crime under attack : the Ford Pinto case and beyond / Francis T. Cullen, William J. Maakestad, Gray Cavender. © 1987.
    Includes bibliographical references and index.
    ISBN 1-59345-955-6 (softbound)
    1. Ford Motor Company--Trials, litigation, etc. 2. Trials (Homicide)--Indiana--Winamac. 3. Trials (Products liability)--Indiana--Winamac. 4. Criminal liability of juristic persons--United States.
    5. Corporations--Corrupt practices--United States. 6. Pinto automobile. I. Cullen, Francis T. II. Cullen, Francis T. Corporate crime under attack.

KF224.F67C85 2006
345.73'0268--dc22   2006025354

Cover design by Tin Box Studio, Inc.

EDITOR Ellen S. Boyne
ACQUISITIONS EDITOR Michael C. Braswell

For:

Paula J. Dubeck and Jordan Cullen

Catherine and Gray Cavender Jr.

Jean Maakestad Wolf

Shelley Paden and Christopher Michael Benson

Table of Contents

Preface

This is a book about corporate violence and the long and mounting effort to bring such harm within the reach of the criminal law. In the early part of the last century, businesses could, with virtual impunity, market defective products and diseased food, place workers in unsafe conditions, and spew pollutants into the air and water that jeopardized the health of the general public. This is no longer the case. Corporations that illegally endanger human life now must negotiate the surveillance of government regulators and risk civil suits from injured parties seeking financial compensation. Of more concern to us, they also may be charged with criminal offenses and their officials sent to prison.

Calling attention to corporate violence is not equivalent to taking an anti-business posture any more than studying street crime is an indictment of all individual citizens. Corporations are a key source of our nation's wealth, of our individual prosperity, and of our quality of life. But because these enterprises, large and small, touch our lives so intimately, they have the power to sicken, injure, and kill. Observers may debate the precise statistics, but the accumulating evidence suggests that the human toll exacted by illegal corporate practices is extensive. It was once believed that, although companies might commit enormously costly thefts—such as price-fixing, insider trading, and defrauding stockholders—"at least they do not hurt anyone." Given the known scope of corporate violence, this view is now considered a myth.

The fight to criminalize business violence is a tale that is at times complicated but always intriguing. How did corporations come to be subjected to criminal penalties when powerful interests were aligned to protect them from such threats? When business practices harm someone, can it be said that the corporate entity "intended" to victimize that person and therefore should be held criminally culpable? When no legal statutes exist that specifically outlaw "corporate violence," what strategies must be invented to prosecute wayward companies? When businesses are attacked through the criminal law, how do they resist being stigmatized as an "offender"? And as we move further into the twenty-first century, will the criminal law be an important, or merely a symbolic, weapon in the campaign to reduce corporate violence? Over the course of this book, we attempt to address these and related questions.

In exploring the criminalization of corporations, we use the landmark "Ford Pinto case" as our centerpiece. Just over 25 years ago, Ford Motor Company was prosecuted for reckless homicide after three teenage girls were burned to death when their Pinto was hit from behind and exploded into flames. A local prosecutor in Elkhart, Indiana, was persuaded that Ford's production of, and subsequent failure to repair, the Pinto's unsafe fuel system was responsible for the girls' deaths. To him, this event was not a tragic accident—as so often occurs on the nation's highways—but rather was foreseeable and could have been prevented had Ford moved quickly to recall and fix the girls' Pinto. Not to do so was to recklessly endanger human life. As a result, he took the pathbreaking step of indicting Ford and of bringing the company to trial.

This is a drama that, we trust, will capture each reader's imagination. But this case is important not simply for the interest it sparks and for the chance it offers to glimpse what it is like to try to prosecute a powerful business enterprise. It is also salient because it signifies a major turning point in the fight to criminalize business violence. Although Ford's prosecution in Elkhart was a unique decision made by a unique district attorney, we attempt to show that this case—the decision to conceptualize and charge Ford with being a "criminal"—would not have taken place even a few years before. The Ford Pinto case, in short, was very much a product of its times.

The first section of the book thus tries to depict how, over the course of the twentieth century, a series of legal and social transformations coalesced to make Ford's prosecution—its potential criminalization—possible. How did we reach the point at which a major American company could be charged with being a reckless killer and put on trial? How did the inconceivable become conceivable? Of course, beyond Ford's trial and the forces that created this prosecution, there is still the matter of what has transpired in the quarter century since the case concluded. Was Ford's prosecution merely an idiosyncratic "blip" of the historical screen, or was it a harbinger of things to come? Has the fight to criminalize corporations—especially when their illegal practices damage or take human lives—been stymied, or has this movement broadened and deepened? What can we expect in the years ahead? In the final part of the book, we take up these significant issues.

It is appropriate to disclose that one of the authors—William Maakestad—was an active participant in the Pinto trial. A lawyer and a (half) brother of the prosecutor (Michael Cosentino), Bill attended many sessions of the trial, lived with the prosecution team during the trial, and made substantive contributions to the prosecution's efforts. Admittedly, his involvement carries both a benefit and risk. We benefit by first-hand knowledge of public testimony in the trial and of events behind the scenes. We run the risk, however, that our in-depth knowledge of the prosecution's members and their experiences will inadvertently bias our account of the trial. Only the reader can judge whether we have committed this error, but we are reassured by the precautions we have taken to avoid presenting a slanted story.

The current enterprise is a revised version of the first edition of *Corporate Crime Under Attack*—an endeavor prompted in part by the Ford Pinto case's twenty-fifth anniversary and our corresponding recognition of the continuing significance of the issues this prosecution raised and of the important developments that have transpired in the intervening years. Beyond a new subtitle, the book has been substantially remodeled and new sections added. In Part I, we have re-ordered and revised the chapters so that the story we are telling about the expanding criminalization of corporations is faster-paced, up-to-date, and arranged in historical sequence. Part II, which contains the chapters on the Pinto case, remains largely unchanged, though it does carry a new epilogue. Part III, however, incorporates material that is almost completely new. It is here that we explore the aftermath of Ford's prosecution. Thus, we both assess the extent to which the criminal law has been used in recent times to fight business violence and illuminate the key issues that will inform future efforts to criminalize harmful corporate behavior.

Let us close with a few final comments. First, we are pleased to engage in the custom of thanking those who have helped us to complete this project. The good people at LexisNexis/Anderson Publishing Co.—especially Ellen Boyne and Mickey Braswell—must be singled out for their continued support and patience. We must also express our appreciation for the assistance given by our colleagues at our respective academic homes: the Division of Criminal Justice at the University of Cincinnati, the School of Justice and Social Inquiry at Arizona State University, and the Department of Management at Western Illinois University. To other individuals, too, we owe debts of all sorts—intellectual, emotional, and practical. The specific contributions are too numerous to describe in detail, but we trust they know what these contributions are and how much they have helped. We feel obliged, in the best sense of the word, to list their names: Kathleen Brickey, Michael Cosentino, Emily Froimsom, Nancy Jurik, Cheryl Lero, Russell Mokhiber, Pete Sorensen, Mark Stavsky, Brenda Vose, John Wozniak, the staff at the Macomb Public Library, and the Legal and Government Documents library staff at Western Illinois University. We further take note of the students in our respective courses who, over the years, have listened, posed probing questions, and asked to hear more about the Ford Pinto case.

Second, this volume has been a truly collaborative project, with each author contributing in distinct and essential ways. Much as a chair needs four legs to stand erect, this revised edition of *Corporate Crime Under Attack* would not have been possible without each author's supportive participation. Although we must list our names in some order on the title page, we trust this necessity will not obscure our equal partnership in the current enterprise.

Finally, we are pleased to dedicate this book to Paula J. Dubeck and Jordan Cullen; Catherine and Gray Cavender Jr.; Jean Maakestad Wolf; and Shelley Paden and Christopher Michael Benson.

Francis T. Cullen
University of Cincinnati

Gray Cavender
Arizona State University

William J. Maakestad
Western Illinois University

Michael L. Benson
University of Cincinnati

Part I

Corporate Crime Under Attack

1

The Criminalization of
Corporate Violence

On August 10, 1978, three teenage girls perished when a rear-end collision caused their Ford Pinto to burst into flames. As we know, this was not the first time a crash had tragically claimed the lives of a group of youths; nor were these girls the first victims of a Pinto-related fire. Yet the teenagers' deaths were unique in the legal reactions they evoked. Scarcely a month after the accident, an Indiana grand jury indicted Ford Motor Company on three charges of reckless homicide, and a local prosecutor embarked on a vigorous crusade to see that Ford paid for its alleged "crime." Indeed, in 1980, Ford's subsequent criminal trial earned national headlines and riveted the attention of all serious students of white-collar crime and corporate ethics. To this day, it remains a landmark legal case—one that has much to teach us about why attempts to criminalize business violence succeed and fail.

This book tells the story of the Ford Pinto trial. Making this story understandable, however, requires more than simply relaying the facts of the case. To be sure, the details are fascinating in themselves: the story's characters are strong-willed and interesting; there is a David-and-Goliath appeal in a county prosecutor taking on a major American corporation; and the plot is sufficiently dramatic and its ending sufficiently uncertain to make the case suspenseful.

Yet a simple account of the facts does not explain why a *criminal* prosecution of this sort was undertaken. Certainly, other options existed. The drivers—or fate—could have been blamed for the tragic accident. Why even consider holding a corporation culpable for the teenagers' deaths? And why contemplate labeling a major American corporation a reckless killer? To some extent, the answers lie in the unique history of the Pinto, which includes allegations that the subcompact had a defective fuel system (a gas tank placed dangerously close to the back bumper). But more is involved; indeed, the idea that a broader perspective is needed to address questions of this sort is the central premise of our book.

Thus, throughout our analysis, we attempt to demonstrate that the Ford Pinto trial is best understood as a sign of the times—the product of a general movement against white-collar and corporate illegality. We argue further that this attack on corporate crime—whether by prosecutors, politicians, or intellectuals—was itself a manifestation of broad legal, social-structural, and ideological changes that, starting in the 1960s, led up to, and then were energized by, the Pinto case.

In a broad way, Ford's prosecution represents a dividing line—some might prefer the imagery of a "tipping point"—between two eras in the social control of corporate misconduct. In the preceding time period, confidence in corporate America was high, awareness of "white-collar crime" was limited, district attorneys were reluctant to prosecute "respectable" members of the business community, and prison sentences were rare and, if imposed, short. The Pinto case, however, reflects an ongoing fundamental social and legal transformation. Today, Americans mistrust the ethics of corporations, the concept of "white-collar crime" is part of our lexicon, prosecutions of the rich and powerful bring reelection if not fame for district attorneys, and convicted corporate executives can count on spending many of their remaining adult years behind bars.

Much of this book is about these remarkable changes and how, as a nation, we moved from a time when corporations could victimize workers, consumers, and the public with near impunity to a time when executives can be given 20-year prison terms. That is, this tale is about the multiple factors that coalesced not simply to expand "control" over wayward business practices but, more significantly, to *expand the criminal culpability of corporations and their executives*. The Ford Pinto case is a conduit for exploring this issue.

But this case is about one more, important matter: *the criminalization of corporate violence*. Although the nature and extent of Ford's culpability are disputed by some, the corporation was prosecuted for *causing the deaths of three teenage girls*. We have grown accustomed to seeing executives hauled into courts for fixing prices, insider trading on the stock market, looting a company's treasury, and massive financial fraud. In this instance, however, a courageous prosecutor was making the argument that when corporations physically harm someone, they should be held accountable by the criminal law just like any other lawless predator. In this case, he was claiming that Ford Motor Company was a reckless killer—three times over—and should be treated as one by the criminal law.

This was—and for some observers remains—a controversial position. In the course of business operations, there are times when defective products harm consumers, when workers are hurt or perish on the job, and when the public is possibly sickened by various emissions. It is one thing to say that the corporation should be sued (in civil court) or subjected to stiffer controls (by regulatory agencies). It is quite another to say that the criminal justice system should be revved up to go after the corporations. Ford's prosecution was important because it reminded the nation that corporations whose decisions have violent consequences can, under certain circumstances, be prosecuted for these acts.

There was then—and is now—much debate over the point at which the line is crossed between a poor business decision and a crime of violence, and over how far the criminal law should expand to attack business practices that have violent consequences. The current project is meant to raise, and to provide an opportunity to reflect on, these critical considerations.

PLAN OF THE BOOK

This book tells three interrelated stories. In Part I, we relay the story of how corporations, which emerged into dominant economic enterprises, relied during their development on their political power and sympathetic jurists to escape control by the criminal courts. This immunity from prosecution, however, was fitfully eroded over the 1900s as the criminal culpability of wayward businesses was expanded. This attempt to criminalize corporations was particularly encouraged by a social movement against white-collar and corporate crime that gained force in the 1970s. These legal and social developments created the opportunity for pathbreaking corporate prosecutions to occur, including in particular Ford's trial on charges of reckless homicide.

Part II tells the story of the "Ford Pinto case." The chapters in this section illuminate what it is like to use the criminal law in an innovative way to attempt to criminalize a major corporation that seemingly has endless resources at its disposal in its efforts to mount a spirited defense. This prosecution was, as we have and will argue, a "sign of the times"; it would not have been possible at an earlier date. But it also is a criminal case that individuals made weighty decisions to initiate (and, on Ford's part, to defend) and that was fought in the unlikely battleground of Indiana. Although the trial has now passed its twenty-fifth anniversary, it is a legal and human drama that remains both compelling in its plot and contemporary in the lessons it has to teach us.

Finally, Part III tells the "rest of the story"—that is, what has occurred in the years following the Ford Pinto case. Was Ford's prosecution a rare occurrence or a harbinger of things to come? As intimated, the post-Pinto era has seen a spate of high-profile business scandals leading to criminal prosecutions, many of which have resulted in prison terms for corporate officials. But whether the criminal law is being used to its full potential to contribute to the control of corporate crime—including violence—is a more complicated matter. The advances in, obstacles inhibiting, and prospects for the criminalization of corporate crime and violence are investigated. This is a story that remains largely hidden from public view. We hope to make a contribution by pulling its various chapters together under one cover.

We use the remainder of Chapter 1 to construct an informational foundation for what is ahead. We pause to define key terms and then move on to show how white-collar and corporate crime were "discovered" in the United Stated. We briefly review the costs of corporate illegality. In particular, we show that beyond enormous financial losses, the dimensions of corporate violence are sufficiently disquieting to warrant public policy attention aimed at effecting its control. The discussion then explores the controversy of whether corporate decisions that have violent impacts are indeed "crimes." This discussion provides a context for examining competing claims about the "criminality" of Ford's production of the Pinto in which three teenage girls perished in a horrible, fiery crash.

CORPORATE CRIME AS WHITE-COLLAR CRIME: DEFINITIONAL ISSUES

In the 1940s, Edwin Sutherland introduced and popularized the concept of "white-collar crime."[1] This idea had the revolutionary effect of sensitizing subsequent students of crime and, ultimately, those outside academic circles to a range of behaviors that had previously escaped careful scrutiny: the illegal activities of the affluent.[2]

Although Sutherland's own research concentrated on the pervasiveness of the unlawful actions of corporations, he proposed a considerably more comprehensive definition of white-collar criminality, which encompassed all offenses "committed by a person of respectability and high social status in the course of his occupation."[3] The very breadth of this definition has been a source of the concept's vitality and ambiguity. The major advantage is that it prompted social commentators to investigate the full range of criminal offenses emanating from the occupations of the rich, including crimes by politicians, crimes by professionals such as physicians, tax cheating, crimes against businesses, such as employee theft or embezzlement, and crimes by corporate organizations themselves. On the other hand, while these various offenses share a common thread—if nothing else, they fall well outside traditional categories of street crime—important qualitative differences exist among them. Thus, the use of a catchall term like "white-collar crime" risks obscuring the differences among many of these offenses: for example, the act of a physician who defrauds the government by billing for false Medicaid payments and that of a multi-million-dollar corporation that markets a defective product. Therefore, when analysts speak generally of "white-collar crime," it is not always clear what they have in mind.[4]

In short, Sutherland's selection of the term "white-collar" to demarcate a realm of occupational behavior was not free of limitations. More controversial, however, was his tendency to characterize the occupational transgressions of the upperworld as "crime." The controversy centered around the reality that many of the actions subsumed under Sutherland's concept of white-collar crime are not often defined by the state as criminal. Although important changes have taken place, criminal sanctions traditionally have been employed only sparingly in the social control of the business, political, and professional deviance of the affluent. Civil courts, where monetary damages can be won, and administrative agencies, which develop and enforce regulations for industry, have been relied upon to control the occupational behavior, particularly the corporate behavior, of those in the upper strata. Critics have thus questioned whether the behavior included in Sutherland's definition can rightly be called "crime."[5]

The most notable criticism, because it was both an early and a forceful critique of Sutherland's view of white-collar criminality, was the 1947 essay by lawyer-sociologist Paul Tappan titled "Who Is the Criminal?"[6] Tappan's chief concern was that Sutherland's concept was frequently used to encompass any means of accumulating profits that commentators might see as socially injurious or morally reprehensible, whether or not the conduct violated existing criminal codes. Therefore, whether an act was defined as a "crime" depended less upon the applicability of legal standards than upon the ideology or idiosyncrasies of any given scholar. Not surprisingly, this state of affairs, in Tappan's view, caused the term "white-collar criminality" to lose its conceptual rigor and to "spread into vacuity, wide and handsome."[7]

Such confusion meant that it was impossible to demarcate what constituted a "crime" among the occupationally advantaged, a condition that precluded systematic scientific investigation. For Tappan, the only solution was to restrict criminological analysis to that set of behaviors which met the criteria imposed by a narrow, legalistic definition of crime. Being more a lawyer than a sociologist, Tappan concluded, "Only those are criminals who have been adjudicated as such by the courts. Crime is an intentional act in violation of the criminal law (statutory and case law), committed without defense of excuse, and penalized by the state as a felony or misdemeanor."[8]

In reaction to Tappan and similar critics of that time, Sutherland was able to make a persuasive argument for the legitimacy of a broad definition of white-collar crime and for the inclusion of a wide range of business violations within criminology. First, he noted that the failure of criminal sanctions to regulate the behavior of the rich and powerful was largely a reflection of the elite's ability to use their position to avoid exposure to prosecution. "White-collar criminals," he stated, "are relatively immune because of the class bias of the courts and the power of their class to influence the implementation and administration of the law."[9] Thus, the absence of criminal convictions among the rich cannot be taken as evidence for the absence of criminality. Second, Sutherland observed that much occupational deviance could ultimately be punished by criminal penalties. In some instances, the exercise of such penalties is contained as a possible option in the legislation proscribing particular business activities (e.g., price fixing); in others, criminal sanctions are available when injunctions to obey the rulings of an administrative agency are ignored. Sutherland included injunctions because such penalties were, by law, "part of the procedure for enforcement"; consequently, their use involved "decisions that the corporations committed crimes."[10] In any event, Sutherland proposed that the appropriate criterion for determining the criminality of an act—whether by someone wearing a white collar or by someone unemployed—is its potential to be criminally sanctioned. "An unlawful act is not defined as criminal by the fact that it is punished," he asserted, "but by the fact that it is punishable."[11]

Our review of Sutherland's attempt to delineate a new realm of criminality serves as a necessary prelude for understanding what is implied by "corporate crime," a term often used but not always defined in the literature. Corporate crime is conceived most accurately as a form of white-collar crime; it is thus a "crime of the rich" or part of "upperworld criminality." Corporate violations, however, differ from other forms of white-collar illegality. The most distinctive feature of corporate crime is that it is organizational, not individualistic. This is not to suggest that corporate acts are not the product of individuals; after all, a corporation cannot do anything but through the acts of its agents. The crucial point, however, is that the individuals involved in corporate criminality are acting in behalf of the organization and not primarily for direct personal gain—although higher corporate profits, including those obtained illegally, may bring executives such personal benefits as promotions, bonuses, and salary increases. Thus, an executive who participates in a price-fixing scheme to stabilize a company's market position is committing a corporate offense; an executive who embezzles funds or profits from an insider-trading scheme is not.

Corporate crimes are organizational in another sense as well: the activation of nearly all corporate policies—whether legal or illegal—requires the coordination of diverse elements within a corporation. Thus, few violations of the law could be committed without the involvement (though not necessarily the culpability) of many persons within the corporate structure.[12]

Corporate illegality is an organizational phenomenon, but in what sense can it be considered a "crime"? We must emphasize again that civil courts and regulatory agencies (like the FTC or FDA) are the traditional mechanisms for the social control of corporate conduct, and that the use of criminal sanctions remains relatively infrequent. Yet, as Sutherland has reminded us, "crime" is distinguished from other types of behavior by its potential to be punished under the criminal law, not by the actual application of a sanction. Later scholars also embraced this conception of criminality, and it will serve to guide our work as well. In this study, corporate crime will be defined as *illegal acts potentially punishable by criminal sanctions and committed to advance the interests of the corporate organization.*[13]

THE DISCOVERY OF WHITE-COLLAR AND CORPORATE CRIME

Corrupt business practices have long existed, but they have not always been publicized and, in particular, conceptualized as a *crime* worthy of state intervention. When public officials campaign to "get tough" on crime, they rarely need to qualify what they mean: the drug sales, robberies, assaults, and shootings that too often transpire on the streets of the nation's inner cities. Leaving aside the accuracy of the portrayal of where such "street crimes" occur, the imagery leaves out the vast array of illegalities and harmful practices perpetrated by businesses. Corporate scandals remind us that we ignore this misconduct at our own peril—that is, at the risk of enormous damages being wrought on innocent victims.

The view of crime as a lower-class problem is long-standing. Since the onset of immigration and the concentration of foreign and minority peoples in urban centers, slum neighborhoods have been viewed as dangerous places and their residents as a dangerous class; the poor, not the rich, are to be feared as society's criminals. A number of ideological movements in the latter part of the nineteenth century consolidated this image in the American mind. In particular, Social Darwinist thought, which emerged in the final quarter of the 1800s, was influential in portraying the disadvantaged as falling to the bottom levels of society because they were the least fit among the combatants in the struggle for survival. Their inability to stay within the strictures of the law was seen in turn as an outgrowth of their biological inferiority and innate moral defects.[14] This thinking contributed to the eugenics movement and to the sterilization of offenders (and others) drawn from poor families.[15]

Closer to the turn of the century, the liberally oriented Progressives offered a more optimistic view of offenders, suggesting that criminality was not a product of innate and irreversible defects, but of defects in the social order, which were amenable to reforms. Yet even though criminogenic forces were no longer seen to rest within the poor themselves, they were not far removed. The origin of society's crime problem was now the pathology or disorganization of slum life. In the words of Anthony Platt, "the city was suddenly found to be a place of scarcity, disease, neglect, ignorance, and 'dangerous influences.' Its slums were the 'last resorts of the penniless and criminal'; here humanity reached the lowest level of degradation and misery."[16]

Over the years, however, various commentators challenged this hegemonic view of crime, calling attention in their writings to the injurious practices that prevailed in the world of business. Influential, concerted efforts to expose the damaging and sometimes ruthless conduct of business people emerged in the early years of this century during the Progressive Era. Termed "muckrakers" by Theodore Roosevelt, such authors as Upton Sinclair, Lincoln Steffens, Ida Tarbell, and Charles Russell passionately dramatized the social misery wrought by the burgeoning of large industrial enterprises and by the capitalistic obsession with profit at the expense of human needs that guided them. Historian Vernon Parrington captured the essence of this Progressive tradition when he observed that these social critics

> were read eagerly because they dealt with themes that many were interested in—the political machine, watered stock, Standard Oil, the making of great fortunes. There was a vast amount of nosing about to discover bad smells, and to sensitive noses the bad smells seemed to be everywhere. Evidently some hidden cesspool was fouling American life, and as the inquisitive plumbers tested the household drains they came upon the source of infection—not one cesspool but many,

under every city hall and beneath every state capitol—dug
secretly by politicians in the pay of respectable businessmen. . . . It was a dramatic discovery and when the corruption of American politics was laid on the threshold of business
. . . a tremendous disturbance resulted.[17]

It is notable that these remarks suggest a certain duality in Progressive thinking. On the one hand, we observe a clear sensitivity to
the evils of "big business." On the other hand, as we recall from our
earlier discussions, commentators of this era—particularly those who
embraced the emerging social sciences—also did much to strengthen
the idea that lower-class conditions were the prime breeding grounds
of criminality. According to historian David Rothman, the link between
these two positions is found in the Progressives' belief that by instituting
reforms aimed at curbing the excesses of business, it would be possible to broaden economic opportunities and thus facilitate the process
of elevating the poor into the noncriminogenic middle class.[18] In addition, it may be fair to conclude that the legacy of the Progressives is
twofold: they fostered mistrust simultaneously toward corporations and
toward the poor. The powerful are corrupt and should be treated
with suspicion; the powerless are dangerous and should be feared—at
least until efforts to transform them into "respectable" citizens prove
successful.

Much like the muckrakers, reformist academics who wrote in this
period also attempted to cast a spotlight on the scandals of big business. In 1912, for example, Thorsten Veblen likened the captains of
industry to the juvenile delinquent in his "unscrupulous conversion of
goods and persons to his own ends, and a callous disregard of the feelings and wishes of others, and of the remoter effects of his actions."[19]

Perhaps the most forceful denunciation of corporate social irresponsibility can be found in the 1907 Progressive tract of sociologist
E.A. Ross, *Sin and Society: An Analysis of Latter Day Inequity*. Ross
began his attack on corporate industrialism with the observation that
new economic relationships create opportunities for "new varieties of
sin"; that is, the emergence of a corporate economy opens the way for
fresh approaches to victimizing the public.

Anticipating many themes that would be embellished by later critics of big business, Ross set out to define the distinctive features of this
developing area of immorality. For one thing, he stated, these new sin-
ners do not fit the traditional image of those who prey on society; they
occupy positions of influence and are "respectable" members of the
community. Further, in contrast to the direct interpersonal nature of
crimes like robbery, the businessman plans his transgressions "leagues
or months away from the evil he causes. Upon his gentlemanly presence the eventual blood and tears do not obtrude themselves. . . . The

current methods of annexing the property of others are characterized by a pleasing indirectness and refinement."[20] As a consequence, Ross believed, the public had not yet come to realize the full magnitude of the social harms emanating from the "moral insensitivity" of big business, and thus failed to display "the flood of wrath and abhorrence that rushes down upon the long-attainted sins."[21] Yet, in Ross's opinion, the harms engendered by the trickery of the industrialist class were immense, and far outweighed those stemming from the immoralities of the poor.

Ross's moral outrage led him to attach the stigma of "crime" to the new varieties of sin, and he branded as "criminaloids" the rich and powerful businessmen who preyed on the unsuspecting public. Despite their malfeasance, these criminaloids had succeeded in hiding behind the "anonymity of the corporation" and in remaining immune from punitive measures. Ross argued that only the threat of prison would constrain their behavior. Indeed, criminal sanctions should be aimed at the very top of the corporate ladder. "The directors of a company," urged Ross, "ought to be individually accountable for every case of misconduct of which the company receives the benefit, for every preventable deficiency or abuse that regularly goes on in the course of the business."[22]

Just over three decades after E.A. Ross attempted to identify as criminal the corrupt business practices of corporate leaders, Edwin H. Sutherland introduced his now-classic concept of "white-collar crime." His initial essay on this topic, titled "White-collar Criminality," published in 1940, began with the sentence, "This paper is concerned with crime in relation to business";[23] and over the course of the subsequent decade he continued to champion the idea that the unlawful occupational behavior of the affluent could rightly be considered criminal. Unlike Ross, however, Sutherland maintained that he was not a reformer embarking on a moral crusade against the sins of the captains of industry. His efforts, he argued, were "for the purpose of developing theories of criminal behavior"—specifically, for showing the advantages of his own theory of differential association—and "not for the purpose of muckraking or of reforming anything except criminology."[24] Some commentators have suggested that Sutherland was disingenuous in making this disclaimer; that because he was writing in an academic context, which displayed a strong preference for "value-free" social science, he saw a need to conceal his real ideological leanings in order to sustain the legitimacy of his work.[25] Whatever his motivations, Sutherland's contributions played a major role in opening up the study of crime by the rich and in revising the notion that crime is exclusively a lower-class phenomenon.

In "White-collar Criminality," Sutherland observed that existing "criminal statistics show unequivocally that crime, *as popularly con-*

ceived and officially measured, has a high incidence in the lower class and a low incidence in the upper class" (emphasis in original).[26] Even so, he cautioned, these official statistics foster a mistaken image of the crime problem because they "are biased in that they have not included vast areas of criminal behavior of persons not in the lower class."[27] Sutherland emphasized that "one of these neglected areas is the criminal behavior of business and professional men"—a glaring omission given that the criminality of those in the upperworld "has been demonstrated again and again in the investigations of land offices, railways, insurance, munitions, banking, public utilities, stock exchanges, the oil industry, real estate, reorganization committees, receiverships, bankruptcies, and politics."[28]

Not until the end of the 1940s, however, could Sutherland present systematic empirical data aimed at verifying his earlier impressions that white-collar crime is a pervasive feature of American society. He reported the data in his 1949 classic *White Collar Crime.* Despite this broad title, Sutherland focused exclusively on corporate crime. In doing so, he completed the first large-scale quantitative study of this mode of white-collar criminality.

Sutherland analyzed the practices of the 70 largest industrial and commercial corporations in the United States, whose life span averaged 45 years. To measure the extent of their criminality, Sutherland "attempted to collect all the records of violations of law by each of these corporations, so far as these violations have been decided officially by courts and commissions."[29] He recognized that some critics might dispute his use of the judgments passed down by civil courts and administrative regulatory agencies as evidence of criminality; yet, as discussed earlier in this chapter, he remained firm in asserting that "violations of law which were attested by decisions of equity and civil courts and by administrative commissions are, with very few exceptions, crimes."[30] Sutherland did note, however, that his use of official statistics would underestimate substantially the true prevalence of illegality in his corporate sample, because "only a fraction of the violations of law by a particular corporation result in prosecution, and only a fraction of the corporations which violate the law are prosecuted." In general, he contended, "few corporations are prosecuted for behavior which is industry-wide."[31]

Despite this observation, even the incomplete official records available to Sutherland revealed that the largest and most powerful businesses in the land operate regularly outside legal boundaries. On the basis of these records, he found that the corporations in his sample had violated the law 980 times. The data also indicated that "every one of the 70 corporations has a decision against it, and the average number of decisions is 14.0."[32] Using language traditionally reserved for discussions of street criminals, Sutherland reported that 98 percent of his sample were "recidivists," bearing "two or more adverse decisions."[33] In keeping with the image of the street criminal, he proposed that most of the corporations could be considered "habitual criminals." After noting that states had enacted laws that "define an habitual criminal as a person who has been convicted four times of felonies," he stated, "If we use this number and do not limit the convictions to felonies, 90 percent of the 70 largest corporations in the United States are habitual criminals."[34] Even if this analysis were limited to adverse criminal decisions, the majority of the sample would still qualify as chronic offenders, in that 60 percent were "convicted in criminal courts and have an average of approximately four convictions each."[35]

As suggested earlier in this chapter, Sutherland's conceptual and empirical contributions have had the enduring effect of sensitizing criminologists to a new realm of criminality—the occupational offenses of the affluent, particularly corporate illegality—and thus of revising dramatically the image of crime. The full impact of his work, however, was not immediately apparent. Although his concept of white-collar crime quickly entered the established lexicon of criminologists and his book has been called "the publishing highlight of the 1940s in criminology,"[36] the initial influence of Sutherland's writing was not great enough to inspire a sustained paradigm for research on lawlessness in the business world. He did lay the groundwork for several notable inquiries, but most of these studies were conducted either by his students and/or shortly after his works were published. Following that initial wave of interest, a long hiatus occurred in the study of corporate criminality.[37]

As will be discussed in Chapter 3, scholars' interest in this subject revived in the 1970s and beyond as part of a general movement against white-collar crime. The events of this period provided a context in which insights like Sutherland's took on new meaning and life.[38] As a result, an increasing number of scholars joined the movement against white-collar crime, and turned their attention from the crimes of the poor to the crimes of the privileged. The efforts of these scholars, as well as those of popular writers, produced investigations that helped to illuminate the extent to which corporate offenses victimize citizens and contribute to the nation's "crime problem." Taken together, these works revealed that corporate crime was a common, not a rare, occurrence—a revelation that raised the corresponding question of why these illegalities were not prompting more criminal prosecutions.

Thus, an investigation by *Fortune* found that 11 percent of a sample of 1,043 companies committed at least "one major delinquency" between 1970 and 1980.[39] In 1982, *U.S. News and World Report* furnished a similar account in its article, "Corporate Crime: The Untold Story." The reporters discovered that "of America's 500 largest corporations, 115 have been convicted in the last decade of at least one major crime or have paid civil penalties for serious misbehavior." The picture was even bleaker when the conduct of the nation's 25 biggest companies was examined. Since 1976, seven had been convicted on criminal charges, and "seven more have been forced into settlements of major noncriminal charges—a total of 56 percent linked to some form of serious misbehavior." On a broader level, the magazine reported that from 1971 to 1980 "2,690 corporations of all sizes were convicted of federal criminal offenses."[40]

Other publications echoed these claims. Disclosures of misconduct were so common that a *Time* article, titled "Crime in the Suites," observed that "the way things are going, *Fortune* may have to publish a 500 Most Wanted List"; according to another *Time* writer, "during 1985 the business pages often looked like the police blotter as investigators uncovered case after case of corporate crime."[41] Newspapers across the nation also voiced concern about the prevalence of corporate brushes with the law. *The New York Times* concluded that "a corporate crime wave appears to be exploding," while the *Peoria Journal Star* ran the headline, "Corporate Crime Was Big Business in 1985."[42]

More systematic academic articles confirmed these conclusions. Thus, a study published in the *Academy of Management Journal* analyzed violations of antitrust laws and the Federal Trade Commission Act by *Fortune* 500 companies between 1980 and 1984. Corporate illegality was measured by the "total number of instances in which firms were found guilty in litigated cases, were parties to nonlitigated consent decrees, or involved in unsettled cases in which the court found substantial merit to the charges against the cited firms." Even though the researchers investigated only a limited area of corporate conduct, they found that the companies in their sample averaged nearly one violation apiece, and "that the mean for those firms which were involved in some type of illegal activity was three acts."[43]

Although these figures indicate that corporate illegality is widespread, it appears that they underestimate the true prevalence of lawlessness in the business community. A more detailed search of records and rulings by a team of researchers headed by Marshall B. Clinard and Peter C. Yeager painted an even bleaker picture. We should note that to this day, Clinard and Yeager's research remains the most systematic analysis of illegal corporate conduct.

These researchers calculated the number of criminal, civil, and administrative actions either initiated or completed by 25 federal agencies against the 477 largest publicly owned manufacturing corporations in the United States during 1975 and 1976. For these two years alone, they discovered that "approximately three-fifths of the . . . corporations had at least one action initiated against them."[44] When offenses were classified according to seriousness, it was found that one-fourth of the firms "had multiple cases of nonminor violations."[45] Further, some corporations were found to be far worse than others: only 8 percent of the corporations in the sample "accounted for 52 percent of all violations charged in 1975–1976, an average of 23.5 violations per firm."[46]

Clinard and Yeager's data also provide a point of comparison with the earlier research of Edwin Sutherland. As noted, Sutherland's study of 70 corporations over a 45-year period led him to conclude that nearly all corporations recidivate and that most are "habitual criminals." Clinard and Yeager reached a similar conclusion on the basis of the number of actions successfully completed (not simply initiated) against the corporations sampled, the criterion of corporate crime employed by Sutherland. In the two years covered by their study, 44 percent of the companies were repeat offenders. Moreover, "if one could extrapolate the number of sanctions over the average equivalent time period used by Sutherland, the result would far exceed his average of 14 sanctions."[47]

Finally, Clinard and Yeager were careful to observe that their statistics represent "only the tip of the iceberg of total violations."[48] Because they could not obtain access to agency records that detailed all actions taken against corporations, the researchers estimated that their figures may undercount such allegations by as much as one-fourth to one-third. In addition, the figures are based only on actions undertaken by federal agencies, and thus do not include transgressions detected by state and local administrators and investigators. Beyond these considerations, Clinard and Yeager relied on "official statistics" to measure illegal corporate behavior: actions initiated or completed by federal agencies. Official statistics invariably underestimate actual violations because they do not reflect the many cases in which court or enforcement officials do not know that an offense was committed. At present we have no way of learning the exact dimensions of the "hidden delinquency" of corporations. When we realize, however, that major corporate misdeeds (such as price fixing) have continued undetected for a decade or more, we have reason to believe that the "hidden" figures of corporate lawlessness are substantial.[49]

Recently, Clinard and Yeager have pondered the question of whether "corporate crime is greater in the 2000s than in the 1970s."[50] In the absence of a replication of their earlier work, they recognize that definitive conclusions are not possible. Even so, revelations of business illegalities are so regular and pervasive that Clinard and Yeager suggest that "corporate lawbreaking is greater than it was and also much more damaging."[51] Indeed, they observe that "there have been serious violations of the law, not only in industrial corporations, but in large accounting firms, banks, investment houses, large insurance companies, and other major financial organizations."[52]

As will be discussed in more detail, there has been a steady flow of executives of high-profile companies prosecuted and, most often convicted; these businesses include, among others, Enron, WorldCom, Adelphia Communications, Tyco International, and HealthSouth. The criminal cases were so extensive that *The New York Times* published "A User's Guide" to "Corporate Scandals."[53] A similar scorecard, called "High Profiles in Hot Water," was presented in *The Wall Street Journal*, accompanied by the explanation that "the list of iconic American companies embroiled in financial controversy seems to grow longer every day."[54] The *Corporate Crime Reporter* had no difficulty in finding candidates for its list of the "Top 100 Corporate Criminals of the Decade," a roster of corporations in the 1990s with criminal convictions.[55] The scandals have been so pervasive that journalists have asked, "Could capitalists actually bring down capitalism?" In response, the federal government declared a "war on fraud,"[56] and at President George W. Bush's behest "formed a task force comprised of senior executives from numerous federal agencies to address the barrage of corporate fraud cases that surfaced in the wake of the Enron scandal."[57] In 2005, the Federal Bureau of Investigation not only issued its analysis of street crimes (the *Uniform Crime Reports*) but also made a *Financial Crimes Report to the Public*, noting in the process that the FBI anticipated that the number of fraud "cases will continue to flourish."[58] But this corporate crime wave did have a silver lining. As *The Wall Street Journal* noted, "corporate malfeasance and executive greed have undermined the stock market and fleeced investors, but they have also proved to be a boon for one sliver of the economy: securities lawyers" ready to sue corporations on behalf of victims.[59] This also was a propitious time for those wishing to write exposés of corporate malfeasance, with much material available and the possibility for enticing titles such as *Infectious Greed*.[60]

The Economic Costs of Corporate Lawlessness

The exact costs of corporate crime are unknown, but by every indication the annual financial loss runs into many billions of dollars. Social commentators agree that the amount of money accumulated illegally by America's corporations dwarfs the amount appropriated through traditional street crimes. They also concur that Sutherland may have understated this difference when he asserted that the cost of business criminality "is probably several times as great as the financial cost of the crimes which are customarily regarded as the 'crime problem.'"[61]

This is not to diminish the seriousness of street crime, which damages property, lives, and the social fabric. But deep concern about these consequences, though deserved, should not lessen our worries about the damage inflicted by corporate lawlessness. As students of white-collar crime have warned, it is erroneous to identify the crime problem as simply a "dangerous class problem"—street crimes committed by the urban poor. We cannot afford to neglect the capacity of corporations, the most powerful actors in the nation, to victimize society. Although corporate crime is usually less spectacular than the typical homicide or robbery, it still does significant harm, and in many respects this harm may far exceed the damage wrought by more traditional modes of criminality.

The tremendous economic impact of corporate lawlessness results in part from the extensive involvement of business in unlawful activities, but it is also due to the reality that the costs of even a single corporate offense are often immense. This fact was illustrated as criminologists attempted to systematically document the costs of corporate illegality in the 1970s and beyond. Thus, in an analysis of presentence reports on offenders convicted in federal courts during the fiscal years 1976, 1977, and 1978, Stanton Wheeler and Mitchell Rothman found that the median economic loss for "eight presumptively white-collar offenses" committed by "organizational offenders" was $387,274. By contrast, the "median take" for individuals who did not use an "organizational role" to commit white-collar offenses barely exceeded $8,000.[62]

The gap becomes even more pronounced when the losses due to organizational crimes are compared with those incurred in traditional street offenses. According to FBI statistics, in 2004, the average economic loss per crime was $1,308 for robbery, $1,642 for burglary, $727 for larceny-theft, and $6,108 for motor vehicle theft.[63] Viewed together, these data suggest, in the words of Wheeler and Mitchell, that "just as the organizational form has facilitated economic and technological development on a scale far beyond that achieved by individuals, so that form has permitted illegal gains on a magnitude that men and women acting alone would find hard to attain." They seem correct in concluding that the "organization [is] the white-collar criminal's most powerful weapon."[64]

Similarly, in her 1984 book *Wayward Capitalists*, Susan Shapiro explored the extent of the economic costs associated with corporate financial frauds—crimes committed by or against corporations.[65] Her research focused on offenses investigated by the U.S. Securities and Exchange Commission (SEC), such as misrepresenting the worth of stocks or of the company issuing them, stock manipulation, self-dealing, and insider trading. Shapiro estimated that the mean cost to victims of SEC offenses was $100,000, with 19 percent of the cases incurring losses in excess of $500,000.[66] For cases that ended in a criminal conviction, the costs were even higher. It is instructive that in their study of white-collar offenders in federal courts, Wheeler and Rothman found that the "median take for persons convicted of SEC fraud was almost half a million dollars"; 20 percent of these cases incurred losses greater than $2.5 million.[67]

The huge magnitude of the economic costs of corporate crime is incontrovertible by scanning the business world over the past half century. Indeed, in each time period, scandals involving massive fraud were perpetrated and unmasked. For example, the 1950s experienced a celebrated case of price fixing that earned the name of the "incredible electrical conspiracy."[68] Throughout most of the 1950s, companies in the electrical industry conspired to fix the prices of as many as 12 different products. The executives who managed their company's division of heavy electrical equipment (which involved such expensive items as turbogenerators) arranged a series of clandestine meetings in which they agreed to sell their goods at artificially inflated prices and to apportion various percentages of the market among themselves. The strategy was quite simple and highly profitable: before submitting supposedly sealed bids on potential contracts, the parties would consult to determine how high the price would be set, and which firm would be allowed to "win" the "competition." When the conspiracy was finally unmasked at the end of the decade, 45 corporate officials were fined a total of $136,000, and seven were imprisoned for a month apiece. The 29 corporations involved in the numerous price-fixing agreements received fines of nearly $2 million, with the stiffest penalties imposed on General Electric ($437,500) and Westinghouse ($372,500).

On the surface these economic sanctions may appear substantial, but they are insignificant in comparison to the costs of this corporate crime. According to Justice Department calculations, the prices of the nearly $7 billion worth of goods sold while the price-fixing schemes were in progress would have been 40 percent lower had a free and not a closed enterprise system been permitted to function. The profits reaped by the corporate conspirators from these criminal arrangements—money illegally taken from the public—approached the "incredible" figure of $3 billion.[69] Gilbert Geis, a criminologist who studied the scandal, noted that "the heavy electrical equipment price-fixing conspiracy alone involved more money than was stolen in all of the country's robberies, burglaries, and larcenies during the years in which the price fixing occurred."[70]

Not long thereafter, the huge losses that may attend an individual corporate offense were evident once again in the fraud perpetrated by the Equity Funding Corporation of America (EFCA). Beginning in the early 1960s, the executives of EFCA introduced a novel concept called the "equity funding program." In this somewhat complex program, the company offered its mostly middle-class clientele the opportunity first to purchase mutual-fund shares and then to use these shares as collateral to secure a company loan to buy an EFCA life insurance policy. The rising value of the mutual-fund shares, it was hoped, would exceed the interest due on the loan and defray at least a portion of the insurance premiums. As early as 1964, top corporate executives began to report exaggerated sales figures and profits. The purpose of this continuing fraud was to inflate artificially the value of EFCA stock, which then could be used as a resource to back the company's plans to expand by acquiring other firms. The executives were successful in achieving these goals, but a nagging question arose: How could they make up the bogus earnings they were reporting and thus balance the company's books?

Initially, loans were obtained, laundered through foreign holdings, and subsequently claimed as profits rather than liabilities. However, this solution worked only temporarily because payment on the loans soon came due. As an alternative, officials legally began to "reinsure" EFCA life insurance policies with other companies. That is, in exchange for a cash settlement, EFCA in effect would sell its customers' policies to another firm. While this plan had the benefit of providing much-needed immediate income, it also engendered a new difficulty: in the years to come, EFCA would not receive premium payments from what would have been its regular policyholders; the payments would go to the reinsuring company.

Faced with a severe and unresolved cash-flow problem, the EFCA executives embarked on their most shocking scheme. They created totally fictitious policies and reinsured or sold these policies to other insurance firms. Eventually, 50 to 100 workers were assigned to manufacture these bogus policies. Before a disgruntled ex-employee exposed this undertaking in 1973, 64,000 phony policies had been sold; EFCA executives had even "killed off" 26 "policyholders" and collected on their claims. In the end, 22 executives were convicted; most received prison sentences. The price tag for this one corporate crime proved to be an astounding $2 *billion*.[71]

The decade of the 1980s brought more highly publicized incidents of business criminality that exacted enormous financial costs. Thus, for a 20-month period beginning in July 1980, E.F. Hutton engaged in a complex check-kiting scheme in which officials at branch offices consistently wrote checks that exceeded funds on deposit in more than 400 commercial banks. By shifting money from one bank account to another, company executives kept their checks from bouncing. The delay between the writing of the initial checks and the time when the overdrafts were covered provided Hutton with the equivalent of interest-free loans. The total operation involved nearly $10 billion; on some days the company enjoyed $250 million in illegal "loans." In a

1985 plea bargain with the Justice Department, Hutton eventually pleaded guilty to 2,000 felony counts of mail and wire fraud, paid the maximum fine allowable under law ($2 million), and established an $8 million restitution fund to repay the banks it victimized.[72] In the end, the scandal and the corresponding depletion of consumer trust led to the sale of E.F. Hutton and the loss of its corporate identity.[73]

The crash of the savings and loan (S&L) industry in the 1980s resulted in losses in the vicinity of $200 billion, a figure that with interest payments and other losses could rise to anywhere from $500 billion to $1.4 trillion by 2021.[74] Observers debate how much of the loss was due to criminal activity as opposed to poor business decisions, but it appears that billions of dollars were appropriated through illegal activities.[75] This looting was encouraged by changes in regulatory standards that increased federal insurance for deposits from $40,000 to $100,000 and that permitted S&Ls—which previously had been limited to making home-buyer loans—to pursue riskier and potentially more profitable investments (e.g., loans for commercial development). S&Ls were now able to induce an infusion of money by offering high interest rates and the promise of federal insurance for deposits up to $100,000—in short, a high return on a no-risk investment. As money poured in and with little oversight by banking regulators, the S&Ls attracted many unscrupulous executives seeking to "get rich quick." These officials not only made irresponsibly poor investments but also engaged in criminal activities such as arranging for kickbacks on loans and the outright theft of funds—monies often used to support lavish lifestyles. Indeed, the U.S. Department of Justice called the scandal an "unconscionable plundering of America's financial institutions."[76] In 1990, it was estimated that the S&L debacle had resulted in 231 convictions.[77]

The 1980s also saw revelations of "insider trading," a scandal popularized by the movie aptly titled *Wall Street*, which was highlighted by actor Michael Douglas's memorable line that "greed is good." This illegal practice involves offenders using "insider" information not available to other investors either to purchase company stocks that are about to rise in value (e.g., due to an impending takeover) or to sell off stocks that are about to fall in value (e.g., due to a profitable drug product that was about to be recalled). In this way, these offenders have an unfair advantage on the stock market because they are able to unload declining stocks on, and to buy rising stocks from, unsuspecting investors. The unraveling of insider schemes led to the conviction of prominent Wall Street figures, including Ivan Boesky (who paid a fine of $100 million and received a three-year prison term) and Michael

Milkin (who made a $600 million settlement and received a 10-year prison term). Milkin's firm, Drexel Burnham Lambert, also pleaded guilty on criminal charges and paid more than $650 million in fines and restitution.[78]

More recently, the nation's financial institutions have been rocked by a series of noted scandals, the most celebrated of which involved Enron, an energy-based firm that traded in a range of commodities. At the time of its collapse, Enron had become the seventh largest corporation in the United States. In August 2000, the company's stock reached a high of $90.56 per share; shockingly, a little over a year later, the stock's value had plummeted to under $1.00. By using a labyrinth of partnerships with companies it created as well as questionable accounting practices, Enron artificially inflated its profits and hid its massive financial liabilities. This misleading, rosy financial picture—often trumpeted by its executives—led to an overvaluing of its stock on Wall Street and to a steady flow of capital being invested in its often-risky ventures. But as losses and external scrutiny mounted, Enron was forced to disclose a third-quarter 2001 loss of $638 million and a decline in shareholder equity of $1.2 billion. And as its financial rating declined and prospects for investments dried up, Enron quickly spiraled into insolvency. Chapter 11 bankruptcy was filed on December 2, 2001.[79]

In the aftermath, federal prosecutors secured 16 guilty pleas from former Enron employees and high-profile criminal convictions on securities and fraud charges of the company's chief executives, Kenneth Lay and Jeffrey Skilling. The costs of Enron's collapse were enormous and included "the loss of $60 billion in market value on Wall Street, almost $2.1 billion in pension plans, and 5,600 jobs."[80] Enron's accounting firm, Arthur Andersen, was also convicted of obstruction of justice (later overturned by the U.S. Supreme Court), paid millions to settle shareholder civil suits, and was on the brink of going out of business. At the time of its conviction in 2002, only 5,000 of Anderson's 26,000 U.S. employees remained with the firm.[81]

Enron did not prove to be an isolated corporate fraud. In a 2002 scandal, the communications conglomerate, WorldCom, was also found to have used shady accounting practices to portray huge losses as a $1.4 billion profit.[82] Meanwhile, executives enriched themselves with millions in compensation. The company's stock share price, which had risen to more than $64, dropped to 9 cents.[83] In the end, the "fraud at WorldCom, which eventually totaled $11 billion, wiped out $180 billion in market capitalization, plunged the company into Chapter 11 bankruptcy-court protection and resulted in 30,000 layoffs."[84] WorldCom's CEO, Bernard Ebbers, was eventually given a 25-year prison sentence "for his role in the biggest accounting fraud in U.S.

history."[85] Similarly, executives at Adelphia Communications, founder John Rigas and his son, Timothy Rigas, received prison terms of 15 and 20 years, respectively, in a scheme that involved misstatements of profits, the extensive pilfering of company funds to support an opulent lifestyle, and, ultimately, the firm's bankruptcy.[86] And at the conglomerate Tyco International, the CEO Dennis Kozlowski and his chief financial officer, Mark Swartz, were sentenced in 2005 to serve up to 25 years in a New York state prison. They were convicted of "enriching themselves by nearly $600 million by taking unauthorized pay and bonuses, abusing loan programs and selling their company stock at inflated prices after lying about Tyco's finances."[87]

The focus on these headline-grabbing scandals is appropriate because they show vividly the huge costs of business lawbreaking. But there are two additional points that must be emphasized. First, although unusual by their sheer size—multi-billion dollar impacts—these celebrated cases are but the "tip of the iceberg." In July 2005, for example, there were reports that the U.S. Department of Justice "had charged more than 900 people in more than 400 corporate fraud cases and that more than 500 people had either been convicted or pleaded guilty."[88] Second, and perhaps more consequential, the understandable focus on economic losses should not obscure how corporate decisions kill, injure, or sicken people. These actions that jeopardize the health and safety of workers, consumers, and the general public are justifiably called *corporate violence*. Whether they could—or should—be considered and treated as *crimes* is what the Ford Pinto prosecution and, more generally, this book is about.

CORPORATE VIOLENCE

Shortly before 8:00 in the morning of February 26, 1972, after a night of rain, a mining-company dam that sat precariously above Buffalo Creek Valley, West Virginia, collapsed and unleashed 130 million gallons of water and coal waste products. A mixture of water and sludge rushed down the slopes at speeds of up to 30 miles an hour. The devastation was sudden and immense: 125 people were drowned or crushed to death, 1,000 homes were ruined, and 16 small communities lining the valley were washed away. The flood destroyed "everything in its path."[89]

Officials of Pittston, the parent company of Buffalo Mining, which constructed and maintained the dam, immediately declared the regrettable disaster "an act of God" Those closer to Buffalo Creek voiced different sentiments. One flood victim remarked, "You can blame the Almighty, all right—the almighty dollar";[90] another said, "All I call the disaster is murder. The coal company knew the dam was bad, but . . . they did not care about the good people that lived up Buffalo Creek."[91] An investigative commission convened by the governor agreed in part, finding that "The Pittston Company, through its officials, has shown flagrant disregard for the safety of residents of Buffalo Creek and other persons who live near coal-refuse impoundments."[92] In the face of a civil suit launched on behalf of several hundred flood victims by Gerald Stern and a staff of fellow lawyers, Pittston agreed to an out-of-court settlement of $13.5 million; eventually the company paid more than $30 million to dispose of claims related to the disaster.[93]

The clearest evidence that Pittston had acted in a reckless manner was uncovered by Gerald Stern and his associates as they prepared their civil case against the giant company. The dam at Buffalo Creek had been constructed by dumping huge piles of solid waste products from the nearby mining operation across the creek bed. This mound of refuse was supposed to contain the large quantities of water that the company disposed of daily after it had been used to clean coal in preparation for shipment to market. Stern learned, however, that the dam had a crucial engineering flaw: it possessed no emergency spillway that could absorb excess water should the need arise—such as on the rainy night preceding the disaster. His investigations also disclosed that other Pittston-managed dams had runoff systems and that corporate executives apparently were aware that the lack of a spillway at the Buffalo Creek impoundment was potentially dangerous.[94]

The survivors at Buffalo Creek lost much more than their property and belongings. Many who had barely escaped the flood and who had watched as friends and relatives were swept away by the onrushing wave of debris and coal-blackened water suffered intense psychic trauma. Kai Erikson, a sociologist who studied the disaster and its aftermath, commented, "Two years after the flood, Buffalo Creek was almost as desolate as it had been the day following, the grief as intense, the fear as strong, the anxiety as sharp, the despair as dark."[95] There was another scarring cost as well: what Erikson has called "collective trauma . . . a blow to the basic tissues of social life that damages the bonds attaching people together and impairs the prevailing sense of communality."[96] After the flood, people were thrown together hurriedly into emergency trailer-court camps, where few of the old communities and communal bonds could be reconstructed. For most residents, life would never be the same. The words of one survivor paint a disheartening but typical portrait:

> This whole thing is a nightmare, actually. Our life-style has been disrupted, our home destroyed. We lost many things we loved, and we think about those things. We think about our neighbors and friends we lost. Our neighborhood was completely destroyed, a disaster area. There's just an open field there now and grass planted where there were many homes and many people lived.[97]

The violent or "physical" costs—the toll in lives lost, injuries inflicted, and illnesses suffered—are perhaps the gravest and certainly the most neglected of the damages that corporate lawlessness imposes on the American people. The events at Buffalo Creek should help to dispel the misconception that corporations "might take some of our money but at least no one gets hurt." Yet it would be wrong to assume from the Buffalo Creek incident that corporate negligence causes injury or death only in unusual circumstances akin to a natural disaster. Every day, in unpublicized and often latent ways, corporations illegally victimize the bodies of workers, consumers, and members of society in general.

Significantly, the *physical costs of violent corporate crime may outstrip the injuries and deaths sustained at the hands of street criminals.* Indeed, a growing number of social commentators have suggested that corporate lawlessness costs more than street crime not only in dollars and cents but also in life and limb.[98] This reality often is hidden by the publicity given to immense corporate frauds and by the mistaken assumption that violence is exclusively an individual predatory act—as this following newspaper editorial displays:

> The idea that we should be easier on people whose crimes mark them as brutal and dangerous to life and limb is crazy. Yet, that is the notion that goes with the idea that somebody who broke the latest rule invented—by the bureaucrats—committed the worst crime. Even as we sizzle about the public officials grabbing for bribes in the latest FBI "Sting" exposé, we ought to face the facts. They are crooked bums but they aren't axe murderers. Neither one deserves much sympathy, perhaps, but reality demands a sane priority between people clearly capable of blowtorch murder and bloody abuse to get what they want and the guy who has a chance to pick up some extra cash effortlessly and can't resist it. . . . We cannot afford to indulge in fantasies that tickle our prejudices. We need to be realistic about dealing with all types of crime and the record speaks for itself. Crimes inflicted with a total disregard for the physical well-being of the victim are the most dangerous to us all . . . and those who commit such are the most persistent criminals among us. Those are proven facts—not ideological fancies.[99]

Although the gravity of traditional crimes of violence should never be minimized, it is wrong to assume that corporations—which touch people's lives in so many ways—cannot inflict harm through negligent and, at times, wanton behavior. It is to these violent costs that our attention next turns.

Workers as Victims

Three decades ago, Ralph Nader alarmingly pronounced that "as a form of violence, job casualties are statistically at least three times more serious than street crime."[100] Although meaningful strides have been made in making working environments safer,[101] his basic point remains substantially true today. In raw figures, the National Institute for Occupational Safety and Health (NIOSH) has estimated that each year, workers suffer approximately 5 million nonfatal injuries, 3.9 million of which require treatment in a hospital emergency room.[102] Approximately 6,000 employees are killed in occupational accidents.[103] Further, NIOSH has indicated that depending on the year examined, the workplace may cause between 330,000 and 430,000 cases of "nonfatal illness" annually.[104]

Admittedly, it would be neither accurate nor fair to indict corporations for all of these casualties. Some job tasks are inherently dangerous, and employees are occasionally negligent about their own well-being. In some areas, too, the government condones the sacrifice of a measure of worker safety and protection in hopes of lowering consumer costs, increasing corporate efficiency, and improving the vitality of the economy. The endangering practices that result might strike some as insensitive, if not immoral, but they are not necessarily illegal.

It is equally clear, however, that a substantial portion of workers' deaths, injuries, and diseases are caused by the violation of prevailing laws and regulations. One source estimated that 30 percent of all industrial accidents are caused by illegal safety violations (and another 20 percent by legal but unsafe conditions).[105] The record may be much worse in some segments of the business world, notably the coal mining industry, in which mishaps have claimed more than 100,000 lives and injured 1.5 million people since 1930.[106] Indeed, NIOSH data reveal that mining workers have a higher "fatal occupational injury rate" (23.5 per 100,000 workers) than members of any other job category.[107] The rate across "all private industry was 4.2 per 100,000."[108]

The 1976 catastrophe in Letcher County, Kentucky, in which 26 people perished, is a tragic illustration of the hazards faced by miners. The disaster in Letcher County began when a malfunction in the mine's ventilation system allowed dangerous quantities of volatile methane gas to accumulate in a shaft 2,000 feet below the surface. Supervisors had failed to monitor the air quality in accordance with established guidelines, and unsuspecting workers entered a section filled with methane. They died in a ball of flame when sparks from machinery ignited the lethal gas.

Before the explosion, the mining operation had been cited for 652 safety violations, including 60 for inadequate ventilation. Moreover, 500 new citations for safety infractions were issued in the following 13 months. In this light, commentary published in *The Nation* seems credible:

> Twenty-six men died under circumstances that reek of carelessness, lack of skill, illegality, incompetence and official neglect, but no noteworthy changes have been induced by the tragedy. . . . If sleepless nights have been endured, it was because of the profits lost during the months when the coal vein was sealed, not because outraged justice demanded it.[109]

Mining deaths in 2006 reveal that these types of hazards remain. The tragedy at the Sago Mine in West Virginia received special attention as a national television audience was initially buoyed by the news that 13 miners had been rescued, only to learn thereafter that 12 of these workers had died. The lone survivor was Randal McCoy. Most of the miners apparently survived an initial blast, but then perished from carbon monoxide poisoning during their 41 hours trapped 260 feet below ground. It was soon revealed that in the year preceding the deaths, the mine had been cited for more than 200 health and safety violations and had to suspend operations 16 times for failing to follow safety rules. "The violations found at Sago included mine roofs that collapsed without warning, faulty tunnel supports and a dangerous build-up of flammable coal dust."[110] These problems led commentators to note that the Bush administration, which appointed mining company executives to key Mine Safety and Health Administration positions, had opposed increased mine safety regulations and had cut funding for safety enforcement. It is perhaps instructive that "since 2000 the coal mining industry has contributed $10.7 million to federal campaigns, 88 percent to Republicans."[111]

The consequences of illegally disregarding employees' health and well-being appear even more profound when we consider the deadly and crippling diseases caused by the workplace. Toxic agents are especially dangerous. Typically they do not take their toll suddenly and openly; they kill silently, over the course of many years, and often in ways that seem indistinguishable from other ailments. Workers do not die dramatically on the job; they simply become ill, and all too often never regain their health.[112]

"Statistics," as Paul Brodeur notes, "are human beings with the tears wiped off"; they do not capture the "agonizing human consequences" of occupationally induced illnesses.[113] With this consideration in mind, we find special significance in the statistics on the effects of toxic agents in the workplace. NIOSH publishes data on "pneumoconiosis," which is a "class of respiratory diseases attributed solely to occupational exposures."[114] These include, for example, byssinosis or "brown lung disease," which stems from the inhalation of cotton, flax, or hemp dusts and causes "chest tightness" and severely impairs lung function. Another disabling respiratory ailment is silicosis, which results from contact with silica dust generated in foundries, abrasive blasting operations, and stone or glass manufacturing. Coal miners suffer from "black lung disease," whereas other workers, exposed to asbestos, suffer from "asbestosis." NIOSH reports that over a three-decade period (1968 to 1999), "pneumoconoiosis was an underlying or contributing cause of 121,982 deaths."[115]

Historically, exposure to asbestos appears to have had especially damaging effects. Asbestosis, a lung disease, can surface 10 to 20 years after initial exposure and has no specific treatment. Victims suffer from "extensive scarring of the lung and progressive shortness of breath." By the mid-1980s, approximately 11.5 million Americans—most of whom worked in asbestos plants, insulation operations, and shipyards during World War II—were exposed to asbestos. Longitudinal studies indicated that 10 to 18 percent of these people will die from asbestosis.[116] The effects of asbestos exposure are not limited to asbestosis; according to NIOSH, this exposure can also lead to lung cancers. A 1985 NIOSH report predicted that "up to 11 percent of workers exposed to asbestos" might eventually develop cancerous mesothelial tumors.[117]

No reliable statistics exist for the proportion of occupationally induced illnesses and deaths that can be attributed to corporate illegality. Even when corporations comply in good faith with existing safety regulations, toxic exposures may take place because of a lack of scientific evidence warning of potential hazards. Yet enough instances of executives' disregard for workers' health have been documented to justify the allegation that corporate negligence is responsible for many health and safety violations; in some cases these laws are broken intentionally.[118]

Indeed, the plight that befell asbestos workers appears to support the conclusion that businesses, in the pursuit of profits, can be negligent in the protection of workers' safety. In his 1985 exposé *Outrageous Misconduct*, Paul Brodeur alleged that although manufacturers had evidence for the deleterious effects of asbestos exposure, they either failed to explore the implications of this evidence or decided consciously to hide this information from their employees. For nearly half a century, the extent of the corporations' knowledge about the inherent dangers of asbestos remained largely secret. Starting in the early

1970s, however, workers brought numerous lawsuits against asbestos manufacturers, and the subsequent probing of the plaintiffs' lawyers unearthed widespread evidence of corporate irresponsibility. A number of juries were convinced that asbestos manufacturers had been "guilty of outrageous and reckless misconduct" in suppressing information from workers. In 10 cases against one company, decided in 1981 and 1982, juries awarded plaintiffs not only compensatory damages but also punitive damages averaging more than $600,000 a case.[119]

Since this time, asbestos lawsuits have continued unabated. A search on Google for "asbestos lawsuits" will reveal many sites devoted to asbestos litigation. It is estimated that by the end of 2002, there had been approximately 730,000 asbestos-related claims filed in state and federal courts, representing the interests of more than 10 million potential victims (each lawsuit can involve multiple plaintiffs).[120] In 2005, President George W. Bush called for legislation to limit asbestos legal claims, arguing that many were "junk lawsuits" that were clogging the courts and threatening to bankrupt companies that ultimately may be shown to be blameless.[121] A month later, however, seven executives of W.R. Grace & Co. were criminally indicted for exposing workers and residents of Libby, Montana, to toxic exposure from asbestos. The company officials faced "ten counts of conspiracy, knowing endangerment, obstruction of justice, and wire fraud."[122] In June 2006, a federal judge limited the scope of the case on a legal technicality, agreeing with the defendants that the key conspiracy charges to endanger workers and the public had not been filed within a five-year statute of limitations.[123]

Libby is a picturesque valley of 8,000 located in northwest Montana (the town of Libby has about one-third of the population). Until 1990 when it closed, a major source of employment was a vermiculite mine and related plant facility owned by W.R. Grace & Co. When heated, vermiculite expands to accordion-shaped, worm-like pieces that can be used for a variety of products, including attic insulation, cat litter, and packing materials. It is also a material that can naturally contain and be contaminated by asbestos.[124] Over the years, W.R. Grace workers, their families, and the community were exposed to toxic dust through emissions, spills, and clothing worn by the workers to their homes. Contaminated vermiculite was used in local school tracks and, once the mining operation closed, company property infested with agents was leased by Grace to youth baseball teams and to businesses. Studies show that approximately 1,200 residents in Libby suffer from asbestos-related health problems, and that the area has a mortality rate from asbestosis that is 40 to 60 times higher than expected. Hundreds have died from toxic exposure.[125]

Stunningly, investigative reports[126] and the prosecution's indictment[127] allegedly reveal that, as in other asbestos scandals, company officials for years had a wealth of health data on employees and evidence from scientific studies showing the toxicity and deleterious effects of exposure to vermiculite. Internal corporate memos discuss strategies to thwart disclosure of the risks and to obstruct government agencies' (NIOSH and the EPA) investigations and regulation. As the U.S. Attorney's indictment charged, W.R. Grace conspired "to conceal and misrepresent the hazardous nature of the tremolite asbestos contaminated vermiculite, thereby enriching defendants and others."[128] Between 1976 and 1990, the after-tax profit for the Grace's Libby operation was about $140 million.[129]

Notably, as a 2004 New York prosecution suggests, it appears that the risks that asbestos poses to workers are now more clearly understood. Father and son owners of a company that removed asbestos from private residences and public facilities (e.g., churches, schools, military housing) were sentenced to 19.5 and 25 years, respectively, in federal prison. The Environmental Protection Agency announced that these were the "two longest U.S. jail sentences for environmental crimes in U.S. history."[130] Rather than follow approved procedures for safely abating asbestos from buildings, the company owners had workers, not equipped with respirators and protective equipment, simply rip out the material in a way that created "snow storms" of asbestos. It is estimated that due to this toxic exposure, "as many as 100 former . . . workers are now substantially likely to develop asbestosis, lung cancers and mesothelioma, a fatal form of cancer."[131]

Two earlier, pathbreaking cases involving employee deaths, one in Illinois and one in North Carolina, also are valuable in highlighting the relationship between corporate illegality and workplace violent victimization. In the early 1980s, the national spotlight focused on a case involving Stefan Golab, a 61-year-old Polish immigrant working for Film Recovery Systems, Inc. (FRS), a company located in the northwest Chicago suburb of Elk Grove Village.[132] FRS was a recycling operation that extracted silver from film negatives by dipping them in a cyanide solution. By 1981, the company was grossing $13 million a year.

The day after Christmas 1982, FRS hired Stefan Golab to clean the vats containing the cyanide solution. On February 10, 1983, Golab staggered from the plant floor into the workers' lunchroom. Collapsing into a chair, he began to shake violently and foam at the mouth; then he lapsed into unconsciousness. A life squad soon arrived, but Golab could not be revived. He died before reaching the hospital.

At first it was believed that Golab had died of a heart attack, but an autopsy showed that the cause of death was poisoning by the plant's cyanide fumes. Subsequent investigations revealed, in the view of Cook County State's Attorney Richard A. Daley (now Mayor of Chicago), that Golab had worked in "a huge gas chamber."[133] A prosecution team headed by Daley's assistant Jay Magnuson charged that conditions at FRS were so hazardous that Golab had been murdered. The prosecution argued that company officials had ignored repeated instances of workers becoming nauseous and vomiting; had hired mostly illegal aliens who could not speak English and had failed to warn them of the dangers of cyanide; had scraped skull-and-crossbones warnings off drums of cyanide; had clearly violated safety regulations by equipping employees with only paper face masks and cloth gloves before assigning them to work over open vats containing cyanide; and had such inadequate ventilation that the plant's air was a thick yellow haze with a distinct cyanide odor, which exceeded safety standards by containing four times the accepted level of cyanide.

Magnuson sought and received homicide indictments against FRS as well as five corporate officials, claiming that "exposing workers to something as dangerous as cyanide gas is no different than firing a weapon into a crowd. You have created a strong probability of death. No intention is needed at that point."[134] After a two-month bench trial, Judge Ronald J.D. Banks agreed that the prosecution had proven its contentions: Stefan Golab's death "was not an accident but in fact murder."[135] On June 14, 1985, Judge Banks found three FRS officials guilty of murder and of 14 counts of reckless conduct. (Midway through the trial, he had dismissed the case against one other official; the governor of Utah refused to extradite the fifth company executive who had been indicted.) Banks also convicted Film Recovery Systems and Metallic Marketing Systems, Inc., which owned one-half of FRS's stock, of involuntary manslaughter and 14 counts of reckless conduct. Two weeks later, he sentenced the three executives to 25 years in prison and fined them $10,000 apiece. The companies were fined $24,000 each. In rendering his decision, Banks commented, "This is not a case of taking a gun and shooting someone. It is more like leaving a time bomb in an airport and then running away. The bomb kept ticking . . . until Stefan Golab died."[136] In 1990, citing the technicality that the corporation and executives were not charged with the same offenses, the Appellate Court of Illinois overturned the executives' convictions and remanded the case for retrial. Eventually, a plea bargain led to two company executives and a foreman receiving prison terms.[137]

A second prominent case occurred in a chicken processing plant—Imperial Food Products, Inc.—located in Hamlet, a town of 5,000 close to North Carolina's southern border. At 8:00 A.M. on September 3, 1991, a hydraulic line above a large vat of grease, which workers had tried to repair, burst, spraying flammable liquid into the 400-degree oil in the vat. A fast-spreading fire erupted that engulfed the plant in smoke-filled soot. The building, which had not been inspected in 11 years by the state's Occupational Safety and Health Administration, was more than 100 years old, had no sprinklers, and had no windows and few doors through which employees might escape. Most tellingly, on the orders of the firm's owner, Emmett Roe, a fire-exit door had been padlocked to keep workers from leaving the premises with pilfered chicken fingers. The metal door was later found to have dents where desperate employees had tried to kick it open. But it would not have mattered. A truck had been parked inches from the door, as extra insurance that employees could not sneak chicken parts out this exit. In the end, of the 90 workers at the plant, 24 died and 56 were injured. An employee of a snack company, servicing vending machines, also perished. Years later, another employee died from complications that stemmed from her injuries.[138]

On March 10, 1992, Roe was indicted on 25 counts of involuntary manslaughter, carrying a potential sentence of 250 years. He eventually pleaded guilty to all counts and received a 19-year, 11-month sentence; he was paroled after serving 4.5 years. In the aftermath, the plant never reopened, leading to the loss of 230 jobs. Survivors, some of whom continued to live with painful ailments, received little financial compensation. More disquieting, "many children were orphaned, and many were left with single parents. Many grandparents and aunts and uncles were pressed into service to rear second families."[139]

The Imperial Food Products case is reminiscent of the infamous Triangle Waist Company fire that occurred on March 25, 1911, in New York City. Located in the top three floors of the Asch Building—a then-new 10-story skyscraper—this garment industry factory manufactured women's "shirtwaists" (i.e., women's blouses). As the workday was ending, a wooden bin containing flammable clothing scraps from the cutting process ignited, with the blaze sweeping across the ninth floor within minutes. In all, 146 people—123 of them women—perished. A funeral march for the victims drew a crowd of 350,000, virtually all dressed in black and silent throughout the procession.[140] Eventually, the loss of life would play an integral role in triggering a rash of labor and fire-safety laws in New York state.[141]

Workplace violence was commonplace in early-1900s America; it is estimated that 100 people a day died on the job.[142] However, a key fact emerged that made this tragedy seem particularly outrageous: a door on one side of the ninth floor had been kept locked on the orders of the corporation's two owners, Max Blanck and Isaac Harris, who wished to prevent workers from unauthorized arrivals and departures. In a stunning development, a Progressive District Attorney, Charles Whitman, secured indictments on manslaughter. Blanck and Harris were acquitted at trial, in large part due to the judge's instructions to the jury that the prosecutor had to prove that the owners knew the doors were locked on this particular day. As we will see, the Triangle case was an unusual development at a time when few corporations were held criminally liable for killing or injuring workers or the public.[143] As we will also see in later chapters, special legal obstacles, such as those that emerged in the Triangle case, often have to be surmounted when prosecutors seek to use the criminal law to hold companies' executives culpable for acts of corporate violence.

Consumers as Victims

Corporate violence extends not only to workers who produce goods but also to those who purchase them. Many products, even when used as recommended by the manufacturers, injure or kill thousands of consumers every year. Statistics on consumer casualties lend credence to this conclusion. One report estimated that dangerous products result annually in approximately 28,000 deaths and 130,000 serious injuries.[144] Data from the U.S. Consumer Product Safety Commission showed that from toys alone, there were 210,300 injuries that required hospital emergency room visits in 2004.[145] The Commission also noted that "deaths, injuries and property damage from consumer product incidents cost the nation more than $700 billion annually."[146]

Again, it is difficult to calculate exactly what proportion of these physical costs can be attributed directly to corporate illegality. Evaluations of product quality and safety, however, lend credence to the assessment that the unlawful victimization of consumers is widespread.[147] One analysis by the Consumer Product Safety Commission demonstrated that 147 out of 847 fabrics failed to meet flammability standards, eight out of 15 models of baby cribs were defective, 753 out of 1,338 toys were hazardous, and 117 out of 148 products were unsafely packaged.[148] In the same vein, the U.S. General Accounting Office found "gross contamination" in 35 of 65 poultry operations it examined, while inspections of meat-processing factories revealed that 18 of 216 plants in North Dakota and 31 of 57 plants in Massachusetts were characterized by unsanitary conditions.[149] These statistics, especially with reference to the meat-packing industry, have led some scholars to conclude that Upton Sinclair's descriptions of conditions in the early 1900s are all too often still valid. Specific examples support this assessment:

> In 1984, Nebraska Beef Processors and its Colorado sub-
> sidiary, Cattle King Packing Company—the largest supplier
> of ground meat to school lunch programs and also a major
> supplier of meat to the Defense Department, supermarkets,
> and fast-food chains—was found guilty of: (1) regularly
> bringing dead animals into its slaughterhouses and mixing rot-
> ten meat into its hamburgers; (2) labeling old meat with
> phony dates; and (3) deceiving U.S. Department of Agricul-
> ture inspectors by matching diseased carcasses with the
> healthy heads from larger cows. . . . In 1979, a New Jersey
> firm was convicted of making pork sausage with an unau-
> thorized chemical which masks discoloration of spoiled meat.
> And in 1982, a California company used walkie-talkies to
> avoid inspectors while doctoring rotten sausage.[150]

Recent accounts continue to paint a disturbing picture about the willingness of companies to market adulterated food products. Many examples could be cited, but two prominent cases serve to illustrate the illegality that regularly occurs. First, in 1998, Odwalla Inc. pleaded guilty and paid a $1.5 million fine for marketing apple juice contam-inated with E.coli bacteria after managers ignored an inspector's warning that apples were too rotten to use in making the product. The food poisoning led to the death of a 16-month-old child and to a life-threatening kidney disease for 14 children. More than 50 people were sickened and are at risk for further health complications in the years ahead. Federal officials hailed this case as "the first criminal convic-tion in a large-scale food-poisoning outbreak."[151]

Second, in 1999, Andrews and Williamson Sales Co. paid $1.65 mil-lion in criminal fines, and its president was incarcerated, for distrib-uting tainted strawberries later linked to a hepatitis A outbreak. The strawberries were sold to a federal school lunch program and sickened at least 200 students and teachers in Michigan and 50 people elsewhere. Students in four other states had to be vaccinated as a health precau-tion after consuming the product. Food used in the federal school pro-gram must be of domestic origin, but the corporation's officials hid the fact that the strawberries were harvested in Mexico in conditions that Food and Drug Administration investigators later showed to be unsanitary. Adverse publicity over the case also had a substantial eco-nomic impact, not only depressing the market for Mexican products but also costing California farmers millions of dollars in lower straw-berry sales.[152]

The willingness to market tainted products is not limited to the food industry. In the past decade, companies manufacturing medical equip-ment have been criminally convicted for selling glucose monitors that give faulty readings, nonsterile plastic covers used to cover medical instruments, unsterilized surgical instruments, and medical devices that had not received FDA approval.[153] In a prominent prosecution decided in 2003, Ednovascular Technologies Inc. pleaded guilty and paid $92.4 million to settle criminal and civil charges. Over a 19-month period, the corporation had failed to disclose to the FDA—as required by federal law—2,628 instances in which its Ancure device, an instrument used in abdominal aortic aneurysm surgery, did not work properly and risked harm to a patient. The unreported incidents included 12 deaths and 57 cases in which more invasive surgery had to be used when the Ancure's delivery system became stuck in a patient's body. The problems with the device were uncovered only when seven employees, whose strenuous complaints about the product's safety had been ignored by company managers, sent a letter voicing their concerns to the FDA after the death of a patient.[154]

Data on the extent of product recalls also point to corporate culpability in the marketing of defective goods. Between 1966 and 1971 alone, the FDA was forced to recall nearly 2,000 different drug products, including "806 because of contamination or adulterations, 752 because of subpotency or superpotency, and 377 because of label mixups."[155] In the decade following its inception in 1972, the Consumer Product Safety Commission recalled more than 300 million dangerously defective products. According to one source, the agency's action may have prevented as many as 1.25 million serious injuries and deaths in a five-year period.[156] The Commission's vigilance remains warranted. In just two days in mid-June of 2006, the Commission issued recall notices for girls' water shoes that were slippery when wet, swivel rockers that broke at the base, steel stands for hammocks prone to collapsing, and children's books whose pop-up felt pieces proved to be a choking hazard. In addition, the Commission posts a "Most Wanted" list of products previously recalled but, if not returned, still pose a safety risk to consumers (e.g., 1.9 million wall heaters that can overheat and catch fire; 12 million cedar chests with locks that can automatically close and had caused the suffocation deaths of at least six children; window blind cords responsible for the strangulation of 160 infants).[157]

Further, when it has been possible to penetrate corporate defenses and obtain more than a cursory look into corporate operations, the historical record has been troubling. Commentators have seen that even leading corporations are sometimes willing to place profits above consumer safety. GM's Corvair, first exposed by Ralph Nader's *Unsafe at Any Speed*,[158] is one of the most celebrated of these cases. From its inception, the Corvair was plagued by rear-end suspension difficulties that caused it to become directionally unstable and to overturn at high speeds. As revealed by John DeLorean, a GM executive of that era who would later have legal difficulties of his own, "these problems with the Corvair were well documented inside GM's Engineering Staff long before the Corvair was offered for sale."[159] Nevertheless, the company launched the Corvair in 1959 and initially resisted attempts by its own staff to introduce a stabilizing bar capable of reducing the car's hazards; at an additional cost of $15 per vehicle, it was deemed "too expensive." DeLorean offers a telling summation of this episode:

> To date, millions of dollars have been spent in legal expenses and out-of-court settlements for those killed or maimed in the Corvair. The corporation steadfastly defends the car's safety, despite the internal engineering records which indicated it was not safe, and the ghastly toll in deaths and injury it recorded.[160]

Another example of corporate insensitivity to consumers' well-being surfaced in an exposé by a former B.F. Goodrich engineer. He recounted how superiors ordered him to falsify test results and to help construct an elaborate document indicating that a company-designed brake for a new Air Force attack plane had satisfied all qualification standards. The deficiencies in the brake assemblies were revealed only after several near-crashes.[161]

Similar scandals have prevailed in the pharmaceutical industry. A study of 17 pharmaceutical companies, for example, disclosed that over a two-year period each company violated the law at least once, and two drug companies committed more than 20 violations; when compared with firms in other industries, the pharmaceutical companies committed 2.5 times their share of total violations.[162] Case studies add further documentation of illegalities in the pharmaceutical industry.[163] One case frequently cited as an example of egregious corporate conduct involves the anti-cholesterol drug MER/29. Employees of the William S. Merrell Company (a subsidiary of Richardson-Merrell) falsified laboratory findings in order to secure FDA approval of MER/29. After the drug was marketed, numerous users suffered negative side effects, including cataracts and loss of hair. Eventually, both the William S. Merrell Company and Richardson-Merrell, as well as three corporate officials (two doctors and a vice-president), pleaded no contest to a variety of criminal charges. The companies were also named in nearly 500 civil suits that reportedly awarded nearly $200 million in damages to victims.[164]

In his book *At Any Cost*,[165] Morton Mintz details the problems associated with another pharmaceutical product: the "Dalkon Shield," an IUD manufactured by A.H. Robbins. According to Mintz, the company marketed 4.5 million Shields in 80 countries on the basis of exaggerated claims for the device's effectiveness and safety. Although advertisements claimed that those wearing the IUD had a pregnancy rate of only 1.1 percent, the actual rate was five times as high. In addition, the Dalkon Shield caused more miscarriages than other IUDs among women who became pregnant, and was more likely to cause potentially lethal septic spontaneous abortions. In the United States, at least 15 women died from such abortions; in Third World countries, where the antibiotics needed to treat this condition often are not available, the toll is unknown but suspected to be much higher, amounting in Mintz's view to "hundreds—possibly thousands—of women."[166] The Shield also caused pelvic infections that subjected thousands of its consumers to extended periods of chronic pain and in some instances irrevocably harmed their reproductive systems. One consultant estimated that of the 2.2 million American women who used this IUD, approximately 87,000 may have suffered physical harm.[167]

The Dalkon Shield remained on the market for more than three years, from January 1971 to June 28, 1974. Mintz alleges that A.H. Robbins failed to recall the device despite growing evidence that it was a safety hazard; the company continues to maintain that its product was no more dangerous than other IUDs. It appears, however, that Dalkon Shield victims and juries have found Mintz's interpretation more compelling. By 1985, more than 14,000 victims had filed either civil suits or nonlitigated claims for compensation while juries had awarded plantiffs $24.8 million in punitive damages.[168] The prospect of sustaining losses in future lawsuits moved A.H. Robbins to file for reorganization under Chapter 11 of the Bankruptcy Code, "so that it could be protected from lawsuits by creditors—Shield victims, above all—while it devised a plan to pay its debts."[169]

Is the Dalkon Shield case an isolated incident of corporate lawlessness? What, Mintz asks, does this catastrophe teach us?

> Not that the A.H. Robbins Company was a renegade in the pharmaceutical industry. Yes, Robbins knowingly and willfully put corporate greed before human welfare, suppressed scientific studies that would ascertain safety and effectiveness, concealed hazards from consumers, the medical profession and government, assigned a lower value to foreign lives than to American lives, behaved ruthlessly toward victims who sued, and hired outside experts who would give accommodating testimony. Yet almost every other major drug company has done one or more of these things, and some have done them repeatedly or routinely, and continue to do so. Some have even been criminally prosecuted and convicted, and are recidivists.[170]

Indeed, there continues to be a steady flow of criminal cases involving pharmaceutical companies, two of which we highlight here. Both of these illegal schemes involved the fraudulent promotion of drugs approved by the FDA for one purpose but marketed as cures for other ailments. This practice of "off-label marketing" not only skirts FDA regulatory procedures but also jeopardizes patients' health by inducing them to take drugs that either may be ineffective or not as effective as approved prescription medicines.

Thus, in 2004, Warner-Lambert pleaded guilty to criminal charges and agreed to pay $430 million to settle criminal and civil charges stemming from its fraudulent marketing of Neurontin, a drug approved for the treatment, in conjunction with other drugs, of epilepsy. To increase Neurontin's profitability, the company used a coordinated, unlawful scheme to market this medicine as a single treatment for epileptic seizures and for a range of other ailments. For one of these problems—bipolar mental disorder—scientific evidence had shown that a placebo worked as well as Neurontin.[171] The company targeted doctors in their successful campaign to boost the drug's off-label sales:

> Warner-Lambert used a number of tactics to achieve its marketing goals, including encouraging sales representatives to provide one-on-one sales pitches to physicians about off-label uses of Neurontin without prior inquiry by doctors. The company's agents also made false or misleading statements to health care professionals regarding Neurontin's efficacy and whether it had been approved by the FDA for the off-label uses. Warner-Lambert also used "medical liaisons," who presented themselves (often falsely) as scientific experts in a particular disease. . . . Warner-Lambert paid doctors to attend so-called "consultants' meetings" in which physicians received a fee for attending expensive dinners or conferences during which presentations about off-label Neurontin were made. These events included lavish weekends and trips to Florida, the 1996 Atlanta Olympics, and Hawaii. . . . [At one educational event], when unfavorable remarks were proposed by a speaker, Warner-Lambert offset the negative impact by "planting" people in the audience to ask questions highlighting the benefits of the drug. . . . These tactics were part of a widespread, coordinated national effort to implement an off-label marketing plan.[172]

In a similar illegal scheme resolved in 2005, Eli Lilly and Company pleaded guilty and paid $36 million to address criminal and civil charges. The case involved Evista, a drug used to treat osteoporosis in postmenopausal women. After poor sales in Evista's first year on the market, the company sought to increase the drug's sales by promoting its off-label use for ailments for which it did not have FDA approval. The company engaged in a variety of practices to induce doctors to prescribe Evista. One of these involved "creating and distributing to sales representatives an 'Evista Best Practices' videotape, in which a sales representative states that 'Evista is truly the best drug for the prevention of all these diseases, referring to osteoporosis, breast cancer, and cardiovascular disease."[173]

The Public as Victims

Participants in a corporate society need not produce or consume goods to risk victimization by corporate violence. Each day, business practices occur that endanger the lives of the general public. Sometimes these physical costs are exacted dramatically, as when the dam collapsed at Buffalo Creek and 125 residents perished. More often, however, the toll is taken by the more silent means of environmental pollution. A *Time* magazine article captures this fact:

> Natural disasters and wars do their damage spectacularly and quickly—shaking, crushing, burning, ripping, smothering, drowning. The devastation is plain; victims and survivors are clearly distinguished, causes and effects easily connected. With the unnatural disasters caused by environmental toxins, however, the devastation is seldom certain or clear or quick. Broken chromosomes are unseen; carcinogens can be slow and sneaky. People wait for years to find out if they or their children are victims. The fears, the uncertainties, and the conjectures have a corrosive quality that becomes inextricably mingled with the toxic realities.[174]

The risks posed increasingly by the nation's air, earth, and water are linked directly with our dependence on industrial processes and chemicals that generate toxic pollutants but also, ironically, provide us with the products, technological advances, cures, and employment that sustain the quality of our lives. The magnitude of this dependence is seen in these statistics: there are "160 million tons of air pollution emitted annually, 225 million tons of hazardous waste generated, [and] 4 million tons of toxic chemicals discharged into waterways and streams."[175]

Over the past two decades, public consciousness has been raised regarding the immense dangers posed by releasing these pollutants into the environment. Environmental groups are responsible in part for focusing attention on the growing health risks created by current disposal practices, but several highly publicized toxic disasters have also helped to identify environmental victimization as a major social problem. One of these turning points in public opinion was the December 3, 1984, catastrophe in Bhopal, India, which forced attention on the possibility that an industrial chemical disaster could take life quickly and on a large scale. The leak of 45 tons of methyl isocyanate from a Union Carbide pesticide plant claimed the lives of more than 2,000 citizens. "Human progress came up against human frailty," commented Roger Rosenblatt. "The air was poisoned, and the world gasped."[176]

The American public has not had to look abroad to see the dangers of pollution. The words "Love Canal" have come to signify the capacity of toxic agents to pose such a severe risk that citizens are driven from their homes.

From the early 1940s to the 1950s, the Hooker Chemical Company dumped 20,000 tons of chemical waste residues in a 15-acre trench located in Niagara Falls, New York. The site was called "Love Canal" after William T. Love, who had started and then abandoned excavations on a canal designed to bypass the falls and join the Niagara River to Lake Ontario. In 1953, Hooker sold the dump site to the city's school board for the token fee of $1, noting in the deed that the "premises have been filled . . . with waste products resulting from the manufacturing of chemicals by the grantor" and that it was transferring liability "for injury to a person or persons, including death therefrom . . . in connection with or by reason of the presence of said industrial wastes."[177] Neither Hooker nor the school board issued a public statement warning citizens of the potential hazards of the chemical wastes in the dump.[178] The land was used eventually for residential housing; an elementary school was also built on the site.

In *Laying Waste,* Michael Brown writes, "Love Canal was simply unfit to be a container for hazardous substances, even by the standards of the day," particularly because it held not only seriously harmful solvents and pesticides but also dioxin, the "most toxic substance ever synthesized by man."[179] Over the years, the wastes seeped gradually into the surrounding earth and its waters, with predictably devastating consequences. To an astonishing degree the community suffered from miscarriages, birth defects, cancer, chromosome damage, skin rashes, headaches, ear infections, nervous disorders, and other ailments. Brown's account of his first visit to the area is disquieting:

> I saw homes where dogs had lost their fur. I saw children with serious birth defects. I saw entire families in inexplicably poor health. When I walked on the Love Canal, I gasped for air as my lungs heaved in fits of wheezing. My eyes burned. There was a sour taste in my mouth.[180]

Indeed, the dangers proved so severe—one study reported that dioxin levels were "among the highest ever found in the human environment"—that hundreds of families were evacuated and their homes purchased by the government and then bulldozed under or closed off as uninhabitable.[181]

The Love Canal incident may be unique in the degree of contamination and the amount of publicity it attracted, but it is not an isolated case. "Each day," a story in *Time* notes, "more and more communities discover that they are living near dumps or atop ground that has been contaminated with chemicals whose once strange names and initials—

dioxin, vinyl chloride, PBB and PCB, as well as familiar toxins such as lead, mercury and arsenic—have become household synonyms for mysterious and deadly poisons."[182] There may be as many as 10,000 of these dangerous waste dump sites.[183]

Moreover, the physical costs suffered by the Love Canal residents have been experienced elsewhere. There is mounting evidence that exposure to toxic agents increases the risk of health problems, including cancer, reproductive complications, kidney failure, and neurological disorders.[184] One estimate warns that contact with dangerous chemicals may cause as many as 45,000 deaths a year.[185] Another report observes that "12,000 people in the United States die from pesticide poisoning" annually; due to underreporting of illnesses, the true incidence might be twice as high. If so, then "pesticide exposure kills anywhere from 50% to 100% as many Americans as homicides in a given year."[186] And still another study of nine major cities found that 3 percent of all deaths could be traced to "outdoor air pollution."[187] Disturbingly, it appears that the toll from environmental pollution falls most heavily on minorities and the poor—those who do not have the resources to move away from toxic hazards and who do not have the power to resist the placement of toxic sites in or near their community. This hidden cost of inequality is sometimes referred to as "environmental racism" or "environmental injustice."[188]

Corporations should not be blamed in all instances for polluting the environment deliberately. Much of the pollution took place while companies were in compliance with governmental regulations and before the dangers of the toxic agents were fully understood. In the case of Love Canal, for example, it is difficult to determine how culpability should be divided between the Hooker Chemical Company and the City of Niagara Falls, which Hooker apparently warned of the dump site's hazards (though Hooker's parent company, Occidental Petroleum, eventually paid $129 million to reimburse the federal government for cleaning up the area).[189] Nonetheless, a number of social commentators argue that corporate lawlessness is responsible for a significant amount of the public's victimization. As Ralph Nader commented about the effects of air pollution:

> The pervasive environmental violence of air pollutants has imperiled health, safety, and property throughout the nation for many decades. . . . The efflux from motor vehicles, plants, and incinerators of sulfur oxides, hydrocarbon, carbon monoxide, oxides of nitrogen, particulates, and many more contaminants amounts to compulsory consumption of violence by most Americans. There is no full escape from such violent ingestions, for breathing is required. This damage, perpetuated increasingly in direct violation of local, state, and federal law, shatters people's health and safety. . . .[190]

The existing evidence lends credence to Nader's view. Thus, in their classic book 1980 book *Corporate Crime*, Clinard and Yeager presented data showing that the violation of environmental protection standards is among the most frequent of all corporate offenses.[191] In a 1985 *Wall Street Journal* article, Barry Meier echoed this finding, citing another study indicating "that one out of every seven companies producing toxic wastes may have dumped illegally in recent years."[192] Meier noted that the wastes are dumped into places—streams and vacant lots, for example—where the risk of contamination is high but the likelihood of detection is slight. Comparing corporate crime "yesterday and today," Clinard and Yeager do not see a marked improvement. They observe that in the "1990s and 2000s," we find similar large-scale oil industry violations."[193] As they illustrate:

> To select a few, Chevron, in 1992, pled guilty to sixty-five Clean Water Act violations, and was given $8 million in criminal and civil fines. . . . In 1991, Marathon Oil pled guilty to criminal violation of the Clean Water Act: it discharged pollutants from its refinery and was fined $900,000. Mobil, in 2004, was fined $5.5 million for oil spills on the Navajo Reservation in Utah. In 1994, Unalocal Corporation was given a criminal fine of $1.5 million for illegally discharging 8.5 million gallons of petroleum thinner over a fifty-year period, whereupon it could pass into state waters. In 1990, Exxon was criminally fined $121 million in state claims over the Exxon Alaskan Valdez oil spill of 11 million gallons of crude oil spilled from the ship, the *Valdez*, which fouled up 700 miles of Alaskan shoreline, killing birds and fish and diminishing the living standards of thousands of Alaskan Americans. There had been other corporate violations by Exxon.[194]

Indeed, there appears to be no current shortage of environmental criminals to detect and punish. As we will see in Chapter 7, the Environmental Protection Agency now refers about 400 cases annually to the U.S. Department of Justice for prosecution; numerous other environmental criminal cases are pursued by prosecutors at the state and local levels.[195]

CONCLUSION: THE FORD PINTO CASE AND BEYOND

The crime problem in America has a dual quality that is not always recognized or understood. Images embedded deeply in our cultural heritage, combined with frequent political rhetoric and constant attention by the media, sensitize us to the ravages of conventional illegal behavior. Certainly conventional criminality is individually and socially devastating, but the natural inclination to equate the "crime problem" with street crime can blind us to a second, seemingly more consequential, aspect of the problem: corporate lawlessness is pervasive and its effects are immense. "Suite crime," as it is sometimes called, disrupts the social and institutional order, and its financial toll outweighs substantially the amounts stolen by street offenders. Most significantly, there is every indication that the physical costs of corporate crime surpass the bodily harm inflicted by those who prey more intimately on their victims. Each day, executives must make life-and-death decisions, and through negligence or intent they sometimes place profits above the safety and well-being of workers, consumers, and the general public. Contrary to what some citizens and policymakers might continue to believe, corporate crime can be violent.

The seriousness of illegal corporate activities focuses attention on the question, "How has this problem been attacked in the past and in more recent times?" In the next chapters, we will explore how a movement against white-collar crime has made corporate crime, including business violence, a larger part of the nation's collective conscience. We also will attempt to show how changes in several areas, including the prevailing socioeconomic context and our understanding of the concept of "person," have shaped the legal responses made in different eras to corporations engaging in socially injurious practices. In particular we will learn why our legal system is now increasingly prepared—in an unprecedented if at times still rudimentary fashion—to bring corporate illegalities, especially those with violent consequences, within the reach of the criminal law.

As we make this inquiry into the fight to criminalize corporate crime and violence, we will, as noted, come to use the Ford Pinto case as a conduit to explore a number of issues at the heart of the control of business illegality. Perhaps the most salient controversy underpinning any analysis of Ford's prosecution is whether the corporation was guilty of a "crime" in its production of the 1978 Pinto that burst into fire on an Indiana highway and claimed the lives of three teenage girls. Was Ford so reckless in its production and marketing of the Pinto as to be responsible for these youths' deaths? Was this a case of "reckless homicide"?

In criminal cases, the outcome of a trial can hinge on demonstrating that the alleged corporate offender, through its executives and other workers, manifested culpability or a measure of intent. Each side—prosecution and defense—attempts to construct a social reality that portrays the corporation either as a callous and calculating offender who places profits above human life (the prosecution's story) or as a good corporate citizen who may have made errors of judgment but never would intend to kill anyone (the defense's story). Each side highlights facts selectively and tries to weave them into a persuasive tale. In the end, and as will be apparent in Part II of this book where Ford's prosecution is probed, juries must decide whose story is more compelling.

Over the years, there have been strenuous differences of opinion about the degree of Ford's culpability, whether in the Indiana case we analyze or, more generally, in the deaths of others who perished in one of its Pintos.[196] For some, Ford was a willful killer—an "amoral calculator" who is the poster child for corporate violence; for others, the company was unjustly cast as a villain by those who have distorted its record in handling the Pinto. It is not our purpose to settle this dispute here, in large part because the two versions of the story are presented in Part II where readers can, in the end, decide for themselves. Even so, we will offer some preliminary thoughts that can frame the analysis of the Pinto case that is presented in the middle part of the book.

As we will see in more detail, the Pinto had a fundamental design flaw: the gas tank was placed six inches from the back bumper and, when pushed forward, would be punctured by sharp bolts protruding from the car's differential housing (a filler pipe also tended to dislodge). This meant that in a rear-end collision the Pinto was prone to gas leakage, which in turn could result in a fire that would rapidly engulf the vehicle in flames. In retrospect, it is puzzling how company engineers could have made such an egregious mistake (the gas tank could have been placed elsewhere or protected by simple measures from the protruding bolts). What is even more inexplicable—from today's perspective—is why Ford, once this potentially lethal hazard was disclosed, did not sprint to recall the Pinto. In today's safety-conscious context, where automakers advertise their vehicles' success on crash tests, it would be virtually unimaginable that it would not do so. As one recent full-page newspaper advertisement boldly stated: "Today, GM announces the next big step in automotive safety."[197]

As Matthew Lee and M. David Ermann's analysis of the Pinto's production and marketing reveals, it is reductionistic to claim that Ford made a single, conscious decision to sell a dangerous vehicle.[198] Rather, the Pinto, like any other automobile, was brought to dealership showrooms through a lengthy, routine process involving many employees located in different subunits of the corporation. Based on interviews and analysis of documents, Lee and Ermann show how a variety of factors coalesced to divert workers from defining the Pinto as having a special, anomalous safety hazard. Thus, Ford employees thought that rear-end crash tests conducted on the Pinto were inconclusive, that the car met all federal regulatory safety standards, that the Pinto was as safe as other subcompacts on the road, and that other features of the Pinto (lack of safety glass in the front window) were of greater concern.

Similarly, the failure initially to pull the Pinto off the road was due largely to the view that the crash information was not sufficiently unusual to meet the company's existing standards for issuing a recall. Lee and Ermann propose that other vehicles might just as easily have been singled out for scrutiny and as being unsafe.[199]

These considerations, however, do not necessarily mean that Ford was blameless or not criminally culpable. Under Lee Iaccoca's management, Ford was imbued with a culture of productivity and profit and not with a culture of safety. Safety, in fact, was not made an overriding priority at Ford, and revelations of safety problems (called safety "conditions" at the company) were not encouraged.[200] Safety anomalies with the Pinto were assessed in a routine way, and the car's deviant features were "normalized"—that is, defined as "acceptable risks."[201] By contrast, federal, industry, and company standards for safety, however reasonable to Ford managers, were not necessarily seen as legitimate by the public and victims of defective automobiles. At this historical juncture, the external environment to the company was changing in such a way that there was growing mistrust of corporations and a social movement against white-collar crime. New expectations of corporate responsibility and what constituted an "acceptable risk" were emerging—ones that today make marketing a car's safety a means to increase sales and earn more profit.[202] At the time, it was this changing context that made Ford vulnerable to the charge that it would put profits above human life. Further, even if no individual made explicit choices to sell or keep an unsafe vehicle on the road, this does not mean that, due to its standard operating procedures, lines of communication, and normative culture, the corporation as a collective entity was not responsible for producing these "decisions." It is instructive that in the Pinto case, Ford as a corporation—and not any of its upper-level executives or managers who dealt directly with the Pinto—was criminally prosecuted.

A key consideration was not simply the design of the Pinto but Ford's intransigence in issuing a recall. Due to its organizational culture, it was blind to the simple fact that, crash statistics aside, it is indefensible to keep a vehicle on the road that has been publicly unmasked to have an obvious, lethal design flaw—one that could be corrected rather inexpensively. This vigorous resistance made the company vulnerable to the charge that it was callous and calculating. Indeed, if Ford had moved more quickly to recall its Pintos, it is almost certain that the three deaths in Indiana would not have occurred. If so, there never would have been a "Ford Pinto case."

We are, of course, getting a bit ahead of the Pinto story, which we tell in Part II. Even so, this discussion is relevant to a more general point that informs our current project: corporate criminal liability often is not a "fact" but a socially and legally constructed reality. The Ford

Pinto trial is important because it was a ring in which adversaries fought not only over Ford's specific guilt but also over whether corporations can be criminalized if they jeopardize people's safety. The stakes were high, which is why the battle was fierce and worthy of national coverage.

In the chapters ahead, we first discuss how the social and legal context developed in the United States to the point at which a powerful corporation, such as Ford, could be charged with reckless homicide and forced to defend its corporate honor. After relaying the details of Ford's prosecution, we then discuss what has transpired in the ensuing 25 years. Although corporate criminal liability remains an evolving and at times frustrated development, the Pinto case marked a juncture at which a significant transformation in the criminalization of business violence and crime was inspired. This account—before, during, and after Ford's prosecution—is, in our view, an intriguing tale. We are ready to begin the story.

NOTES

[1]   Edwin H. Sutherland, "White-Collar Criminality," *American Sociological Review* 5 (February 1940), pp. 1–12; *White Collar Crime.* New York: Holt, Rinehart and Winston, 1949; "Crime of Corporations," in Karl Schuessler (ed.), *On Analyzing Crime.* Chicago: University of Chicago Press, 1973 (paper originally presented in 1948), pp. 78–96; and in the same volume, "Is 'White-Collar Crime' Crime?" (originally published in 1945), pp. 62–77.

[2]   Gilbert Geis and Colin Goff, "Introduction," in Edwin H. Sutherland, *White Collar Crime: The Uncut Version.* New Haven: Yale University Press, 1983, p. xxx.

[3]   Sutherland, *White Collar Crime,* p. 9.

[4]   In order to avoid conceptual confusion, authors have begun to evolve separate terms, such as "business crime" or "organizational crime," to refer to distinct modes of illegality that fall under the more general heading of white-collar crime. See, for example, John E. Conklin, "Illegal But Not Criminal," in *Business Crime in America.* Englewood Cliffs, NJ: Prentice Hall, 1977.

[5]   For an overview of this controversy, see George Vold, *Theoretical Criminology.* New York: Oxford University Press, 1958, pp. 243–261; and Donald J. Newman, pp. 78–96, "White-Collar Crime: An Overview and Analysis," in Gilbert Geis and Robert F. Meier (eds.), *White-Collar Crime.* New York: The Free Press, 1977, pp. 50–64. Compare with Leonard Orland, "Reflections on Corporate Crime: Law in Search of Theory and Scholarship," *American Criminal Law Review* 17 (1980), pp. 501–520.

[6]   Paul Tappan, "Who Is the Criminal?" in Gilbert Geis and Robert F. Meier (eds.), *White-Collar Crime.* New York: The Free Press, 1977, pp. 272–282.

[7]   *Ibid.,* p. 275.

8   *Ibid.*, p. 277.

9   Sutherland, "White-Collar Criminality," p. 7.

10   Sutherland, "Is 'White-Collar Crime' Crime?" p. 66

11   *Ibid.*, p. 66. See also Sutherland, "White-Collar Criminality," p. 6.

12   Marshall B. Clinard and Peter C. Yeager, *Corporate Crime*. New York: The Free Press, 1980, pp. 17–19, 43. See Neal Shover, "Defining Organizational Crime," in M. David Ermann and Richard J. Lundman (eds.), *Corporate and Governmental Deviance*. New York: Oxford University Press, 1978, pp. 37–40; Laura Shill Schrager and James F. Short, Jr., "Toward a Sociology of Organizational Crime," *Social Problems* 25 (April 1978), pp. 407–419.

13   A number of scholars have rejected a narrow legalistic definition of corporate crime. Marshall B. Clinard remarks, for example, that "corporate crime, like white-collar crime (of which it is a part), is defined here as any act punishable by the state, regardless of whether it is punished by administrative or civil law." Similarly, John Braithwaite defines corporate crime "as conduct of a corporation, or individuals acting on behalf of a corporation, that is proscribed and punishable by law." He comments, "I take the view that to exclude civil violations from a consideration of corporate crime is an arbitrary obfuscation because of the frequent provision in law for both civil and criminal prosecution of the same corporate conduct. In considerable measure, the power of corporations is manifested in the fact that their wrongs are so frequently punished only civilly." See Marshall B. Clinard, *Corporate Ethics and Crime: The Role of Middle Management*. Beverly Hills, CA: Sage, 1983, p. 10; John Braithwaite, "Enforced Self-regulation: A New Strategy for Corporate Crime Control," *Michigan Law Review* 80 (June 1982), p. 1466, footnote 1. See also Sheila Balkan, Ronald J. Berger, and Janet Schmidt, *Crime and Deviance in America: A Critical Approach*. Belmont, CA: Wadsworth, 1980, pp. 165–167, and Jeffrey H. Reiman, *The Rich Get Richer and the Poor Get Prison: Ideology, Class, and Criminal Justice*. New York: John Wiley and Sons, 1979, pp. 44–94.

14   Anthony Platt, *The Child Savers: The Invention of Delinquency*. Chicago: University of Chicago Press, 1969; Richard Hofstadter, *Social Darwinism in American Thought*. Boston: Beacon Press, 1955; Stephen Jay Gould, *The Mismeasure of Man*. New York: W.W. Norton, 1981.

15   Harry Bruinius, *Better for All the World: The Secret History of Forced Sterilization and America's Quest for Racial Purity*. New York: Knopf, 2006.

16   Platt, *The Child Savers*, p. 41. See also David J. Rothman, *Conscience and Convenience: The Asylum and Its Alternatives in Progressive America*. Boston: Little, Brown, 1980.

17   Vernon L. Parrington, "The Progressive Era: A Liberal Renaissance," in Arthur Mann (ed.), *The Progressive Era: Liberal Renaissance or Liberal Failure?* New York: Holt, Rinehart and Winston, 1963, p. 8. See also Gilbert Geis and Robert F. Meier, "Introduction," in their edited volume *White-Collar Crime*. New York: The Free Press, 1977, p. 6.

18   Rothman, *Conscience and Convenience*, pp. 48–49.

19   Quoted in Conklin, "Illegal But Not Criminal," pp. 8–9.

20   E.A. Ross, *Sin and Society: An Analysis of Latter-Day Iniquity*. New York: Harper and Row, 1907, pp. 8, 10–11.

21   *Ibid.*, p. 47.

22   *Ibid.*, p. 126.

23   Sutherland, "White-Collar Criminality," p. 1.

24   *Ibid.*, p. 1.

25   Geis and Meier, "Introduction," p. 24; Gresham M. Sykes, *Criminology*. New York: Harcourt, Brace, Jovanovich, 1978, p. 97.

26   Sutherland, "White-Collar Criminality," p. 1.

27   *Ibid.*, p. 2.

28   *Ibid.*, p. 2.

29   Sutherland, "Crime of Corporations," pp. 79–80 (citations to the version contained in *On Analyzing Crime*). Presented one year before the publication of *White Collar Crime*, this essay contained the results of Sutherland's investigation of corporate illegality.

30   *Ibid.*, p. 81.

31   *Ibid.*, p. 94. For a more extended discussion of why "the enumeration of decisions as reported in these sources is certainly far short of the total number of decisions against these 70 corporations," see Sutherland, *White Collar Crime. The Uncut Version*. New Haven: Yale University Press, 1983, pp. 14–15.

32   Sutherland, "Crime of Corporations," p. 80.

33   *Ibid.*, p. 80.

34   *Ibid.*, p. 80.

35   Sutherland, *White Collar Crime. The Uncut Version*, p. 23. For a summary of the statistical findings of Sutherland's research, see pp. 13–25.

36   Geis and Goff, "Introduction," p. xxviii. See also Stanton Wheeler, "Trends and Problems in the Sociological Study of Crime," *Social Problems* 23 (June 1976), p. 528.

37   Geis and Goff, "Introduction," p. xxx; Sykes, *Criminology*, p. 100.

38   See also Marshall B. Clinard and Peter C. Yeager, "Corporate Crime: Issues in Research," *Criminology* 16 (August 1978), pp. 258–262; Sykes, *Criminology*, pp. 100–103.

39   Irwin Ross, "How Lawless Are Big Companies?" *Fortune* 102 (December 1, 1980), pp. 56-64.

40   Orr Kelly, "Corporate Crime: The Untold Story," *U.S. News and World Report* (September 6, 1982), p. 25.

41   Charles P. Alexander, "Crime in the Suites," *Time* (June 10, 1985), p. 56; Stephen Koepp, "The Year of the Big Splashes," *Time* (January 6, 1986), p. 79.

42   Winston Williams, "White-Collar Crime: Booming Again," *New York Times* (June 9, 1985), Section 3, p. 1; Steven P. Rosenfield, "Corporate Crime Was Big Business in 1985," *Peoria Journal Star* (December 15, 1985), p. A-14.

43 Idalene F. Kesner, Bart Victor, and Bruce T. Lamont, "Board Composition and the Commission of Illegal Acts: An Investigation of *Fortune* 500 Companies," *Academy of Management Journal* 29 (December 1986), p. 794. This research was a partial replication of an earlier study. See Barry M. Staw and Eugene Szwajkowski, "The Scarcity-munificence Component of Organizational Environments and the Commission of Illegal Acts," *Administrative Science Quarterly* 20 (September 1975), pp. 345–354.

44 Clinard and Yeager, *Corporate Crime,* p. 116. The results of this research were originally reported in Marshall B. Clinard, Peter C. Yeager, Jeanne Brissette, David Petrashek, and Elizabeth Harries, *Illegal Corporate Behavior.* Washington, DC: U.S. Government Printing Office, 1979.

45 Clinard and Yeager, *Corporate Crime,* p. 118.

46 *Ibid.,* p. 116.

47 *Ibid.,* p. 127. Clinard and Yeager reported that 210 of the 477 corporations in their sample had "two or more legal actions completed against them." Thus, as noted in the text, 44 percent of corporations were repeat offenders.

48 *Ibid.,* p. 111; see pp. 112–113.

49 Some scholars, however, disagree with Clinard and Yeager's conclusions. Favoring a strict legalistic definition of corporate crime rather than the broad definition used by researchers of the Sutherland tradition, Leonard Orland questions whether Clinard and Yeager's study can be used to "support the claim of widespread corporate crime in America." He revives the Tappan-Sutherland debate and chides Clinard and Yeager for trying to assert "that corporate crime is prevalent by pointing to a large number of incidents that have nothing to do with criminal law and even less to do with crime." Instead, he says, the "tabulation of recorded crime should be the starting point for determining the actual extent of crime." See "Reflections on Corporate Crime," p. 108. Orland believes that researchers should focus on "recorded criminal accusations and convictions against America's largest corporations" because of a "significant body of criminology that teaches that tabulation of recorded crime should be the starting point for determining the actual extent of the crime." That is, once the official crime rate is established, an "informed estimate" becomes possible of how much corporate crime goes unreported and unsolved. Notably, Orland observes that the "gap between recorded and actual corporate crime may be even greater than for other forms of crime." See pp. 508–509.

　　Despite this criticism, Orland does not dispute that corporate crime—even when defined by strict legalistic criteria—is a frequent and troubling occurrence: he reports that for the fiscal years 1976–1979, 574 corporate criminal convictions were obtained in federal courts (pp. 501–502, footnote 4). He also inspected filings to the Securities Exchange Commission to determine the number of corporations that had reported being involved in "material legal proceedings." Because criminal cases are not automatically "presumed to be material," SEC filings constitute only a "minimal estimate of corporate criminal convictions." Even so, for 1978 alone, "fourteen of the 100 largest industrial corporations disclosed criminal convictions to the SEC" (pp. 509–510).

50 Marshall B. Clinard and Peter C. Yeager, with the collaboration of Ruth Blackburn Clinard, "Corporate Crime: Yesterday and Today—A Comparison," in *Corporate Crime.* New Brunswick, NJ: Transaction, 2006, p. xvii.

51   *Ibid.*, p. xvii.

52   *Ibid.*, p. xvii.

53   "Corporate Scandals: A User's Guide," *The New York Times* (May 11, 2003), p. 2-wk.

54   "High Profiles in Hot Water," *The Wall Street Journal* (June 28, 2002), p. B1.

55   Russell Mokhiber, "Top 100 Corporate Criminals of the Decade," *Corporate Crime Reporter*, 2006, available at http://www.corporatecrimereporter.com.

56   "In Heart of Corporate World, Bush Declares War on Fraud," *Cincinnati Enquirer*, July 10, 2002, p. A1.

57   Federal Bureau of Investigation, *Financial Crimes Report to the Public*. Washington, DC: FBI, U.S. Department of Justice, 2005, p. B1.

58   *Ibid.* p. B1.

59   Jonathan D. Glater, "From Investor Fury, A Legal Bandwagon," *The New York Times* (September 15, 2002), p. 3-1.

60   Frank Partnoy, *Infectious Greed: How Deceit and Risk Corrupted the Financial Markets*. New York: Time Books, 2003.

61   Sutherland, "White-Collar Criminality," pp. 4–5. For examples of those asserting that corporate and, more generally, white-collar crimes are more costly than conventional criminality, see Balkan et al., *Crime and Deviance in America*, pp. 167–168; Frank Pearce, *Crimes of the Powerful: Marxism, Crime and Deviance*. London: Pluto Press, 1976, pp. 77–79; Conklin, "Illegal But Not Criminal," pp. 2–7; Colin H. Goff and Charles E. Reasons, *Corporate Crime in Canada: A Critical Analysis of Anti-Combines Legislation*. Scarborough, ON: Prentice Hall of Canada, 1978, pp. 11–13; Charles H. McCaghy, *Deviant Behavior: Crime, Conflict, and Interest Groups*. New York: Macmillan, 1976, pp. 204–213; Stuart L. Hills, *Crime, Power, and Morality: The Criminal Law Process in the United States*. Scranton, PA: Chandler, 1971, pp. 167–168; Chamber of Commerce, *White-Collar Crime: Everyone's Problem, Everyone's Loss*, 1974, pp. 4–6; Richard Quinney, *Criminology*. Boston: Little, Brown, 1979, pp. 197–203.

62   Stanton Wheeler and Mitchell Lewis Rothman, "The Organization as Weapon in White-Collar Crime," *Michigan Law Review* 80 (June 1982), p. 1414. It should be noted that Wheeler and Rothman's organizational crimes "need not be the result of corporate misadventure (though most of the organizational illegality...was committed by, or on behalf of, for-profit business organizations)." See p. 1409.

63   Federal Bureau of Investigation, *Crime in the United States 2004: Uniform Crime Reports*. Washington, DC: U.S. Government Printing Office, 2005, p. 259.

64   Wheeler and Rothman, "The Organization as Weapon in White-Collar Crime," pp. 1424, 1426.

65   Susan P. Shapiro, *Wayward Capitalists: Target of the Securities and Exchange Commission*. New Haven: Yale University Press, 1984.

66   *Ibid.*, pp. 31–32.

67   Wheeler and Rothman, "The Organization as Weapon in White-Collar Crime," pp. 1414–1415.

68   For accounts, see Richard A. Smith, "The Incredible Electrical Conspiracy," in Donald R. Cressey and David A. Ward (eds.), *Delinquency, Crime and Social Process.* New York: Harper and Row, 1969, pp. 884–912; John G. Fuller, *The Gentlemen Conspirators. The Story of Price-fixers in the Electrical Industry.* New York: Grove Press, 1962; Myron Watkins, "The Electrical Equipment Antitrust Cases: Their Implications for Government and For Business," *University of Chicago Law Review* 29 (Autumn 1961), pp. 97–110.

69   Fuller, *The Gentlemen Conspirators,* pp. 57, 67.

70   Gilbert Geis, "Deterring Corporate Crime," in M. David Ermann and Richard J. Lundman (eds.), *Corporate and Governmental Deviance.* New York: Oxford University Press, 1978, p. 281.

71   For accounts of the Equity Funding Company of America scandal, see Lee J. Seidler, Frederick Andrews, and Marc J. Epstein (eds.), *The Equity Funding Papers: The Anatomy of a Fraud.* New York: John Wiley and Sons, 1977; Donn B. Parker, *Crime by Computer.* New York: Charles Scribner's Sons, 1976, pp. 118–174; Conklin, "Illegal But Not Criminal," p. 46; and Edward Gross, "Organizational Structure and Organizational Crime," in Gilbert Geis and Ezra Stotland (eds.), *White-Collar Crime: Theory and Research.* Beverly Hills, CA: Sage, 1980, pp. 71–73.

72   Alexander, "Crime in the Suites," p. 57; Merrill Hartson, "E.F. Hutton Pleads Guilty to Fraud," *Cincinnati Enquirer* (May 3, 1985), p. C-8; Barbara Rudolph, "E.F. Hutton's Simmering Scandal," *Time* (July 22, 1985), p. 53; "Capitalist Punishment," *The New Republic* (May 27, 1985), pp. 5–6.

73   Stephen M. Rosoff, Henry N. Pontell, and Robert H. Tillman, *Profit Without Honor: White-Collar Crime and the Looting of America*, 3rd ed. Upper Saddle River, NJ: Prentice Hall, 2004, p. 232.

74   *Ibid.*, p. 327. John Greenwald, "No End in Sight," *Time* (August, 13, 1990), p. 50.

75   Rosoff et al., *Profit Without Honor: White-Collar Crime and the Looting of America*, p. 232. See also Stephen Pizzo, Mary Fricker, and Paul Muolo, *Inside Job: The Looting of America's Savings and Loans.* New York: McGraw-Hill, 1989.

76   Quotes in Rosoff et al., *Profit Without Honor: White-Collar Crime and the Looting of America*, p. 337.

77   Robert Dvorchak, "Northeast to Foot S&L Bill," *Cincinnati Enquirer* (September 3, 1990), p. D5. See also Rosoff et al., *Profit Without Honor: White-Collar Crime and the Looting of America*, pp. 327–344.

78   For accounts of the insider trading scandal, see Mark Stevens, *The Insiders: The Truth Behind the Scandal Rocking Wall Street.* New York: Putnam's Sons, 1987; Connie Bruck, *The Predator's Ball: The Inside Story of Drexel Burnham and the Rise of the Junk Bond Raiders.* New York: Penguin Books, 1988; Laurie P. Cohen, "Public Confession: Milkin Pleads Guilty to Six Felony Counts and Issues an Apology," *The Wall Street Journal* (April 25, 1990), pp. A1, A12; "Milkin's Stiff 10-Year Sentence Is Filled with Incentives to Cooperate with U.S.," *The Wall Street Journal* (November 23, 1990), pp. A3, A8.

79   Details of the Enron scandal were taken from a three-page report on "The Enron Trial" in the "Money Section" of *USA Today* (May 26, 2006), pp. 1–3. See also Rosoff et al., *Profit Without Honor: White-Collar Crime and the Looting of America*, pp. 278-285; Partnoy, *Infectious Greed*, pp. 296–349; Bethany McLean and

Peter Elkind, *The Smartest Guys in the Room: The Amazing Rise and Scandalous Fall of Enron*. New York: Penguin Books, 2003.

80   Julie Appleby, "Many Who Lost Savings, Jobs Pleased," *USA Today* (May 26, 2006), p. 3B.

81   Ken Brown and Ianthe Jeanne Dugan, "Andersen's Fall from Grace Is a Tale of Greed and Miscues," *The Wall Street Journal* (June 7, 2002), pp. A1, A5; Cathy Booth Thomas, "Called Into Account," *Time* (June 24, 2002), p. 52; Rosoff et al., *Profit Without Honor: White-Collar Crime and the Looting of America*, pp. 293–294.

82   Jared Sandberg, Deborah Solomon, and Rebecca Blumenstein, "Disconnected: Inside WorldCom's Unearthing of a Vast Accounting Scandal," *The Wall Street Journal* (June 27, 2002), pp. A1, A12.

83   Rosoff et al., *Profit Without Honor: White-Collar Crime and the Looting of America*, pp. 295–297.

84   Gregg Farrell, "Ebbers Gets 25 Years for Fraud at WorldCom," *USA Today* (July 14, 2005), p. 1B.

85   *Ibid.*

86   Rosoff et al., *Profit Without Honor: White-Collar Crime and the Looting of America*, pp. 299–302; Roger Lowenstein, "The Company They Kept," *The New York Times Magazine* (February 1, 2004), pp. 26–32, 42–43, 62.

87   Associated Press, "High Living CEO Stole from Tyco, Jury Finds," (May 17, 2005), available at http://www.msnbc.msn.com; Rosoff et al., *Profit Without Honor: White-Collar Crime and the Looting of America*, p. 302; Grace Wong, "Koslowski Gets Up to 25 Years," (September 19, 2005), available at http://www.money.cnn.com; Mark Maremont and Laurie P. Cohen, "Executive Privilege: How Tyco's CEO Enriched Himself," *The Wall Street Journal* (August 7, 2002), pp. A1, A6.

88   Greg Farrell, "Sentence's Message: Crime Does Not Pay," *USA Today* (July 14, 2005), p. 2B.

89   This tragic description became the title of a thorough analysis of this disaster and its impact on the lives of those who experienced it. See Kai T. Erikson, *Everything in Its Path: Destruction of Community in the Buffalo Creek Flood*. New York: Simon and Schuster, 1976.

90   Quoted in Gerald M. Stern, *The Buffalo Creek Disaster*. New York: Vintage Books, 1976, p. 12. Stern furnishes a comprehensive account of the disaster and the attempts of its victims to win compensation from Pittston.

91   Quoted in Erikson, *Everything in Its Path,* p. 183.

92   Stern, *The Buffalo Creek Disaster*, p. 70.

93   *Ibid.*, p. 299; "Pittston Settles Claims from '72 Dam Collapse Totaling $4,880,000," *The Wall Street Journal* (January 25, 1978), p. 17. Note that a Special Grand Jury was convened to consider the possibility of criminal charges following the tragedy, but no indictments were handed down. According to Stern, although members of the Grand Jury apparently held strong sentiments against the company, a prosecutor had instructed them that it would be "legally and particularly practically difficult to sustain an indictment against Pittston." See pp. 73–74.

94   Stern, *The Buffalo Creek Disaster,* pp. 148, 151–153.

95   Erikson, *Everything in Its Path,* pp. 183–184.

96   *Ibid.,* p. 154.

97   *Ibid.,* p. 196.

98   Clinard and Yeager, *Corporate Crime,* p. 9; Ronald C. Kramer, "A Prolegomenon to the Study of Corporate Violence," *Humanity and Society* 7 (May 1983), pp. 149–178, and "Is Corporate Crime Serious? Criminal Justice and Corporate Crime Control," *Journal of Contemporary Criminal Justice* 2 (June 1984), pp. 7–10; John Braithwaite, "Challenging Just Deserts: Punishing White-Collar Criminals," *Journal of Criminal Law and Criminology* 73 (Summer 1982), p. 744; Reiman, *The Rich Get Richer and The Poor Get Prison,* p. 82 and, more generally, pp. 44–94; Hills, *Crime, Power, and Morality,* pp. 168–169; Ralph Nader, "Business Crime," *The New Republic* 157 (July 1, 1967), p. 8, and "Corporate Disregard for Life," in his edited volume, *The Consumer and Corporate Accountability.* New York: Harcourt, Brace, Jovanovich, 1973, pp. 151–153.

99   *Peoria Journal Star* (February 18, 1980), p. A-4.

100   Ralph Nader, "Introduction," in Joseph A. Page and Mary-Win O'Brien, *Bitter Wages.* New York: Grossman, 1973, p. xiii.

101   National Institute of Occupational Safety and Health, *Worker Health Chartbook, 2004.* Washington, DC: NIOSH, Centers for Disease Control and Prevention, 2004.

102   *Ibid.,* p. 81.

103   *Ibid.,* p. 45. Between 1980 and 2000, the NIOSH number of "traumatic occupation fatalities"—a count based on death certificates—declined from 7,343 to 4,956. An alternative measure of "fatal occupational injuries" compiled by the Bureau of Labor Statistics noted that fatalities in 1992 were 6,217 and in 2002 were 5,524. See also National Institute for Occupational Safety and Health (NIOSH), *Prevention of Leading Work-related Diseases and Injuries.* Washington, DC: U.S. Government Printing Office, 1985. See section titled "Severe Occupational Traumatic Injuries." This document is composed of articles reprinted from *Morbidity and Mortality Weekly* Report. More generally, see Daniel M. Berman, *Death on the Job: Occupational Health and Safety Struggles in the United States.* New York: Monthly Review Press, 1978; Page and O'Brien, *Bitter Wages*; Carl Gersuny, *Work Hazards and Industrial Conflict.* Hanover, NH: University Press of New England, 1981.

104   NIOSH, *Worker Health Chartbook,* 2004, p. 19; NIOSH, *Worker Health Chartbook, 2000: Nonfatal Illness.* Washington, DC: NIOSH, Centers for Disease Control and Prevention. See also Mark Green and John F. Berry, "White-Collar Crime Is Big Business: Corporate Crime-I," *The Nation* 240 (June 8, 1985), p. 706.

105   Schrager and Short, "Toward a Sociology of Organizational Crime," p. 413.

106   Balkan et al., *Crime and Deviance in America,* p. 171. See also John Braithwaite, *To Punish or Persuade: Enforcement of Coal Mine Safety.* Albany: State University of New York Press, 1985, p. 102; NIOSH, *Worker Health Chartbook, 2000: Focus on Mining.* Washington, DC: NIOSH, Centers for Disease Control and Prevention, 2002, p. v.

107   NIOSH, *Worker Health Chartbook,* 2004, p. 224. See also NIOSH, *Worker Health Chartbook, 2000: Focus on Mining.* Washington, DC: NIOSH, Centers for Disease Control and Prevention, 2002, p. v.

108   NIOSH, *Worker Health Chartbook,* 2004, p. 224.

109   Harry M. Caudill, "Manslaughter in a Coal Mine," *The Nation* 224 (April 23, 1977), p. 497. See also Reiman, *The Rich Get Richer and the Poor Get Prison,* pp. 45–46. Note that 15 miners died in an initial explosion; a second explosion claimed the lives of 11 members of a rescue team.

110   "Were the Deaths of the 12 Coal Miners Preventable? A Look at the History of Safety Violations at the Sago Mine," *Democracy Now* (January 5, 2006), p. 2, available at http://www.democracynow.org. See also Thomas Frank, "Fines in Mining Deaths Cut Back," *USA Today* (January 9, 2006), available at http://www.usa.com/news/nation; Jerry Isaacs, "West Virginia Towns Morn Deaths of 12 Coal Miners," *World Socialist Web Site* (January 6, 2006), available at http://www.wsws.org.

111   Peter Dreier, "Why Mine Deaths Are Up," *The Nation* (June 12, 2006), p. 2, available at http://www.thenation.com.

112   Joel Swartz, "Silent Killers at Work," in M. David Ermann and Richard J. Lundman (eds.), *Corporate and Governmental Deviance.* New York: Oxford University Press, 1978, pp. 114–128.

113   Paul Brodeur, *Outrageous Misconduct: The Asbestos Industry on Trial.* New York: Pantheon, 1985, p. 355. See also Dorothy Nelkin and Michael S. Brown, *Workers at Risk: Voices from the Workplace.* Chicago: University of Chicago Press, 1984.

114   NIOSH, *Worker Health Chartbook, 2004,* p. 151.

115   *Ibid.,* p. 151.

116   NIOSH, *Prevention of Leading Work-related Diseases and Injuries.* See articles titled "Occupational Lung Diseases."

117   *Ibid.* See articles titled "Occupational Lung Diseases" and "Occupational Cancers (Other Than Lung)."

118   Swartz, "Silent Killers at Work," p. 124; Gerald Markowitz and David Rosner, *Deceit and Denial: The Deadly Politics of Industrial Pollution.* Berkeley: University of California Press, 2002.

119   Brodeur, *Outrageous Misconduct,* p. 283.

120   Public Citizen, *Asbestos Cases in the Courts: No Logjam.* Washington, DC: Public Citizen, 2006, pp. 18, 31.

121   Associated Press, "Bush Targets Asbestos Lawsuits." *CBS News* (January 7, 2005), available at http://www.cbsnews.com.

122   Molly Irvins, "Tort Reform: While W. R. Grace Is Indicted, Senate Votes to Curb Lawsuits," *Working For Change,* p. 1, available at http://www.workingforchange.com. See the indictment at *United States of America vs. W.R. Grace et al.,* available at http://www.findlaw.com.

123   "Federal Judge Dismisses Criminal Charge Against W.R. Grace in Asbestos Case," *Jurist* (June 13, 2006), available at http://www.jurist.law.pitt.edu/paper-

chase. See Judge Donald W. Molloy's decision at *United States of America v. W. R. Grace et al.* (June 8, 2006).

124   U.S. Environmental Protection Agency, "Asbestos/Vermiculine," p. 2, available at http://www.epa.gov/asbestos/#vermiculite.

125   *United States vs. W. R. Grace et al.* (Indictment); Exposure Investigation and Consultation Branch, Division of Health Assessment and Consultation, Agency for Toxic Substances and Disease Registry, *Health Consultation: Mortality From Asbestosis in Libby, Montana—Libby Asbestos Site, Libby, Lincoln County, Montana,* December 12, 2000, available at http://www.atsdr.cdc.gov/HAC/PHA/libby; "Asbestos Case in Libby, Montana Comes to a Dramatic Conclusion as a Federal Indictment Is Handed Down to W. R. Grace & Company," *The Mesothelioma Center* (February 14, 2005), available at http://www.mesotheliomacenter.org/news.

126   Andrea Peacock, *Libby, Montana: Asbestos and the Deadly Silence of an American Corporation.* Boulder, CO: Johnson, 2003; Andrew Schneider and David McCumber, *An Air That Kills: How the Asbestos Poisoning of Libby, Montana, Uncovered a National Scandal.* New York: Berkley, 2004.

127   *United States of America v. W.R. Grace et al.* (Indictment).

128   *Ibid.,* p. 9.

129   *Ibid.,* p. 6.

130   "Father and Son Sentenced to Longest U.S. Jail Terms for Environmental Crimes," *EPA Newsroom,* available at http://www.yosemite.epa.gov/opa/admpress.nsf.

131   *Ibid.,* p. 2.

132   Details on the Film Recovery System's case were drawn from the following sources: Nancy Frank, *Crimes Against Health and Safety.* New York: Harrow and Heston, 1985, pp. 21–25; Rena Wish Cohen and Debbe Nelson, "Stefan Golab's Job Was a Death Sentence," *The Daily Herald* (October 30, 1983), pp. 1, 9; John Burnett, "Corporate Murder Verdict May Not Become Trend, Say Legal Experts," *Occupational Health and Safety* (October 1985), pp. 22–26, 58–59; Rick Kendall, "Criminal Charges on the Rise for Workplace Injuries, Deaths," *Occupational Hazards* (December 1985), pp. 49–53; "Murder in the Front Office," *Newsweek* (July 8, 1985), p. 58; Tim Padgett and Leslie Baldacci, "Execs Get 25 Years," *Chicago Sun-Times* (July 2, 1985), pp. 1–2; Bill Richards and Alex Kotlowitz, "Judge Finds 3 Corporate Officials Guilty of Murder in Cyanide Death of Worker," *The Wall Street Journal* (June 17, 1985); Steven Greenhouse, "3 Executives Convicted of Murder for Unsafe Workplace Conditions," *The New York Times* (June 15, 1985), pp. 1, 9; "Convictions May Jolt Corporate World," *Lexington Herald-Leader* (June 16, 1985); Ray Gibson and William Presecky, "Indictments Cite Officials, 3 Firms," *Chicago Tribune* (October 20, 1983), pp. 1, 8; Barry Siegel, "Murder Case a Corporate Landmark," *Los Angeles Times* (September 15, 1985), pp. 1, 8–9.

133   Burnett, "Corporate Murder Verdict May Not Become Trend, Say Legal Experts," p. 22.

134   *Ibid.,* p. 22.

135   Kendall, "Criminal Charges on the Rise for Workplace Injuries, Deaths," p. 49.

[136]   Padgett and Baldacci, "Execs Get 25 Years," pp. 1–2.

[137]   Rosoff et al., *Profit Without Honor: White-Collar Crime and the Looting of America*, p. 186.

[138]   Judy R. Aulette and Raymond Michalowski, "Fire in Hamlet: A Case Study of a State-Corporate Crime," in Kenneth D. Tunnell (ed.), *Political Crime in Contemporary America*, 1993, pp. 171–206; John Paul Wright, Francis T. Cullen, and Michael B. Blankenship, "The Social Construction of Corporate Violence: Media Coverage of the Imperial Food Products Fire," *Crime & Delinquency* 41 (January 1995), pp. 20–36; Clark Cox, "Haunted by Ghosts," *The Pilot*, September 12, 2001, available at http://archives.thepilot.com.

[139]   Cox, "Haunted by Ghosts," p. 3.

[140]   David Von Drehele, *Triangle: The Fire That Changed America*. New York: Atlantic Monthly Press, 2003.

[141]   *Ibid.*, p. 215.

[142]   *Ibid.*, p. 3.

[143]   *Ibid.*, pp. 217–258.

[144]   Joan Claybrook and the Staff of Public Citizen, *Retreat From Safety: Reagan's Attack on America's Safety*. New York: Pantheon, 1984, p. 60.

[145]   U.S. Consumer Product Safety Commission, "Toys," *Consumer Product Safety Review*, 10 (Winter 2006), p. 6. For more data on injuries by product categories, see "NEEIS Data Highlights—2003," *Consumer Product Safety Review* 9 (Fall 2004), pp. 2–6.

[146]   U.S. Consumer Product Safety Commission, "All Terrain Vehicles," p. 1, available at http://www.cpsc.gov/cpspub/pubs/atvpubs.

[147]   Gilbert Geis, "Victimization Patterns in White-Collar Crime," in I. Drapkin and E. Viano (eds.), *Victimology: A New Focus, Volume V., Exploiters and Exploited*. Lexington, MA: Lexington Books, 1974, p. 93; Braithwaite, "Challenging Just Deserts," p. 745.

[148]   Schrager and Short, "Toward a Sociology of Organizational Crime," p. 415.

[149]   Harrison Wellford, *Sowing the Wind*. New York: Grossman, 1972, pp. 17, 29, 130.

[150]   David R. Simon and D. Stanley Eitzen, *Elite Deviance*, 2nd ed. Boston: Allyn & Bacon, 1986, p. 102. See also Neal Karlen with Jeff B. Copeland, "A 'Mystery Meat' Scandal," *Newsweek* (September 24, 1984), p. 31.

[151]   Pam Belluck "Juice-Poisoning Case Brings Guilty Plea and a Huge Fine," *The New York Times* (July 24, 1998), p. 1, available at http://www.query.nytimes.com. John Henkel, "Juice Maker Fined Record Amount for E. Coli-Tainted Product," *FDA Consumer Magazine* 33 (January-February 1999), available at http://www.fda.gov.

[152]   John Henkel, "Food Firm Gets Huge Fine for Tainted Strawberry Harvest," *FDA Consumer Magazine* 33 (March-April 1999), available at http://www.fda.gov.

[153]   Michelle Meadows, "Company Gets a Guilty Reading in Glucose Monitor Cases," *FDA Consumer Magazine* 35 (March-April 2001); John Henkel, "FDA Uncovers Contaminated Covers," *FDA Consumer Magazine* 31 (July-August 1997); Dixie Farley, "Manufacturer Sentenced for Selling Unsterilized Surgical Instruments," *FDA Consumer Magazine* 32 (January-February 1998), all avail-

able at http://www.fda.gov; Office on Consumer Litigation, "U.S. v. Para Tech Industries et al.," available at http://www.usdoj.gov./civil/ocl/cases/ParaTech.

154 Linda Bren, "Company Caught in Coverup of Medical Device Malfunctions," *FDA Consumer Magazine* 37 (November-December 2002), available at http://www.fda.gov; "Press Release," United States Attorney's Office, Northern District of California (June 13, 2003); available at http://www.usdoj.gov/usao/canpress.

155 Clinard and Yeager, *Corporate Crime*, p. 266.

156 Claybrook et al., *Retreat from Safety*, p. 59.

157 See the web site of the Consumer Product Safety Commission at http://www.cpsc.gov.

158 Ralph Nader, *Unsafe at Any Speed: The Designed-in Dangers of the American Automobiles*. New York: Grossman, 1965. Nader's book and its impact will be discussed in Chapter 4.

159 J. Patrick Wright, *On a Clear Day You Can See General Motors: John Z. DeLorean's Look Inside the Automotive Giant*. New York: Avon, 1979, p. 65.

160 *Ibid.*, p. 67. Notably, Lee Iacocca shares the view that the Corvair was an unsafe vehicle. Thus, he commented that "GM had its fiascos, too, like the Corvair. Here I find myself in rare agreement with Ralph Nader: the Corvair really was unsafe." See Lee Iacocca, *Iacocca: An Autobiography*. New York: Bantam Books, 1984, p. 161. On the other hand, GM lost only one Corvair-related civil case that reached trial; other suits, however, were settled out of court. See Brent Fisse and John Braithwaite, *The Impact of Publicity on Corporate Offenders*. Albany: SUNY Press, 1983, p. 64.

161 Kermit Vandiver, "The Aircraft Brake Scandal," *Harper's Magazine* 244 (April 1972), pp. 45–52.

162 Clinard and Yeager, *Corporate Crime*, p. 120.

163 For case studies focusing on the physical costs of corporate illegality, see John Braithwaite, *Corporate Crime in the Pharmaceutical Industry*. London: Routledge and Kegan Paul, 1984, Chapters 3 and 4.

164 *Ibid.*, p. 64. See also Paul D. Rheingold, "The MER/29 Story—An Instance of Successful Mass Disaster Litigation," *California Law Review* 56 (January 1968), pp. 116–148.

165 Morton Mintz, *At Any Cost: Corporate Greed, Women, and the Dalkon Shield*. New York: Pantheon Books, 1985.

166 *Ibid.*, p. 4.

167 *Ibid.*, pp. 3, 242.

168 *Ibid.*, p. 7.

169 *Ibid.*, p. 245. See also p. 242.

170 *Ibid.*, p. 247.

171 "Drug Maker to Pay $430 Million in Fines, Civil Damages," *FDA Consumer Magazine* 38 (July-August 2004), available at http://www.fda.fdac/features/2004.

172   *Ibid.*, p. 2.

173   Press Release, "Eli Lilly and Company to Pay U.S. $36 Million Relating to Off-Label Promotion," (December 21, 2005), available at http://www.usdoj.cov, p. 2.

174   "Living, Dangerously, with Toxic Wastes," *Time* (October 14, 1985), p. 86. More generally, see the October 14, 1985 issue of *Time*, bearing the cover titled, "Toxic Wastes: The Poisoning of America."

175   Clayborn et. al., *Retreat from Safety*, p. 118.

176   Roger Rosenblatt, "All the World Gasped," *Time* (December 17, 1984), p. 20. More generally, see the December 17, 1984 issue of *Time*, bearing the cover titled, "India's Disaster: The Night of Death—A Global Worry."

177   Quoted in Jay S. Albanese, "Love Canal Six Years Later: The Legal Legacy," *Federal Probation* 48 (June 1984), p. 54.

178   Alan A. Bloch and Frank R. Scarpitti, *Poisoning for Profit: The Mafia and Toxic Waste in America*. New York: William Morrow, 1985, p. 40.

179   Michael Brown, *Laying Waste: The Poisoning of America by Toxic Chemicals*. New York: Pantheon, 1979, pp. 10–11, 52. It should be noted that we have drawn a number of specific details about the Love Canal case from Brown's account. See pp. 3–59.

180   *Ibid.*, p. xii.

181   Albanese, "Love Canal Six Years Later," p. 53.

182   Ed Magnuson, "A Problem That Cannot Be Buried," *Time* (October 14, 1985), p. 76.

183   *Ibid.*, p. 76; Rosoff et al., *Profit Without Honor: White-Collar Crime and the Looting of America*, p. 162.

184   Bloch and Scarpitti, *Poisoning for Profit*, pp. 50–51.

185   Green and Berry, "White-Collar Crime Is Big Business," p. 706.

186   Ronald G. Burns and Michael J. Lynch, *Environmental Crime: A Sourcebook*. New York: LFB Scholarly, 2004, p. 5.

187   Rosoff et al., *Profit Without Honor: White-Collar Crime and the Looting of America*, p. 150.

188   *Ibid.*, pp. 155-156; Burns and Lynch, *Environmental Crime: A Sourcebook*, pp. 236-242; Markowitz and Rosner, *Deceit and Denial: The Deadly Politics of Industrial Pollution*, pp. 267–270.

189   Rosoff et al., *Profit Without Honor: White-Collar Crime and the Looting of America*, p. 144.

190   Ralph Nader, "Introduction," in John C. Esposito, *Vanishing Air*. New York: Grossman, 1970, pp. vii–viii. See also Ralph Nader, "The Profits of Pollution," *The Progressive* 34 (April 1970), pp. 19–22, and Markowitz and Rosner, *Deceit and Denial: The Deadly Politics of Industrial Pollution*.

191   Clinard and Yeager, *Corporate Crime*, pp. 116–117. More generally, see Jonathan Lash, Katherine Gillman, and David Sheridan, *A Season of Spoils: The Story of*

the Reagan Administration's Attack on the Environment. New York: Pantheon, 1984.

192   Barry Meier, "Dirty Job: Against Heavy Odds, EPA Tries to Convict Polluters and Dumpers," *The Wall Street Journal* (January 7, 1985), p. 1.

193   Clinard and Yeager, "Corporate Crime: Yesterday and Today—A Comparison," p. xx.

194   *Ibid.*

195   Michael L. Benson and Francis T. Cullen, *Combating Corporate Crime: Local Prosecutors at Work*. Boston: Northeastern University Press, 1998. See also Donald J. Rebovich, "Environmental Crime Prosecution at the County Level," in Mary Clifford (ed.), *Environmental Crime: Enforcement, Policy, and Responsibility*. Gaithersburg, MD: Aspen, 1998, pp. 205–227.

196   See, for example, Mark Dowie, "Pinto Madness," *Mother Jones*, 2 (September-October 1977), pp. 18–32; Richard A. Epstein, "Is Pinto a Criminal?" *Regulation* 4 (March-April 1980), pp. 15–21.

197   Advertisement in *Cincinnati Enquirer* (January 31, 2005), p. A4.

198   Matthew T. Lee and M. David Ermann, "Pinto 'Madness' as a Flawed Landmark Narrative: An Organizational and Network Analysis." *Social Problems* 46 (February 1999), pp. 30–47.

199   *Ibid.* See also Dennis A. Gioia, "Pinto Fires and Personal Ethics: A Script Analysis of Missed Opportunities." *Journal of Business Ethics* 11 (May 1992), pp. 379–389.

200   Gioia, "Pinto Fires and Personal Ethics: A Script Analysis of Missed Opportunities," p. 381.

201   For a pathbreaking analysis of the concepts of "culture of production" and "normalization of deviance," see Diane Vaughan, *The Challenger Launch Decision: Risky Technology, Culture, and Deviance at NASA*. Chicago: University of Chicago Press, 1996.

202   On changing standards of risk and how this affects potential legal action, see Lawrence M. Friedman, *Total Justice: What Americans Want from the Legal System and Why*. Boston: Beacon Press, 1985. With regard to how risks of environmental pollution are now interpreted very differently than they were before disasters such as Bhopal and Love Canal, see Markowitz and Rosner, *Deceit and Denial: The Deadly Politics of Industrial Pollution*, pp. 299–300.

2

Corporate Criminal Liability: From Immunity to Culpability

As we noted in Chapter 1, many U.S. corporations have been involved in criminal activity on a continuing basis. Corporate crime, like criminal behavior generally, is costly and harmful to society. We seem to be besieged by reports of dangerous products or by disclosures of corporate misbehavior that disregards our quality of life or that violates our basic values. And yet, despite the seriousness of these acts and their costs to us, the law—especially the criminal law—has often provided insufficient redress for the socially harmful behavior of corporations.

In this chapter, we will trace the development of the corporation from its beginnings as a limited collective entity to its present state as the dominant form of business enterprise worldwide. We will consider why and how the corporation has historically enjoyed a degree of immunity from the provisions of the criminal law. Finally, we will see that gradually this immunity has been eroded so that corporations are increasingly held responsible, even by the criminal law, for their socially harmful behaviors. We also will see, however, that there is a constant struggle to regulate corporate misbehavior with the criminal law.

LAW AND THE SOCIAL ORDER

Law is a social institution that regulates human behavior. Along with other mechanisms of social regulation, such as custom and religion, law is characterized by norms and sanctions, that is, by expectations of behavior and a reward-punishment scheme that encourages compliance with these expectations. Notions of social harm tend to pervade discussions of law. It is commonly assumed that strongly held social values, those that are basic to the very existence of society and that proscribe the most harmful behavior, fall within the ambit of the criminal law.[1] Crime violates these values, and the penal sanction is the societal response to the violation.

The content of law varies over time, as does the format of the penal sanction. The purpose or justification for the sanction has changed over the years as well. Punishment has existed in a variety of formats, including imprisonment and all sorts of torture and methods of execution. Rationales for the penal sanction have included (1) retribution in its various forms, such as deserved punishment and punishment as a symbolic expression of social reprobation; (2) incapacitation, or the isolation of offenders from society; (3) deterrence of either a specific offender or of the general population; and (4) rehabilitative programs designed to effect changes in the behavior and values of offenders. To some extent, all of these rationales have coexisted over the years and exerted a combination of influences on the administration of penal sanctions. For example, although rehabilitation was the official justification for the penal sanction during much of the twentieth century, it co-existed with the other rationales, for example, the more pernicious variants of retribution such as racially biased executions. Beginning in the late 1970s, a more straightforwardly punitive view of sanctioning policy emerged, although it, too, was grounded in retribution, incapacitation, and deterrence.[2]

Until fairly recently, these various aspects of the system of penal sanctions were applicable to conventional crime but less so to corporate criminality. It was perhaps paradoxical even to speak of corporate crime. For reasons that we will discuss in this chapter, historically the actions of corporations were neither considered within the purview of nor subject to the usual sanctions of the criminal law. In part, this is why the trial of the Ford Motor Company for reckless homicide was a landmark case.

According to a strict legalistic definition, crime presumes a prohibited act and a penal sanction, that is, an act prohibited by the criminal law and for which the law specifies a punishment. Paul Tappan articulated this definition in an important criminological debate 60 years ago, a debate that was occasioned by a discussion of corporate crime. The debate began in 1940 when Edwin Sutherland used the term "white-collar crime" in his presidential address to the American Sociological Association. In 1949, Sutherland published *White Collar Crime*, wherein he argued that a number of major corporations regularly engaged in behaviors that would be considered crimes if undertaken by individuals. Sutherland applied the term "white-collar crime" to these behaviors, and even called the corporations recidivists. Tappan responded with his legalistic definition because he argued that Sutherland's sociological approach would result in a vacuous definition of crime that would impede criminological analysis.[3]

The academic debate over the meaning of corporate crime (and how to regulate it) remains lively today. For example, although Tappan's view dominates legal thinking, the legalistic approach exhibits circular reasoning—crime is whatever the criminal law says it is. Moreover, definitions of crime reflect power and privilege. Equally important, the debate about crime generally, and corporate crime in particular, forces us to consider the notion of social harm, an important issue when we ask, "What *is* the definition of crime? What *should* it be?"

The somewhat philosophical "is versus ought" issue is addressed only partially (or perhaps is evaded) by the assumption that the criminal law reflects society's most basic values. By implication, the criminal law proscribes those acts that are the most detrimental or harmful to society. However, this view fails to explain why many corporate actions are not considered criminal even though they are socially harmful.

One of two responses is usually offered. First, the social harm produced by corporations and their responsibility for these harms are difficult to perceive. The point is not merely that corporate crime is complex, which it often is, but rather that a kind of Parkinson's law describes our understanding of crime: our comprehension is greatest when the phenomenon is simplest.[4] While crime is defined as a violation of *social* norms and arguably as *socially* harmful, our understanding of unlawful conduct tends to be fixated at the *individual* level. The entire crime-punishment nexus is highly individualistic. In the traditional model, one person harms another and is punished. Criminal activity at a more complex level—i.e., a collective entity being punished for harming great numbers of scattered victims—is hard to grasp and was inconceivable under common law. The early law was designed to regulate the behavior of individuals as natural persons, not a collective entity like the corporation. In a strict legalistic sense, the corporation had no mind to form the requisite intent to commit a prohibited act and no body to punish,[5] so no matter how grave the social harm, the corporation could not commit a crime.

The second answer reflects the assumption that the criminal law reflects and protects strongly held social values. Criminal behavior, according to this view, is an official statement of society's moral boundaries. If an act is not a crime, arguably it does not violate the boundaries. Of course, at a certain point in their development, corporations became powerful enough to influence the law and to protect themselves from criminal responsibility.[6] In any case, boundaries change as society changes. A behavior may be considered within a society's moral boundaries at one time and outside them at another. Certain actions of corporations may not have been considered harmful enough to violate the moral boundaries under common law, but later they were viewed as serious enough to deserve the label "criminal."[7]

These two responses are usually given to the question of why corporate misbehavior historically was not considered a violation of criminal law. Crime, according to the traditional view, is highly individualistic, and/or the moral boundaries (i.e., what is regarded as seriously wrong or harmful) have shifted so that corporate malfeasance that formerly was acceptable now provokes more widespread disapproval. We use the "and/or" conjunction because these answers need not be mutually exclusive and because each is probably correct as far as it goes. But these answers still beg the question and generate yet another set of inquiries. Why is our perception of crime individualistic? Why did the moral boundaries shift?

To answer these questions and to address the more fundamental issue of the corporation's historical exclusion from the purview of the criminal law, we must analyze the development of the corporate form. This analysis must be sensitive to the historical context of law's development.

The Historical Context of Law

We propose an analysis of law that is historically specific and applicable to the development of corporations. Historical periods are characterized by different perceptions of behavior, including crime; by different perceptions of responsibility for behavior; and by particular conceptualizations of justice, the ultimate aim of law.[8] Within historical periods we can comprehend specific connections and also discover general interrelationships among law and other social phenomena.

These interrelationships are a long-standing topic of discussion for academics; indeed, many prominent scholars analyzed these interrelationships during the formative years of social sciences such as sociology. For example, we have mentioned the claim that the criminal law reflects the most strongly held social values and that a relationship exists between law and the moral sentiments of society's members. The French sociologist Emile Durkheim developed a frequently cited framework for understanding this relationship. Writing during the late 1800s and early 1900s, Durkheim addressed the degree to which law reflected values that were common to the average member of society. In his framework, however, legal norms and penal sanctions were not simply the mirror image of social values, especially in complex societies, but also were informed by increasing social complexity, a decreasing role for religion in the regulation of behavior, and the degree of centralization of political authority.[9]

Scholars differ as to which factors they consider most important for an understanding of legal norms or the transformations of these norms. Some writers de-emphasize values in favor of other social factors. For Karl Marx, a German social scientist and Durkheim's contemporary, the key factor was the mode of production, that complex set of relations that surrounds the economy of society. Marx's framework is best understood via an architectural metaphor: the base/superstructure model. Law and other social institutions (including our social consciousness) are a part of a superstructure that is built upon the economic base, which is the foundation of society. The institutions in the superstructure change when the economic base changes.[10]

The economy also was an important consideration for Max Weber, a German scholar who made his intellectual contributions at about the same time as Marx and Durkheim. Weber was concerned with the autonomy of law, the development of the legal profession, and their relationship to the rise of the bureaucratic state. He argued that the modern political organization, legitimated by the legal order, provided the rationality or predictability necessary for the emergence of capitalism as a sophisticated economic system.[11]

Clearly, Durkheim, Marx, and Weber offer different views, but they also show points of convergence. They see law as a social institution that is intertwined with other institutions; law is sensitive to changes in other institutions, and facilitates or contributes to the changes. These three scholars established the intellectual framework for much of the contemporary theoretical analysis that addresses the interrelationship of law and other social institutions.

We are interested in a related, albeit more specific, issue: the emergence and the law's treatment of the corporation. Our review of the historical record prompts us to focus on three factors that are of primary importance to an analysis of the corporation's development: the centralization of political authority in the state, the shift in the economic structure from feudalism through mercantilism to capitalism, and changes in "person" as a legal concept. Two of these factors draw on the analytic frameworks of the pioneering scholars whom we have discussed. The centralization of political authority is a significant issue for both Durkheim and Weber, and the economic structure is a central theme for Weber and Marx. The third factor, the concept of person, is especially relevant because new dimensions of the meaning of person and the meaning of personal responsibility accompanied the emergence of the corporation as a legal entity. In sum, we can best understand the emergence of the corporate form and its relationship to the criminal law through a historical analysis that is keyed to three factors: the state, the economy, and person as a legal concept.

THE DEVELOPMENT OF THE CORPORATION

Corporations are the dominant business form in the world today; they are pervasive and wield tremendous economic power. Their prevalence is reflected in the sheer number of corporations and in a diversity of size and organization that ranges from the individual entrepreneur to the multinational conglomerate. Their economic power is evidenced by wealth and productivity that sometimes exceeds the gross national product of nations.

Yet, ironically, their pervasiveness causes us to view corporations somewhat myopically. Notwithstanding its considerable impact on our lives for good and bad, the corporate form is a relatively recently development. The dominance of the corporate form and the explosive growth that produced it in the United States date to about 150 years ago. As recently as the early 1800s, the corporation was a rarity in the United States.

The development of the corporation followed a complex and circuitous route, accompanying significant and interrelated transformations in the economic structure of society, the nature of political authority, and the concept of person. The emergence of the corporation is best understood within the context of the large-scale social changes that occurred through the Middle Ages and into the Industrial Revolution.

Early History

The history of the corporation begins in England and other parts of Europe in the Middle Ages, when feudalism was the dominant institutional feature of society. Feudalism entailed a way of life that differed greatly from the conditions that had prevailed in earlier centuries. In earlier times, society was comprised of small groups of people, often kinship groups, who banded together to ensure survival. These groups were a homogeneous population with little economic or political division of labor.

These patterns changed in the feudal period. Economically, feudalism was defined by an agrarian existence linked to the ownership of land parceled into feudal estates. Social and legal interactions—that is, the rights and responsibilities that people owed one another—were informed by this arrangement. The relationships within feudalism were hierarchical, and included definite superiors (the feudal lords) and subordinates (the serfs). Sir Henry Maine, a nineteenth-century legal historian, described this as a "status relationship," that is, one's place in the hierarchy was determined at birth and was rarely transcended.[12] Rights and responsibilities existed as a set of reciprocal obligations and expectations between the serfs, who owed their basic existence and fealty to the feudal lord (as had their parents to the previous lord), and the feudal lord, who inherited the fidelity and labor of the serfs along with the duty of providing for their subsistence.

Feudalism was characterized by a decentralized pattern of political authority; power resided in the feudal estates rather than in the collective population. There was no powerful state yet, and the most significant development of centralized authority existed in the church. The regulation or maintenance of social order that accompanies political power was in the hands of the feudal lords and the church. They enjoyed different spheres of influence—the secular and the sacred—although there was overlap and occasional conflict.

In times long before the feudal period, social regulation was aimed at restoring the social order that was disturbed when someone violated a norm. Sanctions tended to be collective both in purpose and administration. Violations that threatened the group (e.g., breaking a taboo) were sanctioned to appease the supernatural, and even individual disputes often produced a collective response. Whether a violation threatened the group or only a few members, responsibility for wrongdoing was a matter of strict liability. "Liability was founded on the act of doing damage rather than on any subjective state of, or degree of care exercised by, the defendant."[13] The key issue was injury, and liability was imputed through a variety of vicarious and indirect methods. A person might be held responsible for an injury because he or she was nearby when it occurred. Oracles and other supernatural signs were important in assigning liability.[14]

During the feudal period, by contrast, responsibility was less collective in the sense of kinship groups, but was a far cry from the internal, individual matter that it would later become. Because criminality as embodied in the legal concept of *mens rea* remained undeveloped, internal volition and subjective intent were less important than the external, objective relationship between a violation and the person held accountable. The maintenance of social order persisted as the basis of sanctions, although that order was defined by the feudal lord who administered the sanction. Feudalism shaped not only the view of social harm—defined as a disturbance of the feudal order—but also the administration and purpose of sanctions.

The concept of person was simple and limited during the feudal period. It denoted the rights and responsibilities of an individual as a natural person, and was rarely applicable to a collective entity. Partnerships existed, but merely as assemblages of individuals, each with their own rights and responsibilities. Corporations did not exist.

Wealth in the feudal period consisted primarily of land separated into feudal estates and owned by individuals. Rights and responsibilities and the political authority that governed them were largely a function of the feudal arrangement. The concept of person was limited and individualistic, with little place for forms of collective ownership. This pattern began to change, however, amid the societal upheavals of the Middle Ages.

The Middle Ages

The economic structure of Europe was shaped by feudalism early in the Middle Ages. Wealth meant land, but the right to own land was limited to those few who were born to it. During the fourteenth and fifteenth centuries, however, feudalism gave way to mercantilism and an economy based on trade. Commerce within and between nations appeared, and with it came the merchants who displaced the feudal lords as the primary economic players. Merchants, too, owned property, but that ownership included commercial interests, not just land.

Shipping, the heart of the trading economy, flourished with continual advances in shipping technology. Ships became larger, faster, and more profitable. However, they also became more expensive to outfit, and trading ventures were costly. For a variety of reasons (e.g., pirates), such ventures became riskier as well. Merchants were forced to pool investments, and more complex and increasingly collective business forms were developed to accommodate these ventures. The trading company was an important collective entity of the shipping economy.

Technological advances were not limited to shipping; they occurred in other modes of transportation and in other business sectors as well. Manufacturing eventually became as important as shipping, and economies prospered during the seventeenth and eighteenth centuries with the transition to capitalism. With the coming of the Industrial Revolution, the capitalists became the significant economic players in society. Like the merchants and traders before them, they combined their resources or capital to achieve maximum growth. The collective business enterprise (e.g., the joint stock company) facilitated the necessary concentration of capital. (Later in this section we will discuss more fully the trading company and the joint stock company as business forms, and also in terms of their relationship to the centralization of political authority and their ramifications for the legal concept of person.) With the transition to capitalism, property took on yet another meaning: it changed from physical possession for one's own use to a source of value in exchange.[15]

In a few centuries, the economic structure of England and the rest of Europe was transformed from feudalism through mercantilism to capitalism. The transformation was massive and paradoxical as well. Amid unprecedented economic growth and prosperity, the old social order was disrupted and ultimately broke down. Accordingly, the upheavals that occurred in the Middle Ages included a transition in the nature of political authority and the establishment of a new social order. A relocation of political authority accompanied the transformation in the economic structure of society. We will avoid the potentially reductionistic argument about which was the more significant change (with the implication that one caused the other) by simply suggesting that the political and the economic transformations each contributed to and were influenced by the other.

The political power of the feudal lords was by no means unchecked, even in feudalism. As noted, the church was a powerful force during that period, and an uneasy truce existed between the two. The church facilitated the decline of the feudal lords' authority. More important, however, as the economic dominance of the feudal lords waned, political power shifted to the state. The shift occurred with the strong support of the bourgeoisie, the increasingly powerful merchants of the emerging middle class, who supported the interests of the monarchy—the centralized state—against the feudal lords and the church. Their growing economic power made their political support significant. Moreover, the Middle Ages witnessed the emergence of political doctrines such as the social contract, which justified both the ownership of property by the bourgeoisie and the concentration of political power in the state.[16]

The shift of political power was a complex phenomenon. To suggest that power simply vested in the state misses much of that complexity. The notion of state included both the monarchy and local authorities. During the mercantile period in England, for example, the political authority of the feudal lords dissipated but remained somewhat local, residing for a time in the boroughs and counties, primarily in the hands of justices of the peace. The crown could tax the localities and grant or withhold business privileges, so even then the centralization of political authority was under way.[17]

That pattern continued throughout the Middle Ages. As the centralized state became stronger, its willingness and ability to regulate the population grew more pronounced. The expansion of state control occurred throughout England and the rest of Europe in both civil and criminal law. In civil matters the English Crown extended its control over local authorities and business interests via the royal charter, an official grant that conferred legal existence. With respect to the criminal law, the state's consolidation of power proceeded through several stages. Initially, the Crown merely sought to limit blood feuds by encouraging victims or their kin to accept a compensatory payment rather than engage in retaliatory acts against an offender. Later the Crown became a public prosecutor for violations that disturbed the "King's Peace," thereby displacing local criminal jurisdiction. Eventually the Crown prosecuted and sanctioned criminals for offenses against the monarchy; the state had become the definer of legal norms.[18]

In both the civil and criminal spheres, the centralization of political authority culminated in the codification of laws and ultimately in lawmaking by legislation. For Sir Henry Maine, legislation represents the highest stage of legal development, and it exists only in modern, dynamic societies.[19] The modern legal system, with its formally rational laws, is also central to Max Weber's analysis. Such a legal apparatus is an essential element of the modern bureaucratic state, and, in Weber's model, is a condition precedent to the development of Western capitalism.[20]

The changes in the economic structure of society and in the nature of political authority were interrelated with the third significant transformation that occurred during the Middle Ages—the meaning of person as a legal concept. The meaning of the concept of person changed in two respects: first, it expanded beyond the limited definition of a natural person to include collective entities that were recognized as juristic persons; second, the nature of personal responsibility changed.

An early case involving the legal recognition of a collective entity was occasioned by a dilemma that concerned the ownership of churches in the waning days of feudalism. Traditionally, the feudal lord built a church on his estate and selected the priest; he also enjoyed property rights in it. But by the thirteenth century, the decline of feudalism was under way, and the power of the feudal lord had begun to diminish on a number of fronts, including ownerships of churches and associated property. The law was confronted with a dilemma: if the feudal lord no longer owned the church and related property as an individual, who did? Eventually it was concluded that the church owned itself, namely, the building, the property, and any income it generated. Those who managed its affairs could transact business in its name, essentially as guardians. The church was not a natural person but rather enjoyed a special status, that of a juristic person. The law recognized the church and also protected it, almost as a legal infant, from those who managed it as guardians.[21]

The concept of a juristic person was extended during the thirteenth and fourteenth centuries to include English boroughs or townships. Boroughs incurred both financial rights and responsibilities as they gained political authority. The responsibilities included debts, usually rents and fines, that were owed to the Crown. The rights included the privilege of levying tolls and selling franchises. These revenue-producing assets were transferable. The status of a juristic person facilitated these financial transactions by creating an entity that could conduct business as if it were a natural person. At the same time, the recognition of that special status reflected the increasing centralization of political authority: that special status was conferred by the Crown through the royal charters.[22]

This point is significant for two reasons. First, the collective entities that were recognized as juristic persons, including the corporation, developed largely at the pleasure of the state. Second, during its early development, the corporation acted in a quasi-governmental capacity, in this case, collecting tolls. As we shall see, the first U.S. corporations operated under state charters, and their activities were often quasi-governmental. This situation may partially explain the preferential treatment enjoyed by corporations; they were a child of the state and in many instances performed the duties of the state.

One of the best examples of the complex interaction of business interests, political authority, and the development of a collective entity is the English trading company. The trading company emerged in the sixteenth century as a business form that allowed merchants to pool investments and conduct business on a larger scale. At first, the companies resembled partnerships: members conducted business as individuals even though they had combined their resources. As trading ventures became more elaborate, the companies developed into collective entities trading on joint stock. For a time, companies existed for a single venture, but eventually they became permanent enterprises.

Although business was their primary purpose, trading companies shared with other phases of corporate development a secondary, quasi-governmental role. A significant share of the English economy was built on trade with other nations and on colonizing new lands. The companies facilitated trade, and, in new territories, served in a political capacity until England established a colonial government.[23] The trading companies were created by the state (through royal charters), furthered its economy, and even acted as an arm of the state.

This symbiotic relationship was evidenced by the passage of the Bubble Act in 1719, which prohibited unchartered joint stock companies. The unchartered joint stock company was an accommodating, if informal, type of enterprise that owed its existence to prevailing business practices. Ironically, it became more widespread after the passage of the prohibitory legislation. The Bubble Act generated a financial panic that caused the collapse of some chartered companies; as a result, the demand for charters declined. Following the loss of confidence in chartered companies, the legal community devised a number of ingenious methods that circumvented the restrictions of the Bubble Act and made the unchartered joint stock company even more popular. Lawyers often created the companies through contractual agreements, essentially using a deed of settlement that was adopted from the fourteenth-century trust. The companies were virtually immune from suit, and members enjoyed an unofficial limited liability. Increasingly, the joint stock company resembled the modern corporation, and a specialized corporate bar was created as an indirect result.[24]

Other kinds of collective entities were developed between the fourteenth and sixteenth centuries. Some were unrelated to the trend toward centralization but nonetheless contributed to an extension of the concept of juristic persons. The trust, for example, was a legal device that became popular in the fourteenth century. The trust was initially a vehicle for passing land or the profits from land to one's heirs while avoiding the legal and financial restraints that attached to an inheritance. The owner conveyed to trustees the legal title to land by deed of settlement; the trustees held it for the owner's benefit during life and, upon death, for the benefit of the designated beneficiary (*cestui que* trust). Akin to a juristic person, the trustees held legal title not as individuals but as an ongoing juristic entity.[25]

The willingness to recognize a juristic as distinguished from a natural person was further evidenced in the sixteenth century. Again the issue was a legal dilemma, but in this case, one with political overtones. The dilemma concerned the conveyance of land by the King who, as a minor, lacked the legal capacity to engage in such a transaction. As a resolution, English law recognized the Crown as two persons: one, the current King as a natural person, and the other, the Crown as a political entity with legal standing that transcended the King as an individual.[26] With this solution, English law in effect recognized the "corporation sole," in which an individual and the individual's successors became more than a natural person, guaranteeing a legal entity's existence in perpetuity through incorporation.

A third example, the concept of *universitas*, was uncovered amid a revival of interest in Roman law among legal scholars. A *universitas* was an association that was treated as an entity rather than as a group of individuals. It gave a collective status to guilds and professional organizations. Under Roman law, these groups could only be created by the sovereign, which reinforced the link between a collective entity and the state.[27]

The interest in Roman law resurrected even more significant concepts. These concepts contributed to the second change in the legal concept of person that we mentioned earlier—a change in the nature of personal responsibility. English and European legal scholars redis-covered the concepts *culpa* and *dolus*. These concepts addressed the notion of intent, an internal and subjective state: *culpa* connoted fault or negligence; *dolus*, connoting more intent, implied guile or deceit. *Culpa* and *dolus* were part of a new legal doctrine that appeared dur-ing the Middle Ages, a doctrine that included the emergence of *mens rea*—a guilty mind or criminal intent—and a theory of criminal neg-ligence.[28] The legal focus for criminal responsibility shifted to the individual.

The church had long advocated moral guilt for individual sin, a con-cept of culpability that entailed a mental element. But during earlier times a sort of strict liability prevailed, and neither intent nor individual responsibility were important considerations with respect to blame. Sim-ilarly, during the feudal period, the imputation of accountability for a wrong was an external, objective concern. In both periods, the restoration of order was the primary issue. The secondary issue of who should be sanctioned was a matter of kinship, whim, physical proximity, or a variety of other means whereby the determination was made.

That state of affairs changed in the Middle Ages. The transition to mercantilism and then to capitalism signaled an end to the agrarian life and a social order based on the reciprocal obligations between feudal lord and serf. The population steadily moved from the countryside to towns and eventually to cities, and wage labor became an important element of economic life. The nature of political authority also changed as the feudal lords lost power to the increasingly powerful centralized state. In short, an old order ended and a new one appeared. As the importance of kinship groups or the position within the feudal hierarchy faded, the individual became the focal point of society. Sir Henry Maine described the change as a shift from "status to contract." A per-son was no longer locked at birth into the rigid feudal structure in which relationships were based on status, but instead experienced the mobil-ity and freedom of legal relationships based on contract.[29] The person became a citizen, not a subject.

The rights and responsibilities of citizens vis-à-vis other citizens and the centralized state were expressed in a new theory of political oblig-ation—the social contract. Social contract theory explained the legit-imacy of the state and the obligation to obey its laws. It provided a philosophical justification for the equality and freedoms of citizens and for their expanding rights, including a right to own property.[30] The legit-imacy of the centralized state was enhanced by the modern legal appa-ratus with its formally rational laws that applied to all citizens as individuals. The individualization of a citizen's responsibility under the social contract also prevailed with respect to criminal liability. For most crimes, *mens rea* became a necessary condition for conviction and pun-ishment. As the legal scholar Blackstone noted, "to constitute a crime against human laws, there must first be a vicious will."[31] The issue of who would be sanctioned was now internal and subjective.

Corporate Development: A Summary

The corporation emerged as the transition from feudalism to capitalism generated demands for collective entities that could accommodate the combined resources of individuals and facilitate business on a grand scale. The state created these entities, which it then recognized as juristic persons.

The state maintained support and control of its population through political authority that was grounded in social contract doctrine. Individuals enjoyed the rights of citizenship, which carried a reciprocal obligation: obedience to the state's laws. The theory of political obligation legitimated the centralized state's exercise of political power, and, at the same time, reflected the individualization of responsibility that occurred with the transition to capitalism. This individualization entailed a focus on *mens rea* in the criminal law, and, in the civil sphere, the sanctity of the wage labor contract.

Our analysis of corporate development emphasized the transformations with respect to economic structure, political authority, and the legal concept of person. This is not to suggest the absence of other contributing factors. Religion, a factor stressed by Durkheim and Weber, fostered the demise of the feudal lord's political authority and the development of an individualized moral culpability in the criminal law. With Weber, we recognize the importance of an autonomous legal apparatus, especially the legal profession. Recall the Bubble Act and the role of the "corporate bar" in perpetuating and expanding the joint stock company, a forerunner of the corporate form. The legal profession and the law more generally created the notion of limited liability of managers and investors, which facilitated corporate growth in England and the rest of Europe, and, as we will see, in the United States.[32] Charles Perrow, a commentator who also focuses on the United States, suggests that the modern bureaucratic organization is the key to understanding the growth of the corporation.[33] Despite these interesting arguments, however, we suggest that the interaction of the three more encompassing factors had a significant impact on corporate development.

By the eighteenth century, the corporation was an established fact, a juristic person that derived its existence from the state and was legally recognized as more than the sum of its individual members. It could transact business, own assets, and transfer shares, and by the nineteenth century its members enjoyed a limited liability for collective debts.[34] Always a child of the state and often a functionary as well, the corporation benefited from the preferential treatment that attended its status as a special person. It was a juristic person for business purposes, with many of the rights of citizenship. However, with respect to criminal law, it was not a natural person and was incapable of the individualized intent that was the essence of *mens rea*. The corporation was not within the regulatory scope of the criminal law.

CORPORATIONS IN THE UNITED STATES

In many respects, the history of the corporate form in the United States parallels developments in England and the rest of Europe. This parallelism is not surprising for two reasons. First, much of what would become the United States was claimed and governed as territories or colonies by England and other European nations. Many of the juristic persons that were forerunners of the corporation were recognized in civil or common law, and their usage was extended to this country during colonization. Even after independence from England, the common law exerted a strong influence on legal development in the United States.

Second, the United States experienced many of the transformations that we described above, and the impact of these on the development of the corporate form was significant here as well. The United States entered the historical picture after those transformations were underway, so situational differences existed. There was, for example, no true feudal period in this country, but the economic structure of the United States did undergo transitions from an agrarian existence in colonial days through an era of commerce and trade to capitalism, and ultimately, to the Industrial Revolution. Moreover, these economic changes were accompanied by battles over the nature of political authority in the new nation, battles that inevitably centralized power in the state.

By the time the United States gained independence, the individualization of responsibility that characterized the shift from "status to contract" was virtually completed, and *mens rea* was an established element of the criminal law. These features were incorporated into the legal system along with the social contract notions of citizenship and political obligation. The concept of person would undergo an even more important change in the late 1800s when due process guarantees were extended to the corporation. As we will see, the interaction of economic and political factors, as well as the interrelated concept of "person," shaped the development of the corporation throughout the nineteenth century.

The Early 1800s

In the seventeenth century, England and some European nations expanded their economic and political influence by colonizing "The New World." Trading companies, such as the Virginia Company and the Massachusetts Bay Company, were the vehicles through which England extended its influence. They reflected the stage of legal development of collective entities. They existed at the pleasure of the state, performed governmental and business activities, and were a mixture of individual and collective enterprise.

Collective entities operated under charter during the colonial period; churches and boroughs were common examples. Collective entities were rare, however, and the civil law applied more to individuals than to collectivities. Although the Bubble Act operated in the colonies, it had less regulatory impact there than in England. The few corporations that existed were relatively small and often operated in a quasi-governmental capacity.[35]

The corporation became increasingly popular in the decades following independence, as more companies were chartered for business purposes. As in England, the corporate form facilitated the combination of capital that was essential for the complex enterprises of the late eighteenth and early nineteenth centuries. The significance of those economic issues is best appreciated if we consider the concept of a legal person and the interrelated changes in the nature of political authority, an especially important consideration in the early years of the nation.

The decades following the American Revolution were a unique historical period in which the United States began its existence, although the slate was not blank, to be sure. A common law heritage survived independence from England, as did social contract doctrine, which had not only supplied the philosophical rationale for the revolution but also informed the concept of citizenship in the new nation.[36] Still, much remained to be decided. Although the new government was to reflect contractarian principles, the specific form was a matter of intense debate. That debate exemplified social contract thinking in a practical sense because there were actual, not hypothetical, discussions about the form of government that would follow.

The central issue in the debate was the disagreement between the Democrats and the Federalists on the degree of centralization of political authority. Democrats such as Benjamin Franklin and Thomas Jefferson were critical of the English monarchy and opposed a strong central government. They trusted the common sense of the common people. The Federalists, including George Washington and Alexander Hamilton, favored a strong national government. They were less trustful of the common people, preferring a system wherein elites would have influence. As one Federalist put it, "Those who own the country ought to govern it."[37]

The Democratic position carried the day at the first Constitutional Convention. Although the Articles of Confederation (1777) created a national government, the powers of the executive were weak, there was no federal judiciary, and the government was subordinate to the sovereign states. However, this situation was short-lived. Limited trade with England and restrictive trade barriers between states produced an economic depression, which caused a crises in the Confederation. A second Constitutional Convention was convened, and the centralization of political authority was reconsidered. By blaming decentralized government for the economic crises, the Federalists fared better.

Alexander Hamilton, the chief architect of federalism, argued that the nation's survival and prosperity depended on its political economy. He envisioned an alliance between a strong national government and a powerful national economy.[38] The second Constitutional Convention produced the Constitution (1787) and a form of government that realized Hamilton's vision.

The United States government had a strong executive, an independent judiciary, and national law-making power. It enjoyed the exclusive right to establish tariffs, coin money, and maintain a military force—a power that would repeatedly prove useful in the alliance between government and business. And although the philosophical foundations of the government were steeped in social contract doctrine and the attendant rights of citizens, many of the important political institutions were "protected" from the common people. Citizen input was limited through the selection of a president by the electoral college, the appointment of a federal judiciary, and a Senate that gave a disproportionate voice to a small Eastern aristocracy.[39] Suffrage also reflected that elitism.

Government support of business was the key to Hamilton's dream of a national economy. The support included direct subsidies of money, land grants, and the construction of canals. The U.S. Supreme Court also facilitated the development of the corporate form and the alliance of government and business.

Approximately 200 new corporations were chartered in the decade after the ratification of the Constitution. The incorporation of so many new businesses foretold the coming era of large-scale collective enterprises, although at that time certain constraints limited the influence of the corporate form. The Federalists had proposed a federal incorporation provision at the second Constitutional Convention, but it was rejected in favor of incorporation at the state level. This requirement allowed state legislatures to scrutinize each charter request so as to ensure that the prospective corporation complied with restrictions on corporate purpose, size, and duration.[40]

That situation might have undermined corporate growth had the Federalists not found another means for shaping the political economy—the Supreme Court. Under the leadership of Chief Justice John Marshall, a staunch Federalist, the Supreme Court rendered throughout the formative early 1800s decisions that strengthened the federal government and the national economy.

The significant cases began with *Marbury v. Madison*.[41] Marshall created the power of judicial review: the Supreme Court would be the final arbiter when legislative action was suspected of contradicting the Constitution. The Marshall Court's interpretation of the Constitution resulted in "the enlargement of the powers of the central government and diminution of state power to control economic activity."[42] Marshall accomplished those Federalist objectives through his interpretation of two constitutional provisions: the contract clause and the commerce clause (in the Constitution, see Article I, Sections 8 and 10).

Although the contract clause was written into the Constitution to protect existing property rights that were threatened by the demise of the Articles of Confederation, its inclusion bordered on a moral imperative with respect to property and contract.[43] Marshall invoked the contract clause in two notable cases. In *Fletcher v. Peck*,[44] the Court prevented the Georgia legislature from annulling a land transaction of the previous legislature; the contract stood even though the earlier legislature had fraudulently transferred the land. In *Dartmouth College v. Woodward*,[45] the Court held that a royal charter to Dartmouth College was a contract and, as such, could not be altered by the New Hampshire legislature. Both cases preserved the sanctity of contracts but, more important, elevated the federal government above the popularly elected state legislatures in legal matters that affected business.

Marshall relied on the commerce clause in *Gibbons v. Ogden*[46] and *Brown v. Maryland*[47] to strike down state regulations of interstate commerce. He interpreted the commerce clause broadly to restrict economic protectionism by individual states and to empower Congress to regulate interstate business activity. Congress alone could regulate such business. Because there was little federal regulation, corporations were virtually unfettered in their development.

Along with the absence of constraining legislation, other dynamic forces contributed to economic success. Business historian Alfred Chandler argues that the first westward expansion of the population (in the early 1800s) was a significant stimulant. Chandler suggests that population shifts combined with government policy to facilitate the development of "big business."[48] Corporations flourished during Marshall's tenure as Chief Justice. The Court eliminated many restrictive state regulations, and Congress, through subsidies and other indirect contributions, provided a supportive business environment. The interaction among economic interests, the centralization of political authority, and the social contract's notion of "person" all encouraged corporate growth early in the nineteenth century.

The Mid-1800s

The corporation was integral to the political economy when Marshall left the bench in 1836. It became even more important in the mid-1800s. Of course, substantial changes accompanied economic prosperity in the United States. Urban populations grew, and the westward expansion continued. Technological advances in communication and transportation, especially the railroads, facilitated expansion and fostered industrial development.

The corporation was integral to those developments and became more dominant during that period of industrialization. Almost half the businesses incorporated between 1800 and 1860 were chartered in one decade—the 1850s.[49] As corporations grew in number they also grew in size, edging toward the large-scale collective enterprises that would eventually dominate economic life worldwide. Much of the organizational structure that eventually characterized big business emerged during this period.

> The railroads, with their huge capital outlay, their fixed operating costs, the large size of their labor and management force, and the technical complexity of their operations, pioneered in the new ways of oligopolistic competition and large-scale, professionalized, bureaucratized management.[50]

The federal government remained supportive of corporate development acting through Supreme Court decisions that further centralized political authority in economic matters. The Court's pro-corporate stance continued even though Marshall's successor, Chief Justice Roger Taney, was not enthusiastic about the growing power of corporations. A Jacksonian Democrat who favored judicial restraint with regard to judicial review, Taney believed that the commerce clause did not preclude all state laws regulating business; he held a limited view of the contract clause as well.[51] Nonetheless, the Taney Court's rulings favored a national economy with the corporation as the principal business form.

Three cases exemplify the Taney Court on economic matters. In *Bank of Augusta v. Earle*,[52] the Court ruled that a corporation chartered in one state could do business in another, although states could regulate the entry of such "foreign" corporations. By the time of

Earle, states vied for corporations by easing incorporation requirements. Incorporation had became a matter of general law rather than the special charter that had been scrutinized by legislatures in the past.[53] In *Swift v. Tyson*,[54] the Taney Court attempted to create a national law of commerce. Previously, when no question of federal law was at issue in a case, federal courts applied applicable state law, but in *Swift*, the Court ruled that federal courts should apply national laws of commerce, not state laws, which might be inconsistent with these general rules. The notion of national law arose again in *Cooley v. Board of Wardens*.[55] Although Taney had expressed the opinion that the commerce clause did not prohibit state regulation of business, the Court held in *Cooley* that certain types of business, to be determined by the Court, demanded uniform laws and could not be regulated by individual states.

Bolstered by the Supreme Court's protection and the fertile environment of an expanding economy, the corporate form flourished. Ironically, that success threatened corporations. As industrial corporations grew, so did the number of workplace accidents. Personal injury suits against corporate defendants increased markedly. Plaintiffs in these cases alleged that they were injured because corporate defendants negligently failed to conduct their businesses in a reasonable manner. The damages sought tended to be substantial because industrial accidents produced serious and often widespread injuries.

Corporations often evaded liability through tort defenses that emerged in England. One defense was assumption of risk: plaintiffs could not recover damages if they voluntarily incurred the risk. The standard interpretation was that employees had accepted the possibility of these accidents by working for industrial employers. Contributory negligence was a second defense: as fault was the issue, plaintiffs could not recover damages if they contributed to accidents through their own negligence. Similarly, plaintiffs were barred from recovery if their injuries were due to the negligence of co-workers. Finally, some plaintiffs were denied recovery under the common law doctrine that tort actions died with the plaintiff. This tort defense was rare in the United States until the mid-1800s, when some state courts invoked it to hold for railroads who were defendants.[56]

Corporate defendants successfully interposed such defenses in state courts in the mid-1800s. Their success in escaping liability for industrial accidents evidenced their special status. There was the economic reality that courts were unwilling to burden business. Courts treated the corporate juristic person as just another individual, one whose responsibility for accidents was no greater than that of any other individual, including employees. That individualization would become even more advantageous to corporations in the coming decades. Along with the notion of limited liability, this preferential treatment allowed corporations to "externalize" their costs, that is, to pass on costs that they had created to people who lacked the power to protect themselves.[57]

The Late 1800s

Expanding markets, friendly government policies, and protection from tort liability continued, and, by the end of the Civil War, the corporation was an established fixture. Nonetheless, the situation was not entirely rosy. Corporations needed predictable prices and markets to facilitate long-range planning and to maximize growth, but normal competition and cut-throat practices undermined predictability. The dilemma had an obvious solution: reduce the uncertainties of competition through greater control over the immediate business environment.[58] Chandler describes the process. Small manufacturers merged to form larger companies. Large, successful corporations—for example, oil and railroads—controlled every facet of their operations through horizontal combination and vertical integration. Companies consolidated ownership of raw materials and component parts to assure control over the sources of supply and the entire production process. Some controlled their environment with business combinations such as trusts and holding companies. The Standard Oil Trust, for example, was involved in the production of crude oil, pipelines, and refineries.[59]

These business combinations made enemies as they neutralized competition and increased their economic power. Their enemies included smaller companies that were at a competitive disadvantage, farming interests, and populists who feared the centralization of economic power in the trusts. The oil and railroad companies were the most frequent targets of calls for reform.

By the late 1800s, growing public sentiment prompted Congress to enact two pieces of regulatory legislation: the Interstate Commerce Act (1887), which dealt with railroad rates and business combinations among the railroads, and the Sherman Antitrust Act (1890), which was directed primarily at the oil companies and outlawed trusts that restrained trade. With the passage of those laws, Congress *appeared* to be responsive to popular demands for reform. The reality proved to be far different.

The Interstate Commerce Act created the Interstate Commerce Commission (ICC), a federal agency that regulated the railroads. The Act also centralized economic policy in the federal government, and, once control was centralized, the ICC tended to protect rather than regulate the railroads. Interestingly, for example, during debate about the

ICC, the president of a railroad sought advice from a friend, the United States Attorney General, about the posture railroads should adopt with respect to the ICC. The Attorney General advised against opposition from the railroads, noting that the creation of the ICC had satisfied public demands for reform, that the agency would protect the railroads from hostile legislation, and that the courts would limit the ICC's power.[60] Within a few years, the Supreme Court, applying a "rule of reasonableness," limited ICC power to regulate railroad rates.[61]

The history of the Sherman Antitrust Act resembles that of the Interstate Commerce Act. Although proffered as a reform that outlawed oil industry combinations that restrained trade, the Sherman Act was a reform that regulated very little.[62] Oil companies grew more powerful, and mergers flourished as corporate lawyers used the holding company in lieu of the trust. When business combinations were prosecuted, the Supreme Court applied its "rule of reason": the Court would determine whether a business combination was an *unreasonable* restraint of trade.[63] Economist John Commons called the Supreme Court "the first authoritative faculty of political economy in the world's history."[64] The Court continued to breathe life into Alexander Hamilton's dream.

Santa Clara County v. Southern Pacific Railroad[65] demonstrates the Court's role in the political economy. The Court held that corporations were persons within the meaning of the due process clause of the Fourteenth Amendment. With this recognition, the evolution of the concept of person with respect to the corporate form was completed: the corporation now enjoyed the constitutional protections of a natural person. Throughout the late 1800s, the Court employed the concept of a corporate person to create a new constitutional protection—liberty of contract. Liberty of contract, as expounded through the opinions of Justice Stephen Field, read into the Constitution the economic doctrine of *laissez faire*. This constitutional protection had no legal foundation and was ironic in its application. Powerful corporations and business combinations were treated as individuals in need of protection from their employees and from health and safety laws.

These decisions were justified by legal ratiocinations and by the popular ideology of "rugged individualism." Thurman Arnold, a law professor who had headed the Justice Department's Antitrust Division, explained that *laissez faire* was accepted because of the personification of the corporation that existed in the public eye and in the legal mind.

> The origin of this way of thinking about organization is the result of a pioneer civilization in which the prevailing ideal was that of the freedom and dignity of the individual engaged in the accumulation of wealth. The independence of the free man from central authority was the slogan for which men

fought and died... Since individuals are supposed to do better if left alone, this symbolism freed industrial enterprise from
regulation in the interest of furthering any current morality.[66]

Ironically, this individualization occurred when corporations were
the most powerful force in the economy. Even when popular sentiment
turned against them and the myth of rugged individualism declined, corporations thrived. The continued centralization of the political economy, mergers and other business combinations, and the Supreme
Court, with its application of due process guarantees to corporate persons, its "rule of reason," and the economic doctrine of *laissez faire* via
liberty of contract, propelled the corporation into the twentieth century.

The Twentieth Century

By the turn of the twentieth century, the United States was an
industrial giant. The economy was a national marketplace, linked by
communication and transportation—initially the railroads and eventually the automobile.[67] If the marketplace had become national, so had
the corporation.

The corporation was firmly established as a large-scale enterprise
characterized by vertical integration and a widely diversified product
line. They were highly bureaucratized organizations with centralized
management that coordinated the activities of interdependent departments and divisions. An important aspect of the management hierarchy was a sophisticated accounting system. The comptroller generated
data that were indispensable to the operation of such complex organizations; these data were the information base for cost control and centralized planning. Authorities such as Max Weber and Alfred Chandler
identify the accounting function as a defining feature of the modern
business form.[68] Chandler notes that, by the early 1900s, cost cutting
was more important to business than competition, especially in oli-
gopolistic industries.[69] The competition that existed, especially among
the producers of consumer goods, was directed at creating new customers. The advertising and marketing divisions had become important features of the corporation.[70] The most significant innovation yet
to come was the application of emerging technologies to business
purposes, and the attendant appearance of research and development
divisions.[71]

As the United States moved into the twentieth century, it had a
viable national economy driven by large-scale corporations. Similarly, the state had become a powerful force by the turn of the century.
As Alexander Hamilton had predicted in the early days of the republic, the unique historical relationship whereby the state both regulated

and protected business had produced a strong central government that would become even stronger in the twentieth century. The state penetrated deeper than ever into all facets of social existence. In some respects, this intensified involvement was prompted by public demand. In the economic sphere, for example, people remained concerned about the power of big business.

> The socially uncontrolled entrepreneurial initiative that led to America's leap into world predominance as an industrial power in the last third of the nineteenth century was accomplished by a ruthless spirit of competition that left little room for concern about the welfare or working conditions for those at the bottom.[72]

Although the heyday of mergers was past, resentment against big business, notably the oil and railroad trusts, continued. Legislation such as the Sherman Antitrust Act had been ineffectual, but public demand for regulatory reform persisted and even became an important issue in several presidential campaigns in the early 1900s. Concern about the negative impact of business extended to issues such as unsafe conditions in the workplace. As an ironic by-product of the burgeoning industrial economy, serious industrial accidents were becoming more prevalent, but little compensation was granted when workers or others were injured. Accordingly, demands were made for reform, primarily by organized labor.

In addition to matters of industrial safety, there were calls for state action in other areas; for example, the state also addressed health and safety concerns in consumer-goods industries and regulated the sale of food and drugs. The state began to provide financial assistance to the needy and became more involved in education. In short, citizens were more dependent on government.

The state played a larger regulatory role in the early 1900s with respect to the economic sector in general and the corporation in particular. The Supreme Court, however, was less important than it had been in earlier years, in part because of the ascendancy of the presidency. In the twentieth century, the executive branch grew in power, often at the expense of the judiciary. The Court also yielded its influence in economic matters to Congress, even as it continued to favor business interests. In *Standard Oil Co. of New Jersey v. U.S.*[73] the Court applied its "rule of reason" to protect a corporation from the provisions of the Sherman Act, but as a matter of statutory interpretation. The Court deferred to Congress.[74] Responsibility for matters of economic policy shifted from the Supreme Court to the executive and legislative branches of the federal government.

The Federal Trade Commission Act (1914) and the Clayton Act (1914) represented a further effort by Congress to prohibit business activities that restrained trade. The Clayton Act was intended to resolve some of the ambiguities that had plagued Sherman by proscribing specific types of practices that restrained competition. The Federal Trade Commission Act created a federal agency that would monitor business practices and sanction anticompetitive behavior via fines.[75]

These federal regulatory efforts were prompted in part by public demands that something be done about the giant corporations. At the same time, however, deeper Congressional involvement in economic policy reflected the complex interaction whereby the state both regulated and protected business. Congress prohibited conduct that restrained trade while guaranteeing the stability and predictability that was essential for rational planning and continued corporate growth in a national economy.

> The provisions of new laws attacking unfair competitors and price discrimination meant that the government would now make it possible for many trade associations to stabilize, for the first time, prices within their industries, and to make effective oligopoly a new phase of the economy.[76]

These legislative enactments quieted the clamor for reform by making the government appear to be responsive to the public interest. These laws also frequently were endorsed by the leaders of major corporations and by professional business organizations.

The history of workers' compensation legislation illustrates the complexities that surrounded efforts to effect reforms in the economic sector. As noted, the industrial workplace of the early 1900s was characterized by hazards and workplace accidents. Organized labor was concerned about workplace injuries and about the lack of corporate liability for them. Labor challenged these defenses as suits were filed again and again in state courts for personal injury compensation because of industrial accidents. Corporate defendants evaded liability in many cases, but plaintiffs sometimes recovered damages, and the pressure for reform continued.

The National Civic Federation (NCF), a national organization that spoke for the business community, mounted a campaign that was designed to secure passage of workers' compensation laws in various state legislatures. The NCF drafted model legislation and lobbied for it among state governments. Prominent corporate leaders joined the campaign. The NCF also acquired the public support of two presidents: Theodore Roosevelt and William Howard Taft. Congress passed a limited workers' compensation law in 1908, a number of state legislatures soon followed suit, and by 1920, most states had enacted such legislation.

These laws benefited a number of interests, including accident victims, business, and government. Workers enjoyed a statutory remedy that overrode tort defenses, and they could now receive compensation for personal injuries arising out of industrial accidents. Corporations could project an image as responsible citizens who were concerned about their employees while avoiding the uncertain outcome of litigation because the amount of recovery was fixed by statute: the legislation made for predictability. Federal and state legislatures addressed a serious social and political issue and appeared to be responsive to the public interest. State courts, which had favored corporate defendants in these cases, escaped the criticism of labor and of political leaders such as President Roosevelt.[77]

The campaign for workers' compensation legislation provides a case history of social and economic reform in the first two decades of the twentieth century. It provides two other important insights that are also relevant to our analysis of the emergence of corporate criminal responsibility. First, early in the 1900s, the nature of government involvement in matters of economic policy changed somewhat. The passage of workers' compensation triggered an upsurge of activity in such matters at the state level. Second, this legislation evidenced a trend in the law with respect to corporate responsibility for socially harmful behavior. Corporations were increasingly held accountable for their actions.

Edging Toward Criminal Culpability

Throughout its evolution, the corporation enjoyed a virtual immunity from criminal and sometimes civil liability. This preferential treatment was the legacy of several factors, including the special relationship wherein the corporation was created by and existed at the pleasure of the state and frequently performed quasi-governmental functions. The early corporation experienced many of the benefits and suffered few of the burdens of citizenship.

Historically, the idea of citizenship benefited the corporation. Citizenship was individualistic as manifested in laws that addressed the behavior of individuals as natural persons, not of juristic entities such as the corporation. This is apparent with *mens rea*, a concept that focused attention on individual criminal culpability. The emergence of *mens rea* marked an important change in the issue of personal responsibility, and it became an essential element in the definition of crime. However, *mens rea* served as an exculpatory mechanism because the corporation, as a juristic person, was incapable of forming the requisite intent for the imputation of criminal responsibility.[78]

This advantageous situation for corporations had begun to change during the late 1800s and early 1900s. In tort law, the likelihood that a plaintiff would recover damages increased due to judicial activity and statutory enactments. Two legal doctrines emerged that favored plaintiffs in tort cases. The doctrine of *res ipsa loquitur* created a rebuttable presumption that a defendant was negligent in certain accidental injury cases. The "last clear chance" doctrine allowed even a negligent plaintiff to recover damages if the defendant could have prevented an injury after discovering the risk of an accident.[79] Workers' compensation legislation meant that prohibitory tort defenses no longer barred recovery of damages for many accident victims. Several states enacted legislation that raised the standard of care required for chronic defendants in tort litigation, especially the railroads.[80] As immunity in the civil sphere dissipated, corporations were increasingly held liable when their conduct caused injuries.

Corporate criminal responsibility developed in a similar fashion. Corporations enjoyed an immunity from the criminal law largely because of the notion of *mens rea*. Executives might be prosecuted as individuals, but corporations as organizations were incapable of forming the intent that was an essential element in most crimes. This immunity was eroded, however, initially through the imposition of liability that was related to civil law, and later by an expansion of the legal concept of person with respect to corporations and the criminal law.

States raised the standard of care imposed on selected populations in the late 1800s. Statutes specified duties that were required in areas that affected the public (e.g., the operation of railroads, the sale of food) and appropriate sanctions if a member of the targeted population failed to exercise the prescribed standard of care. These laws created a new category of crime—the public welfare offense.[81]

Corporations were now accountable in criminal law for such offenses as selling adulterated food or for failing to maintain safety equipment. However, judges treated these offenses as civil matters akin to a public nuisance arising from the failure to perform a required duty. Penalties were usually fines; proof of intent was not a necessary element. *Mens rea* remained an element of crimes like homicide, so a corporation lacked the requisite intent for such offenses.[82]

Even corporate immunity from homicide began to wane early in the 1900s, and in a manner that was consistent with the development of public welfare offenses. In some cases, corporate responsibility grew out of regulatory legislation. In *U.S. v. Van Schaick* (1904),[83] a court held that a steamship company could be guilty of manslaughter when deaths resulted from the failure to provide life preservers as required by statute. In other cases, criminal responsibility reflected an extension of civil liability through principles of negligence. In *People v. Rochester Railway and Light Co.* (1909),[84] a New York court applied the doctrine of *respondeat superior*—an agent's liability is imputed to the corporation—in a manslaughter case that resulted when the defendant's agent improperly installed a gas device.

In these cases, *mens rea* was less important than the meaning of "person" in the applicable statutes. A standard definition of homicide was the "killing of one person by another." The issue was whether a corporation was within the definition of a person. In *Rochester Railway*,[85] an indictment was dismissed because a statute defined homicide as "the killing of one human being by the act, procurement or omission of another." The court construed "another" to mean a human being, not a corporation. *Commonwealth v. Illinois Central Railroad Co.*[86] had a similar result. In *State v. Lehigh Valley Railroad Co.*,[87] however, a court rejected a limited definition of person and upheld an indictment for criminal homicide against a corporate defendant. Using language couched in terms of negligence and nonfeasance, the *Lehigh Valley* court endorsed corporate criminal responsibility unless something in the nature of the offense or the sanction made such liability impossible. In a later case, *People v. Ebasco Services, Inc.*, (1974),[88] a New York court was willing to uphold an indictment for negligent homicide, emphasizing the importance of the state legislature's intent to include corporations within the purview of criminal law. However, the indictment was dismissed on other technical grounds.

By the second decade of the twentieth century, legislation and judicial opinion recognized corporate criminal responsibility for some socially harmful behavior. The dissipation of corporate criminal immunity confirms the analysis that we have proffered throughout this chapter. The corporation had become the dominant form of business enterprise and affected many aspects of life in the United States. We were a nation of consumers, and corporations supplied the consumer goods. We were a nation of industry, and corporations provided the raw materials and the production processes that fueled industrialization. Ironically, the same activities that produced corporate growth and economic prosperity often caused accidents, and even death. Accordingly, the state at various levels increased the standard of care that was required of corporations as well as their accountability when the standard was not met. This change occurred in both the civil and the criminal law.

The willingness to impose greater liability and, in a sense, "take on the corporation," reflects the maturity of the state and the autonomy of the legal order. This is consistent with Weber's view that the legitimacy of the law, and ultimately of the state, is partially due to the autonomy of the legal order, which operates independently of either the political or the economic system.[89] From the late 1800s onward, state court judges manifested such independence by holding corporations to greater accountability in criminal matters. Often their decisions were based on the interpretation of statutes or on legal precedent. Public welfare offenses, for example, were grounded in the application of liability in the law of nuisance to quasi-public entities such as municipal corporations. Sometimes, however, judges addressed issues of broad social policy and predicated their decisions on such issues *despite* legal precedent or statutory language. The court's opinion in the *Lehigh Valley Railroad* case illustrates the predominance of policy considerations over legal precedent.

> We need not consider whether the modification of the common law by our design is to be justified by logical argument: it is confessedly a departure at least from the broad language in which the earlier definitions were stated, and a departure made necessary by changed conditions if the criminal law was not to be set at naught in many cases, by contriving that the criminal act should be in law the act of a corporation.[90]

Similarly, a federal district court in *Van Schaick* focused on social policy rather than on specific statutory language. The court held that the absence of any appropriate punishment, traditionally a bar to corporate criminal liability, was simply an inadvertent omission and not an indication of legislative intent to grant corporate defendants an immunity from prosecution.[91]

Commentators have discussed the expansion of corporate criminal responsibility in terms of social policy considerations.[92] They suggest that the law changed to meet the growing complexities of modern life and the changing social conditions of the twentieth century. The legal pendulum swung from the protection of individual interests, defined as freedom from government interference, to the protection of social interests through increased regulation.[93] The language of their opinions demonstrates that the judges realized the importance of corporate criminal responsibility to the social order.

Notwithstanding these social policy considerations, by the end of the twentieth century the corporation had become an even more powerful economic force. We have discussed several interrelated factors that facilitated this success throughout its evolution. These same factors, however, also fostered a situation wherein a corporation may be held legally liable for its criminal acts. The law is a dynamic social institution, and the development of corporate criminal responsibility that we have presented is not the end of the story. Social conditions continue to change, and the issue of corporate criminality once again became a salient issue on the public agenda.

CONCLUSION

> The industrial corporation provided a vehicle for the con-
> centration of risk capital as well as the organizational struc-
> ture for economic coordination and bureaucratic
> rationalization. Corporations provided an investment outlet
> for small as well as large investors, with limited personal lia-
> bility dispersing the risks and transferable ownership increas-
> ing their speculative attractiveness.[94]

The giant corporations that dominate business today descended from those small and initially rare collective forms that we describe in this chapter. Over the years, the corporation became increasingly popular and successful. Facilitated by interrelated changes in the economy, the centralization of political authority, and the concept of person, the corporation developed as an essential vehicle for complex business endeavors.

Throughout that development, the corporation enjoyed a special status in the law. As a juristic person, the corporation drew its existence from the state, and was a creation and a protectorate of the state. For much of its history, it has contributed to the economic vitality of the state and, in many instances, performed quasi-governmental duties. Today, we again find ourselves in an era of privatization in which for-merly governmental functions are performed by corporations.[95] Now and historically, the corporation has benefited from its preferential treat-ment in the law. Indeed, commentators such as Charles Perrow suggest that the shift from the noncorporate to the corporate form that now dominates world economies was occasioned by law: "legal decisions by the courts, statutory laws by the legislatures, and administrative rul-ings by governmental bodies."[96]

For some time, the corporation was recognized as and enjoyed the constitutional protections of a person, but without many of the respon-sibilities and obligations that represent the "burdens" of the social con-tract. Limited liability, for example, means that, in terms of civil law, corporations can shift bad behavior onto others.[97] In terms of crimi-nal law, conventional wisdom held that a corporation could not com-mit a crime: it had neither a mind to fulfill the *mens rea* requirement nor a body to take punishment. That limited view of criminal respon-sibility may now be more understandable in view of the history of the corporate form.

During the twentieth century, however, the corporation lost some of its immunity from criminal responsibility, initially for nonfeasance or regulatory violations and eventually for some other crimes. The law now recognized the criminal culpability of corporations, and the legal stage was set for further extensions of corporate liability.

Moreover, as we noted earlier, public awareness and concern about the socially harmful behavior of corporations seems to have increased with the recent disclosures of business practices that threaten us economically and physically. The trial of the Ford Motor Company for reckless homicide emerged from this setting. In the chapters to follow, we will discuss this trial, its background, and its implications.

NOTES

1   Emile Durkheim, *The Division of Labor in Society*. New York: The Free Press, 1964 (originally published in 1893).

2   David Garland, *The Culture of Control: Crime and Social Order in Contemporary Society*. New York: Oxford University Press, 2001.

3   See Paul Tappan, "Who is the Criminal?" in Gilbert Geis and Robert F. Meier (eds.), *White-Collar Crime*, rev. ed. New York: The Free Press, 1977, pp. 272–282 (originally published in 1947); Edwin Sutherland, "White-Collar Criminality," *American Sociological Review* 5 (February 1940), pp. 1–12; Edwin Sutherland, *White Collar Crime*. New York: Holt, Rinehart and Winston, 1949; Marshall Clinard, "Criminological Theories of Violations of Wartime Regulations," *American Sociological Review* 11 (June 1946), pp. 258–270.

4   Cyril Northcote Parkinson, *Parkinson's Law*. New York: Ballantine Books, 1957, pp. 39–49.

5   Glen A. Clark, "Corporate Homicide: A New Assault on Corporate Decision-Making," *Notre Dame Lawyer* 54 (June 1979), pp. 911–913.

6   Charles Perrow, *Organizing America: Wealth, Power, and the Origins of Corporate Capitalism*. Princeton: Princeton University Press, 2002.

7   For an interesting application of the "shifting boundaries" argument with respect to the Ford Pinto situation, see Victoria Lynn Swigert and Ronald A. Farrell, "Corporate Homicide: Definitional Processes in the Creation of Deviance," *Law & Society Review* (No. 1, 1980–1981), pp. 161–182.

8   Iredell Jenkins, *Social Order and the Limits of Law*. Princeton: Princeton University Press, 1980, pp. 334–336.

9   Emile Durkheim, "Two Laws of Penal Evolution," *Economy and Society* 2 (1973), pp. 285–308.

10 See James Inverarity, Pat Lauderdale, and Barry Feld, *Law and Society: Sociological Perspectives on Criminal Law*. Boston: Little, Brown, 1983; also see Maureen Cain and Alan Hunt (eds.), *Marx and Engels on Law*. London: Academic Press, 1979.

11 David Trubek, "Complexity and Contradiction in the Legal Order: Balbus and the Challenge of Critical Social Thought About Law," *Law & Society Review* 11 (Winter 1977), p. 540.

12 Henry Sumner Maine, *Ancient Law*. Edited by Fredrick Pollock. London: John Murray, 1930 (originally published in 1861), pp. 180–182.

13 John Davis, "The Development of Negligence as a Basis for Liability in Criminal Homicide Cases," *Kentucky Law Journal* 26 (1937–1938), p. 209.

14 J. Robert Lilly and Richard A. Ball, "A Critical Analysis of the Changing Concept of Criminal Responsibility," *Criminology* 20 (August 1982), p. 171.

15 John Commons, *Legal Foundations of Capitalism*. Madison: University of Wisconsin Press, 1959 (originally published in 1924), pp. 25–54.

16 Wolfgang Friedman, *Legal Theory*, 5th Edition. New York: Columbia University Press, 1967, p. 123.

17 Russell Hogg, "Imprisonment and Society Under Early British Capitalism," *Crime and Social Justice* 12 (Winter 1979), pp. 4–17.

18 Egon Bittner and Anthony Platt, "The Meaning of Punishment," *Issues in Criminology* 2 (1966), pp. 87–89; Davis, "The Development of Negligence as a Basis of Liability in Criminal Cases," p. 210.

19 Maine, *Ancient Law*, pp. 180–182.

20 David Trubek, "Max Weber on Law and the Rise of Capitalism," *Wisconsin Law Review* (Summer 1972), pp. 720-753.

21 James S. Coleman, "Power and the Structure of Society," in M. David Ermann and Richard J. Lundman (eds.), *Corporate and Government Deviance*. New York: Oxford University Press, 1982, pp. 39–40.

22 James Willard Hurst, *The Legitimacy of the Business Community in the Law of the United States, 1780–1970*. Charlottesville: University of Virginia Press, 1970, pp. 3–4.

23 Harry Henn, *Corporations*. St. Paul: West, 1961, pp. 13–14.

24 *Ibid.*, pp. 14–15.

25 Coleman, "Power and the Structure of Society," pp. 42–44.

26 *Ibid.*, pp. 41–42.

27 Henn, *Corporations*, p. 10.

28 Emilio Binavince, "The Ethical Foundation of Criminal Liability," *Fordham Law Review* 33 (1964), p. 16; Louis Westerfield, "Negligence in the Criminal Law: A Historical and Ethical Refutation of Jerome Hall's Arguments," *Southern Law Review* 5 (1979), pp. 183–184.

29 Maine, *Ancient Law*, pp. 180–182.

30 W. Friedman, *Legal Theory*, p. 137.

31 William Blackstone, *Commentaries on the Laws of England, IV*. London: Dawsons of Pall Mall, 1966 (originally published in 1803), p. 21.

32 Lawrence Mitchell, *Corporate Irresponsibility: America's Newest Export*. New Haven: Yale University Press, 2001, p. 47.

33 Perrow, *Organizing America: Wealth, Power, and the Origins of Corporate Capitalism*.

34 Coleman, "Power and the Structure of Society," p. 50; also see Mitchell, *Corporate Irresponsibility: America's Newest Export*, Chapter 2.

35   Lawrence Friedman, *A History of American Law*. New York: Simon and Schuster, 1973, pp. 166–169.

36   W. Friedman, *Legal Theory*, p. 127.

37   Quoted in Wallace Mendelson, *Capitalism, Democracy, and the Supreme Court*. New York: Appleton-Century-Crofts, 1960, p. 7.

38   *Ibid.*, pp. 6–18.

39   Francis Fox Piven and Richard A. Cloward, *The New Class War: Reagan's Attack on the Welfare State and Its Consequences*. New York: Pantheon, 1982, pp. 66–80.

40   Henn, *Corporations*, p. 16.

41   1 Cranch 137 (1803).

42   Arthur Selwyn Miller, *The Supreme Court and American Capitalism*. New York: The Free Press, 1968, p. 21.

43   *Ibid.*, pp. 19, 36–37.

44   10 U.S. 87 (1810).

45   4 Wheaton 518 (1819).

46   9 Wheaton 1 (1824).

47   12 Wheaton 419 (1827).

48   Alfred Chandler, Jr., "The Beginnings of 'Big Business' in American Industry," *Business History Review* 33 (Spring 1959), pp. 2–3.

49   Miller, *The Supreme Court and Capitalism*, p. 44.

50   Chandler, "The Beginnings of 'Big Business' in American Industry," p. 5; similarly, Perrow, *Organizing America: Wealth, Power, and the Origins of Capitalism*, notes that the large bureaucratic organization that characterized the railroads eventually came to dominate the modern corporation.

51   Mendelson, *Capitalism, Democracy, and the Supreme Court*, pp. 36–38.

52   13 Peters 519 (1839).

53   Perrow, *Organizing America: Wealth, Power, and the Origins of Corporate Capitalism*, p. 36, notes that, in 1837, Connecticut made incorporation a matter of registration rather than of special charter.

54   16 Peters 1 (1842).

55   53 U.S. 299 (1851).

56   For a more detailed discussion of these tort defenses, see L. Friedman, *A History of American Law*, pp. 409–415.

57   Mitchell, *Corporate Irresponsibility: America's Latest Export*, p. 47.

58   Gabriel Kolko, *The Triumph of Conservatism: A Reinterpretation of American History*. New York: The Free Press, 1963, p. 3; Lawrence Friedman and Jack Ladinsky, "Social Change and the Law of Industrial Accidents," *Columbia Law Review* 67 (January 1967), pp. 395–414.

59   Chandler, "The Beginnings of 'Big Business' in American Industry," pp. 11, 17, 26.

60   Miller, *The Supreme Court and American Capitalism*, pp. 65–66.

61   *Smyth v. Ames*, 169 U.S. 466 (1898); Perrow, *Organizing America: Wealth, Power, and the Origins of Corporate Capitalism*, p. 129, notes that the ICC did not regulate railroads as much as it adjudicated conflicts among them, and thus brought stability to the industry.

62   Harry V. Ball and Lawrence M. Friedman, "The Use of Criminal Sanctions in the Enforcement of Economic Legislation: A Sociological View," *Stanford Law Review* 17 (January 1965), p. 200.

63   *Standard Oil of N.J. v. U.S.*, 221 U.S. 1 (1911).

64   Commons, *Legal Foundations of Capitalism*, p. 7; also see Perrow, *Organizing America: Wealth, Power, and the Origins of Corporate Capitalism*, p. 199.

65   118 U.S. 394 (1886); also see Mitchell, *Corporate Irresponsibility: America's Newest Export*, p. 42.

66   Thurman Arnold, *The Folklore of Capitalism*. Garden City, NJ: Blue Ribbon Books, 1941 (originally published in 1937), pp. 185–186 and 189.

67   Chandler, "The Beginnings of 'Big Business' in American Industry," pp. 27–28.

68   *Ibid.*, p. 16; Randall Collins, "Weber's Last Theory of Capitalism: A Systematization," *American Sociological Review* 45 (December 1980), p. 926.

69   Chandler, "The Beginnings of 'Big Business' in American Industry," pp. 27–28.

70   Alfred Chandler, Jr., *The Visible Hand: The Managerial Revolution in American Business*. Cambridge, MA: Harvard University Press, 1977, pp. 290–299.

71   *Ibid.*, pp. 240–244.

72   James Weinstein, *The Corporate Ideal in the Liberal State: 1900–1918*. Boston: Beacon Press, 1968, p. 40.

73   221 U.S. 1 (1911).

74   Miller, *The Supreme Court and American Capitalism*, p. 63.

75   Inverarity, Lauderdale and Feld, *Law and Society: Sociological Perspectives on Criminal Law*, pp. 235–237.

76   Kolko, *The Triumph of Conservatism: A Reinterpretation of American History*, p. 268.

77   Friedman and Ladinsky, "Social Change and the Law of Industrial Accidents," pp. 60–65; Weinstein, *The Corporate Ideal in the Liberal State: 1900–1918*, pp. 40–61.

78   Henry Edgerton, "Corporate Criminal Responsibility," *Yale Law Journal* 36 (1926–1927), pp. 827–828.

79   L. Friedman, *A History of American Law*, p. 418.

80   *Ibid.*, pp. 70–73.

81   Francis Bowes Sayre, "Public Welfare Offenses," *Columbia Law Review* 33 (January 1933), pp. 55–58.

82   *Ibid.*, pp. 70–73.

83   134 F. 592 (2nd Cir. 1904).

84   195 N.Y. 102, 88 N.E. 22 (1909).

85   *Ibid.*

86   152 KY 320, 153 S.W. 459 (1913).

87   90 N.J.L. 372, 103 A. 685 (1917).

88   77 Misc.2d 784, 354 N.Y.S.2d 807 (1974).

89   Trubek, "Complexity and Contradiction in the Legal Order," p. 540.

90   90 N.J.L. 373, 103 A. 685 (1917).

91   134 F. 592 (1904).

92   Sayre, "Public Welfare Offenses"; Clark, "Corporate Homicide: A New Assault on Corporate Decision-Making"; James Elkins, "Corporations and the Criminal Law: An Uneasy Alliance," *Kentucky Law Journal* 65 (1976), pp. 73–129.

93   Sayre, "Public Welfare Offenses," p. 68.

94   Inverarity, Lauderdale and Feld, *Law and Society: Sociological Perspectives on Criminal Law*, p. 221.

95   Nancy C. Jurik, "Imagining Justice: Challenging the Privatization of Public Life," *Social Problems* 50 (February 2004), pp. 1–15.

96   Perrow, *Organizing America: Wealth, Power, and the Origins of Corporate Capitalism*, p. 199.

97   Mitchell, *Corporate Irresponsibility: America's Newest Export*, p. 57.

3

The Movement Against
White-Collar Crime

"Crime in the Suites: A Spree of Corporate Skulduggery Raises Questions and Concerns"

"Corporate Crimes: Criminal Prosecution Gaining More Favor"

"Justice for White-Collar Crooks"

"Public Gives Executives Low Marks for Honesty and Ethical Standards"

"White Collar Crime: Booming Again"[1]

* * *

"ImClone Founder Pleads Guilty to 6 Charges"

"2 Ex-Officials at WorldCom Are Charged With Fraud"

"2 Top Tyco Executives Charged With $600 Million Fraud Scheme"

"Officers Flee Crown Vics' Fiery Crashes

"Enron Traders Gleeful at Ripping off Grandmas"

"U.S. Gets Tough on Corporate Crime"[2]

The first set of headlines opened this chapter in 1987. The second set comes from newspapers more recently. Apparently, some things do not change very much. Such headlines still are standard fare in the morning newspaper or the weekly news magazine. They are noteworthy for two reasons. First, they preview an array of interesting stories that feature crime as a connecting theme. Crime news is sensational, and these stories are dramatic because they recount crimes that were committed by powerful individuals and organizations. Stories about celebrities and other elite figures elicit a certain voyeurism, which is even more pronounced when the theme is the melodrama of crime. The crimes of business and political leaders make for good copy.

Second, the very appearance of these stories contradicts conventional wisdom. Journalists, media scholars, and criminologists tend to agree that the public prefers the gory details of street crime over reports about the complicated wrongdoing of the powerful. Perhaps a cynical public dismisses business or political corruption with the comment, "They're all a bunch of crooks." Or, maybe some morally problematic practices are not viewed as crimes. Maybe the public thinks, "That's just politics" or "That's just business." As we note in Chapter 2, historically, many questionable activities that were commonplace among the powerful were not defined as crime and did not mobilize the state's criminal justice machinery. In any case, the conventional view is that the depredations of business and political elites arouse neither the ire of the state nor the moral indignation of the public. "They lack the brimstone smell."[3]

Yet, over the past 25 years, we have seen an increasing number of stories like those previewed in our opening headlines, and they cannot be explained away as just another media-generated news theme. The stories depict crimes and criminals that seldom appeared in typical crime news in the past. Conventional wisdom notwithstanding, the public now regularly learns about the crimes of elites and the state's efforts to redress them. These stories and the cases they report suggest that something has changed with respect to the crimes of the powerful.

Much of the argument in this book rests on the premise that something has indeed changed, and to such an extent that many economic and political institutions in our society have come under attack by the legal system and on a number of other fronts as well. In addition to criminal and civil cases, criminological research and citizen interest generated by media exposure reflect a concern with white-collar crime in general and corporate crime in particular. We suggest that the concern over malfeasance within economic and political institutions is a manifestation of changes in the prevailing social and political context that have sensitized people to the crimes of the powerful.

These considerations are essential for understanding the story that our book tells: why a conservative county prosecutor charged Ford

Motor Company with reckless homicide for the deaths of three young women in 1978, and why that trial of 25 years ago still matters. To be sure, the Ford Pinto trial had its peculiarities, and, as a celebrated incident, contained unique legal and policy implications. But as we will argue, the Pinto case was as much a product of the times as it was special. Indeed, scarcely a decade before, the deaths of three teenagers probably would have been labeled a tragic accident and then forgotten by all but their families and friends. Instead, the accident began a powerful tale that can be tracked in these media headlines: "Ford Indicted in Crash," "The Pinto, the Girls, the Anger," "Ford Seeks Dismissal of Criminal Charges," "Pinto Criminal Trial of Ford Motor Co. Opens Up Broad Issues," "Pinto Death Case About to Begin," and, in the end, "Three Cheers in Dearborn."[4]

Our purpose is to understand why corporate crime came under attack. We will suggest that the United States experienced a broad social movement against white-collar criminality, and that the movement, although cyclical in nature, persists today. We will consider the source of this movement, how it fostered a flurry of academic research on elite crime, and what has happened in the years since the trial and since the publication of the first edition of this book.

In Part II, we will set forth the specifics of the Ford Pinto case. This interesting trial serves a useful heuristic function, offering an actual case as a vantage point from which we may assess the potential of the criminal sanction as a mechanism for suppressing corporate misbehavior.

THE SOCIAL MOVEMENT AGAINST WHITE-COLLAR CRIME

Something *has* changed in our society with respect to the crimes of the powerful. The best indicator of this change is the increased attentiveness to white-collar crime on a number of fronts, including in the media, academic research, and the legal system.

To support this view, we draw upon the social movement concept, which is an analytic vehicle for understanding the nature and the breadth of social change. We offer two definitions.

> A social movement is a collectivity acting with some continuity to promote or resist a change in the society or group of which it is a part. [To paraphrase], the salient characteristics include shared values that are sustained by an ideology, a sense of membership, norms, and a division of labor.[5]

> A social movement is a set of actions of a group of people. These actions have the following characteristics: they are self-consciously directed toward changing the social structure and/or ideology of a society, and they either are carried on outside of ideologically legitimate channels of change or use those channels in innovative ways.[6]

A synthesis of these definitions suggests that the focal concern of a social movement is social change: change is resisted or promoted by a group of people motivated by shared values or an ideology. Herbert Blumer, a sociologist and a pioneer in the field of social movements, emphasized a sense of collectivity or "we-consciousness" as a defining characteristic of such a group. Social movements typically emerge from a background of general unrest or dissatisfaction; they are concerned with individuals' rights and privileges.[7] Other formulations depict the background of social movements as a generalized sense of injustice and a pursuit of equal justice that serves as the motivating ideology for social change or resistance to change.[8]

Blumer identified several types of social movements; two of these are relevant to our analysis. The first is a "specific social movement," especially one of its subtypes, the "reform movement." Reform movements are parsimonious in their aim, which is to effect change in some restricted portion of the social order. The foundations of that order—power and resources and their distribution throughout society—go unchallenged by this sort of movement. Those who constitute a reform movement assent to the political institutions of the state, and the means whereby they attempt reform are within those prescribed by the state.[9] They employ legitimate methods such as public speeches or lobbying legislators to accomplish their goal. Reliance on legitimate methods may guarantee an aura of respectability for a reform movement. The reform movement in Blumer's typology exemplifies a social movement in its purest form: a definite organization that includes membership, leadership, a division of labor, "we-consciousness," and sustaining values (e.g., the Temperance Movement, MADD).[10] Although limited in its methods and goals, the reform movement is defined by rigorous criteria.

Blumer's second category, the "general social movement," is characterized by more flexible criteria and is more accommodating for our analysis. A general social movement is unorganized in both structure and identity, is composed of people in different areas, and is essentially "an aggregation of individual lines of action based on individual decisions and selection."[11] Some scholars argue that the general movement is so diffuse and so lacking in the important element—identity—that it is not a social movement at all. In Blumer's view, however, the general movement is the background from which specific social movements (e.g., reform movements) develop with their defining characteristics, including an organizational identity.[12]

A general social movement is an emergent shift in cultural values that has yet to converge into a well-defined reform movement. This type of movement will provide the framework for our analysis.

THE SOCIAL MOVEMENT FRAMEWORK APPLIED

Sociologist Jack Katz applied this framework as he argued that the United States experienced a social movement against white-collar crime beginning in the 1970s. He detailed the significant increase in the number of business and political elites who were prosecuted for bribes, fraud, and corruption.[13] Katz argued that white-collar crime displaced street crime as a political issue, a shift that reflected this movement. He contrasted the 1960s and the "war on crime" in the streets with the 1970s and the Watergate proceedings, the inclusion of white-collar crime as a campaign issue, and the commitment of the Carter administration to make the crimes of the rich and powerful a top priority for the U.S. Justice Department.[14]

Katz said that the movement focused on the prosecution of individual cases and, although the movement was largely decentralized, the Justice Department provided some leadership, especially during the Carter administration. They expanded the scope of criminal law to include activities of business and political elites who were not traditionally covered by criminal law.[15] Such defendants had enjoyed an unofficial, if not a legal, immunity from criminal prosecutions. Federal prosecutors were the catalysts or moral entrepreneurs of the movement. Moral entrepreneurs are a driving force behind social movements; they attempt to produce some socially beneficial outcome, though they may pursue individual, self-serving ends as well. These prosecuting attorneys illustrated both goals: they were motivated by a commitment to equal justice and by career advancement that might accrue from high-profile prosecutions. Katz noted that their activities differed from earlier social movements. The decentralized, individual case motif of the prosecutions impeded a sense of collectivity or the development of a division of labor within a collectivity. And, unlike social movements of the past, the movement against white-collar crime generated little corrective legislation or institutional reform.[16]

Katz's characterization of these prosecutors varies from the criteria that typically define social movements. However, if we include a broader spectrum of activities, the analysis becomes a useful starting point for a consideration of the social movement against white-collar crime. In addition to the prosecutors, other sources contributed to a milieu in which white-collar crime became an issue of public concern. These other sources are reminiscent of earlier social movements.

Katz dismissed the media, which played a key role in earlier social movements. Muckraking journalists mobilized the public through stories that condemned entire institutions and advocated sweeping reforms. Upton Sinclair's popular novel, *The Jungle*, aroused pubic indignation about deplorable conditions in the meat-packing industry and contributed to the passage of pure food laws.[17] Katz argued that contemporary reporters have abandoned such broad institutional themes and focus instead on individual cases. Even so, the public became more aware and less tolerant of white-collar crimes because of media coverage of sensational cases of the sort that are reflected in the headlines with which we opened this chapter.[18]

For example, media stories about the Ford Pinto appeared in newspapers, in magazines, and on television programs such as "60 Minutes."[19] Criminologists Victoria Swigert and Ronald Farrell contend that the media coverage culminated in an investigation of the Pinto by the National Highway Traffic Safety Administration, a recall of Pintos by Ford, successful personal injury lawsuits against Ford, and, ultimately, a State of Indiana criminal prosecution of the Ford Motor Company for reckless homicide.[20] We will say more about the media's role generally in social movements, and particularly in the Pinto matter, later in this chapter.

The Ford Pinto scenario sensitizes us to the role of other moral entrepreneurs and their interactions with respect to white-collar crime. A good example is Ralph Nader, a recent presidential candidate whose long-term involvement in consumer issues resembles the activities of the muckraking Progressive reformers of the past. His credits as a reformer include attacks on the auto industry and on corporate crimes.[21] Nader publicized an early media exposé of the Pinto gas tank. The publicity and Nader's credibility contributed to the actions against Ford described above. Moreover, the activities involved a network of people: plaintiff's lawyers, expert witnesses, county prosecutors, volunteer law professors and law students, and the media. Their interactions combined with the larger social milieu to produce the Ford Pinto trial, one event in the larger movement against white-collar crime.[22]

Another related activity contributed to the general social movement against white-collar crime: criminological research. This research corresponded to similar activities in earlier social movements. Scholars often formulate the sustaining ideology or shared values that are essential to a social movement's organizational identity.[23] Academics lend credibility and also establish the terms of discourse and the agenda for reform in the early phases of a social movement. For example, the American Social Science Association, later the American Sociological Association, began as an academic association of scholars oriented toward social reform during the Progressive era (late 1800s).[24] Although these scholars joined other reform-minded groups, they claimed a certain expertise as academics who studied social problems.

The discipline of criminology enjoys a similar heritage. Indeed, many reforms of the Progressive era addressed issues of crime and delinquency, and the activist, social-science stance that prevailed contributed to criminology's development. Although Katz did not consider criminology in his social movement analysis, we note that white-collar crime has become an important area of criminological research. Indeed, this research increased concurrently with the prosecutions documented by Katz. They represent diverse aspects—the applied and the academic—of the general social movement against white-collar crime.

In summary, we suggest that the concept of a general social movement facilitates our analysis of the increased salience of white-collar crime. In this chapter, we discuss two aspects of this movement: criminal prosecutions and academic research. While neither activity alone constitutes a social movement, both may be understood as part of the larger context of such a movement. We cast these activities as a purported change of orientation in the legal profession and in academic criminology, which occurred within a milieu of shifting values.

The remainder of this chapter is organized around four themes that pertain to the general social movement against white-collar crime. We suggest (1) that the emergence (and maintenance) of this movement is a reflection or product of a crisis of legitimacy; (2) that the movement tends to revitalize the legal system and academic criminology; (3) that the movement is cyclical; and (4) that the movement is symbolic. These four themes will be detailed in our analysis of the social movement against white-collar crime.

GENESIS OF THE MOVEMENT

Katz cited three interrelated factors that explained his conceptualization of the emergence of the social movement against white-collar crime. The first was the long-term development of several relatively autonomous federal enforcement agencies (e.g., the Justice Department) that provided an institutional setting for the movement. Second, the careers of the attorneys who staffed those agencies were furthered by the prosecution of high-profile cases involving business and political leaders. Third, Watergate and other scandals implicated and weakened the leadership of those agencies, thereby creating a political power vacuum that permitted advancement when aggressive staff attorneys battled business and political corruption.[25]

Katz situated his social movement in the context of a crisis that followed the Watergate affair, a view that conforms to the social movement literature. Social movements arise from a general dissatisfaction about individual rights or a generalized sense of injustice.[26] A period of political unrest followed in the wake of Watergate. Although we accept Katz's explanation for the moral entrepreneurship of U.S. attorneys, our analysis includes a rationale for the prosecutions and the research, and is more compatible with the literature on social movements.

The notion of a "legitimation deficit" or "crisis" is central to our analysis. "Legitimation" refers to the authority of the state as it exercises political power, and the public's acceptance of state actions. Legitimation connotes both a process and an output dimension.[27] A process exists whereby the state works to produce legitimacy, and legitimation is the product of this process. Legitimation is never really accomplished; it is an ongoing process. Our consideration of legitimation deficits and crises provides a structure for understanding the shifts in orientation that occurred within law and criminology. This notion also addresses the general background of unrest and the sense of injustice that is the milieu of this movement.

For many years, we have experienced an endless flow of events that have challenged our faith in major social institutions. The list includes discrimination and inequities faced by women, people of color, gays, and many others. It includes an unequal distribution of power and resources that denies many citizens an opportunity to achieve "the good life" or even minimal subsistence (e.g., health care). The list includes Vietnam and destabilizing incursions into other countries (e.g., Chile). It includes political scandals like Watergate and Iran/Contra wherein leaders were corrupted by their greed for power.[28] The list also includes the disclosure of business practices that are shocking in their illegality and reprehensible in their disregard for our lives. Yet, these powerful criminals appear to have enjoyed special privileges; the law seemed not to apply to them. The result has been cynicism and an erosion of confidence in law and in many of our institutions.[29]

Some academics stress the significance of triggering events in the production of a legitimation crisis, that is, events that produce a crisis and then generate activities such as legislation or revolution. Others see such crises as a tendency inherent in our political economy. Max Weber, the German scholar discussed in Chapter 2, was an early analyst in this matter. Weber was especially interested in the interconnections between capitalism as an advanced economic system and the centralized state with its autonomous legal order.[30] He observed that the modern state enjoys a virtual monopoly on the use of coercive force to maintain the political economy but governs most effectively when citizens accept its legitimacy. The state's authority is enhanced by law and the legal order. Law enjoys its own legitimacy because of several characteristics, which ideally include neutrality (one person or group is not favored over another), autonomy (the legal apparatus is not influenced by the political or the economic system), and formal rationality (the legal apparatus applies its own decision criteria, which can be generalized and predicted).[31] Law contributes to the legitimacy of the state in capitalist society.

Today, legitimacy is more problematic because the state has extended its sphere of influence deeper into all facets of social existence. The state is heavily involved in the economic sector and the sociocultural sphere. Some consider the state's expansion into these areas to be an abomination; others regard it as a social necessity. Jurgen Habermas, a German scholar, suggests that the state's expansion necessitates increased legitimation to justify its incursion. Traditional techniques of legitimation are largely ineffective because they have been displaced by the state's growing intervention—the very action that created the need for greater legitimation in the first place.[32] Once the state intervenes, it creates the expectation that it will continue to do so. These demands sometimes go unsatisfied because of the fiscal crisis that confronts government and because of ideological questions posed by conservatives and libertarians about the state's expanding role.[33] Thus, state intervention is complicated by the state's ability to meet the demands it has created. As a result, the legitimacy of the state tends to be least when its need for legitimacy is greatest.[34] Intervention in the economic sector is particularly dicey. As Habermas puts it, the state's legitimation problem is "how to distribute the...social product inequitably and legitimately."[35]

Even in the best of times, contradictions exist in the political economy that foster a tendency toward deficits or crises of legitimation. And, these are not the best of times. It is commonplace to read about corporate scandals (e.g., Enron or the pharmaceutical industry), about police brutality against people of color, about sexism and even rape in our military academies, or about torture in military prisons. These events may be seen as the trigger for a legitimation crisis or, alternatively, as manifestations of such a crisis. In either case, they call into question important social institutions.

More important for our analysis, these events challenge the legitimacy of law and the legal apparatus and, ultimately, the legitimacy of the social order. Law and the legal apparatus have been hit hard by scandals that question the legal system as a mechanism for assuring compliance to our underlying values. For a variety of reasons, the law, especially criminal law, has not been particularly effective in regulating the crimes of elite groups. When elites who violated the law were caught, they often received no sanction or one that was lenient when compared to the penalty for conventional criminals. The legal apparatus was playing favorites; disclosures of that bias undermined the law's neutrality and challenged its legitimacy. This was true when our book appeared in 1987, and, sadly, it remains true today.

Katz situated the prosecutions of business and political leaders within the context of a post-Watergate crisis. We locate these prosecutions within a general movement amid a crisis of legitimation. When a legitimation deficit exists, the state may be expected to respond with actions that vindicate its legitimacy. The prosecutions of white-collar offenders demonstrate the efficacy, autonomy, and neutrality of law and thereby contribute to the legitimacy of the state's authority. The law is legitimated in a general sense, and specific agencies of the legal apparatus are seen as credible as well. These prosecutions enhance legal careers but within a larger context that has produced a shift of professional orientation—the legal profession's recommitment to equal justice. For Katz, the background of the prosecutions of business and political elites was a post-Watergate crisis in government; for us, it is a more long-term crisis of legitimation.

Academic criminology's contribution to the general movement against white-collar crime also may be understood as a professional reorientation that is set against the background of a legitimation crisis. Because criminologists and prosecuting attorneys share a social milieu, they experienced the same disturbing events that produced a crisis of legitimation. And because their professional environment is concerned with crime, criminologists were affected by the disclosure of serious wrongdoing by business and political elites. As an academic discipline, criminology furnishes the framework within which crime-related matters are considered. That framework rarely included analyses of the crimes of the powerful. Repeated revelations of these crimes undermined the intellectual legitimacy of criminology and jeopardized the discipline's "ownership" of crime as a public problem.[36]

Criminological research on white-collar crime is the academic side of a general social movement. In a sense, this research was directly related to the state's emphasis on white-collar crime. The U.S. government is a major source of research funding; during the period of increased prosecution, criminologists could secure grants for research into white-collar criminality, which enhanced academic careers. This research resulted from a professional reorientation that reflected an intellectual tension during a disciplinary crisis. (We do not suggest that criminology as an academic discipline confronted a legitimation crisis. Habermas's concept entails a more deep-seated societal malady. Rather, because criminology had neglected the crimes of elites, it suffered a threat to its credibility as an academic discipline. The threat happened to occur within the context of the larger societal crisis of legitimation.)

The crisis of intellectual credibility produced a certain uneasiness in criminology during the 1960s and 1970s, as evidenced by the criticism of much that was conventional wisdom, the exploration of alternative paradigms, and an attentiveness to topics such as white-collar crime. Notably, neither the sense of uneasiness nor the call for a new agenda were confined to criminologists of a particular political ideology; they were spread throughout the discipline. This suggests the pervasive shift that Herbert Blumer describes as the background of a general movement.[37]

Criminologists on the political right criticized the long-standing focus on etiology (causation of criminal behavior). They suggested that a search for the root causes of crime (e.g., poverty or social disorganization) had focused the research agenda on conditions that were so deeply ingrained in society as to be immutable. Criminology, having fixated on these unalterable factors, had become irrelevant to crime policy.[38] These criminologists advocated a more policy-relevant agenda. Research should focus on factors and conditions that could be manipulated to reduce crime, (e.g., deterrence research).[39]

Scholars on the political left criticized the assumption, implicit in prior theories, that crime was a lower-class phenomenon.[40] They argued that there was too much deterrence research; criminology had abdicated its intellectual autonomy to become a tool (i.e., a purveyor of rationalization) of the repressive state that maintained the capitalist order. They advocated a redirection of criminology's intellectual agenda to focus on capitalism and on its connection to crime.[41] Some on the left did suggest that criminology had abdicated its policy role to the political right. They advocated strategies that might guide the formulation of crime policy.[42]

Liberal criminologists critiqued positivism as criminology's theoretical underpinning and challenged the assumption that criminal behavior was caused by factors beyond the individual's control. They debunked the myths of humanitarianism and scientific expertise, arguing that they had justified an expansion of state control over vulnerable populations. Their solution was to redirect criminology's agenda in one of two ways: criminology should pursue an interactionist approach,[43] or, alternatively, criminology should adopt a legalistic stance.[44] An analysis of the adverse, criminogenic effects of the criminal justice system would be a priority on the interactionist agenda;[45] a concern with the abuse of discretion would be a priority on the legalistic agenda.[46]

The sense of uneasiness within the discipline reflected a concern about the relevance of criminology to the formulation of crime policy.

Criminology was an applied discipline, and doubt about its policy relevance posed a threat to its intellectual credibility; even theoretical critique reflected this concern. On the one hand, criminology was condemned for an alleged failure to generate theory and practice that would help reduce crime; on the other hand, it was criticized for its inexcusable neglect of crimes by the powerful. Research on white-collar crime emerged amid this tension. With this focus, criminology manifested a new policy relevance that addressed white-collar crime and the crimes of elites.

Like the legal apparatus, criminology underwent a professional reorientation in response to its own crisis of intellectual legitimacy. That reorientation contributed to and was fueled by a general social movement against white-collar crime.

White-Collar Crime as a Revitalization Movement

Disclosures about the crimes of the powerful combined with other triggering events to reveal serious contradictions in our social order and threaten the credibility of the legal apparatus and criminology. Lawyers and criminologists responded to the crisis with prosecutions of and research into white-collar crime. Although they expanded their agendas to include white-collar crime, this reorientation was informed by well-established professional traditions. In a sense, the social movement against white-collar crime took the form of a revitalization movement rather than a commitment to a genuinely new direction in these professions.

The term "revitalization movement," which we borrow from anthropology, denotes a "conscious, organized effort by members of a society to construct a more satisfying culture."[47] Revitalization movements resemble social movements—for example, they represent an effort to effect significant changes or reforms in a society—although anthropologists typically use the term to describe reformative religious movements that arise in disorganized societies. Such movements, which originate in situations of social and cultural stress, are attempts to devise a new culture that will resolve conflicts. While the new culture exhibits its own dogma, myth, and ritual, some elements may be carried over from the conflict-ridden society and transformed to fit the new order.[48] We employ the concept because it highlights the continuity between old traditions and a new culture.

Anthropologist Anthony F.C. Wallace likened revitalization movements to chemical reactions that produce new compounds. In his analogy, just as certain substances combine to form a new compound when mixed with a catalyst and heated, independent and sometimes incompatible social traits will synthesize into a new culture when catalyzed by the prophet of a revitalization movement and heated by social disorder.[49] We extend his analogy to include the activities that were directed against white-collar crime. A social movement against white-collar crime emerged, fueled by disturbing social contradictions and by crises of legitimacy, and catalyzed through the entrepreneurial efforts that we have described. Much as a troubled society is reinvigorated by a revitalization movement, the movement against white-collar crime revitalized the legal order as well as criminology. The movement and the new form it entails exhibit a certain dogma, myth, and ritual; these elements reflect the traditions of these professions. The customs and ideologies of the legal order and criminology received new life and legitimacy.

The continuity of customs and ideology is apparent in the prosecutions of white-collar crime. Katz credited the ideal of equal justice as a motivation for prosecutors, a commitment that is prominent amid a social crisis.[50] In terms of a social movement, this commitment gave prosecutors a sustaining ideology that was grounded in a generalized sense of injustice. U.S. jurisprudence is steeped in the notion of equal justice, so its assertion by the legal profession maintained a fundamental, historical link. The revival of the ideology of equal justice, especially with respect to the crimes of the powerful, reaffirmed the law's neutrality and autonomy. The case motif as the vehicle for prosecuting white-collar criminals reflected the customs of the federal legal apparatus. Those customs included investigations of alleged wrongdoing, grand juries, criminal indictments, and trials.[51] The reliance on statutes and the precedent value of case law maintained the traditions of the legal order and contributed to its legitimacy by reaffirming the formally rational character of law.

The reorientation within criminology revitalized ideals and customs of that profession. In an early text, Edwin Sutherland, the dean of U.S. criminologists, defined criminology as a body of knowledge about crime as a social phenomenon that addresses the process of making laws, breaking laws, and reactions to the breaking of laws.[52] His definition established the agenda for criminological research. For a time, Sutherland and others studied white-collar crime, but interest in the topic gave way to a focus on street crime. Even so, the proliferation of white-collar crime research renewed an earlier inquiry, and was consistent with the orienting themes Sutherland developed long ago. In a sense, white-collar crime research maintained the traditional dogma, myth, and ritual of the criminological enterprise.

Some criminologists analyzed the process of law-making. They considered the distinction between criminal and civil wrongs and the attempt to define as criminal the acts of the rich and powerful.[53] Others analyzed the nature, extent, and costs of white-collar crime, as well as theoretical dimensions. The studies addressed issues such as the rationality and responsibility of offenders, and were consistent with a key theme in criminology: the etiology of crime.[54] A third line of inquiry considered the reaction to crimes of elites. This ranged from discussions of prevention to the philosophical justifications for the criminal sanction with respect to white-collar crime.[55] The research contributed valuable data about white-collar crime and helped to broaden thinking about the nature of the U.S. crime problem. At the same time, the research respected criminological tradition.

Criminologists and U.S. attorneys experienced a professional reorientation that rendered white-collar crime a salient issue. Both groups responded in a manner that was consistent with their profession. They contributed to a social movement against white-collar crime while revitalizing traditional ideologies of the legal order and academic criminology.

A CYCLICAL MOVEMENT

In a recent treatise on corporate crime, criminologist Sally Simpson observed that, "At the beginning of a new century, the corporate crime front is fairly quiet."[56] She noted that, although criminal law is now used more frequently against corporate crime, that usage peaked in the 1980s and waned in the 1990s. She labels as debatable the view that the social movement against corporate crime has had any long-term institutional effect.[57]

Simpson's observations raise important questions about a general social movement against white-collar crime. In this section, we ask, "What has happened to the social movement against white-collar crime in the years since that criminal trial in Indiana in 1980? We address the issue of an ebb in the movement, the reasons for it, and the prospects for a renewal of the social movement against white-collar crime. We suggest that this movement is cyclical in nature.

We begin this reconsideration with a brief statement about social movements. In the years since our book appeared in 1987, sociologists and political scientists have produced a tremendous volume of research about every feasible dimension of social movements. While much of the research is beyond our scope of consideration, several aspects of this discussion are relevant for our analysis. As often occurs in academic debates, there is a good deal of defining of terms, in this case, arguments about what constitutes a social movement. Some scholars argue that the distinctions between social movements and other organizations (e.g., interest groups) are not all that clear, and that they reflect the scholarly tendency to categorize things. They advocate more flexible criteria for a determination that an organization constitutes a social movement.[58] Others analyze the ebb and flow of social movements, and why this process occurs.[59] One explanation (and a significant issue in the social movement literature) focuses on political opportunity, that is, shifts in the political environment that facilitate or impede social movements.[60] Scholars also analyze public opinion with respect to social movements. They focus on the role of the media, the law, or legal cases in generating the discourse that surrounds a social movement and that may affect its success.[61]

Insights from this literature help us understand what has occurred with the social movement against white-collar crime over the past 25 years. The call for flexible criteria for defining social movements is helpful to our analysis because it reaffirms our initial characterization of a general social movement against white-collar crime. As we will see, it also supports our claim that such a movement still (or perhaps once again) is underway.

Political opportunity is key to our analysis, as is the awareness that there may be an ebb and flow of social movements. We grounded our initial analysis in the milieu of the late 1970s: the political environment of that period was fertile ground for a movement against white-collar crime. Amid the backdrop of the Watergate scandal, candidate and then President Jimmy Carter made the crimes of business and political elites a priority for his Justice Department. However, Carter was a one-term president, and the political environment (and opportunities) changed when he left office. During the Reagan years, there was more of a concern with business success than with business excess, and street crime, especially the "War on Drugs," displaced corporate crime as a rhetorical concern in the Reagan and G.H.W. Bush administrations.[62]

Of course, political opportunity entails more than rhetoric; it involves other decisions that determine how the law is implemented. As we saw in Chapter 2, many of the efforts to regulate corporate excesses in the late 1800s and early 1900s produced little success. One means of manipulating political opportunities is to provide less funding for regulatory agencies. Another mechanism is to appoint as agency heads and staff individuals who are unfriendly to regulation. The Reagan administration used both mechanisms to weaken regulatory efforts against corporations, and the Bush administration's Competitiveness Council reviewed (and prevented or watered down) prospective federal regulations.[63] More recently, there was speculation that U.S. Securities and Exchange Commission staff would water down the rules that implement the Accounting Industry Reform Act, which Congress passed in the wake of the Enron scandal.[64]

Political opportunities are not static: they come, they go, and they generate new opportunities and counter-movements. This certainly is the case with respect to corporate crime. Corporations were not the passive objects of a social movement against white-collar crime; instead, they actively challenged the legal and political environment. Innovative attorneys used existing legal doctrines to protect corporations. For example, when an ABC investigative reporter took a job at the Food Lion Grocery Chain and photographed problematic practices (e.g., changing expiration dates on meat), Food Lion sued ABC for criminal trespass.[65] Corporations also required the business equivalent of "loyalty oaths" as a condition of employment or for retirement benefits. Such agreements precluded employees from disclosing illegal corporate acts. In a high-profile case, a former employee of the Brown and Williamson Tobacco Company who had signed a "no-tell" agreement made allegations against the company in a "60 Minutes" interview. Brown and Williamson threatened to sue CBS for suborning a breach of contract. Initially, "60 Minutes" did not air the segment, but did so later after widespread coverage of the incident. The story is depicted in the film, *The Insider*.[66]

Contributions to political campaigns are another means whereby corporations try to control political opportunities. It is speculative to contend that contributions "buy" favorable legal treatment. However, some politicians, more than others, are friendly to corporations, and corporations do make campaign contributions to politicians who support their interests. When President Clinton's National Traffic Highway Safety Administration considered a recall of GM pickup trucks because of gas tank placement problems, *The Wall Street Journal* speculated that such an action would not have occurred in the first Bush administration.[67]

Political opportunities changed in the years following the Pinto case. Corporations went on the offensive, and Presidents Reagan and Bush were less supportive of the activities that had facilitated the social movement against white-collar crime. Some of these issues were relevant to criminology as well.

Criminologists responded to a crisis of legitimacy by incorporating white-collar crime in the discipline's research agenda. By the 1990s, however, other areas of inquiry were in vogue. Criminology turned its attention to what David Garland calls "the new criminologies of everyday life" (e.g., routine activities and life course theories).[68] This research did not supplant corporate crime, but did affect it. Sometimes, even when corporate crime was discussed, it was as an adjunct to other matters. For example, one debate between Carey Herbert, Gary Green, and Victor Larrogoite, and Gary Reed and Peter Yeager revolved around whether Hirschi and Gottfredson's General

Theory of Crime explained corporate crime or whether corporate crime represented an exception that challenged the theory.[69]

Criminology also is affected by political opportunity: U.S. crime policy determines which areas of inquiry will be funded through research grants. In an era when universities are moving toward academic capitalism, criminologists, like other scholars, find their research agendas "following the money."[70] The political climate was less favorable for research into the crimes of elites during the Reagan and Bush administrations, and, by the Clinton years, the condemnation of street crime had become a standard item in the politician's campaign tool kit. Conventional crime was increasing, the public was afraid, grants were available, and criminology's research agenda returned to street crime.[71]

Taken together, these political, legal, and criminological shifts provide a basis for understanding Simpson's observation about a diminution in the social movement against white-collar crime in the 1990s. At the same time, however, we disagree that the movement disappeared or that it has been inconsequential. Serious, important activity was directed at white-collar crime in the 1990s and in the new century. The U.S. Sentencing Guidelines were revised in 1991; the revisions targeted individuals and organizations that committed organizational-level crimes. While the sanctions were more lenient than penalties for many conventional criminals, they were more severe than in the past.[72]

In addition to the Sentencing Guidelines, a number of high-profile criminal prosecutions occurred in the 1990s. Charles Keating, along with Neal Bush, President George W. Bush's brother, was implicated in the savings and loan (S&L) scandal of the late 1980s. Keating was convicted in a California court in 1991 of securities fraud; other activities included campaign contributions of more than one million dollars to senators who were to intervene on his behalf with regulatory agencies.[73] A similar fate awaited another Arizonian, Governor Fife Symington, who was convicted of fraud, stripped of his office, and sentenced to prison.[74] A more violent example of corporate crime occurred in 1991 when 25 workers burned to death in the Imperial Chicken Processing plant because the owner and the managers had locked plant doors from the outside; the owner pleaded guilty to manslaughter.[75] Symington was pardoned by President Clinton, and Keating's and the Imperial manager's convictions were reversed on appeal. Interestingly, although some of these cases were prosecuted by U.S. attorneys, others occurred at the state level. In other words, groups of government lawyers beyond those identified by Katz were active in white-collar crime prosecutions.

As a caveat, the defendants in these criminal trials were individuals, and perhaps these high-profile cases were exceptions. In that sense, these cases may not argue against Simpson's thesis about the social movement against white-collar crime. However, even amid shifting political opportunities, there still were mechanisms for redressing corporate wrongdoing. Sociologist Tim Bartley notes that, as government becomes a less effective regulator, other mechanisms often emerge and fill the void.[76] We suggest that as the political environment (and law) became less supportive of criminal sanctions against corporations, civil lawsuits surged against corporate defendants (see Chapter 2), representing an alternative mechanism of the sort that Bartley describes.

Some lawsuits were traditional wrongful death tort cases. For example, the estate of a Georgia teenager sued General Motors (GM), alleging that GM's negligent placement of the gas tank on its pickup trucks had caused the teen's death. A Georgia jury awarded the plaintiffs $101 million in punitive damages and $4.2 million in compensatory damages in 1993.[77] In 1999, GM was hit with a punitive damages award of $4.9 billion in a case where six family members were severely burned after their Chevrolet Malibu exploded during a rear-end collision.[78] In both cases, jurors said they were angry because GM had denied that there was a problem with its vehicles, and had valued human life too lightly.[79]

Equally relevant to our argument is the proliferation of class action suits. For example, in 2000, hundreds of deaths were attributed to faulty Firestone tires. When prosecutors declined to prosecute, large class action lawsuits were filed around the country.[80] Interestingly, some of these civil prosecutions invoke notions of criminality. In a case involving a Ford Bronco rollover, a state court of appeals restored a jury verdict for plaintiffs of $285 million, comparing defendant Ford's actions to "involuntary manslaughter."[81] Some class action activities are interesting for other reasons. For example, groups of state prosecutors joined with groups of plaintiffs' lawyers to broker a settlement wherein a number of major tobacco companies agreed to pay hundreds of millions of dollars to participating states.[82] The tobacco settlement and the lawsuits that we have discussed maintain the pressure on corporations. They also represent coalitions of people, which, absent government action, pursue private (but organized) redress against corporations.

There are similar issues with respect to criminological research. The shift to other lines of inquiry did not mean that the discipline abandoned white-collar crime research altogether. Perhaps there was less emphasis on the incidence of white-collar crime or on efforts to demonstrate its seriousness, but these claims are well established. As always, "the devil is in the details," and criminologists in the 1990s devoted attention to the details of white-collar crime. Earlier, we mentioned a debate about whether Hirschi and Gottfredson's General Theory of Crime applies to corporate criminality. Despite a focus on the General Theory, two scholars in that debate, Peter Yeager and Gary Reed, provide a thoughtful discussion of several topics that are relevant to corporate crime research: the unit of analysis in measuring the incidence of corporate crime; how opportunity and motivation should be conceptualized as social constructions that are negotiated in institutional settings; and the relationship between conventional socialization in the United States and organizational norms that facilitate deviance.[83]

Diane Vaughan's analysis of the decision to launch the Challenger space craft offers an excellent account of how organizational deviance occurs. Employing the concept of "the normalization of deviance," Vaughan provides a nuanced understanding of the incremental process of organizational decisionmaking and deviance. NASA used her analytic framework in its evaluations of the tragic loss of the Columbia space craft.[84] Moreover, the appearance of revised editions of earlier books (e.g., Coleman's *The Criminal Elite*, 5th edition; Erman and Lundman's *Corporate and Governmental Deviance*, 5th edition; Simon's *Elite Deviance*, 7th edition; along with general texts such as Rosoff, Pontell, and Tillman's *Profit Without Honor: White Collar Crime and the Looting of America*) demonstrate the vitality of the concept of white-collar crime for scholars and for students in university courses.[85]

Another area of inquiry addresses the media. Scholars highlight the media's importance in framing the discourse of social movements. We suggest that the media have played a continuing role in the social movement against white-collar crime. Recall, for example, Swigert and Farrell's conclusion that media coverage created an unfavorable impression of the Ford Pinto, which led to regulatory pressure to recall the car and to legal action against Ford. Swigert and Farrell's analysis of this discourse addressed media condemnations of Ford in the language of moral deviance.[86]

Law professor Gary Schwartz offers a similar observation in an analysis of the Pinto case. Schwartz identifies a number of "misunderstandings" about the car, about Ford's decisionmaking, and about the trial, but he also concludes that the Pinto case has become, in a sense, mythic.[87] The myth is premised on a belief held by judges, scholars, and laypersons alike (including jurors) that "it is wrong for a corporation to make decisions that sacrifice the lives of its customers in order to reduce the corporation's costs, to increase its profits."[88] Schwartz argues that the Pinto narrative deals with fundamental notions of right and wrong—he refers to these as "elemental" or "essential"—which is why the Pinto case captured the public's attention.[89]

We agree. The mythic nature of the Pinto case has a direct bearing on the social movement against white-collar crime. First, as a landmark case, the Indiana criminal trial has become a legal reference point. For example, the Pinto was a frequent reference point during the continuing controversy over the fuel tank explosions in the Ford Crown Vic-

toria and in the media coverage of those wrongful death tort cases that
we mentioned earlier.[90]

There is a second and perhaps more interesting point. Notwithstanding the outcome of the Indiana criminal trial, the criticisms of that
trial, or, for that matter, the critiques of our book, the Ford Pinto is so
deeply ingrained in our culture and language that it has become a trope.
The phrase "Ford Pinto" has a symbolic meaning in the public vocabulary that stands for organizational wrongdoing or shoddy products.
The standard usage reflects variations on this theme: "This ___ is the
Ford Pinto of ___." Here are several examples: This was the Ford Pinto
of a baseball game; The State Elections board doesn't keep track but
pretty soon more politicians will have been recalled than Pintos; If
America Online were a car, it would be a Ford Pinto; He [a pro golfer]
was experiencing the type of golf season only a Ford Pinto owner could
appreciate; Hepatitis B vaccine is the Ford Pinto of the vaccine world.[91]
The Ford Pinto has become a legal and a public point of reference.

Of course, the Ford Pinto is but one example—albeit one of the
best—of this symbol system. Revelations of other crimes and scandals
in the years since the Pinto trial, especially cases sensationalized by the
media (e.g., the movie *Erin Brockovich*, or the best seller and movie,
A Civil Action), are the equivalent of booster shots that keep such
wrongdoing in the public eye. Thus, despite an ebb in the movement
that Simpson suggests, when disclosures appeared about Enron or
securities fraud on Wall Street or corrupt practices in the pharmaceutical
industry, there was an available frame of reference, that is, a discourse, for recognizing and naming these actions: corporate crime.[92]
Law professor Lawrence Mitchell commented on National Public
Radio that, as a result of these scandals, Americans have lost trust in
business.[93] And, because of the cozy relationship between these corporations and some of our political leaders, this loss of trust affects the
public perception of law and justice. Once again, the legitimacy of
important institutions has been challenged.

Once again, groups of individuals are "going after" white-collar
crime. Moreover, these groups extend beyond those named by Katz and
even beyond those that we discussed in the first edition of this book.
State Attorneys General like Eliot Spitzer in New York are prosecuting not only individuals but corporations as well (e.g., Merrill Lynch).[94]
Often, these state attorneys are networked with other regulatory agencies, further broadening the movement.[95] Pension fund managers constitute another interesting network. In the aftermath of accounting
scandals and amid allegations that some corporations pay excessive
salaries to top management, pension fund managers (e.g., people who
manage state retirement funds) have begun to network and to press for
reforms. These managers control billions of dollars in assets, so their
calls for reform carry weight.[96]

A social movement added white-collar crime to the public lexicon. The examples of corporate wrongdoing that we have mentioned in this section have created political opportunities that renew and sustain a new cycle in the social movement against white-collar crime. Today, white-collar crime is again a part of the public's agenda.

The Symbolic Movement Against White-Collar Crime

With respect to the crimes of the powerful, something changed: there emerged a social movement against white-collar crime. Indiana's criminal prosecution of the Ford Motor Company both reflected this social movement and galvanized it. Legal cases as well as the media generate the discourse that popularizes a social movement.[97]

Social movements, though, may produce outcomes that are more symbolic than they are real. Politics often are symbolic: laws or other regulations that are promulgated in the name of the public interest may lose that commitment in their implementation.[98] Recall our discussion in Chapter 2 of hollow regulatory efforts, and that the rules of implementation may be watered down in the aftermath of regulatory legislation.

This symbolic dimension is relevant to our analysis of the movement against white-collar crime. Symbolic politics affect crime policy. By the 1980s, for example, citizens feared crime and were angry at criminals because of rising crime rates and media coverage of crime.[99] Crime became a top priority on the public's agenda, and politicians raced to enact "get tough" laws. In legislative hearings and through media interviews, politicians condemned crime in expressive, symbolic language that criminologist David Garland calls "sound bite policies."[100]

White-collar crime was displaced by street crime during these years. It might be argued that the social movement against white-collar crime waned because the public was less outraged by organizational-level deviance than by street crime. Simpson argues that the criminal law is most appropriate for acts that outrage the community and for which someone obviously is blameworthy.[101] But, there is a potential loop in this argument. In part, elected officials respond to public sentiments, but public sentiment is shaped by official views of crime. The agenda of public discourse is responsive to political agenda-setting and to media themes.[102] Paul Burstein notes that social movements are constrained by electoral politics and by limits on the ability of citizens (and legislators) to attend to multiple issues at the same time.[103] With respect to crime, it is as if the public, the legislators, and the media could attend to only one type of crime: street crime.

The media's role in this is complicated. The media offer sensational depictions of crime, but in a manner that tends to spotlight the individual, even in stories about organizational deviance. The Iran/Contra scandal is illustrative. Despite evidence of widespread organizational deviance—the Reagan administration sold weapons to Iran and diverted the profits to the Nicaraguan Contra—the media individualized the coverage to the president. In their search for "the smoking gun" that would implicate President Reagan, the media took up a refrain from the Watergate hearings and repeatedly asked, "What did the president know and when did he know it?"[104] Criminologist Albert Cohen notes that this tendency to ask, "Who did it? and Why?" shifts attention from the interactions that produce such crimes to more traditional notions of blameworthiness. Cohen suggests that a better question with respect to organizational deviance is, "What made it happen?"[105] Diane Vaughan addresses this question in her analysis of the Challenger launch decision, which is why it is such a compelling account.

Nevertheless, symbols circulate images, and high-profile criminal cases keep alive the notion that white-collar crime exists and is problematic. This is true even if the cases are "individualized" in the media or become political rhetoric. The congressional hearings that followed the Enron scandal and the passage of the Accounting Industry Reform Act are a case in point. These hearings were an occasion for lawmakers to condemn Enron and its accounting firm, Arthur Andersen. The hearings and the condemnations, covered in stinging detail by the media, bordered on status degradation ceremonies.[106] Perhaps these condemnations were mere rhetoric; perhaps some of those moralistic lawmakers had taken campaign contributions from Enron. Even so, the condemnations symbolically restated society's moral boundaries, and, in so doing, revitalized that discourse that would re-inscribe the social movement against white-collar crime on the public agenda.[107]

CONCLUSION

The public is more aware that white-collar crime is a socially harmful phenomenon that poses a serious threat to our society. The concept of a social movement is a useful framework for understanding this emergent concern. The concern with white-collar crime constitutes a particular type of movement—a general social movement. This more diffuse, uncoordinated type of movement better accommodates the diverse activities that we describe.

Jack Katz argued that the social movement against white-collar crime was initiated by attorneys who staff federal enforcement agencies. We expand his position and include criminologists. The attorneys and criminologists reoriented their professional agendas and addressed white-collar crime in a manner that was consistent with the long-standing ideals and customs of their professions. For the lawyers, this entailed a recommitment to the ideology of equal justice through the case motif. For criminologists, it involved an adherence to the research agenda prescribed by noted criminologist Edwin Sutherland, and a renewed concern with the policy implications of their research.

The social movement against white-collar crime waned somewhat in the 1980s and 1990s. The Reagan and Bush administrations were friendly to corporations and created a political environment that was less conducive to corporate regulation via the criminal sanction. In the language of the social movement literature, political opportunities changed. Amid rising crime rates, government at all levels devoted more attention to street crime. Criminology turned its intellectual agenda to street crime as well.

At the same time, however, once white-collar crime became a topic on the public's agenda, it never really disappeared. Even during the 1990s, the U.S. Sentencing Guidelines specified criminal sanctions for organizational crime, and a number of high-profile members of the elite were convicted of crimes and remanded to prison. Wrongdoing also resulted in costly civil verdicts against corporations, both in traditional wrongful death cases and in class action suits; indeed, it was almost as if the plaintiffs' attorneys filled the gap vacated by U.S. prosecuting attorneys.

Sometimes the social movement against white-collar crime has been largely symbolic. Although symbolic politics may empty political action of all but rhetoric, we must not underestimate the importance of this symbolic dimension. Recall the notion of the Ford Pinto as a mythic narrative or trope, or the powerful condemnations that accompanied the Enron-related congressional hearings.

Enron and related business scandals illustrate the cyclical dimension of the social movement against white-collar crime, and how such movements ebb and flow with shifts in political opportunity. In the 1980s and 1990s, when the political climate favored the corporations, the movement ebbed. Recently, however, corporate crime on a grand scale has again undermined the public's trust in business. A framework for understanding and condemning these behaviors was available, if dormant. That framework was embraced by more actors than the federal prosecutors and academic criminologists. Legislation that criminalized such actions quickly passed. The activities of state attorneys (e.g., Eliot Spitzer in New York) demonstrate that prosecutorial zeal against corporate crime is no longer limited to U.S. Attorneys.[108] Moreover, new and very different networks in the social movement against white-collar crime have appeared: for example, pension fund managers.

These activities—sentencing and legislative regulation—counter claims that the social movement against white-collar crime has produced no lasting reforms. Perhaps what has happened is that some business and political elites were emboldened by a decade or so of a seemingly unfettered political environment, and simply went too far. The social pendulum has swung, and now more tangible reforms are appearing.

There are, of course, many impediments to this movement. Corporations have phenomenal power and resources, and their reach into politics and their success at undermining regulation are taken-for-granted. This realization breeds apathy and cynicism. At the same time, the legitimacy of law has been and continues to be fairly well established, primarily because the legal order sometimes does live up to its promises. The noted historian E.P. Thompson has addressed this issue:

> The essential precondition for the effectiveness of law, in its function as ideology, is that it shall display an independence from gross manipulation and shall seem just. It cannot seem to be so without upholding its own logic and criteria of equity; indeed, on occasion, by actually being just.[109]

Legal historian Douglas Hay puts it more dramatically, observing that the legitimacy of the law has been maintained by the occasional hanging of a nobleman.[110] Hanging a nobleman was a spectacle that spoke to law's majesty and fairness. Perhaps the congressional condemnation (and criminal prosecutions) of Enron, Arthur Andersen, and others are such a spectacle.

As Habermas has observed, formally democratic institutions and procedures are defining features of the modern state, which enjoys generalized mass loyalty by virtue of the universal rights of citizenship.[111] The ideological foundation of these rights is the notion of equal justice, a popular ideology to which the public is strongly committed. Given the strength and diffusion of this commitment, we anticipate that the public will demand the fulfillment of these ideological promises, especially those such as equal justice, which are the essence of the state's claim to legitimacy. In other words, the state must use the law to regulate socially harmful behavior regardless of who commits it, at least sometimes.

This climate was responsible for the passage of the Accounting Industry Reform Act with its criminal sanctions. As we will see in later chapters, it also made prosecutions like Ford's possible. Despite setbacks, we now have a discourse wherein corporate (and political) actions can be conceptualized as wrongs, and more, as wrongs that we as a society need not tolerate. These cases and the media's coverage of them (in the news but also in film, in cartoons, even in talk show humor) have established white-collar crime as an ongoing important issue on the public's agenda.

NOTES

1   These headlines, which appear in the first edition of this book, came from the following sources: "Crime in the Suites: A Spree of Corporate Skulduggery Raises Questions and Concerns," *Time* (June 10, 1985), p. 56; "Corporate Crimes: Criminal Prosecution Gaining More Favor," *Chicago Tribune* (September 9, 1984), Section 7, p. 1; "Justice for White-Collar Crooks," *Chicago Tribune* (December 3, 1976); "Public Gives Executives Low Marks for Honesty and Ethical Standards," *The Wall Street Journal* (November 2, 1983), p. 31; "White-Collar Crime: Booming Again," *The New York Times* (June 9, 1985), Section 3, p. 1.

2   These new headlines came from the following sources: "ImClone Founder Pleads Guilty to 6 Charges," *The New York Times* (October 16, 2002), pp. C1, 3; "2 Ex-Officials at WorldCom Are Charged in Huge Fraud," *The New York Times* (August 2, 2002), pp. A1, C5; "2 Top Tyco Executives Charged With $600 Million Fraud Scheme," *The New York Times* (September 13, 2002), pp. A1, C3; "Officers Flee Crown Vics' Fiery Crashes," *The Arizona Republic* (August 26, 2002), pp. A1, 14; "Enron Traders Gleeful at Ripping off Grandmas," *The Arizona Republic* (June 3, 2004), p. A15; "U.S. Gets Tough on Corporate Crime," *The Arizona Republic* (January 9, 2003), Business Section, p. D3.

3   Sandra Evans and Richard Lundman, "Newspaper Coverage of Corporate Price-Fixing: A Replication," *Criminology* 21 (November 1983), p. 529.

4   "Ford Indicted in Crash," *Peoria Journal Star* (September 14, 1978), p. C13; Dennis Byrne, "The Pinto, the Girls, the Anger," *Chicago Sun-Times* (September 17, 1978) pp. 5, 50; "Ford Seeks Dismissal of Criminal Charges," *Peoria Journal Star* (October 25, 1978), p. D3; Andy Pasztor, "Pinto Criminal Trial of Ford Motor Co. Opens Up Broad Issues," *The Wall Street Journal* (January 4, 1980), pp. 1, 23; "Pinto Death Case About to Begin," *Indianapolis Star* (December 2, 1979), Section 3, p. 15; "Three Cheers in Dearborn," *Time* (March 24, 1980), p. 24.

5   Ralph Turner and Lewis Killian, *Collective Behavior*, 2nd ed. Englewood Cliffs, NJ: Prentice Hall, 1972, p. 246; Lewis Killian, "Social Movements: A Review of the Field," in R. Evans (ed.), *Social Movements*. Chicago: Rand McNally, 1973, p. 16.

6   Roberta Ash Garner, *Social Movements in America*, 2nd ed. Chicago: Rand McNally, 1977, p. 1.

7   Herbert Blumer, "Collective Behavior," in A.M. Lee (ed.), *Principles of Sociology*. New York: Barnes and Noble, 1951, pp. 200–202.

8   Ralph Turner, "The Public Perception of Protest," *American Sociological Review* 34 (December 1969), p. 819; Turner and Killian, *Collective Behavior*, p. 259.

9   Blumer, "Collective Behavior," p. 212; Garner, *Social Movements in America*, p. 6.

[10]   Blumer, "Collective Behavior," p. 202.

[11]   *Ibid.*, pp. 200–201.

[12]   *Ibid.*, p. 202.

[13]   Jack Katz, "The Social Movement Against White-Collar Crime," in Egon Bittner and Sheldon Messinger (eds), *Criminology Review Yearbook*, vol. 2. Beverly Hills, CA: Sage, 1980, p. 162.

[14]   *Ibid.*, p. 161.

[15]   *Ibid.*, p. 167.

[16]   *Ibid.*, pp. 165–169.

[17]   Upton Sinclair, *The Jungle*. New York: Signet Classics, 1905.

[18]   Michael L. Benson and Francis T. Cullen, *Combating Corporate Crime: Local Prosecutors at Work*. Boston: Northeastern University Press, 1998, p. 49.

[19]   Mark Dowie, "Pinto Madness," *Mother Jones* 2 (September–October 1977), pp. 18–32; Jack Anderson and Les Whitten, "Auto Maker Shuns Safer Gas Tank," *Washington Post* (December 30, 1976), p. B7; "Is Your Car Safe?" "60 Minutes," CBS Inc. (June 11, 1978).

[20]   Victoria Swigert and Ronald Farrell, "Corporate Homicide: Definitional Processes in the Creation of Deviance," *Law & Society Review* 15 (Number 1) 1980–81, pp. 160–182.

[21]   Ralph Nader, *Unsafe at Any Speed: The Designed-In Dangers of the American Automobile*. New York: Grossman, 1965; Ralph Nader and Mark Green, "Crime in the Suites: Coddling the Corporations," *The New Republic* 166 (April 29, 1972), pp. 18–21; Ralph Nader and Mark Green, *Corporate Power in America*. New York: Grossman, 1973.

[22]   Francis T. Cullen, William J. Maakestad, and Gray Cavender, "The Ford Pinto Case and Beyond: Corporate Crime, Moral Boundaries, and the Criminal Sanction," in Ellen Hochstedler (ed.), *Corporations as Criminals*. Beverly Hills, CA: Sage, 1984, pp. 107–130.

[23]   Turner and Killian, *Collective Behavior*, p. 265.

[24]   Blake McKelvey, *American Prisons: A Study in American Social History Prior to 1915*. Revised and reprinted edition. Montclair, NJ: Patterson Smith, 1968 (originally published in 1936), pp. 118–119.

[25]   Katz, "The Social Movement Against White-Collar Crime," pp. 167–175.

[26]   Blumer, "Collective Behavior," pp. 172–200; Turner, "The Public Perception of Protest," p. 819; Turner and Killian, *Collective Behavior*, p. 259.

[27]   David O. Friedrichs, "The Legitimacy Crisis in the United States: A Conceptual Analysis," *Social Problems* 27 (June 1980), pp. 540–541.

[28]   Michael Schudson, *Watergate in Memory*. New York: Basic Books, 1992; Gray Cavender, Nancy C. Jurik, and Albert K. Cohen, "The Baffling Case of the Smoking Gun: The Social Ecology of Political Accounts in the Iran-Contra Affair," *Social Problems* 40 (May 1993), pp. 152–166.

29 Richard Stivers, *The Culture of Cynicism: American Morality in Decline*. Cambridge, MA: Blackwell, 1994; Robert Putnam, *Bowling Alone: The Collapse and Revival of American Community*. New York: Simon and Schuster, 2000.

30 Randall Collins, "Weber's Last Theory of Capitalism: A Systematization," *American Sociological Review* 45 (December 1980), pp. 925–928.

31 David Trubek, "Max Weber on Law and the Rise of Capitalism," *Wisconsin Law Review* (Summer 1972), pp. 720-753; David Trubek, "Complexity and Contradiction in the Legal Order: Balbus and the Challenge of Critical Thought About Law," *Law & Society Review* 11 (Winter 1977), pp. 538–541.

32 Jurgen Habermas, *Legitimation Crisis*. Boston: Beacon Press, 1975, pp. 69–72.

33 See James O'Connor, *The Fiscal Crisis of the State*. New York: St. Martin's Press, 1973.

34 Habermas, *Legitimation Crisis*, p. 69.

35 *Ibid.*, pp. 47–48; Thomas McCarthy, *The Critical Theory of Jurgen Habermas*, Cambridge, MA: MIT Press, 1978, p. 368.

36 Joseph Gusfield, *The Culture of Public Problems: Drinking-Driving and the Symbolic Order*. Chicago: University of Chicago Press, 1981, p. 10.

37 Blumer, "Collective Behavior," p. 200.

38 James Q. Wilson, *Thinking About Crime*. New York: Vintage Books, 1975, pp. 52–57.

39 *Ibid.*, pp. 58–70.

40 Ian Taylor, Paul Walton, and Jock Young, *The New Criminology: For a Social Theory of Deviance*. New York: Harper and Row, 1973, pp. 268–281.

41 David M. Gordon, "Capitalism, Class, and Crime in America," *Crime & Delinquency* 19 (April 1973), pp. 163–186; Steven Spitzer, "Towards a Marxian Theory of Deviance," *Social Problems* 22 (June 1975), pp. 638–651; William Chambliss, "Toward a Political Economy of Crime," *Theory and Society* 2 (Summer 1975), pp. 149–170.

42 Ian Taylor, *Law Against Order: Arguments for Socialism*. London: Macmillan, 1981; Stanley Cohen, "Guilt, Justice and Tolerance: Some Old Concepts for a New Criminology," in D. Downes and P. Rock (eds.), *Deviant Interpretations*. New York: Barnes and Noble, 1979, pp. 20–49.

43 David Matza, *Becoming Deviant*. Englewood Cliffs, NJ: Prentice Hall, 1969.

44 Frederick Kellog, "From Retribution to Desert," *Criminology* 15 (August 1977), pp. 179–192.

45 Edwin Schur, *Radical Non-Intervention: Rethinking the Delinquency Problem*. Englewood Cliffs, NJ: Prentice Hall, 1973.

46 Norval Morris, *The Future of Imprisonment*. Chicago: University of Chicago Press, 1974.

47 Anthony F.C. Wallace, *Religion: An Anthropological View*. New York: Random House, 1966, p. 30.

48   Anthony F.C. Wallace, "Revitalization Movements," *American Anthropologist* 58 (March 1956), pp. 264-281.

49   Wallace, *Religion: An Anthropological View*, pp. 210–211.

50   Katz, "The Social Movement Against White-Collar Crime," p. 165.

51   *Ibid.*, pp. 167–169.

52   Edwin Sutherland, *Principles of Criminology*, 2nd ed. Philadelphia: Lippincott, 1934, p. 3.

53   Christopher D. Stone, *Where the Law Ends: The Social Control of Corporate Behavior*. New York: Harper and Row, 1975; John E. Conklin, *"Illegal But Not Criminal": Business Crime in America*. Englewood Cliffs, NJ: Prentice Hall, 1977; Stephen Blum-West and Timothy Carter, "Bringing White-Collar Back In: An Examination of Crimes and Torts," *Social Problems* 30 (June 1983), pp. 545–554.

54   Stephen Yoder, "Criminal Sanctions for Corporate Illegality," *Journal of Criminal Law and Criminology* 69 (Spring 1978), pp. 40–55; John Braithwaite, "Inegalitarian Consequences of Egalitarian Reforms to Control Corporate Crime," *Temple Law Quarterly* 53 (1980), pp. 1127–1146.

55   John Braithwaite and Gilbert Geis, "On Theory and Action for Corporate Crime Control," *Crime & Delinquency* 28 (April 1982), pp. 292–314; John Braithwaite, "The Limits of Economism in Controlling Harmful Corporate Conduct," *Law & Society Review* 16 (No. 3 1981–82), pp. 481–504; David Ermann and Richard Lundman, *Corporate Deviance*. New York: Holt, Rinehart and Winston, 1982.

56   Sally S. Simpson, *Corporate Crime, Law, and Social Control*. New York: Cambridge University Press, 2002, p. 153.

57   *Ibid.*, pp. 16–18.

58   Paul Burstein, "Social Movements and Public Policy," in Marco Giugni, Doug McAdam, and Charles Tilly (eds.), *How Social Movements Matter*. Minneapolis: University of Minnesota Press, 1999, p. 8.

59   Verta Taylor and Nancy Wittier, "Collective Identity in Social Movement Communities: Lesbian Feminist Mobilization," in Aldon Morris and Carol Mueller (eds.), *Frontiers in Social Movement Theory*. New Haven, CT: Yale University Press, 1992, p. 8.

60   Doug McAdam, "Conceptual Origins, Current Problems, Future Directions," in Doug McAdam, John D. McCarthy, and Mayer Zald (eds.), *Comparative Perspectives on Social Movements: Political Opportunities, Mobilizing Structures, and Cultural Framings*. Cambridge, UK: Cambridge University Press, 1996.

61   Valerie Jenness and Ryken Grattet, *Making Hate a Crime: From Social Movement to Law Enforcement*. New York: Russell Sage Foundation, 2001, pp. 4–5.

62   James William Coleman, *The Criminal Elite: Understanding White-Collar Crime*. Fifth edition. New York: Worth Publishers, 2001, p. 87; Katherine Beckett, *Making Crime Pay: Law and Order in Contemporary American Politics*. New York: Oxford University Press, 1997, pp. 5–6.

63   Coleman, *The Criminal Elite: Understanding White-Collar Crime*, pp. 139–140.

64   Stephan LaBaton and Jonathan Glater, "Staff of S.E.C. Is Said to Delete Rule Changes," *The New York Times* (January 2, 2003), pp. A1, C2.

65   Food Lion sued ABC after the network aired a 1992 "Primetime Live" program about the grocery chain's practices. Food Lion was awarded a $5.5 million judgement in federal district court (later reduced to $315,000). Characterizing Food Lion's attempt as "an end run" around the First Amendment, a federal appeals court reduced the damages to $2. See Felicity Barringer, "Appeals Court Rejects Damages Against ABC in Food Lion Case," *The New York Times* (October 21, 1999), p. A1.

66   *The Insider.* Touchstone Pictures (1999).

67   "Is U.S. Recall Request On GM Trucks Driven by Safety or Politics?" *The Wall Street Journal* (April 29, 1993), pp. A1, 7.

68   David Garland, *The Culture of Control: Crime and Social Order in Contemporary Society.* New York: Oxford University Press, 2001, pp. 127–128.

69   Gary E. Reed and Peter Cleary Yeager, "Organizational Offending and Neo-Classical Criminology: Challenging the Reach of a General Theory of Crime," *Criminology* 34 (August 1996), pp. 357–382; Carey Herbert, Gary S. Green, and Victor Larragoite, "Clarifying the Reach of a 'General Theory of Crime' for Organizational Offending," *Criminology* 36 (November 1998), pp. 867–883; Peter Cleary Yeager and Gary E. Reed, "Of Corporate Persons and Straw Men: A Reply to Herbert, Green, and Larrogoite," *Criminology* 36 (November 1998), pp. 885–897.

70   Roland Chilton, "Viable Policy: The Impact of Federal Funding and the Need For Independent Research Agendas—The American Society of Criminology 2000 Presidential Address," *Criminology* 39 (Number 1, 2001), pp. 1–8; Sheila Slaughter and Larry Leslie, *Academic Capitalism: Politics, Policies, and the Entrepreneurial University.* Baltimore: Johns Hopkins University Press, 1997.

71   Chilton, "Viable Policy: The Impact of Federal Funding and the Need for Independent Research;" Garland, *The Culture of Control: Crime and Social Order in Contemporary Society.*

72   Associated Press, "U.S. Gets Tough on Corporate Crime," *The Arizona Republic* (January 9, 2003), p. D3; Coleman, *The Criminal Elite: Understanding White-Collar Crime,* p. 232; Simpson, *Corporate Crime, Law, and Social Control,* p. 13.

73   Coleman, *The Criminal Elite,* p. 30. Keating also was convicted in federal court of 73 counts of racketeering and fraud violations; these convictions also were reversed on appeal. He had served more than four years in a California prison.

74   William Carlile, "Symmington's Exit Roils Arizona GOP: Resignation Opens Doors for Democrats, Hurts Business-oriented Republicans," *Christian Science Monitor* (September 5, 1997), p. 3. Symmington's conviction was reversed on appeal. Federal prosecutors planned to retry Symmington, but President Clinton pardoned him.

75   John P. Wright, Francis T. Cullen, and Michael B. Blankenship, "The Social Construction of Corporate Violence: Media Coverage of the Imperial Food Products Fire," *Crime & Delinquency* 41 (January 1995), pp. 20–36.

76   Tim Bartley, "Certifying Forests and Factories: States, Social Movements and the Rise of Private Regulation in the Apparel and Forest Products Fields," *Politics & Society* 31 (September 2003), pp. 433–464.

77   Warren Brown, "GM Found Negligent in Fuel Tank Case: Jury Awards $105 Million to Parents of Teen Who Died in Truck Crash," *The Washington Post* (February 5, 1993), pp. A3, 4.

78   Andrew Pollack, "$4.9 Billion Jury Verdict in GM Fuel Tank Case," *The New York Times* (July 10, 1998), p. A8.

79   Peter Applebome, "G.M. Is Held Liable Over Fuel Tanks In Pickup Trucks," *The New York Times* (February 5, 1993), pp. A1, 16; Andrew Pollak, "$4.9 Billion Jury Verdict in G.M. Fuel Case," p. A8.

80   J. Nealy-Brown, "Two More Suits Target Ford, Firestone," *St. Petersburg Times* (June 30, 2001), p. B3.

81   Myron Levin, "State Reinstates Huge Ford Verdict," *The Los Angeles Times* (June 29, 2002), Part 3, p. 1.

82   This combination of private and state attorneys allowed plaintiffs' lawyers to join forces to better compete with the powerful defense teams that represent corporate defendants. The approach is reminiscent of the "prosecutorial team" in the Indiana Ford Pinto trial in 1980.

83   Yeager and Reed, "Of Corporate Persons and Straw Men: A Reply to Herbert, Green, and Larragoite."

84   Diane Vaughan, *The Challenger Launch Decision: Risky Technology, Culture and Deviance at NASA*. Chicago: University of Chicago Press, 1996. Also see John Schwartz and Matthew Wald, "Echoes of Challenger: Shuttle Panel Considers Longstanding Flaws in NASA's System," *The New York Times* (April 13, 2003), p. A15.

85   Coleman, *The Criminal Elite*; M. David Erman and Richard J. Lundman (eds.), *Corporate and Governmental Deviance: Problems of Organizational Behavior in Contemporary Society*, 5th ed. New York: Oxford University Press, 1996; David Simon, *Elite Deviance*, 7th ed. Boston: Allyn & Bacon, 2002; Stephen M. Rosoff, Henry N. Pontell, and Robert Tillman, *Profit Without Honor: White-Collar Crime and the Looting of America*. Upper Saddle River, NJ: Prentice Hall, 1998.

86   Swigert and Farrell, "Corporate Homicide: Definitional Processes in the Creation of Deviance," p. 179.

87   Gary T. Schwartz, "The Myth of the Ford Pinto Case," *Rutgers Law Review* 43 (1991), pp. 1013–1068.

88   *Ibid.*, p. 1035.

89   *Ibid.*, p. 1014.

90   Teresa Baldas, "Suits Allege Fatal Flaw in Ford's Cop Cars," *National Law Journal* 24 (July 29, 2000), p. A1; Nikki Tait and Tim Burt, "Carmakers Count the Cost of Rising Damages Awards," *Financial Times* (July 16, 1999), p. 3.

91   Ken Davidoff, "Stumble and Grumble," *Newsday* (August 8, 2001); Mike Nichols, "Debate, Not Fascist Control-Freaks, Provokes Recall Petition of Town of Saukeville Board," *Milwaukee Journal Sentinel* (July 21, 2000), p. B1; John Schwartz, "AOL: Technically, America's Most Hated Company?" *The Washington Post* (January 16, 2000), p. H1; Aaron Lopez, "In Search of His Swing," *Rocky Mountain News* (July 29, 2002), p. N36; Lisa Sukaj, "A Skirmish Over the Hepatis B Vaccination," *The New York Times* (July 18, 1999), NJ sec., p. 1.

92   When we account for our actions as a part of everyday social life, our accounts have to make sense. We offer accounts and social audiences understand them within a relevant framework of accounts. See John Heritage, *Garfinkel and Ethnomethodology.* Cambridge, UK: Polity Press (1984). In noting that the Ford Pinto has become a trope, we suggest that the car and the famous Indiana criminal trial have become a relevant framework for understanding corporate crime.

93   "Morning Edition," National Public Radio (June 11, 2003).

94   Richard Perez-Pena and Patrick McGeehan, "War on Wall St. Lifts Profile of Albany Attorney General," *The New York Times* (November 11, 2002), pp. A1, 22; Raymond Hernandez, "Finding Fraud on Wall St. May Be a Step to a Higher Post," *The New York Times* (April 29, 2003), p. C4.

95   Benson and Cullen, *Combating Corporate Crime: Local Prosecutors at Work,* p. 235.

96   "Morning Edition," National Public Radio (June 11, 2003).

97   Jenness and Grattet, *Making Hate a Crime: From Social Movement to Law Enforcement,* pp. 4–5; William Gamson and Andre Modigliani, "Media Discourse and Public Opinion on Nuclear Power: A Constructionist Approach," *American Journal of Sociology* 95 (July 1989), pp. 1–37.

98   J. Craig Jenkins, "Non-profit Organizations and Policy Advocacy," in Walter Powell (ed.), *The Non-Profit Sector: A Research handbook.* New Haven: Yale University Press (1987), p. 309; Murray Edleman, *Constructing the Public Spectacle.* Chicago: University of Chicago Press, 1988.

99   Garland, *The Culture of Control: Crime and Social Order in Contemporary Society,* pp. 10–11.

100 *Ibid.,* p. 13.

101 Simpson, *Corporate Crime, Law, and Social Control,* p. 63.

102 Edelman, *Constructing the Public Spectacle,* pp. 12–13.

103 Paul Burstein, "Social Movements and Public Policy," p. 4.

104 Cavender, Jurik, and Cohen, "The Baffling Case of the Smoking Gun: The Social Ecology of Political Accounts in the Iran-Contra Affair," p. 161; also see Gray Cavender and Aogan Mulcahy, "Trial By Fire: Media Constructions of Corporate Deviance," *Justice Quarterly* 15 (December 1998), pp. 501–521.

105 Albert K. Cohen, "Criminal Actors: Natural Persons and Collectivities," in David Altheide, Gray Cavender, John Hepburn, John Johnson, Nancy Jurik, Pat Lauderdale, Michael Musheno, and Marjorie Zatz (eds.), *New Directions in the Study of Justice, Law, and Social Control.* New York: Plenum Press, 1990, p. 116.

106 Sandra Sobieraj, "Tough Wall St. Talk: Bush Seeks New Penalties for Cooking Books," *San Francisco Chronicle* (July 7, 2002), pp. A1, 9; Richard Oppel, Jr., "Senate Backs Tough Measures to Punish Corporate Misdeeds," *The New York Times* (July 11, 2002), pp. A1, C6; David Barboza, "From Enron Fast Track to Total Derailment," *The New York Times* (October 3, 2002), pp. C1, 5; also see Harold Garfinkel, "Conditions of Successful Status Degradation Ceremonies," *American Journal of Sociology* 61 (1956), pp. 420–424.

107   Emile Durkheim, *The Division of Labor in Society*. New York: Free Press; for an update about the media from a Durkheimian perspective, see Gus Schattenberg, "Social Control Functions of Mass Media Depictions of Crime," *Sociological Inquiry* 51 (No. 1, 1981), pp. 71–77.

108   Benson and Cullen, *Combating Corporate Crime: Local Prosecutors at Work*, pp. 234–236.

109   E.P. Thompson, *Whigs and Hunters: The Origin of the Black Act*. New York: Pantheon, 1975, p. 263.

110   Douglas Hay, "Property, Authority and the Criminal Law," in Douglas Hay, Peter Linebaugh, John G. Rule, E.P. Thompson, and Cal Winslow (eds.), *Albion's Fatal Tree: Crime and Society in Eighteenth-Century England*. New York: Pantheon, 1975, pp. 33–34.

111   Habermas, *Legitimation Crisis*, p. 36.

Part II

The Ford Pinto Case

4

Assessing Blame

"Watch out! There's going to be an accident," yelled Albert Clark, as he glanced at the oncoming traffic on Highway 33. A moment later, his anticipation turned to horror. "It was like a large napalm bomb. It was nothing but flames. I couldn't see anyone in the vehicle. It was nothing but a big ball of flames."

Hurriedly, he pulled his mini motor home to the side of the road and sprinted across the highway. His wife, Pauline Clark, followed close behind.

First they saw Robert Duggar, one of the drivers involved in the collision. Fearing that his Chevy van would also be engulfed in flames and wanting to help, Duggar had jumped from his seat and run toward the burning vehicle ahead. At the sight of the inferno, he dropped to his knees and began to pound the ground with his fists. "Take care of him. Get him out of here," instructed Albert. Pauline grabbed Duggar by the arm and made him sit by the side of the road. When asked if he was hurt, the sobbing Duggar could only reply, "No. Help them. Help them."

As he approached the fiery car, Albert Clark was joined by a local farmer, Levi Hochstetler. They were shocked at the sight of the driver, Judy Ulrich. Badly burned, her foot was still caught in the car door, which had jammed with the force of the collision. Now she was pleading for help.

The searing heat from inside the auto drove them back as they tried to pry the door loose. Finally, on the third attempt, they were able to pull her free. As she lay on the ground, waiting for the ambulance to arrive, Judy suddenly called out, "Girls, the girls, are they okay?" A bystander answered comfortingly, "Yes, they're okay. We got them out of the car." Soon after that, Judy was rushed to the hospital with third-degree burns over 95 percent of her body. She died approximately eight hours later. She was 18 years old.

"The girls," however, did not escape the car. Judy's 16-year-old sister, Lyn Ulrich, and her cousin, Donna Ulrich, visiting from Illinois and born just a day apart from Judy, were trapped inside the burning vehicle. With the temperature of the fire over 1,000 degrees, Albert Clark, Levi Hochstetler, and the others at the scene could only watch in horror. The two girls perished seconds after their car had burst into flames.[1]

The Ulrichs crashed and died on August 10, 1978. Although their ages and the manner of their deaths make this a particularly tragic event, they were part of a larger phenomenon: the carnage that occurs each year on the nation's highways. Judy, Lyn, and Donna were three of the 50,145 Americans killed in automobile wrecks during 1978.[2]

Yet in another sense the girls' crash proved unique. For the first time in the nation's history, the legal arm of the state did not attribute a highway death either to a mistake or to outright recklessness on the part of a driver. Instead, a little more than a month after the fiery collision, a local county prosecutor secured an indictment suggesting that a major American corporation, Ford Motor Company, should be held criminally liable for the Ulrichs' deaths.

Why did the state seek to blame Ford for robbing three teenagers of their lives? The state could have concluded that the collision was an accident case in which inattention, sloppy driving, and perhaps bad luck combined to produce tragic consequences on Indiana's Highway 33. The conservative prosecutor, Michael Cosentino, might have singled out Robert Duggar and argued that he was responsible for the crash. After all, Duggar would have made a good candidate to take the rap; only recently this 21-year-old man had reacquired his driver's license, which had been suspended after he received tickets for speeding (twice), failing to yield, and running a stop sign. Not only had Duggar's Chevy van, with "Peace Train" emblazoned on its front hood, rammed the Ulrichs' car from behind, but investigations also revealed that his vehicle contained two half-empty beer bottles, five grams of pot, rolling papers under the seat, and pills in the ashtray.

In assessing blame, however, Cosentino and his staff decided that the collision was not merely an accident and that Duggar was not the real culprit; instead, they saw it as a case of reckless homicide on the part of Ford. To some extent, their interpretation of the accident and the action it demanded were idiosyncratic. In a different locale and with different personalities involved, thoughts of corporate criminality might not have emerged. However, to understand why the prosecutor officially blamed Ford for the Ulrichs' deaths, we must consider more than personalities and unique circumstances. We must also consider the context in which the crash occurred.

Two circumstances form the background to Ford's indictment on charges of reckless homicide. First, the automobile in which the Ulrich girls were incinerated was a 1973 Pinto. As will be seen below, questions about dangers in the Pinto's design had arisen by the time of the collision, and many people across the nation—including members of the legal profession—were prepared to believe that Ford had sacrificed safety in pursuit of profits. Second, and more broadly, the events of the decade preceding the crash had transformed Americans' view of corporations as well as the government's possible reactions to the conduct of big business. Had the Ulrichs perished just a few years earlier, it is unlikely that an attempt at a criminal sanction of Ford would have been made. Had they died a decade earlier, it is doubtful that even the prospect of a prosecution would have been entertained.

Thus, while Ford's indictment was a special event—indeed, so unusual that its announcement drew considerable national attention—it is best seen as a product of the times. Described differently, the "Pinto case" signified the social and legal changes that had placed corporations under attack and made them vulnerable to criminal intervention in an unprecedented way.

In the pages to follow, this theme will furnish the framework for our analysis of why Michael Cosentino blamed Ford for the three deaths on Highway 33—a tragedy that took place miles away from Ford's headquarters in Dearborn, Michigan, and from the New Jersey plant that had manufactured the Ulrichs' Pinto five years before.

A SIGN OF THE TIMES

For much of its history, as we have seen in previous chapters, the American corporation enjoyed near immunity from legal intervention by the state. Yet, in more recent times, this protected status has been threatened as repeated assaults have edged the corporation toward increasing criminal culpability. Though variations exist in different jurisdictions, the opportunity to fight wayward businesses with criminal sanctions is now clearly present.

This opportunity is important in two respects. On the one hand, it means that prosecuting a corporation is not legally impossible; thus, the idea of initiating a criminal action is not dismissed immediately as unfeasible. On the other hand, this growing opportunity can motivate prosecutions by showing the possibility of success in an action that formerly would have promised few, if any, rewards.[3] Thus, as the law evolves so as to suggest that corporations are not immune from criminal penalties—as more and more business enterprises and their executives are brought before the court—the practical outcome of prosecuting a corporation appears more favorable. Taking on a corporation no longer seems a fruitless effort, but an important, possibly intriguing, challenge with a reasonable chance for a payoff. Further, as this perception spreads, interest may increase, and a "movement" against "corporate crime" may take shape. As discussed in Chapter 3, we believe this movement had begun in the 1970s.

These observations become significant when we consider the timing of the indictment of Ford on charges of reckless homicide. After reviewing the evidence surrounding the Ulrichs' deaths, Michael Cosentino was convinced that Ford made a conscious decision "to sacrifice human life for private profit."[4] Yet, aside from his moral outrage, this question remains: What allowed Cosentino to jump from this insight to the conclusion that it was legally possible for him to prosecute a major corporation on charges of reckless homicide?

In part, he based this judgment on his knowledge that the recently revised Indiana criminal code contained a provision for "reckless homicide," which might be used to indict and try Ford for manufacturing the Pinto in which the Ulrichs were incinerated. He instructed his staff to research this possibility and consulted with William Conour of the Indiana Prosecuting Attorney's Office, who had been involved in drafting the "reckless homicide" statutes.[5] Both Cosentino's staff and Conour agreed that a prosecution under the statute was legally permissible.

However, these facts, taken by themselves, fail to explain why Cosentino even began his search for an applicable statute and entertained the idea that as prosecutor he might bring Ford within the reach of the criminal law. As we will see presently, moral outrage, the history of the Pinto, and the lack of civil redress all entered into Cosentino's thinking at some point.[6] Something else was present as well: a changing legal context. Granted, he would break new legal ground by being the first to prosecute a corporation for violence stemming from the reckless design of a consumer product, but he also confronted the Ulrichs' deaths at a time when the law had clearly edged toward corporate criminal culpability. Pragmatically, this meant that the law was sufficiently developed to make conceivable the innovative step of taking on Ford—it would no longer be dismissed out of hand as legally impossible. Additionally, corporations were now appearing regularly in civil courts in product liability cases and, increasingly, in criminal courts on charges such as price fixing and dumping hazardous wastes. On a professional level, Cosentino would not only be joining a movement within his occupation but also embarking on an adventure. Some of his colleagues might consider him a bit misguided, but the times were such that others would consider him a celebrity (indeed, his profession would eventually honor him).[7]

Thus, the changing legal environment removed the constraints that traditionally would have precluded the prosecution of Ford. Cosentino had sufficient legal precedent on his side, and was operating at a historical juncture when members of his profession were not only applying criminal sanctions to corporations but also writing in law journals about the pressing need to make "the punishment fit the corporation."[8] In this light it is not surprising that he considered the possibility of prosecuting Ford.

Another issue remained, however: Could he anticipate that people outside his staff would support the idea of hauling a corporation into court? Could he reasonably expect that in conservative Elkhart County he would be able to win an indictment and then a conviction? Was it politically feasible for him, an elected official, to devote time and resources to taking on Ford? At first, Cosentino was uncertain what the public reaction would be. Therefore, he decided not to try to sway the members of the grand jury toward indicting Ford when he brought the circumstances of the case before them; they would be his barometer of community sentiment. After the announcement of the grand jury's decision to charge Ford with three counts of reckless homicide, Cosentino felt that the local residents were divided evenly about the wisdom of his pursuing the case. Later, as the facts surrounding the Ulrichs' deaths were publicized, he believed that the vast majority of citizens backed his actions.[9]

What if the collision on Highway 33 had occurred a decade, or perhaps two decades, earlier? Apart from recent legal developments that had made corporations more vulnerable, would Cosentino (or any similar prosecutor) have risked accusing Ford (or any similar major company) of homicide? Would he have had any confidence that a grand jury would return an indictment and that the electorate would support his calling a corporation a reckless killer? To be sure, Cosentino's righteous anger at the girls' deaths may have prompted him to pursue a case against Ford, regardless of how foolhardy it seemed. But we believe that his initial uncertainty about the public's reaction would have been much greater, and would have constrained him from stepping outside his "normal" role as a local prosecutor to become a corporate crime fighter. A decade or two before the Ulrichs' Pinto crash, the idea of criminally sanctioning corporations was only beginning to take hold.

By contrast, the social context of the late 1970s had become increasingly conducive to the prosecution of questionable corporate conduct. Indeed, as one commentator wrote in 1977, "the corporation, which touches us all, is under attack as never before."[10] Of course, it would be unrealistic to assert that the "corporation" as a business form was on the brink of collapse or even of fundamental transformation; however, this commentator's remark makes us aware that the reputation of corporations and their executives had been sullied. People had come to mistrust big businesses and to suspect that they were willing to step outside the law in the pursuit of profit. This context made the prosecution of Ford possible; it increased the likelihood that citizens in Elkhart would believe that Ford, like other companies, was capable of doing wrong. For Michael Cosentino, this trend meant that his prosecution would express rather than violate the public will.

Why was the public ready to doubt the trustworthiness of corporations? In particular, why was it ready to blame a company like Ford for killing three teenagers? As Peter Berger has observed, "what people see as plausible largely depends on their social experiences."[11] An explanation or interpretation of a situation only "makes sense" to the extent that it confirms the "reality" of a person's everyday life. When an explanation does not resonate with this reality—or, to use Alvin Gouldner's terms, when it violates a person's "background assumptions" about the nature of society—it simply does not "ring true" or seem believable.[12]

These considerations help to provide a framework for understanding why corporations such as Ford were vulnerable to attack. As noted briefly above and in more detail in earlier chapters, the events of the decade before the Ulrichs' Pinto crash upset the social order and challenged the legitimacy of America's central institutions. Living through this period changed many people's "reality" and led them to revise their basic assumptions about America. Seymour Martin Lipset and William Schneider have argued that for many citizens these new "assumptions" were rooted in an unprecedented "confidence gap" or "cynicism toward all major institutions in American society," which emerged in response to the events of the day. On the basis of voluminous data drawn from opinion polls, they concluded that

> the decline of confidence after 1965 was a response to events, or to the perception of events. Beginning in the mid-1960s, the country experienced an unremitting barrage of bad news. In the initial period—roughly 1965 to 1974—most of this bad news flowed from disastrous events in the political system rather than the economy—the Vietnam War, protest movements, Watergate, exposés of corruption in high places, and urban violence. Beginning with the oil embargo at the end of 1973, bad news about the economy tended to command the country's attention, albeit accompanied by a regular smattering of social conflicts, foreign policy disasters, and polit-

ical scandals. . . . In order for confidence in institutions to be restored to a significantly higher level, we will need a sustained period of good news. . . . A durable restoration of trust in institutions will require something more than a shift in the ideological posture of government; it will require an improved level of performance.[13]

Big business did not escape the influence of this general erosion of confidence. To be sure, the legitimacy crisis had not grown so far as to support the sentiment that America's capitalist system should be scrapped in favor of a socialist economy. Faith in the ideal of a free-enterprise system still remained high.[14] Yet as Upset and Schneider discovered, "the period from 1965 to 1975 . . . was one of enormous growth in anti-business feeling."[15] Echoing this theme, a more recent column in *The Wall Street Journal* reported that "a huge share of Americans have adopted a cynical view of the ethics practiced by the country's leaders in the professions as well as in business. . . . [The] public gives executives low marks for honesty and ethical standards."[16]

Empirical indicators of the declining confidence in corporate America are readily available:

> In 1965, an average of 68 percent of citizens polled on their attitudes toward eight major industries stated that they had "very" or "mostly" favorable feelings. By 1977, that figure had dropped to 35.5 percent.

> On the basis of studies conducted every second year between 1975 and 1981, only 15.5 percent of the respondents answered that they possessed a "high" amount of "trust and confidence in large companies." Similarly, a mean of only 33 percent rated the "ethical and moral practices of corporate executives" as "excellent or good."

> Asked how much "confidence" they had in the "people running major companies," less than one-third of a national sample contacted in 1973 and 1974 answered "a great deal." By the early 1980s, this had slipped even further to 26 percent.

> Roper surveys in the late 1970s indicated that two-thirds of the public agreed with the statement, "American industry has lost sight of human values in the interest of profits."

> Asked to assess the occupational prestige of business executives, less than one-fifth of a 1981 national sample gave the rating "very great." Executives were ranked ninth out of 15 occupations behind scientist, doctor, minister, lawyer, engineer, teacher, athlete, and artist. Moreover, fully 78 percent of a 1979 sample felt that the "presidents of major business corporations" are "generally overpaid."[17]

The pervasive cynicism and antibusiness feelings suggested by these findings were fertile ground for a movement against corporate crime. Lacking confidence in the integrity of business leaders, many citizens believed that neither law nor morality would prevent companies, particularly large and powerful companies, from engaging in socially injurious conduct when profits were at stake. As Lipset and Schneider observed, the public had come to associate "bigness with badness" and to assume that "businesspeople . . . will act in a socially responsible way only when the public interest coincides with their self-interest, that is, when there is something in it for them."[18] Considering this climate of opinion, we can understand why even a conservative prosecutor like Michael Cosentino could expect jurors and voters in Elkhart County to back the bold idea of accusing a corporation of reckless homicide. In addition, when we consider that the prevailing climate had helped to quicken legal developments that moved the corporation toward increased criminal culpability, it is equally apparent why Cosentino's prosecution of Ford can be seen as a *sign of the times.*

Changing circumstances made a case against Ford socially and legally possible, but one other fact must be added to explain why Cosentino decided to seek an indictment: the Ulrichs were driving in a Pinto. Had they perished in any other automobile, it is doubtful that thoughts of reckless homicide would have emerged, even in 1978. By that time, however, Ford's Pinto had been investigated by the national media and, for many, it symbolized the worst side of corporate America. Indeed, as we will see below, a crusade against the Ford Pinto was well under way by the time Cosentino first learned of the deaths of three teenage girls and began to assess the blame for this tragic event.

THE PINTO CRUSADE

Profits Versus Safety

In 1965, Ralph Nader published his penetrating and widely discussed book, *Unsafe at Any Speed.* As noted in Chapter 2, this book called attention to structural defects in GM's Corvair that caused the vehicle to become uncontrollable and to overturn at high speeds. This would have been an important revelation in itself, but Nader's exposé accomplished much more. Apart from showing the Corvair's defects, Nader challenged his readers to think beyond the dangers inherent in one automobile to the dangers inherent in the nature of corporate decisionmaking. People needed to understand, he argued, that strong, unfettered forces prevailed within big business—including the automobile industry—and led executives to sacrifice human well-being for profits.

This message came at a time when the "confidence gap" was beginning to grow and when mistrust of corporate executives was spreading. Thus, it fell upon increasingly receptive ears and helped to shape the thinking of citizens and of many elected officials regarding corporate misconduct. A decade after the appearance of *Unsafe at Any Speed,* Nader's message that companies traded lives for profits clearly affected what people would believe about Ford's handling of the Pinto.

Nader began his critique of the motor vehicle industry by noting that "the automobile has brought death, injury, and the most inestimable sorrow and deprivation to millions of people."[19] This observation raises the question of who is responsible for the "gigantic costs of the highway carnage." According to Nader, the major car manufacturers have invariably had a ready answer: "If only people would take driver education and were not so careless when behind the wheel, then the highway death toll would be minimal." But Nader offered a different interpretation. Attributing accidents to "driver fault," he warned, was merely a case of blaming the victim.[20] As long as the victims of the crashes—the drivers—are held responsible for their own fates, he stated, attention is diverted away from the industry's role in producing cars that are "unsafe at any speed." Such ideology protects corporate interests, but only at the cost of continuing to jeopardize human lives:

> The prevailing view of traffic safety [blaming drivers] is much more a political strategy to defend special interests than it is an empirical program to save lives and prevent injuries. . . . [U]nder existing business values potential safety advances are subordinated to other investments, priorities, preferences, and themes designed to maximize profit.[21]

Nader contended that the push for profits, not poor driving, explains why people are perishing in cars like the Corvair. In offering this explanation Nader was not so naive or dogmatic as to accuse executives of consciously setting out to make dangerous vehicles. Rather, he was asserting that the blind pursuit of profits creates conditions within corporations that are conducive to the production of defective cars. Specifically, he understood that companies place a high priority on two factors that they see as essential to high sales and profit: style and cost. Although nobody wants an unsafe product, conflict inevitably arises when a design feature that would increase safety, such as a rear-end stabilizer or a larger windshield for better vision, makes a car look less attractive or increases its purchase price.[22] As Nader observed, the rewards within companies are given ultimately to those who are prepared to advance corporate sales, not to those who are excessively bothersome about safety. Clearly, then, the organizational context encourages decent, if ambitious, executives to risk cutting corners on safety in hopes of boosting sales and advancing their careers. Nader concluded:

> In the making of the Corvair, there was a breakdown in this flow of both authority and initiative. Initiative would have meant an appeal by the Corvair design engineers to top management to overrule the cost-cutters and stylists whose incursions had placed unsafe constraints on engineering choice. There are, however, deterrents to such action that regularly prompt the design engineer to shirk his professional duty. It is to the keepers of those most sacred totems—cost reduction and style—that corporate status and authority accrue.[23]

These realities made it clear to Nader that the automakers could not be trusted to protect consumer interests. The failure of the industry to police itself demanded that outside regulation be imposed:

> A great problem of contemporary life is how to control the power of economic interests which ignore the harmful effects of their applied science and technology. The automobile tragedy is one of the most serious of these man-made assaults on the human body. . . . The accumulated power of decades of effort by the automobile industry to strengthen its control over car design is reflected today in the difficulty of even beginning to bring it to justice. The time has not come to discipline the automobile for safety; that time came four decades ago.[24]

Again, Nader's words were not without consequence. Fearing that his book might threaten Corvair sales, GM hired detectives to investigate Nader in hopes of discrediting him. Snooping into his background not only failed to reveal any damaging evidence, but when GM's probe became public, it stained the company's reputation. (GM eventually issued a public apology to Nader and paid $425,000 to settle a civil action he had brought on grounds of invasion of privacy.)[25] Ironically, the investigation seemed to confirm Nader's indictment of the auto industry's attenuated morality, and the whole affair helped to turn him into a national figure.

As we know, Nader did not decline this opportunity to promote his agenda and to launch a consumer movement that flourished and that continues today.[26] His influence was felt across corporate America,[27] but he had a special impact on car makers. "Largely as a result of exposés by Ralph Nader," comment Clinard and Yeager, "the auto industry has been the subject of increasing criticism for its lack of ethics, violations of law, and general disregard for the safety of the consumer."[28]

In this light, it is not coincidental that in 1966, the year after the publication of Nader's best-selling book, the U.S. Congress passed the Highway Safety Act, which mandated federal regulation of the automotive industry and led to the creation of an enforcement agency, the National Highway Traffic Safety Administration (NHTSA). Indeed, Brent Fisse and John Braithwaite have observed that "this Act is largely a legacy of *Unsafe at Any Speed*" and of Senate hearings to consider industry regulation, during which GM executives were grilled about prying into Nader's background.[29] As one writer commented in 1966:

> The hearings were a sensation, and did as much as anything to bring on federal safety standards. "It was the Nader thing," said one senator whom I asked how it had all come about. "Everyone was so outraged that a great corporation was out to clobber a guy because he wrote critically about them. At that point, everybody said the hell with them." "When they started looking in Ralph's bedroom," said another Hill man, "we all figured they must really be nervous. We began to believe that Nader was right."[30]

As evidenced by GM's reaction to Nader, consumerism and federal safety regulations were not greeted kindly by the major automotive corporations. Their initial grumblings grew more intense as the industry's control of the market was threatened by a combination of escalating gasoline prices and an influx of inexpensive, fuel-efficient foreign imports. By the beginning of the 1970s, the costs of meeting NHTSA regulatory standards were perceived as a serious danger to the profitability of the American auto industry, and thus had to be resisted. "Safety" had become a dirty word in the headquarters of the big auto manufacturers.

This attitude about safety is illustrated well by conversations drawn from the Watergate tapes. On April 27, 1971, between 11:08 and 11:43 A.M., Henry Ford II and Lee Iacocca (then president of Ford Motor Company) talked with Richard Nixon and John Ehrlichman in the Oval Office. The Purpose of this visit was to ask the President to help Ford Motor Company obtain relief from the pressing problems created by the safety standards imposed by the Department of Transportation (which housed NHTSA).[31]

In the first moments of the meeting, President Nixon quickly set the tone, commenting:

> But we can't have a completely safe society or safe highways or safe cars and pollution-free and so forth. Or we could have, go back and live like a bunch of damned animals. Uh, that won't be too good, either. But I also know that using this issue, and, boy this is true. It's true in, in the environmentalists and it's true of the consumerism people. They're a group of people that aren't really one damn bit interested in safety or clean air. What they're interested in is destroying the system. They're enemies of the system. So what I'm trying to say is this: that you can speak to me in terms that I am for the system.

He then continued:

> I try to fight the demagogues, uh, to the extent we can. Uh, I would say this: that I think we have to know that, uh, the tides run very strongly. I mean, you know, the, it's the kick now. You know, the environment kick is in your ads, of course. You're reflecting it. Kids are for it and all the rest, they say. Uh, the safety thing is the kick, 'cause Nader's running around, squealing around about this and that and the other thing. . . .
>
> Now, tell me the problems you've got with, uh, the industry, with the Department of Transportation, and all these things and let me listen.

Soon after these remarks Henry Ford II began to outline his concerns:

> I think the thing that concerns us more than anything else is this total safety problem. And, uh, what we're worried about really, basically, is—this isn't an industry problem—is really the economy of the United States, if you want to get into the broad picture because, uh, we represent the total automotive [unintelligible] supply, industry supplies, dealers, dealer [unintelligible] the whole bit, about one-sixth of GNP. Now, if the price of cars goes up because emission requirements is gonna be in there, even though we, though we've talked about this morning, safety requirements are in there, bumpers are in there. And these things are, and that's leaving out inflation and material costs increases, which are also there.

Nixon responded:

> In other words, it'll, it'll kick up the prices of cars and of all of them, the inexpensive ones and the others too.

Henry Ford:

> We see the price of a Pinto . . . going something like fifty percent in the next three years with inflation part of it, but that's not the big part of it. It's the safety requirements, the emission requirements, the bumper requirements . . .

> If these prices get so high that people stop buying cars . . . they're gonna buy more foreign cars; you're going to have balance-of-payment problems.

Nixon:

> Right. I'm convinced.

Lee Iacocca now entered the conversation, focusing on the problems that attended the implementation of safety regulations by the Department of Transportation:

> I'm worried about the, the fact the Department of Transportation, not willfully, but maybe unknowingly, is really getting to us. . .

> And I keep saying, "The clock is running and we are wasting money." It, it just kills me to see it starting with Ford. We are becoming a great inefficient producer, and what they're doing to us.

> But I think for the basic safety standards, now, the key officials over there—I've talked to 'em now, for two years constantly . . . and they're dedicated—and they say, "Well, we're gonna get on to this, but we've had problems." And they talk about Naderism, and, uh, you know, the . . . the great pressure on them and so forth.

He then focused on the incursions of foreign competitors into American markets:

> And, and, and ya say, "Well, what has this to do with safety?" Well it has one big thing to do with it. They [foreign competitors] are gonna put whatever is demanded by law in this country on at a buck fifty an hour, and we're, we just cracked seven dollars an hour.

Returning to the regulatory issue, Iacocca remarked:

> We are in a downhill slide, the likes of which we have never seen in our business. And the Japs are in the wings ready to eat us up alive. So I'm in a position to be saying to Toms and Volpe [DOT officials], "Would you guys cool it a little bit? You're gonna break us." And they say, "Hold it. People want safety." I say, "Well, they, what do you mean they want safety? We get letters. . . . We get about thousands on customer service. You can't get your car fixed. We don't get anything on safety! So again, give us a priority." We cannot carry the load of inflation in wages and safety in a four-year period without breaking our back. It's that simple, and, and that's what we've tried to convey to these people.

Later, Nixon promised to review Ford's situation:

> . . . let me take a look at the whole, uh, John, what I can do here. But the other thing is I want to see what the hell the Department [of Transportation] is doing in the future.

Echoing the Ford officials' reasoning, Nixon then stated:

> I'll have a look at the situation, and I will on the air bag thing and the rest. And, uh, and uh, but, but I think this is an element that had, you see, goes beyond the DOT because it involves America's competitive position, it involves the health of the economy, uh, it involves a lot of things. . .

> I want to find out, I want to find out what the situation is, if cost-effectiveness is the word.

Nixon continued:

> . . . a lot of, what, what it really gets down to is that uh, . . . it, it is uh, . . . progress, . . . industrialization, ipso facto, is bad. The great life is to have it like when the Indians were here. You know how the Indians lived? Dirty, filthy, horrible. [Followed by laughs in the room].

At the end of the meeting, Nixon gave Ford the name of a "contact person," but reserved final judgment on matters brought before him:

> Now, John [Ehrlichrnan] is your contact here. . .

> . . . and, uh, particularly with regard to this, uh, this air bag thing. I, I don't know, I, I may be wrong.

> I will not judge it until I hear the other side.

When juxtaposed with the themes in *Unsafe at Any Speed,* these conversations illuminate the conflict over the appropriate balance of safety and profits that raged as America moved into the 1970s. In Nader's view, big companies were callously and recklessly endangering human life in their efforts to maximize profits. Cost-effectiveness, not the Golden Rule, was their governing morality. Corporate leaders dismissed such talk as naively or maliciously undermining the nation's economy. Safety was now the fad of those on the political left; if not resisted, it had the potential to cripple industries that were already struggling to fight off foreign competitors.

It was in this context that the Ford Pinto was conceived and produced. Under Lee Iacocca's direction, Ford moved quickly to market the Pinto before Volkswagen and the Japanese manufacturers monopolized small-car sales. Iacocca's formula for success was simple but rigid: the vehicle must weigh under 2,000 pounds and cost under $2,000. "Lee's car," as the Pinto was known at Ford, was rushed through production, taking only 25 months as opposed to the normal 43.[32] The 1971 model rolled off the production line and into showrooms in September 1970. It cost only $1,919 and weighed in under the 2,000-pound limit.[33]

Though pleased by this success, Ford executives were still concerned about the price of safety. The Pinto had won the initial battle with cost, but faced a war against rising expenditures and vigorous competition. As we have seen, this is one reason why Henry Ford II and Lee Iacocca traveled to Washington to meet with President Nixon. During this time, too, Ford executives made the decision not to guard against potential fuel-leakage problems caused by the placement of the Pinto's gas tank, which made it vulnerable to puncture in rear-end collisions. In an internal company memo dated April 22, it was recommended that Ford "defer adoption of the flak suit or bladder on all affected cars until 1976 to realize a design cost savings of $20.9 million compared to incorporation in 1974."[34] Whether Ford was reckless in its calculation that improved safety precautions were not worth a substantial reduction in profit would be questioned increasingly in the years ahead.

Pinto Problems

After six years of sales, there were more than 1.5 million Pintos on the nation's roads. Although "Lee's car" was the most popular American make, all was not right with the Pinto. Concern about the Pinto's safety had grown, beginning modestly but then escalating in intensity. By August 10, 1978—the day the Ulrichs died in the burning wreck of their 1973 Pinto—the car's problems had received exposure in the national media, and NHTSA had pressured Ford to issue a recall notice to Pinto owners. A crusade against Ford's Pinto was under way.

Jack Anderson and Les Whitten were perhaps the first to claim that Ford, despite having the technology to do so, had consciously refused to fix the potentially lethal hazard posed by the placement of the Pinto's gas tank. They began their December 30, 1976, column in *The Washington Post* by claiming, "Buried in secret files of the Ford Motor Co. lies evidence that big auto makers have put profits ahead of lives." This "lack of concern," they lamented, "has caused thousands of people to die or be horribly disfigured in fiery crashes." All this, they said, was preventable: "Secret tests by Ford have shown that minor adjustments in the location of the fuel tank could greatly reduce the fiery danger." Moreover, "repositioning of the tank would cost only a few dollars more per car"—not much of a price when human lives are at stake. "In the long run," they warned, "the auto makers are saving little with this 'cost cutting.'"[35]

Nine months later, these criticisms were elaborated in Mark Dowie's scathing condemnation of Ford, called "Pinto Madness." This award-winning report, which appeared in the September-October issue of *Mother Jones*, detailed Ford's allegedly cold and calculating decision to market a "firetrap." Again the message was clear: in the name of profits, "Ford Motor Company sold cars in which it knew hundreds of people would needlessly burn to death."[36] To make certain that this message would not remain buried in the pages of *Mother Jones*, Dowie announced the publication of "Pinto Madness" at a Washington, DC, press conference attended by Ralph Nader. The gathering was held on August 10, 1977—ironically, exactly one year before the three Ulrich girls were incinerated in their Pinto.

"Are you driving the deadliest car in America?" To this rhetorical question, Dowie supplied a frightening answer: "By conservative estimates, Pinto crashes have caused 500 burn deaths to people who would not have been seriously injured if the car had not burst into flames. The figure could be as high as 900."[37] But what made the Pinto "burst into flames" even when the impact of a collision was not great enough to inflict severe bodily harm on its occupants? According to Dowie, the lethal defect in the Pinto was the placement of the car's gas tank only six inches from the rear bumper. When hit from behind—even at speeds as low as 30 mph—the bumper was pushed forward into the tank, creating two potential hazards. First, the tube leading from the tank to the gas cap often was ripped away, thus causing fuel to gush out. Second, the bumper could propel the tank forward into the car's differential housing (the bulge in the middle of the rear axle). If that happened, four bolts on the housing would puncture the gas tank, again allowing fuel to spill. At that point, all that was needed to ignite the fuel and to create an inferno was a spark—from steel against steel or from steel against pavement.

In Dowie's opinion this was not merely an unfortunate or unavoidable engineering mistake. Ford, he claimed, knew about the defect and knew how to fix it. In fact, as "internal company documents" revealed, "Ford has crash-tested the Pinto at a top-secret site more than 40 times and . . . every test made over 25 mph without special structural alteration of the car has resulted in a ruptured fuel tank."[38] Eight of these tests, moreover, were made before the vehicle was delivered to dealerships across the nation. Other tests conducted before marketing showed that it was possible to eliminate fuel leakage in one of four ways: by placing a piece of steel between the gas tank and the bumper; by inserting a plastic protective device between the tank and the bolts on the differential housing; by lining the tank with a rubber bladder; or, as with Ford's Capri, by positioning the gas tank over the rear axle. Although Ford had the technology to minimize the Pinto's hazards, they chose, Dowie observed, not to do so.

Why would Ford consciously endanger the lives of their customers? Dowie offered a simple but damning answer: cost-effectiveness. Inside Ford, Dowie's sources told him, it was well understood that profit was the guiding principle and that safety didn't sell. When asked whether anyone had gone to Lee Iacocca and informed him of the Pinto's problems, a high-ranking company engineer responded, "Hell no. That person would have been fired. Safety wasn't a popular subject around Ford in those days. With Lee it was taboo."[39] To exacerbate matters, the Pinto was being produced under rigid price and weight restrictions ($2,000 and 2,000 pounds), and under a time schedule that made delays intolerable and changes costly. The pressure was on. "Whenever a problem was raised that meant a delay on the Pinto," Dowie's engineer informant said, "Lee would chomp on his cigar, look out the window and say, 'Read the product objectives and get back to work.'"[40]

Even so, Dowie noted that the Pinto could have been made safe at relatively little expense. Lining the gas tank with a rubber bladder would have only cost $5.08 per car, and Ford knew this as early as January 15, 1971. Ford's concern, however, was not with saving lives but with cost-effectiveness. In the end, Dowie contended, they determined that it would be cheaper to fight or settle any civil suits stemming from fiery Pinto crashes than to fix the car.

To back this assertion, Dowie published a chart developed by Ford that related to leakage in fuel systems when a car rolled over in a crash. The company used this chart in lobbying against proposed federal regulations that would have mandated more stringent fuel-leakage standards. Placing the value of a human life at $200,000 and the cost to preventing leakage at $11 a vehicle, they concluded that the cost-benefit ratio was not favorable to dictating improved safety.[41] The exact calculations, as reported by Dowie, are presented in the display below.

$11 vs. A BURN DEATH

Benefits and Costs Relating to Fuel Leakage
Associated with the Static Rollover
Test Portion of FMVSS 208

BENEFITS

Savings: 180 burn deaths, 180 serious burn injuries,
   2,100 burned vehicles.
Unit Cost: $200,000 per death, $67,000 per injury,
   $700 per vehicle.
Total Benefits: 180 x ($200,000) + 180 x ($67,000) +
   2,100 x ($700) = $49.5 million.

COSTS

Sales: 11 million cars, 1.5 million light trucks.
Unit Cost: $11 per car, $11 per truck.
Total Cost: 11,000,000 x ($11) + 1,500,000 x ($11) =
   $137 million.

In Dowie's view, Ford used this kind of analysis to reach the conclusion that it was impractical initially to fix, or later to recall, the Pinto. Instead, they adopted a strategy of sustained resistance against any safety regulations that threatened profits. "Ford succeeded beyond its wildest expectations," Dowie observed, for it was not until 1977 that NHTSA imposed a rear-end collision standard that would minimize the potential of fuel leakage. Yet Dowie remained troubled, remarking that the new standard would "never force the company to test or recall the more than two million pre-1977 Pintos still on the highway. Seventy or more people will burn in those cars for many years to come. If the past is any indication, Ford will continue to accept the deaths." Dowie concluded by wondering "how long the Ford Motor Company would continue to market lethal cars were Henry Ford II and Lee Iacocca serving 20 year terms in Leavenworth for consumer homicide."[42]

Dowie's exposé was the most important factor in triggering a crusade against Ford's "Pinto madness." In reflecting on the Pinto affair, Ford executives told Brent Fisse and John Braithwaite that the article was "the real watershed." Fisse and Braithwaite agree that "the adverse publicity began in earnest" at this point.[43] The most immediate effect, however, was on NHTSA. In the prevailing social climate, they could not ignore the claim that profits were being placed above human lives. The day after the Washington, DC, press conference announcing Dowie's charges against Ford, NHTSA undertook a preliminary evaluation of the Pinto's dangers. As a result, a month later (September 13) they initiated "a formal defect investigation . . . to determine whether the alleged problem constitutes a safety-related defect within the meaning of the National and Motor Vehicle Safety Act of 1966."[44]

Soon the Pinto was capturing media headlines again. In mid-February 1978 came the astonishing report that a jury had awarded Richard Grimshaw, a Pinto burn victim, $125 million in punitive damages, "the largest award ever made by a jury in a personal injury case."[45] This amount was added to $2.8 million in compensatory damages awarded to Grimshaw; another $666,280 was allocated to the family of Lily Gray, who had died in the accident. *Time* magazine called the total judgment "Ford's $128.5 Million Headache."[46]

On May 28, 1972, Grimshaw was riding with his 52-year-old neighbor, Lily Gray, when her Pinto stalled on Interstate 15 near San Bernardino, California. They were hit from behind by a vehicle traveling approximately 35 mph. Within moments their car was engulfed in flames. Ms. Gray died two days later. Grimshaw, then 13, survived the crash although he suffered burns over 90 percent of his body and lost his nose, his left ear, and much of his left hand.[47]

At the civil trial, Mark Robinson, Grimshaw's lawyer, presented the jury with evidence that Ford had conducted five crash tests before marketing the Pinto, which showed that the car was susceptible to fuel leakage. Then he exhibited a Ford memo stating that the company would delay fixing the Pinto's gas tank in order to save $20.9 million. He also used company records to prove that the gas-tank defect could have been remedied for merely $10 a car. "We were charging," he said at the end of the case, "that Ford Motor Company had consciously, knowing that those tests had failed, put out that model to save 10 bucks a car at the risks of hundreds of human lives and hundreds more injuries like Grimshaw's."[48] For "willfully neglecting" his client's safety, he asked for $100 million in punitive damages—the amount of money he estimated Ford had saved from not fixing the defective Pintos manufactured before 1977.

The jury agreed with Robinson's logic and went one step further. They did not think that $100 million was enough; this amount would allow Ford to break even. Therefore they raised the punitive damages to $125 million. The foreman of the jury justified this action by asserting, "We wanted Ford to take notice. I think they've noticed."[49]

As a footnote, a judge later reduced Grimshaw's total award, including punitive damages, to $6.6 million. In May 1981 the California Court of Appeal upheld this award, declaring that "Ford's institutional mentality was shown to be one of callous indifference to public safety. There was substantial evidence that Ford's conduct constituted 'conscious disregard' of the probability of injury to members of the consuming public."[50] Ford's subsequent appeal to the state's Supreme Court was set aside. While contemplating a further appeal to the U.S. Supreme Court, the company settled with Grimshaw for $7.5 million (the $6.6 million plus interest). Grimshaw, who had endured nearly 70 operations to remedy his fire-related injuries, made this response to the outcome of the case:

> It could have been more just. Not that I'm greedy. But there was no punishment. It was no sweat to Ford. You always wish you could be that way you were in the beginning. And someone dying in the accident. You can never replace that.[51]

After the initial Grimshaw decision, the crusade against the Pinto continued to mount. The American Trial Lawyers appealed to Ford to recall all defective Pintos still on the highways. In Alabama, a class-action suit on behalf of the owners of 1971–1978 models asked for $10,000 in damages for each plaintiff because the cars "were negligently designed and engineered so that they are dangerously vulnerable." Pinto owners in California filed a similar suit; meanwhile, individual victims across the nation continued to bring Ford into court, seeking large punitive awards. Fearing possible civil actions, employers in Oregon began to take Pintos out of service. The State of Oregon withdrew more than 300 of the cars, while Multnomah County, in which Portland is located, took 65 off the road. Salem sought to solve its Pinto problem by instructing employees who drove the car to avoid highways and to stay under 35 mph. Northwest Bell Telephone, unwilling to take any chances, impounded and sold its six Pintos.[52]

The pressure against Ford did not abate. In May 1978, NHTSA sent a letter to Lee Iacocca, informing him of the agency's evaluation of the Pinto's safety. For Ford, the news was not good. "Based on our investigations," NHTSA wrote, "it has been initially determined that a defect which relates to motor vehicle safety exists in these 1971–1976 Ford Pintos and 1975–1976 Mercury Bobcats." Specifically, NHTSA stated that the fuel tanks and filler necks (leading from the tank to the gas cap) "are subject to failure when the vehicles are struck from the rear. Such failure can result in fuel leakage, which in the presence of external ignition sources can result in fire." The "fire threshold" in a rear-end collision was placed "at closing speeds between 30 and 35 miles per hour." Further, because the fuel tank design was similar on the

1975–1976 Mercury Bobcat, that car was also subject to possible recall. NHTSA then told Ford that a public hearing on the safety defect would be held on June 14, at which time the company could "present data, views, and arguments respecting this initial determination."[53]

To justify their conclusions, NHTSA attached an "Investigation Report" that contained, among other things, the results of crash tests conducted by Dynamic Science, Inc., of Phoenix. These "fuel tank integrity collision tests" left few doubts of the Pinto's hazardous design. When hit from behind at 35 mph by a Chevrolet Impala, the first two Pintos tested (a 1971 and a 1972 model) exploded into flames. Eight other Pintos in the evaluation leaked, averaging a fuel loss of two gallons per minute. NHTSA called this a "significant leakage." By contrast, six crash tests conducted on the 1971 Chevrolet Vegas— a vehicle comparable to the Pinto—produced "no fires" and minimal gasoline loss when compared with that sustained by the Pintos.[54]

In the face of this evidence and the impending public hearing scheduled by NHTSA, Ford announced that it was recalling 1.5 million 1971–1976 Pintos and 1975–1976 Bobcats. Although they denied any wrongdoing in their press release, Ford promised to equip each vehicle with both a polyethylene shield to prevent the bolts on the differential housing from puncturing the gas tank and with a longer filler pipe and a seal to reduce the chance that the pipe would be dislodged in an accident.[55] They said it would take them three months— until September—to send official recall notices to owners.[56] This date was too late for the Ulrich girls; the letter from Ford did not reach their household until February 1979, months after their deaths on August 10, 1978.

Two days after Ford declared its recall, the Pinto received national exposure again. [Permission for the following excerpt comes from CBS Inc. © 1978 All rights reserved. Originally broadcast June 11, 1978, over the CBS Television Network on 60 MINUTES: IS YOUR CAR SAFE?] On Sunday evening, June 11, viewers of "60 Minutes" were greeted with Mike Wallace's question, "Is your car safe?" He answered, "Well, if you're driving a Ford Pinto, vintage 1971 to '76, the answer seems to be: Not as safe as it could be." Wallace then proceeded to tell the Pinto story.

Richard Grimshaw was the first to be interviewed. The audience learned that he had been in the hospital for four months following his Pinto burn accident, and had returned for "about 65 major surgeries." Reading from the brief for Grimshaw's case, Wallace noted that Grimshaw's lawyers were claiming that Ford "deliberately and intentionally . . . made a high-level corporate decision which they knew would kill or maim a known and finite number of people." He added, "Now that is one extraordinary allegation." The lawyer replied, "Well, we had a lot of proof."

Soon afterward this view was corroborated by Harley Copp, a former $150,000-a-year executive engineer who had worked at Ford for 30 years. Copp observed that style, not safety, was the dominant consideration in making cars at Ford and elsewhere in the industry. Engineers who spoke out about safety didn't "get that promotion" or "salary increase." This observation was not surprising, given the attitudes of those in charge of the company. As Henry Ford II told Copp, "this safety business is all a bunch of politics; it's going to go away, and we're going to handle it in Detroit." The Pinto, Copp asserted, was a product of this thinking. Mike Wallace commented, "I find it difficult to believe that top management of the Ford Motor Company is going to sit there and say, 'Oh, we'll buy 2,000 deaths, 10,000 injuries, because we want to make some money or we want to bring in a cheaper car.'" Copp replied, "You can't buy that?"

Herbert Misch, a 23-year veteran and vice president of environmental and safety engineering at Ford, was quick to take issue with this view. "I have never known a decision to be made to build an unsafe product or an unsafe characteristic of a product because of cost, or for any other reason, for that matter." Wallace immediately challenged this contention by noting the cost-benefit chart published in Dowie's "Pinto Madness." Misch countered by saying that the value placed on human lives was set by the government, not by Ford, and that the memo has "been taken totally out of context, and people led to believe that the Ford Motor Company is so callous that we wouldn't spend eleven dollars to save that many lives, and it's an untruth."

But Wallace would not let go. Did not a Ford document state that the company would save $20.9 million by deferring the repair of the Pinto? Were not Ford engineers told not to locate the gas tank over the rear axle because it would cost $10 more? Had not Ford trumpeted its Fiesta in Europe as safer because the tank was "located forward of the rear axle to avoid spillage in the event of a collision"? And had not the company omitted this information from the American Fiesta advertisements and then taken the trouble to delete all references to gas-tank placement from the car's European brochure? At the end of this interrogation, Misch could only answer: "Well, I—and I—I don't know that. And I don't—the reasons why it was taken out."[57]

Like Mike Wallace, other reporters found the Pinto matter a fascinating and eminently newsworthy upperworld scandal. Indeed, as Victoria Swigert and Ronald Farrell have observed, the case gained growing notoriety. Based on a content analysis of newspaper reports, their data show that the attention given to the Pinto's problems escalated markedly after Dowie's article and the announcement of the Grimshaw decision. Other changes took place as well during the Pinto crusade; the stories not only increased in quantity but also changed in quality. Early reports tended to focus on the defect in the Pinto's gas tank; later columns described the crash victims who were incinerated or horribly burned. In Swigert and Farrell's terms, harm was now being "personalized." These later accounts also stressed that this harm was being done "willfully" in an effort to maximize corporate profits, and that Ford, in denying any culpability, was "unrepentant" for having manufactured a dangerous automobile. Ford was portrayed much like a conventional sociopathic criminal: hurting people in the pursuit of money and feeling no guilt. As described by Swigert and Farrell,

> The emerging public imagery of the manufacturer was confirmed in media accounts of its production policies. Newspapers reported that the company was aware of the defectively constructed fuel tank and of the death and injury that it produced. Based on a cost-benefit analysis, however, Ford chose to continue production and sale of the vehicle. This depiction of the corporation, along with the application of a vocabulary of deviance and the personalization of harm, had the effect of transforming a consumer problem into a crime. At issue was no longer bad-faith sales to unwitting consumers, but reckless violence against individuals in exchange for corporate profit.[58]

In summary, by the time of the Ulrichs' crash in August 1978, Ford was under attack from Pinto victims, wary owners, a federal regulatory agency, consumer leaders such as Ralph Nader, and members of the magazine, newspaper, and television media. This many-sided "crusade" against the Pinto publicized the view that Ford had willingly moved far beyond the moral boundaries that ought to constrain corporate conduct.[59] As Swigert and Farrell noted, a "vocabulary of deviance"[60] had been introduced. In this portrayal, Ford was not called careless, but ruthless. Even the prospect of people tragically and terribly burned to death could not stop their quest for profit. Something had to be done. Perhaps, as Mark Dowie suggested, the only solution was to do what we do with other killers: lock them up.[61]

A new way of describing Ford's moral character was not the only by-product of the Pinto crusade. Both the civil cases and the NHTSA investigation had unearthed damning evidence, ranging from internal company documents to crash tests. This information was now in the public domain and being publicized by reporters who were anxious to show that crime occurred in corporate suites, not just in city streets. Farther, all of the anti-Pinto activity helped to create a pool of experts, such as Harley Copp, who were willing to testify against Ford.

It was at this point that Michael Cosentino faced the task of assessing blame for the Ulrichs' deaths. Though initially he did not know much about the Pinto, he quickly learned, in the context of the Pinto crusade, the whole story. This knowledge, along with the specifics of the accident and the existence of a larger social and legal context increasingly conducive to holding corporations accountable for their misbehavior, led Cosentino to two conclusions. As a man of good conscience, he thought that Ford had gone too far and was to blame for the fiery crash on Highway 33. As a pragmatic elected official, he was beginning to realize that it was indeed feasible for him to bring Ford Motor Company into court and to make them pay for their "crime."

Blaming Ford

The Accident

It was a happy time, full of promise, for the Ulrich family. Judy had just recently graduated from high school and was waiting to study interior design at a commercial college in the fall. Her sister, Lyn, was looking forward to her junior year at Penn High School, where she had been a straight-A student. And it was always a special occasion when cousin Donna visited from Illinois. The visits offered the chance to have fun and to share their excitement about and commitment to Christianity.[62]

It was past 5:30 when the three teenagers hurried out the door of the Ulrichs' brick ranch house. They were leaving to play volleyball at a Baptist church located in Goshen, some 20 miles away. The temperature hovered over 80 degrees, but was accompanied by a slight breeze and few clouds. It seemed an ideal evening to ride through the Indiana countryside.

Perhaps out of courtesy to her cousin, but more likely because she knew what was expected of the youngest, Lyn hopped into the back seat of her sister's yellow Pinto. The auto was a used 1973 model, but Judy was happy to have her first car and happy that her parents were helping her with the payments as a graduation present. Once Donna had settled into her seat, Judy was ready to drive off. The trip to Goshen would take the girls from the small town of Osceola (where the Ulrichs lived) toward Elkhart by way of Highway 33.

As later accounts would reveal, they made a fateful stop on their brief journey. The gas was running low, and Judy pulled into a self-service Checker station. When they drove away, they apparently left the gas cap on the roof of the car.

About a mile and a half down the road, the cap flew off the roof and landed on the other side of the five-lane highway. Judy cautiously made a U-turn and flipped on her four-way emergency flashers. Then she drove back westward, slowing as the Pinto approached the lost gas cap. It was impossible to pull completely off the road to avoid the traffic because Highway 33 was bordered by an eight-inch-high curb.

Meanwhile, Robert Duggar was approaching from behind in his Chevy van. He had just passed a police car coming in the opposite direction and equipped with radar. Quickly checking his speedometer, he was relieved to see that he was going 50 mph, well within the posted limit of 55 mph. Feeling the urge for a cigarette, he glanced down and reached for his pack, which had fallen on the floor of the van. When he looked up, he was shocked to see the Ulrichs' Pinto only 10 feet in front of him.

There was no time to avoid a collision. The van's front bumper, a thick pine board, rammed into the Pinto's rear. Duggar immediately smelled gasoline; an instant later the Pinto burst into flames.

The Accident Scene

Interpreting the Accident

Shortly before 6:30, state trooper Neil Graves received a call from the dispatcher. The news was not good; there was an accident on Highway 33, just north of Goshen. As a six-and-a-half year veteran of the force, investigating crashes was nothing new for Graves. He had already witnessed the aftermath of 987 accidents.

As sociologist David Sudnow has observed, the experience of participants in the criminal justice system leads them to gain "knowledge of the typical manner in which offenses of given classes are committed, the social characteristics of the persons who regularly commit them, the features of the settings in which they occur, the types of victims often involved, and the like."[63] Offenses that coincide with this knowledge are viewed as "normal crimes," and the participants know how to react when they confront such cases. The procedure is less clear, however, when the conduct in question violates the expected parameters—for example, when one confronts an elderly criminal.

Neil Graves's experiences on the road had taught him that there was a "normal" accident that resulted in loss of life, involving high speeds, alcohol or other substance abuse, broken bodies, and substantial damage to all vehicles involved in the crash. As he drove up Highway 33, he expected to find these circumstances.

From the beginning, however, Graves was troubled by the oddness of this accident; certain things did not fit the normal pattern. As he pulled onto the scene at 6:39, the firefighters had just finished extinguishing the Pinto's fire. It struck Graves that this was only the third fire he had seen in nearly 1,000 collisions, and all of those had involved extremely high speeds. He had the difficult job of being the first to look inside the Ulrichs' vehicle, and found that what the bystanders suspected was tragically true: two charred bodies were inside. For Neil Graves it was a heart-wrenching picture that would give him nightmares in the coming months. As he commented later, "that's a sight indelibly burned on my mind. I'll never forget it for the rest of my life."

Recovering from this initial shock, he proceeded to check the interior of the car. The water used to douse the fire had accumulated in the front floor, but Graves noticed that it was mixed with something else. He dipped his fingers in the liquid and took a small sample to sniff. Then it dawned on him: he was smelling gasoline. Somewhat bewildered, Graves could not understand how this could have happened. As lab tests would reveal later, the passenger compartment had been splashed with gasoline before the fire had ignited.

This was not the only unusual aspect of the accident. All the witnesses of the crash told Graves that both vehicles were moving when they collided and that the speed difference was at most 30 mph. They felt that this would only be a fender-bender, but then, suddenly, the Pinto exploded into flames.

Graves was also puzzled by the difference in the damage to each vehicle. Duggar's van sustained only minor dents, a pushed-in front grill, and one cracked headlight. By contrast, the back of the Pinto had collapsed like an accordion, and only the burned-out shell of the car remained. Graves, a veteran investigator of highway wrecks, found it hard to believe that the two vehicles had been in the same accident.

"Consciously or subconsciously," as Graves would later put it, another factor was at work. Six months before that evening he had picked up a copy of *Mother Jones* magazine from a newsstand. That issue had featured Dowie's "Pinto Madness." In retrospect, Graves could not say how much that article shaped his investigation of the accident. In any event, his memory would be jogged by the next day, and the odd aspects of the accident scene would begin to make sense.

Meanwhile, Terry Shewmaker, Cosentino's 30-year-old assistant prosecutor, had just returned home. He was greeted with a call from a local television station asking him about the accident. This was the first he had heard of the tragedy, and he called the Elkhart County sheriff's office to learn more. The details were disturbing: two dead, one burned critically. Shewmaker hung up and immediately dialed his boss at home. Because of the gravity of the case, Cosentino instructed him to treat the accident as a potential homicide.

Struck by the horrible deaths of the three teenage girls, the local citizens and media searched to assess blame. Some felt that Highway 33, with its treacherous eight-inch curbs, was at least partially at fault. However, when it was learned that pills, suspected to be amphetamines (though they proved to be caffeine), were found in his Chevy van, the local consensus was that Robert Duggar was to blame. By 4:00 on Friday, the day after the accident, Duggar had been arrested on charges of possessing an illegal drug.

On the national level, word of the Pinto burn deaths received a very different interpretation. On Friday, while working at a part-time job that helped make ends meet, Neil Graves repeatedly received calls. As expected, the local media tracked him down. But this was not all; he was also contacted by such national media sources as UPI, AP, and CBS's Dan Rather. These callers did not ask about the possibility of a drugged-up driver but about the defects in an automobile. Combined with the oddities of the accident and Dowie's article, these questions made Graves begin to think that the Pinto, and not Duggar, might be to blame for the Ulrichs' deaths the night before.

Graves's next step was to get in touch with Mark Dowie. Dowie retold the particulars of the "Pinto Madness" story and offered to forward a reprint. He also gave Graves the names of Harley Copp, the ex-Ford engineering executive, and Byron Bloch, a safety expert. Both Copp and Bloch had worked against Ford in Pinto civil cases (such as the Grimshaw trial), and Copp had appeared on the "60 Minutes" segment on the Pinto. In effect, Graves, and thus Cosentino, now belonged to the network of people who were crusading against the Pinto.

Over the weekend, the evidence gathered at the accident site was processed and prepared for examination. Cosentino sat down with Graves, Shewmaker, and the rest of his staff to consider what, if anything, the prosecutor's office should act upon. The others quickly came to share Graves's gut feeling—formed the night of the crash—that this was not a normal case. When he viewed photographs of the vehicles, Cosentino could not believe the disparity in the damages to the Pinto and to the van. He was also bothered by the eyewitness testimony indicating that this should have been just a minor crash. Most troubling were the pictures of the dead girls; they were, as Terry Shewmaker remarked, "incredible." Those at the meeting could not help feeling that no one should have to die in this way. It was clear that the case deserved further investigation.

In the days that followed, calls and information continued to flow into the prosecutor's office. Lawyers with civil cases pending against Ford for its handling of the Pinto contacted Cosentino and offered to furnish him with damaging corporate documents. Some may have acted out of altruism, but there was also a pragmatic motive: a criminal decision against Ford would hurt the company's chances in civil trials and thus would bolster the lawyers' bargaining power in out-of-court settlements. As Cosentino noted later, his office became a "clearinghouse" for Pinto documents.

This information would be valuable, of course. Yet while Cosentino was considering how to proceed, the repeated offers to share "inside" tests and memoranda had other, perhaps more significant, effects. For one thing, they revealed that Ford's corporate shield had been pierced. Cosentino would not have to start from scratch; he would have some documents, a good idea of where to look for others within Ford, and some confidence that the corporate giant could be forced to relinquish secret materials. Building a case against the company was not out of the question; if civil lawyers could do it, then so could he.

In addition, each outside contact—whether from lawyers or from the media—sensitized Cosentino to a way of thinking about the accident: Ford knew that the Pinto was dangerously defective, consciously chose to place profits over safety, resisted all attempts to make the company fix the car, and showed no signs of remorse over what it had done.[64] In short, it was said, the company had gone too far. Disregarding normal moral boundaries, it had placed its own needs above the welfare of innocent citizens. For a "law and order" prosecutor, this idea had a familiar ring and suggested a well-conditioned response: immoral offenders should pay for their crimes.[65]

Thus, Cosentino became increasingly convinced that Ford was to blame for the Ulrichs' deaths. The abnormal aspects of the crash, Dowie's article, input from safety experts, internal Ford documents, and media interest—when taken together—firmly reinforced this conclusion. One issue remained, however: was it possible under Indiana law to prosecute a corporation for the violence that resulted when it knowingly produced and failed to repair a hazardous consumer product? Recently the state had revised its criminal code, which now included an enabling statute providing for corporate criminal liability and a statute for reckless homicide (in fact, this had become effective 41 days before the Ulrichs' deaths on August 10, 1978). Cosentino knew the law and felt certain that Ford could be taken to criminal court under these statutes. To test his view, he asked his staff to research the question. He also requested an opinion from William Conour of the Indiana Prosecuting Attorney's office, who had been involved in drafting the reckless homicide provision. The response was unanimous: Ford could be held criminally liable under Indiana law.

"Reckless homicide" is one of several general categories of homicide that have been established by legal tradition and written into modern criminal statutes to address the wrongful taking of human life. Unlike the charge of murder, which is considered the most serious category of homicide and thus deserving of the harshest punishment, the charge of reckless homicide does not require the prosecutor to prove that the accused intended to kill anyone. It is enough to show that a death—even if unintended—resulted from the reckless behavior of the accused, and that a reasonable person would have known that the behavior was life-threatening. Because Cosentino would be trying to prove essentially that the Ulrich girls' deaths were caused by Ford's reckless choice of profits over safety—the company's management obviously did not intend to kill any of its customers—reckless homicide was the most logical offense category for the prosecution to consider using against Ford.

Scarcely two weeks after the accident, then, Cosentino was prepared to seek a pathbreaking indictment against a major American corporation and to join the crusade against the Pinto. He was now convinced that Ford had acted immorally, and he was fully capable of explaining its conduct with a term—"reckless homicide"—previously reserved for conventional criminals. With evidence and expert witnesses (such as Bloch and Copp) available, he also knew that it was feasible to develop a case against Ford. Finally, as mentioned above, Indiana law seemed to offer the option of bringing the company within the reach of the criminal sanction.

Yet Cosentino was, after all, a prosecutor in a conservative county. On the brink of making legal history, he was reluctant to move too hastily. He would put his feelings to one final test before taking on the fourth largest corporation in the world.

The Grand Jury

Elkhart County is located in northern Indiana just east of South Bend and a few miles south of Interstate 80. In 1980, its population of more than 125,000, including the city of Elkhart with about 45,000, was composed of typical "middle Americans." Conservatives outnumbered liberals by more than two to one, and secular influences had yet to erode the deep spiritual commitment of many citizens. Indeed, because of the strong Mennonite and Amish heritage in the region, religion continued to flourish, often with a fundamentalist flavor. Elkhart residents were proud that the county was the "mobile-home capital of the world" and that a number of other industries were also doing well. More than a few self-made millionaires were born, raised, and still lived in Elkhart, and this fact was evidence enough to the local people that in America hard work and smart entrepreneurship could still be parlayed into success.

This context surrounded Mike Cosentino as he considered the prospect of prosecuting Ford. As an elected official, he had to be sensitive to what the public would think about this bold action. To be sure, he was running unopposed in the upcoming November election, and thus any political liability would not be immediate. In addition, under Indiana law, he had the power to file charges against a defendant without grand jury approval. But Cosentino, a conservative man, was not comfortable about embarking on a case that would not be supported by his community both inside and outside the courtroom.

Would conservative citizens with a firm faith in capitalism believe that Ford could be a criminal? Cosentino thought they might, but some doubts remained. One possible solution suggested itself: to bring the case before a grand jury. As a small sample of the community, a grand jury could be a "sounding board," Cosentino believed. He could present the evidence but not try to sway the jury—as prosecutors often do—to return an indictment. In this way the jurors would provide a good indication of the average citizen's feelings about criminalizing corporate conduct.

Yet other considerations remained. On a general ideological level, Cosentino was not anti–big business; he "had no burning desire to prosecute Ford." He was motivated by his belief that people in the system have a moral obligation to play by the rules of the game. There was also an economic element: Cosentino, then a 41-year-old father of two, was a part-time prosecuting attorney with a salary of $23,000. The balance of his income came from a lucrative civil practice in which he often represented corporate clients (his law partners included his retired predecessor as prosecutor, C. Whitney Slabaugh, and assistant prosecutor Terry Shewmaker). He was concerned that a time-consuming trial might hurt his and the firm's income, and that attacking a corporation might cause some accounts to seek counsel elsewhere. His partners, however, promised to carry the load at the firm, and Cosentino was confident that his civil clients would understand his actions against Ford once he explained his reasoning. After all, he felt that in "99.9 percent" of all cases, the criminal law should not be invoked to control business enterprises. It was only when giant corporations—like Ford, not like those he typically represented—had shown that they were immune to normal regulatory and civil actions that criminal penalties should be considered.

Perhaps the deciding factor in Cosentino's thinking was the sentiment expressed by Mattie and Earl Ulrich, the parents of Judy and Lyn. Had they opposed any further action, Cosentino says, he would have ended the case. The Ulrichs, however, supported the idea of prosecuting Ford and offered to help in any way possible. As deeply religious people they were motivated less by retributive feelings than by a sense that there must have been some higher purpose for their daughters' fate. Maybe the case against Ford would give meaning to their tragic loss.

With all barriers finally swept aside, Cosentino convened a six-member grand jury to consider what action, if any, the state should take. Word of his decision spread quickly to Ford headquarters in Dearborn, Michigan. Three in-house lawyers were sent to inform Cosentino of the wisdom of abandoning the course he was about to follow. Visiting him in his Elkhart office, they allegedly threatened to halt the case through a federal restraining order and arrogantly (in Cosentino's opinion) dismissed his case as a joke that had already proceeded too far. After all, didn't he know who he was dealing with?

The meeting was brief, and the Ford lawyers, with their condescending approach, miscalculated the situation. Mike Cosentino had a strong will and was not about to back down from a fight. Difficult circumstances were not new to him. Raised in a broken home by a mother who supported the family by working as a waitress, Cosentino worked hard to become a high school football standout. His athletic prowess earned him a scholarship to Beloit College, where he majored in philosophy. After a stint in the military service, he tended bar in the evenings to help put himself through law school at the University of Wisconsin. In 1967 he joined the law firm and prosecutorial staff of C. Whitney Slabaugh. When Slabaugh retired, Cosentino ran for the county prosecutor's office on a "law and order" platform. He captured the Republican primary by less than 100 votes; in conservative Elkhart, this victory was tantamount to winning office.

By the time the Ford lawyers came to dissuade him from pursuing a grand jury investigation, Mike Cosentino, the epitome of the "American dream," had become a successful man. His civil practice was flourishing; he was a popular elected official. He was also known for his intense, flamboyant courtroom manner. Competitive by nature, he was proud that he had tried 25 homicide cases and had won a conviction in every instance. He was not pleased to be told by "slick" corporate lawyers that he didn't know what he was doing. After all, who the hell did Ford and its lawyers think *they* were dealing with?[66]

Undaunted by Ford's attempt to block his efforts, Cosentino pressed on with the grand jury hearings. Again, from a desire not to depart too radically from community norms, he tried consciously not to manipulate the jury into indicting Ford; he would let the evidence speak for itself. Further, any action would be directed against the corporation as a whole. Establishing the culpability of individual executives seemed too complex a task, especially because he considered it unlikely that Michigan would extradite top Ford officials to Indiana.

Behind closed doors, the six jury members were shown physical evidence from the crash site and internal Ford documents. Byron Bloch, the automotive safety expert, was brought in to analyze the particulars of the Ulrichs' accident and to comment on the Ford memos and reports. The jurors learned about Ford's crash-testing policies from Harley Copp, the former Ford engineering executive who was forced to retire from the company at age 55. The company said the action was necessary because of Copp's excessive absenteeism; others, however, believed he was forced out because he was too outspoken about safety issues.

On September 6 the grand jury issued summonses to Henry Ford II and Lee Iacocca. They wanted to hear Ford Motor Company's side of the story. At first the automaker hinted that it would refuse to obey any such dictates, but through a compromise achieved a satisfactory arrangement: Ford would send two of its engineers to explain why the company was not culpable in its handling of the Pinto.

The grand jury did not accept Ford's interpretation and decided that there was enough evidence to suggest that the company was to blame for the Ulrichs' burn deaths. On September 13, 1978, they voted unanimously to hand down three felony indictments against Ford for reckless homicide.[67] They decided, however, not to take any criminal action against Robert Duggar, the driver of the Chevy van. Though he may have been careless, eyewitness testimony confirmed that he was not speeding, and blood tests revealed no trace of alcohol or other drugs. Finally, the grand jury recommended that the eight-inch curbs on Highway 33 be removed; this was done some 10 months later.

The indictment, which William Conour helped Cosentino and his staff draft, asserted that "Ford Motor Company, a corporation," had caused the Ulrichs' deaths "through the acts and omissions of its agents acting within the scope of their authority with said corporation."

It charged that Ford "did recklessly design and manufacture a certain 1973 Pinto . . . in such a manner as would likely cause said automobile to flame and burn upon rear-end impact," permitted the Pinto "to remain upon the highways and roadways of Elkhart County, State of Indiana," and "did fail to repair and modify said Pinto." This "reckless disregard for the safety of other persons," the indictment concluded, led the Ulrichs to "languish and die by incineration."[68] With these words, legal history had been made. For the first time a major corporation in the United States had been indicted (and, ultimately, prosecuted) on the charge of reckless homicide for making and failing to recall an allegedly defective product that resulted in a consumer's death.[69]

Local reaction to this news was mixed. Some Elkhart citizens supported the action; others were cynical about Cosentino's motives. It was suspected that indicting Ford was a publicity ploy to gain the fame he needed to run for a higher office.

Perhaps the most common response was one of confusion. As David "Scoop" Schreiber, a reporter for the *Elkhart Truth,* observed, many people were genuinely puzzled by the action of their "law and order" prosecutor and wondered "why Mike would do this." Schreiber also suggested that community outrage was diminished somewhat by the fact that the Ulrichs lived in Osceola, which is located just over the Elkhart line in St. Joseph's County. The Ulrichs did not attend Elkhart schools, were not known well by many residents, and thus in a sense were outsiders.

Cosentino believed that public opinion was divided evenly. Neil Graves, however, conducted an informal poll in a South Bend mall; his numbers were 70 percent against prosecuting Ford, 30 percent in favor. Graves also found some opposition among other state troopers, and his superiors initially opposed the idea of assigning him to the case full-time. Nonetheless, Cosentino and Graves were fairly confident. Both were respected professionals, and both felt that sentiments would change as soon as people—like the grand jury—learned the facts about Ford's handling of the Pinto. By their accounts, public opinion had indeed shifted markedly in favor of the prosecution by the time the Pinto case had ended.

On the national level, the response was quite different. Cosentino received some hate mail decrying his action, but generally the feedback was encouraging. The news media, recognizing that historical firsts make good copy, flooded his office with calls and highlighted his attack on Ford in prominently displayed stories. Those who were already familiar with the Pinto's problems took advantage of the situation to celebrate Cosentino's wisdom and courage. A delighted Ralph Nader remarked that Ford's indictment "is going to send tremors through the highest levels of the executive suites throughout the country."[70] Similarly, *Mother Jones,* the magazine that published Dowie's "Pinto Madness" story, issued a press release stating that it "salutes the Elkhart Grand Jury for this indictment." The magazine's editors, however, added this caveat:

> We . . . respectfully suggest that criminal investigations be commenced immediately on the roles played in this [Pinto marketing] decision [by three Ford vice-presidents,] Ford President Lee Iacocca, and Chairman of the Board Henry Ford II.[71]

Meanwhile, Ford Motor Company, stung by the news of the indictments, was mobilizing its immense resources to put a stop to Cosentino's game plan. To be sure, Ford stood to suffer only a minimal penalty from a conviction: a maximum fine of $30,000–$10,000 for each count of reckless homicide. Because Ford was a corporation, it could not, as in the case of an individual offender, be incarcerated. A $30,000 fine was insignificant to the fourth largest corporation in the world. The case had other possible ramifications, however, and Ford had reason to fear these: the use of a criminal conviction against Ford in Pinto-related civil cases in which enormous punitive damages were at stake; the loss of consumer confidence resulting in declining sales; and the specter of a trial precipitating more stringent federal safety regulations (see Chapter 5 for an extended review of these issues). Although these points were only a matter of speculation, the automaker did not wish to take this kind of risk. Cosentino may have had some success in his own backyard, but now Ford intended to hire the best legal minds available to see that this Pinto matter was quickly put to rest.

CONCLUSION

In his best-seller *Megatrends,* John Naisbitt observed that "most of the social invention occurs in just five states." These "bellwether" states, "again and again the places where new trends begin," are California, Florida, Washington, Colorado, and Connecticut.[72] It is not surprising that Indiana does not appear on this list; the state and its people may have many admirable qualities, but Hoosiers are not generally thought to be social trendsetters.

Yet even if Indiana is not one of the five "bellwether states" that signal what is to come, it may be a place that tells us what has arrived—what changes have taken hold sufficiently to penetrate deeply into the American social fabric. Thus, it seems significant that Ford was indicted not in a jurisdiction that experimented constantly with new social policy but in a community—Elkhart—that took pride in traditional values and practices. This fact suggests that the movement against white-collar crime and, more specifically, the attack on questionable corporate conduct had reached the heart of middle America. Social, political, and legal circumstances had combined to create the possibility that even a Republican "law and order" prosecutor in a conservative county would seek—and win—an indictment against a giant corporation. Seen in this light, the Ford Pinto case assumed importance not merely for the legal precedent it would set, but also because it was fundamentally a sign of the times.

NOTES

[1]   This account of the accident was drawn from Lee Patrick Strobel, *Reckless Homicide? Ford's Pinto Trial*. South Bend, IN: And Books, 1985, pp. 7–16; Dennis Byrne, "The Pinto, the Girls, the Anger," *Chicago Sun-Times* (September 17, 1978). pp. 5, 50; and the following articles by local reporter David Schreiber that were published in the *Elkhart Truth*: "Eyewitnesses Tell of Pinto Crash" (January 17, 1980), "Witness Saw Pinto Become Ball of Flame" (January 18, 1980), "Duggar Describes Tragic Pinto Scene" (January 22, 1982).

[2]   Hugh McCann, "The Pinto Trial," *Detroit News Magazine* (January 6, 1980), p. 23.

[3]   This point was taken from Cynthia Fuchs Epstein's observation that female interest in law and in legal specialties previously reserved for males was not merely the result of changing sex roles but also of the emergence of opportunities that prompted women to pursue nontraditional career paths. As Epstein has commented, "The opening up of opportunities proved immediately effective in creating interest. And, contrary to popular myths, it was not necessary for women to go through long years of 'resocialization,' retraining, or reorientation to prepare for their new roles." See *Women in Law*. Garden City, NY: Anchor Books, 1984, p. 380.

[4]   David Schreiber, "Cosentino Defends Charges," *Elkhart Truth* (October 25, 1978).

[5]   Interview with Michael Cosentino, June 1983.

[6]   *Ibid.*

[7]   Cosentino was a keynote speaker at the 1980 meeting of the American Bar Association. He was also featured prominently in a series of articles on the case that appeared in the *National Law Journal*.

[8]   See, for example, John C. Coffee, Jr., "Making the Punishment Fit the Corporation: The Problems of Finding an Optimal Corporation Criminal Sanction," *Northern Illinois University Law Review* 1 (1980), pp. 3–36. The legal literature debating the wisdom of criminally sanctioning corporations has grown remarkably since the mid-1970s and is now voluminous.

⁹   Interview with Michael Cosentino, June 1983.

¹⁰   John L. Paluszek, *Will the Corporation Survive?* Reston, VA: Reston, 1977, p. 3.

¹¹   Peter L. Berger, *The Heretical Imperative. Contemporary Possibilities of Religious Affirmation.* Garden City, NY: Anchor, 1966.

¹²   Alvin W. Gouldner, *The Coming Crisis of Western Sociology.* New York: Avon, 1970, p. 29.

¹³   Seymour Martin Lipset and. William Schneider, "Confidence in Confidence Measures," *Public Opinion* 6 (August-September 1983), p. 44.

¹⁴   Seymour Martin Lipset and William Schneider, *The Confidence Gap: Business, Labor, and Government in the Public Mind.* New York: Free Press, 1983, p. 72. See also Kathy Bloomgarden, "Managing the Environment: The Public's View," *Public Opinion* 6 (February-March 1983), pp. 47–51; "Opinion Roundup: the Balance Sheet on Business," *Public Opinion* 5 (October-November 1982), p. 21.

¹⁵   Lipset and Schneider, *The Confidence Gap*, p. 31.

¹⁶   Roger Ricklefs, "Public Gives Executives Low Marks for Honesty and Ethical Standards," *The Wall Street Journal* 64 (November 2, 1983), p. 31.

¹⁷   Lipset and Schneider, *The Confidence Gap*, pp. 35, 78, 171; "Opinion Roundup: No Reduction in Pop Cynicism," *Public Opinion* 6 (December-January 1984), p. 32; "Opinion Roundup: Occupational Prestige," *Public Opinion* 4 (August-September 1981), p. 33.

¹⁸   Lipset and Schneider, *The Confidence Gap*, pp. 380, 382.

¹⁹   Ralph Nader, *Unsafe at Any Speed: The Designed-in Dangers of the American Automobile.* New York: Grossman, 1965, p. vii.

²⁰   For a discussion of the concept of "blaming the victim," see William Ryan, *Blaming the Victim.* New York: Random House, 1971.

²¹   Nader, *Unsafe at Any Speed*, p. 236.

²²   The question of whether "safety sells" has remained controversial since Nader's initial writings. For contrasting, though not entirely contrary views, see Marshall B. Clinard and Peter C. Yeager, *Corporate Crime.* New York: The Free Press, 1980, p. 259, and Lee Iacocca with William Novak, *Iacocca: An Autobiography.* New York: Bantam, 1984, p. 297.

²³   Nader, *Unsafe at Any Speed*, p. 40.

²⁴   *Ibid.*, pp. ix, xi.

²⁵   After his settlement with GM, Nader decided to use the proceeds (minus legal expenses) for the "continuous legal monitoring of General Motor's activities in the safety, pollution and consumer relations area." See "GM and Nader Settle His Suit Over Snooping," *The Wall Street Journal* (August 14, 1970), p. 4. For accounts of GM's reaction to Nader, see J. Patrick Wright, *On a Clear Day You Can See General Motors: John Z. DeLorean's Look Inside the Automotive Giant.* New York: Avon, 1979, p. 64, and Brent Fisse and John Braithwaite, *The Impact of Publicity on Corporate Offenders.* Albany: SUNY Press, 1983, pp. 30–33.

26   By the time of Ford's prosecution, the impact of the consumer movement was clearly being felt. Thus, in a 1981 review of opinion studies, Joseph Nolan concluded that "by 1990, if not before, the notion that companies are responsible for their products in perpetuity will be firmly embedded in the public consciousness—and to an increasing extent, in our laws." See "Business Beware: Early Warning Signs in the Eighties," *Public Opinion* 4 (April-May 1981), p. 57. See also "Opinion Roundup: Taxes and Regulation," *Public Opinion* 5 (October-November 1982), p. 23; *The Chronicle of Higher Education* (February 1, 1984), p. 14; and Timothy Harper, "Environmental Issues Gaining Importance," *Cincinnati Enquirer* (August 29, 1984), p. A-10.

27   In two samples, for example, large proportions (89% and 62.8%) of business executives disagreed with the statement that "consumerism or the consumer crusade has not been an important factor in changing business practices and procedures." See Thomas J. Stanley and Larry M. Robinson, "Opinions on Consumer Issues: A Review of Recent Studies of Executives and Consumers," *Journal of Consumer Affairs* 14 (No. 1, 1980), p. 215.

28   Clinard and Yeager, *Corporate Crime,* p. 254.

29   Fisse and Braithwaite, *The Impact of Publicity on Corporate Offenders,* p. 35.

30   Quoted in Fisse and Braithwaite, *The Impact of Publicity on Corporate Offenders,* pp. 35–36.

31   All quotes cited below are taken from "Watergate transcripts" prepared by The National Archives and titled "Part of a Conversation among President Nixon, Lide Anthony Iacocca, Henry Ford II, and John D. Ehrlichman in the Oval Office on April 27, 1971, between 11:08 and 11:43." This information was acquired initially by lawyer Foy Devine for use in a civil suit against Ford conducted in Georgia (*Stubblefield v. Ford Motor Company*).

32   Mark Dowie, "Pinto Madness," *Mother Jones* 2 (September-October 1977), p. 21.

33   Strobel, *Reckless Homicide?* p. 82. Some accounts have placed the actual weight of the Pinto at 2,030 pounds. See Robert Lacey, *Ford: The Men and the Machine.* Boston: Little, Brown, 1986, p. 575.

34   *Ibid.,* p. 88.

35   Jack Anderson and Les Whitten, "Auto Maker Shuns Safer Gas Tank," *The Washington Post* (December 30, 1976), p. B-7.

36   Dowie, "Pinto Madness," p. 18.

37   *Ibid.,* p.18.

38   *Ibid.,* p. 20.

39   *Ibid.,* p. 21.

40   *Ibid.,* p. 21. Dowie also noted another major obstacle in fixing the safety defects of the Pinto: to reduce the time required to get the Pinto on the market, Ford had begun to tool the machines that would produce the car's parts while product development was yet to be completed. Thus, any design changes would be more costly than usual because of the investment already made in the tooling process. In addition, for Lee Iacocca's view of the Pinto, see *Iacocca: An Autobiography,* pp. 161–162.

41   *Ibid.*, p. 24. For the original Ford memorandum and chart, see E.S. Grush and C.S. Saunby, "Fatalities Associated with Crash Induced Fuel Leakage and Fires." Significantly, this document assessed fuel leakage in a rollover test and not in rear-end collisions. Although the problems that arose during rear-end impacts caused the controversy surrounding the Pinto, Dowie did not highlight this distinction. Even so, the most damning aspect of the Ford document was its suggestion that the company would willfully sacrifice human life in the effort to maximize profits.

42   *Ibid.*, p. 32.

43   Fisse and Braithwaite, *The Impact of Publicity on Corporate Offenders*, p. 43.

44   Office of Defects Investigation Enforcement (NHTSA), *Investigation Report, Phase I, C7-38: Alleged Fuel Tank and Filler Neck Damage in Rear-end Collision of Subcompact Passenger Cars (1971–1976 Ford Pinto, 1975–1976 Mercury Bobcat)*, (May 1978), pp. 1–2.

45   Roy Harris, Jr., "Jury in Pinto Crash Case: 'We Wanted Ford to Take Notice,'" *The Washington Post* (February 15, 1978), p. A-2.

46   "Ford's $128 Million Headache," *Time* (February 20, 1978), p. 65.

47   Harris, "Jury in Pinto Crash Case," p. A-2.

48   "Award $128 Million Damage Suit," *AP News Release* (February 14, 1978).

49   Harris, "Jury in Pinto Crash Case," p. A-2.

50   "Award Upheld in Pinto Fire Suit," *Los Angeles Times Wire Service* (May 30, 1981).

51   "Pinto Crash Victim Picks Up the Pieces," *Beacon News* (January 24, 1983), p. A-5.

52   Victoria Lynn Swigert and Ronald A. Farrell, "Corporate Homicide: Definitional Processes in the Creation of Deviance," *Law & Society Review* 15 (No. 1, 1980–1981), p. 172; Reginald Stuart, "Pintos Withdrawn in Oregon Dispute Over Tank Safety," *The New York Times* (April 21, 1978), pp. D-1, D-13.

53   Letter to L.A. Iacocca from Howard Dugoff, Deputy Administrator, NHTSA, U.S. Department of Transportation (May 8,1978).

54   Office of Defect Investigation Enforcement (NHTSA), *Investigatory Report, Phase I*, pp. 11–12, Figure 1. See also Strobel, *Reckless Homicide?* pp. 22–23.

55   Strobel, *Reckless Homicide?* pp. 23–24.

56   Larry Kramer and Charles S. Rowe, Jr., "Nader Hits Ford on Recall," *The Washington Post* (August 2, 1978), p. B-3.

57   All quotes taken from the transcript of "Is Your Car Safe?" *60 Minutes* 10 (No. 40, June 11, 1978), CBS Television Network. It should be noted, however, that Misch later charged that his interview was "cut and spliced"; and thus did not accurately present his responses or views of the Pinto's safety. See Strobel, *Reckless Homicide?* p. 222.

58   Swigert and Farrell, "Corporate Homicide," p. 181.

59   More generally, see Chapter 1. See also Joseph R. Gusfield, "Moral Passage: The Symbolic Process in Public Designations of Deviance," *Social Problems* 15 (Fall 1967), pp. 178–188.

[60]   Swigert and Farrell, "Corporate Homicide," pp. 170–172.

[61]   Dowie, "Pinto Madness," p. 32. Although the accuracy of Dowie's account has been debated, the key point here is that the narrative he supplied was enormously influential in socially constructing Ford as a corporate criminal. For an alternative interpretation of Ford's marketing of the Pinto, see Matthew T. Lee and M. David Ermann, "Pinto 'Madness' as a Flawed Landmark Narrative: An Organizational and Network Analysis." *Social Problems* 46 (February 1999), pp. 30–47.

[62]   The account of the accident and the response to the accident were based largely on June 1983 interviews with Michael Cosentino, his assistant Terry Shewmaker, State Trooper Neil Graves, and newspaper reporter David Schreiber. One of the authors of this book, William J. Maakestad, had acquired much first-hand information from his involvement with the prosecution during the subsequent case against Ford. We also relied on Schreiber's news reports and on excellent descriptions contained in Strobel's *Reckless Homicide?* Finally, although reconstructing a social situation several years after its occurrence is not without risks, we have made every effort to ensure that our account contains no misstatement of any major fact and as few inaccuracies as our method of analysis allows.

[63]   David Sudnow, "Normal Crimes: Sociological Features of the Penal Code in a Public Defender Office," *Social Problems* 12 (Winter 1965), p. 259.

[64]   Swigert and Farrell, "Corporate Homicide," pp. 174–176. Also instructive is Lee Iacocca's statement on the Pinto: "We resisted making any changes, and that hurt us badly." See *Iacocca: An Autobiography*, p. 162.

[65]   For a discussion of the nature of conservative "law and order" criminal justice ideology, see Francis T. Cullen and Karen Gilbert, *Reaffirming Rehabilitation*. Cincinnati: Anderson, 1982, pp. 36–42, 91–104. See also Francis T. Cullen, Gregory A. Clark, John B. Cullen, and Richard A. Mathers, "Attribution, Salience, and Attitudes Toward Criminal Sanctioning," *Criminal Justice and Behavior* 12 (September 1985), pp. 305–331.

[66]   This interpretation of Cosentino's encounter with Ford's lawyers was drawn from our June 1983 interview with him in his Elkhart office. It was our impression that Cosentino resented the condescending attitude of the lawyers as manifested in their implication that he did not really know what he was embarking upon. See also Strobel, *Reckless Homicide?* pp. 33–34.

[67]   The grand jury also indicted Ford on one misdemeanor charge of "criminal recklessness." Cosentino later dropped this charge, however, so that it would not be possible for a trial jury to compromise and convict Ford of this lesser offense.

[68]   Quotes taken from the indictments returned by the Elkhart Superior Court Grand Jury on September 13, 1978, *State of Indiana v. Ford Motor Company*.

[69]   As noted in Chapter 2, other corporations had previously been indicted on charges of murder and negligent homicide. The Ford indictment, however, was unique because it was recent, it involved the fourth largest corporation in the world, and it was fundamentally a product liability case. Thus, in *Corporate Crime*, p. 261, Clinard and Yeager observed that "the case was the first ever in which an American corporation had been criminally prosecuted in a product liability matter." Similarly, according to Strobel in *Reckless Homicide?* p. 29, "And yet the idea was without precedent. No American manufacturer or individual executive had ever

been criminally charged in connection with the marketing of an allegedly unsafe product." See also Malcolm E. Wheeler, "In Pinto's Wake, Criminal Trials Loom for More Manufacturers," *National Law Journal* (October 6, 1980), p. 27.

[70]   Quoted in Byrne, "The Pinto, the Girls, the Anger," p. 50.

[71]   Press release titled "Indiana Grand Jury Brings 3 Counts of Reckless Homicide Against Ford Motor Co./*Mother Jones* Responds."

[72]   John Naisbitt, *Megatrends. Ten New Directions Transforming Our Lives*. New York: Warner Books, 1984, pp. xxvii–xxviii.

5

Getting to Trial:
The Obstacle Course Begins

Many persons told us they believed the prosecution to be "silly"—and that was their word for it—since the maximum potential penalty to Ford under the criminal statute was a fine of $30,000, $10,000 per count. The Ford Motor Company, as might be expected, disagreed with the prosecution too. It variously labeled the prosecution bizarre, novel, destructive, sinister, and (borrowing the criminal defendant's old trick of accusing the accuser) reckless. Ford never once, however, contended that the prosecution was silly because only $30,000 was at stake.

—Michael Cosentino[1]

A strategic response to the landmark indictment was not long in coming from Ford headquarters; the plan was to avert a jury trial at all costs. To this end, Ford spared no expense; the company immediately retained Mayer, Brown, and Platt—a 185-member law firm with its principal offices in Chicago—to develop a legal strategy by which to quash the indictment. Roger Barrett headed a team of about 10 attorneys charged with primary responsibility for the case. Soon afterward, Ford added the prestigious national law firm of Hughes, Hubbard, and Reed to its legal stable. Philip Lacovara, who had served as a Watergate prosecutor while based in the firm's Washington office, was among the lawyers from that firm who worked on the Pinto indictment. It is not unusual for a corporate giant to employ outside counsel, often called "hired guns," for such specialized cases. As we shall see, this was only the first of many displays of the tremendous resources at Ford's disposal. The pretrial legal obstacle course, which would take the prosecution almost a year to complete, had begun.

FEARS AT FORD

As noted, Ford management was not concerned with the less-than-daunting prospect of a $30,000 fine. The comment by Cosentino that introduces this chapter makes a point that has been substantiated by Brent Fisse and John Braithwaite in their book, *The Impact of Publicity on Corporate Offenders*. In their chapter on the Pinto prosecution, the authors note that Ford management was concerned with both the short-term and long-term effects of standing trial in criminal court before the entire country.

Regarding *short-term* financial effects, several observers have noted that at the time of the indictment, the Pinto had just begun to recover from a 40 percent drop in sales following the June recall.[2] In an article that appeared, ironically, just two days before the indictment, *The Wall Street Journal* stated flatly that the Pinto "still threaten[ed] to become the company's biggest albatross since the ill-fated Edsel of two decades ago."[3]

In addition, as reporter Lee Strobel remarked, the company was troubled by other Pinto concerns:

> With the number of Pinto and Bobcat lawsuits continuing to rise toward 50, and total damages of more than one billion dollars being sought, Ford lawyers feared a conviction could cause plaintiffs' lawyers to hold out for higher civil court settlements and even encourage new lawsuits. The evidence disclosed during a criminal trial also might be used by lawyers in civil lawsuits to strengthen their cases if they wound up in front of a jury.[4]

Fisse and Braithwaite discuss in greater depth four major *long-term* effects that Ford feared with regard to a criminal trial: tarnishing the corporate image, lowering the personal reputations of executives, creating worry about longer-term effects on sales, and arousing concern about legislative implications. Let us examine these in order.

First, Ford executives were clearly concerned that extended media coverage of a homicide trial in which Ford was the defendant would tarnish the corporate image, affecting investors' funds and the public trust. Considering the cumulative effect of recurrent newspaper, magazine, radio, and television accounts of Pinto investigations, recalls, and civil lawsuits (such as *Grimshaw*), the company regarded the coverage of such a landmark criminal trial as potentially devastating, regardless of the ultimate legal verdict. Ford knew that the coverage of a corporate homicide trial would be extensive, not only because of the legal issues and implications but also because a "morality play" scenario—an evil corporate giant pitted against grief-stricken parents and an outraged prosecutor—was being established. In addition, the fire of public debate was stoked at this time by Henry Ford II's highly publicized quote: "The lawyers would shoot me for saying this, but I think there's some cause for the concern about the car. I don't even listen to the cost-figures—we've got to fix it."[5]

Second, although the Elkhart County grand jury did not return individual indictments against any executives who were involved with the development of the Pinto, as the company had feared, the fact remained that corporate officers would be forced to testify at trial and to explain internal decisions and operations under cross-examination by a criminal prosecutor. One view of this scenario was expressed as follows:

> Even though no executives were formally charged, prosecutors had to present evidence that the car had been defectively designed and that the corporation had been reckless in failing to warn consumers. A corporation acts through its executives, and so the prosecutors, in effect, would be trying individual members of Ford management for their decisions regarding the Pinto. Ford executives, accustomed to receiving community respect commensurate with their high social status and lucrative salaries, cringed at such a degrading possibility. Even if they felt they had done nothing wrong, the idea of undergoing public interrogation and insinuations was a humiliating thought.[6]

It also has been argued, however, that Ford executives actually welcomed the opportunity to "set the record straight" on the Pinto and that the existence of a "one big family" attitude among those within the Detroit auto industry made the prospect of industry-wide condemnation unlikely; perhaps this attitude even led to a kind of "hometown support" for Ford employees.[7] One must conclude, however, that if Ford management had been given the choice of defending its product and honor with the aid of attorneys in a highly publicized criminal trial or using the skill of public relations personnel in a creative advertising campaign, they surely would have chosen the latter.

Third, the long-term effect on sales feared by Ford was twofold: (1) the questions raised publicly about the safety of the Pinto would rub off on other Ford models, thus calling their safety into question, and (2) another substantial downturn in Pinto sales would raise the company's fleet fuel economy average above the level required by federal law, forcing Ford to restrict sales of its highly profitable full-size autos. According to Fisse and Braithwaite, "Ford's sensitivity on [the safety] issue was particularly acute since its executives worried that adverse publicity from the Pinto trial could trigger resistance to the new Escort, a car essential to the company's recovery in the 1980s."[8] As for fuel economy, the Energy Policy and Conservation Act of 1975 had influenced the number of larger cars that could be sold by requiring that the average fuel economy figure for all cars sold fall within certain guidelines. As a result, if sales of more fuel-efficient cars such as the Pinto decreased, the company would be forced to restrict the marketing and sales of cars from its larger—and, at that time, more profitable—lines.[9]

Finally, company executives feared a federal legislative response. As one possible consequence, NHTSA might promulgate more rigorous safety standards regarding rear-end collisions, which would affect not only Ford but also its competitors. Another possibility might be action by Congress to designate certain corporate activities influencing consumer safety as criminal violations of federal law; thus, they would transfer the responsibility for future corporate prosecutions of this type to federal prosecutors, who had access to much greater resources. The implications, of course, would reach far beyond the automotive industry to affect manufacturers throughout the country.

In sum, Ford was ready, willing, and able to commit its massive corporate resources to the Pinto case not because of any threat posed by the criminal penalties of the State of Indiana, but because of the number and variety of longer-term countervailing forces that could be unleashed against the company as a result of the trial. With this possibility in mind, the officers and directors of Ford were determined neither to take any chances nor to cut any corners.

BUILDING A LOCAL TEAM

In Elkhart, the celebration over the indictment did not last long. Although the first hurdle had been negotiated successfully, Cosentino knew that many more obstacles would have to be overcome. Grand jury proceedings clearly favor the prosecutor, but once the trial process begins, the criminal rules of procedure and evidence shift in favor of the defendant.[10] In addition, Ford's tremendous resources would certainly be brought to bear against the tight budget and small staff of the prosecution team. Up to this point, essentially two men, a part-time prosecutor and his chief deputy, had furthered the prosecution against the multinational corporate defendant.

Once the glow of the landmark indictment and the subsequent headlines had faded, Cosentino and Shewmaker soberly assessed the obstacles created by the disparity between the economic and human resources available to each side. This was an unfamiliar position for a prosecutor, especially because many of the criminal trials in state courts involve an indigent defendant.[11] Normally the prosecutor's office not only has the economic advantage in budget, staff, and support services, but it also has a head start on investigations, witness interviews, laboratory analyses, and other pretrial preparations.[12] In this case, however, the prosecution had far fewer resources than its corporate opponent. As Shewmaker remarked, "Somehow we've got to find a way to imitate a 100-man law firm; otherwise, we won't stand a chance."[13] Knowing that Ford had retained at least two large firms to help the company prepare for battle, the prosecutors spent several days gathering whatever economic and human resources they could.

On the economic side, Cosentino requested and received a $20,000 stipend from the Elkhart County Council to supplement the normal operating budget of this office. He was pleased with the Council's decision, especially in light of the fact that the county's renowned mobile-home industry had been devastated by the recession and the escalating gas prices of the late 1970s. Yet he also knew that he would probably have to forego an experimental crash test on a 1973 Pinto, because it would cost approximately $10,000 and consume half his budget, and forego certain expert witnesses, who were demanding their normal fees of at least $750 per day. In addition to the $20,000 stipend, the prosecution received a commitment from the Indiana State Police to provide the use of planes, helicopters, and crime lab facilities at no expense. As a further means of cutting costs, Cosentino learned that the federal government would turn over, without charge, its cache of internal Ford documents, NHTSA films, and investigatory reports regarding the Pinto.[14]

With respect to human resources, Cosentino and Shewmaker obtained commitments from each of the following individuals within days of the indictment:

> *Neil Graves.* As the Indiana State trooper who was the first investigator on the scene of the accident and a prime influence on the decision to prosecute, Graves was assigned full-time to the case by his state police supervisor. Throughout the case,

he worked closely with Cosentino and the prosecutor's chief investigator, Billie Campbell.

William Conour. After providing early assistance in drafting the indictment from his Prosecuting Attorney's office in Indianapolis, Conour offered further help by interpreting the statutory language that was to be applied to a corporate rather than a living person. As noted, Conour had been one of the drafters of the newly revised Indiana Criminal Code.

Bruce Berner. A highly regarded criminal law professor at nearby Valparaiso University, Berner was recommended to Cosentino by a student law clerk working in his office. After a series of consultations with the prosecutors, he was appointed Special Deputy Prosecuting Attorney and given primary responsibility for the legal theories that would be applied in the case. To assist him in this task, Berner received a large amount of research support from a small but dedicated group of law students at Valparaiso.

Terry Kiely. A former law professor of Shewmaker's at DePaul University, Kiely was a logical choice because of his expertise in product liability and corporate governance. Like Berner, he made a commitment to serve *pro bono publico* as a Special Deputy Prosecuting Attorney. In the division of labor that was established, Kiely handled evidentiary issues, including the crucial Ford documents. A core group of law students from DePaul also volunteered a significant amount of time in assisting Kiely with this task.

John Ulmer. A trial attorney and close friend of Cosentino from nearby Goshen, the hometown of two of the Ulrich girls, Ulmer took a leave of absence from his civil practice to volunteer his assistance with trial preparation. Ulmer was also appointed Special Prosecuting Attorney.

A few observations may be made about this unpaid staff that came to Elkhart to join Shewmaker's "imitation 100-man law firm." First, at the time they committed themselves, these volunteers could not have known that they would ultimately dedicate nearly 14 months of their lives to the prosecution. (Of course, there was no possibility of sharing in any contingency fee, because this was a criminal case.)[15] Second, although the law professors and their students initially became interested in the case because of its theoretical issues and national implications, their academic involvement was eventually transformed into a kind of moral commitment. According to Berner, he and Kiely "got religion" after seeing the photographs of the deceased girls and then reviewing the content of Ford's own internal documents. In Berner's words:

> Originally, of course, I got involved because of the novel legal questions presented by the indictment. It was only after I became involved that I saw the photographs and met the families of the girls. It is nonetheless hard for me to separate the motivating force of the legal issues from that of the personal aspect of the tragedy. They were at all times during the prosecution mutually reinforcing. Part of what we were saying is that a corporation like all other persons must be forced at times to look at the very personal tragedies it causes. . . . All I can say about the photos [of the girls at the accident scene] was that they immediately made me ill and that I cannot, to this day, get them out of my head.[16]

As a result, the volunteer prosecutors grew stronger in their resolve. This feeling became especially important when Ford's relentless legal machinery and massive economic resources threatened to overwhelm them.

Third, Cosentino made a conscious decision to keep the prosecution primarily a matter of "local talent." Although a handful of law professors from various parts of the country had begun to call and offer their assistance on a part-time, long-distance basis, Cosentino decided to limit the decision-making staff to those who had joined forces early.[17] The reasons for this decision were not provincial but practical. The smaller-scale coordination and communication to which Cosentino was accustomed as Elkhart County Prosecutor could not be maintained with a rotating advisory counsel that constantly needed orientation and updating. In addition, the case was being tried in the state court system under the new Indiana Criminal Code, and only limited legal information or knowledge could be gained from those unfamiliar with Indiana law and practice. Finally, additional transportation and telecommunication costs could have bankrupted the already strained budget of $20,000, which had to pay for expert witnesses, preparation of evidence, and other costs attending the trial preparation of such a large and complex case.

A final observation concerns the diversity of backgrounds among the individual prosecutors. As already noted, Cosentino was a conservative, law-and-order Republican prosecutor who counted several corporations among his civil practice clients—hardly the type of character one would expect to be heading a case that was often associated with liberal, "Nader-like" causes and reforms.[18] On the other hand, Berner and Kiely were law professors with liberal political and social views and virtually no criminal trial experience. After a period of adjustment, during which the three men struggled to overcome personal differences, they developed a deep mutual respect and a strong working relationship while striving toward the same goal: a conviction of Ford on all three counts of reckless homicide.

Although the volunteer attorneys, law professors, and students who became such an integral part of the prosecution team may have initially viewed their involvement as a unique opportunity to influence the course of a landmark criminal case, the moral content of the prosecution soon served as a binding force for everyone involved. Cosentino and Shewmaker, who had previously attempted to express the moral outrage of an entire community by themselves, were now joined by a diverse group of committed individuals. Each contributed something different to the Herculean effort of negotiating the obstacles set up by Ford, and each was bound to the effort by the strong sense that a moral crusade was unfolding.

AUTOMAKERS AND LIABILITY FOR DEFECTIVE PRODUCTS: EDGING TOWARD CRIMINAL CULPABILITY?

> The [prosecution] seeks to transform an incident that traditionally is judged under the civil law into a basis for criminal prosecution. . . . There is neither a need nor a proper basis for this court to strain to entertain these criminal charges which . . . are a novel and unprecedented effort to stretch the criminal process to fit the allegations of a product liability case.
> —from a Ford memorandum in support of its motion to dismiss the indictment[19]

As we indicated in Chapter 2, a criminal prosecution, whether viewed from a utilitarian or a moral perspective, represents only one means of controlling corporations outside the framework of regulatory agencies. Indeed, private civil suits have been used far more extensively than criminal prosecution in response to the individual and social harm caused by business. The law of product liability deserves special attention in this regard; the development of the law in this area has led to an explosion of litigation between consumers and business and to a plethora of debates concerning the social costs and benefits of safety in modern industrial society.[20]

The following survey of leading civil cases in this field reveals the role of the auto industry in the development of product liability theory. This review also shows the relationship of automaker-related cases to two goals or functions of law: the "distributive" function, in which the law is used to remedy harm already caused by making wrongdoers pay restitution to private citizens and/or to society in general, and the "reductive" function, in which the law is used to reduce harmful behavior by deterring its from occurrence in the first place. Implicit in our discussion is the proposition that it was consistent, both historically and symbolically, for Ford to be the defendant in a landmark *criminal* case that extended traditional notions of corporate illegality because American automakers have frequently appeared as defendants in landmark *civil* cases that applied new product liability theory. This discussion sets the context for understanding the significance of this legacy of product liability as applied to the Pinto prosecution.

The problems related to product liability in the early twentieth century are rooted in *Winterbottom v. Wright*,[21] an English case decided in 1842. In that case, the defendant contracted with a Postmaster General to supply what might be considered a precursor to the automobile, a coach, and to maintain it in good condition. The plaintiff, a hired coachman, was injured when a defective wheel collapsed while he was making his mail deliveries. The English court held that the seller was not liable to the coachman, for the duty to maintain the coach was owed only to the party with whom the seller had contracted—even though it was foreseeable that someone other than the buyer would drive the coach. In a sense, the court extended the concept of *caveat emptor* ("let the buyer beware"), substituting "employee" for "buyer" and restricting rights of action to those with whom the defendant/manufacturer had a direct contractual relationship.

As the industrialization of society and the distribution of mass-produced goods made remoteness of manufacturers from consumers the rule rather than the exception, the result was virtually a "liability insulation" for manufacturers. However, this refuge from legal responsibility, which reflected the widespread nineteenth-century policy of promoting industrial expansion and innovation at the expense of human life and limb, was relatively short-lived in the United States. The history of product liability law in the twentieth century records the insistent efforts of American courts to displace the policy of *Winterbottom* and the early cases in the United States that followed its lead.

MacPherson v. Buick Motor Company,[22] decided in 1916, was perhaps the most influential decision ever rendered on product liability. In *MacPherson*, the plaintiff was thrown from his new Buick and injured when a wooden wheel crumbled. The feisty Scotsman promptly sued Buick for negligent inspection, even though he had purchased the auto from a dealer and thus had no privity of contract with the manufacturer. In allowing the plaintiff to recover damages from Buick, New York Superior Court Judge Benjamin Cardozo's opinion imposed upon industry the legal duty not to place negligently any product with an "*imminently* dangerous defect" into the stream of commerce. Before *MacPherson*, the general rule of nonliability had been limited by only a narrow exception, which applied only when "*inherently* dangerous products" like mislabeled drugs, adulterated foods, and faulty explosives caused an injury.[23] *MacPherson* opened the door to a much broader judicial interpretation and application of negligence theory; by 1946 every state had adopted the New York court's reasoning and applied it not only to automobiles but to a great variety of consumer and industrial goods.[24]

In practice, however, the negligence theory had its limitations. Foremost among them was the practical difficulty of proving the *specific* acts or omissions that constituted negligence on the part of the manufacturer. This procedure frequently required the plaintiff to enter the manufacturer's plant, examine the production process, and pinpoint the carelessness that led to the defect in the product.[25] Considering the time and expense involved in such a discovery process, plaintiffs' attorneys more often than not determined that the costs and risks of such a negligence suit outweighed the potential benefits. Thus, even though the automotive industry's tremendous growth led to a sharp rise in injuries and deaths related to auto defects, a large number of potential claims went uncontested. It became clear that further development of the law of personal injury was necessary and could be justified on the basis of welfare economics and utilitarian morality.[26] As a result, the courts and legislatures gradually recognized two alternative theories which made it possible for a plaintiff to win his or her case without the requirement of proving negligence: implied warranty and strict liability in tort.

Implied warranty, the first of these "no fault" theories to be recognized, was grounded in contract rather than tort law. Stated simply, this theory protected the ultimate buyer by imposing, *as a matter of law,* a guarantee by the manufacturer and the seller that the product would be reasonably suitable and safe for the general purpose for which it was manufactured and sold.[27] As a part of the codified commercial law that was replacing the common law of contracts in the field of sales, this protection extended a manufacturer's liability for many kinds of injuries and deaths caused by defective products. Under prevailing freedom of contract principles, however, these broad legal protections were initially subject to disclaimer; as a result, it was common for manufacturers simply to waive them and/or substitute far more restrictive warranties in their preprinted sales contract. A typical example was the limited "90 day or 4,000 mile" warranty offered by American automakers in the late 1950s. The effect of this "protection," the concept and language of which were developed by the Automobile Manufacturers Association, was to waive any and all warranties implied by law and to substitute a promise only to replace any defective parts returned by the consumer. The "90 day or 4,000 mile" warranty, then, protected the car and its parts—but not the driver and the passengers—from the consequences of a defect. However, in the 1960 landmark *Henningsen v. Bloomfield Motors,*[28] which involved a defective steering column, the Supreme Court of New Jersey held that such attempts by an automaker to eliminate virtually all protections and obligations other than the replacement of defective parts were contrary to recent developments in the law, violative of public policy, and legally void. Other states soon followed New Jersey's lead, and the broader protections intended by the courts and legislatures to be embodied in implied warranty theory were eventually restored.

The second response to the limitations of negligence theory—and to those of implied warranty as well—was strict liability in tort.[29] The theory was first sanctioned judicially for use in product liability in *Greenman v. Yuba Power Products,*[30] a 1963 California case involving a defective power tool. The California Supreme Court held that a manufacturer could be held strictly liable for any physical injuries that were caused by *"unreasonably* dangerous" product defects. The court made it clear, however, that strict liability was not the same thing as absolute liability; that is, the fact that a defective product caused an injury would not in itself result in an automatic judgment. A plaintiff was required to prove that the injury-causing defect (1) existed at the time it left the control of the manufacturer and (2) caused the product to be not merely dangerous but *unreasonably* dangerous.[31] Although this theory was eventually used in product liability suits against manufacturers of a wide range of consumer and industrial goods, it was used perhaps most consistently and most successfully against automakers, whose products were associated with the most frequent and most visible cause of deaths and injuries to the public at large: highway accidents.

Although for several years the concept of "unreasonably dangerous" was restricted generally to mechanical or design defects that actually caused an automobile to become involved in an accident, a federal court in the 1968 case of *Larsen v. General Motors*[32] set a new course for product liability law: it imposed a duty upon automakers to design their vehicles in such a way as to prevent the *aggravation* of injuries. While noting that an automaker is certainly under no duty to design a "crash-proof" vehicle, the court held that the unfortunate realities of accident statistics meant that collisions, though not preventable by automakers, are foreseeable; therefore, a duty existed to provide not only a means of transportation but a reasonably safe means. The rule in this decision, often referred to as the "crashworthiness" or "enhancement" doctrine, broadened the concept of "unreasonably dangerous" and has since been applied in a clear majority of the states, including Indiana.[33]

The three product liability theories just sketched—negligence, implied warranty, and strict liability in tort—require automakers to provide a remedy in the form of *compensatory* damages in the case of injury or loss of life caused by dangerously defective products. Thus, the three theories have provided the means by which the distributive function of law is served in the field of product liability. In the 1980s, however, there arose a new phenomenon in product liability law: the widespread imposition of additional, *punitive* damages designed to punish and deter (or reduce) market behavior that reflects a flagrant indifference to public safety and welfare. In cases in which plaintiffs' claims for punitive damages have been successful, it has generally been shown that manufacturers, including automakers, abused their responsibility concerning product safety in at least three ways:

1. Failing to take even the most basic steps to acquire efficient safety information through tests, inspections, or postmarketing monitoring.

2. Neglecting to remedy dangerous conditions known to exist in the product and refusing to adopt feasible and inexpensive corrective measures plainly needed in light of the substantial risk of harm presented.

3. Misleading the public by concealing known, substantial dangers in order to enhance the marketability of the product.[34]

While the criminal law—at least before the Pinto prosecution—had left these kinds of marketing misconduct virtually untouched, punitive damages were increasingly used in a quasi-criminal manner to serve the reductive or deterrent function of law. Once again we can point to a case involving an automaker, *Grimshaw v. Ford Motor Company* (see our discussion in Chapter 4), to demonstrate the effect of new developments in product liability theory. Although the record $125 million punitive damage award was eventually reduced on appeal, the jury's message to corporate boardrooms was clear: punitive damages could and would be used to make a powerful statement that would deter corporations from designing, manufacturing, and marketing potentially dangerous products.

The movement in American law away from the insulating effect of early contract law theory and toward the distributive and reductive effects of strict liability theory (and, increasingly, punitive damages) did not occur in neat, linear stages. In addition, many gray areas have emerged in the complex field of product liability. Nonetheless, to borrow a concept introduced in Chapter 2, the application of new liability theories to dangerously defective products reflects social and legal developments that have *edged corporations closer and closer to criminal culpability in a nonregulatory context*. As the first homicide prosecution of a manufacturer for its business decisions regarding the design and marketing of a product, the Pinto case might thus be seen as a logical and even foreseeable consequence of this historical and theoretical movement.

Although a prosecution like the Pinto case may have been foreseeable on the American legal horizon, it hardly guaranteed that the first actual case would meet with unqualified success. It should be remembered, however, that in landmark cases success is often judged by different standards. In the context of a "normal" criminal trial, for example, one in which well-established statutory provisions are applied within a familiar factual context, a conviction is the only acceptable measure of success.[35] On the other hand, in a case that explores uncharted legal waters, the real success is often the legitimation of the breakthrough effort, which occurs when a court decides to recognize and apply new legal theory, regardless of the trial verdict.[36]

Of course, the legitimation of new theory can be sought by either the prosecution, the defense, or both in any particular case, and history ultimately becomes the judge of its legal significance. In the Pinto case, it was the prosecution that sought to legitimate its theory of corporate homicide in what would normally be the context of a product liability suit and thus to write a new page in the history of corporate criminality. The final sections of this chapter analyze the many pretrial obstacles that faced Cosentino and his staff in their efforts to gain such legitimacy through the Indiana judicial system.

THE INDICTMENT OF AN AMERICAN CORPORATION: FACING THE OBSTACLES

> A decision to apply the criminal process to manufacturers whose products may be involved in an accident which results in injury presents so major a policy question that it must, in the first instance, be addressed by the legislature. Such an application of the criminal law would drastically expand common conceptions of criminal responsibility and would wipe out the basic distinctions between civil wrongs and criminal offenses.
>
> The present indictment is not authorized by anything the Indiana legislature has intended to criminalize, and the prosecution of this case as a "groundbreaking" experiment violates several basic constitutional provisions.
>
> —from a Ford memorandum in support of its motion to dismiss the indictment[37]

For months after the grand jury had handed down the indictment, Ford's hired legal staffs spent considerable time and effort in attempting to avert a jury trial. Ford's primary attack on the indictment took the form of a comprehensive motion to dismiss, which drew upon statutes, cases, administrative regulations, and constitutional principles at both state and federal levels. The legal obstacles created through this motion, prepared and submitted by the giant Mayer, Brown, and Platt law firm, generally followed two premises: first, that the indictment was *conceptually* unsound because corporations have neither the legal nor the physical capability of committing the crime of reckless homicide; second, that the indictment was *constitutionally* flawed because several fundamental rights afforded to corporations as persons under the law had been denied. Either premise, if proven to the satisfaction of the Indiana court, would have sounded the death knell for the indictment. Like any good team of defense attorneys, Ford's lawyers were simply making use of every means at their disposal to get the case thrown out of court and, even more important, out of the public eye.

For Cosentino, Ford's attack presented the most challenging task of the case: to research and develop a broad base of legal support for his corporate homicide theory that would overcome each of the pretrial objections raised by Ford. It was time to organize the volunteer staff of professors and their students and put them to the test. Valparaiso's Berner and DePaul's Kiely were assigned to respond to different aspects of the conceptual and constitutional attacks on the indictment. In the manner of any law firm with associates, they would delegate in turn certain research responsibilities to the students who had volunteered their time and effort. This task often caused everyone involved to work late into the night and to travel long distances on weekends. With DePaul in downtown Chicago, Valparaiso in rural northwest Indiana, and Elkhart in north central Indiana, Cosentino's coordination of efforts and meetings became a major undertaking. Not all the students who initially volunteered stayed on through the many months of research, but the few who did remain received once-in-a-lifetime experience and the highest of commendations from their professors:

> The students were absolutely fantastic. They were highly motivated and were highly competent. I think an impartial observer of the research would conclude we had the better of it even though knowing the massive research resources Ford had. It is hard now to know why this is so. It's fun to talk about people who are pure of heart having the strength of ten, but it doesn't help. If [our students] had been on the Ford team, we probably would have been out-researched. It just happens that we were lucky enough to have top-flight people at the time.[38]

The ensuing "battle of the legal memos" produced a mountain of research that explored Ford's conceptual and constitutional challenges. Although these lengthy legal briefs were being prepared for the benefit of a single trial court judge at the local level in Elkhart County, the adversaries conducted a prodigious amount of research: the numerous memoranda submitted by the parties averaged nearly 50 pages per document. In addition, the scholarship reflected in the briefs is frequently outstanding. Indeed, many sections of the briefs read more like scholarly articles than trial court memoranda. One of the advantages often cited for our adversary system of justice is that a judge cannot really know the strength of an argument until he or she has heard it from lawyers who have dedicated all the powers at their disposal to its formulation. It is clear that the adversary system was serving its purpose in this sense; Ford's and Cosentino's staffs exchanged no fewer than four major volleys of pretrial motions, and in the process they created an impressive legacy of research and argumentation pertaining to corporate criminality.

We will examine this legacy in three parts. The first section addresses the *conceptual* issues attendant to corporate homicide by (1) reviewing general common-law principles of corporate criminal liability; (2) surveying the few cases in United States history before the Pinto case that considered criminal indictments of corporations for homicide; and (3) analyzing specific arguments made by Ford and the prosecution pertaining to the conceptual difficulties of applying corporate homicide theory under Indiana law. The second section examines the *constitutional* dimensions of the case by (1) noting the corporation's status within the general context of constitutional protections and (2) detailing specific arguments made by the adversaries regarding key constitutional issues. The third section concludes the chapter by discussing the Indiana court's final resolution of these conceptual and constitutional challenges.

CONCEPTUAL OBSTACLES

Common Law Development of Corporate Criminal Liability: Another View

As seen in Chapter 2, English common law stood clearly for the proposition that a corporation could not commit a crime.[39] This policy was based on both theoretical and practical premises. First, the fact that a corporation had no mind meant that it could not entertain the appropriate criminal intent (*mens rea*) required for all common-law crimes. Second, the absence of a physical being precluded imprisonment, the primary punishment available under common law.

This blanket rule of nonliability for corporations, however, was abolished relatively early in the United States. Units of local government were among the first collective entities considered to be juristic persons (recall Chapter 2); they also were the first juristic persons to be held criminally responsible. The master/servant analogy was applied to this situation: just as a master was responsible for the actions of a servant, municipal corporations were adjudged criminally liable when the actions of their officials (their "servants") created a public nuisance—as when, for example, they failed to maintain public roads. A subsequent and similar development was the attachment of criminal liability to business corporations Early in the nineteenth century, private corporations were typically chartered to fulfil! public functions, such as building or maintaining roads. They, too, were held criminally liable for creating public nuisances if they failed to perform their duties adequately.[40]

Principles that alter traditional common-law doctrine are normally assimilated quite slowly and in piecemeal fashion by state courts, and recognition of corporate criminal liability was no exception. Even so, the final vestiges of *de jure* (legally sanctioned) immunity for corporations from liability for common-law crimes eventually disappeared after the corporation grew to become a dominant force in American business and society. Virtually all prosecutions of corporations before 1900 occurred in response to nonfeasance and regulatory offenses. The modern view that a corporation could be held accountable for crimes of intent committed by its agents was adopted in the 1909 landmark case of *New York Central Railroad v. U.S.*[41] In upholding a conviction under federal laws, the U.S. Supreme Court dismissed the broad claim of corporate criminal immunity advanced by the railroad:

> It is true that there are some crimes which in their nature cannot be committed by corporations. But there is a large class of offenses . . . wherein the crime consists in purposely doing the things prohibited by statute. In that class of crimes we see no good reason why corporations may not be held responsible for and charged with the knowledge and purposes of their agents, acting within the authority conferred upon them.[42]

When the Supreme Court finally discredited any lingering doubts cast by the common-law rule of nonliability, the foundation had been laid for a wider range of corporate criminal prosecutions under both state and federal law. Even though strict liability regulatory statutes continued to be the primary source of prosecutions, the *New York Cen-*

tral decision led to a more intense examination of the relationship between corporations and the criminal law during a period marked by populism and a distrust of "big business," and may have served as a precedent for many of the corporate criminal provisions written into later health and safety legislation.[43]

Even today, however, questions remain about the applicability of certain criminal statutes—especially those requiring proof of criminal intent—to corporations. Generally, whether a corporation is subject to criminal liability under a given statute is determined by the nature of the offense and the perceived legislative intent for promulgating the law.[44] The following section provides a historical survey of different courts' responses when confronted with the issue of corporate culpability for homicide, the most serious of all common-law crimes.

Corporate Homicide in American Courts

One writer has observed that corporate criminal liability for homicide is an enigmatic concept. The ambiguity stems from two factors: the definition of homicide and the infrequency of criminal prosecutions against corporations for this offense.[45] As we noted briefly in Chapter 2, literal readings of statutory definitions of manslaughter and reckless homicide have occasionally created conceptual difficulties for judges faced with applying homicide statutes to corporate defendants.[46] Even so, a historical survey of corporate homicide cases indicates that most of the courts that have considered the issue have demonstrated a willingness to overcome such difficulties.

Before we review these cases, one comment is necessary. Though we presented several of the cases in our discussion of the historical development of corporations (see Chapter 2), we have chosen to reexamine them in greater detail in this chapter because of their special significance as legal precedents cited by the prosecution and by Ford during their crucial pretrial arguments.

Surprisingly, it appears that the first American case to recognize corporate homicide was decided by a New Hampshire court 125 years before the Ford Pinto prosecution. In *B., C. and M. Railroad v. State*[47] an indictment was returned in 1855 against a public carrier for causing the death of a citizen through the "negligence and misconduct" of its agents. In rejecting the defendant corporation's argument that "additional and onerous" liabilities would flow from such an interpretation of the law, the court emphasized a corporation's unique ability to create hazards to the very public that had granted its existence. *B., C. and M.* is an early and isolated case that could hardly be said to characterize a general recognition of the corporate homicide concept in the mid-nineteenth century. The decision deserves special attention, however, for at least two reasons. First, it represents an early example of judicial recognition of a social imperative justifying the application of strong legal sanctions against corporations that created serious and unnecessary risks to the public safety. Second, it provides a representative example of the important historical role that railroads played in the development of corporate criminal liability. Indeed, the railroad industry's "contributions" to this area of the criminal law might be seen to parallel those that helped define and expand concepts of tort law during the mid- to late 1800s.[48]

Nearly 50 years passed before another corporate homicide case was reported in the United States. In *U.S. v. Van Schaick*,[49] decided in 1904, a U.S. District Court addressed one of the oldest obstacles to corporate criminal liability: the absence of an appropriate statutory punishment. In upholding an indictment for the death of 900 passengers caused by the defendant corporation's failure to make its vessel seaworthy, the court skirted the issue of the inappropriateness of imprisonment (the only statutorily prescribed punishment) by suggesting that the social utility of corporate homicide outweighed a legislative oversight.

> A corporation can be guilty of causing death by its wrongful act. It can with equal propriety be punished in a civil or criminal action. It seems a more reasonable alternative that Congress inadvertently omitted to provide a suitable punishment for the offense, when committed by a corporation, than that it intended to give the owner immunity simply because it happened to be a corporation.[50]

In 1917, New Jersey became the next state to consider the conceptual issues surrounding corporate homicide. In *State v. Lehigh Valley R.R. Co.*,[51] while the court admitted that difficulties might arise occasionally regarding a corporation's liability for such specific intent crimes as treason or murder, it distinguished the offense of negligent homicide and upheld the indictment by stating:

> A corporate aggregate may be held criminally liable for criminal acts of misfeasance or nonfeasance unless there is something in the nature of the crime, the character of the punishment prescribed therefor, or the essential ingredients of the crime, which makes it impossible for a corporation to be held. Involuntary manslaughter does not come within any of these exceptions. . . . [W]e can think of no reason why it cannot be held for the criminal consequences or its negligence or its nonfeasance.[52]

B., C. and M., Van Schaick, and *Lehigh Valley* all involved privately run corporations that provided public transportation for profit. This fact may have been a consideration in each court's determination that social welfare mandated the application of common-law criminal concepts—not merely regulatory statutes—to these corporations. As we noted in Chapter 2, however, not every prosecutor's attempt to obtain a corporate homicide indictment has withstood similar scrutiny by the appellate courts. In the following two cases, indictments returned by grand juries were quashed because of strict judicial construction of statutory language. (As we shall see, Ford relied heavily on each of these cases.)

People v. Rochester Ry. and Light Co.,[53] a New York case dating from 1909, concerned a manslaughter indictment obtained after the "grossly improper" installation of gas devices in a home resulted in the occupant's death. Although the court dismissed the indictment, it did so only because the statute defined homicide as "the killing of one human being . . . by another," thus manifesting legislative intent to exclude corporate entities. While emphasizing that its decision rested on definitional rather than policy grounds, the New York court's dicta indicated that there would be no inherent problems in the application of a revised homicide statute that prohibited corporate recklessness:

> We have no doubt that a definition of certain forms of manslaughter might have been formulated which would be applicable to a corporation, and make it criminally liable for various acts of misfeasance and nonfeasance . . . similar to that here charged against the respondent.[54]

In *State v. Pacific Power Co.,*[55] the explosion of an unattended load of dynamite on a parked company truck caused a pedestrian's death. In this 1961 case, an Oregon court held similarly that a proper reading of its criminal code led to the conclusion that a corporation simply could not commit manslaughter as it was then defined. The legislative intent reflected in the wording of the statute made it clear that only *human* deviations from acceptable behavior were anticipated. Furthermore, because the penalty for manslaughter was both a fine and imprisonment, the court concluded that an appropriate administration of the sanctions was impossible. As in *Rochester,* however, the court's dicta expressed a sympathetic attitude toward the increased use of corporate criminal sanctions and noted the historical trend away from the broad immunities of the common law.

Before the Pinto case, the most recent appellate decision addressing the issue of corporate homicide was rendered by a New York court in 1974, 65 years after the *Rochester* decision had been handed down in the same state. In *People v. Ebasco Services, Inc.,*[56] two men were killed when a cofferdam collapsed. The corporation responsible for its installation was indicted for negligent homicide. Recalling the court's earlier decision in *Rochester,* the defendant argued that the same reasoning should apply, preventing indictments for corporate homicide. The *Ebasco* court, however, recognized the linchpin of the *Rochester* decision as that court's determination of the legislative intent behind the homicide statute. After carefully reviewing the relevant provisions of the revised New York Penal Code, the court distinguished *Rochester* by pointing out three important statutory changes contained in the updated Code. First, the definitional section for homicide stated: "A person is guilty of criminally negligent homicide when, with criminal negligence, he causes the death of another person."[57] Second, a related explanatory provision noted: "'Person,' when referring to the victim of a homicide, means a human being who has been born and is alive."[58] Third, a general definitional section added: "'Person' means a human being, and where appropriate, a public or private corporation."[59]

Placing the indictment within this context, the court held that the explanatory provision's more limited definition of a "person" as a living human being (which excluded corporations) was clearly intended by the legislature to apply only to the victim of a homicide, and not to the offender. Furthermore, the court observed that the only purpose of the limitation was to exclude abortions from the definition of homicide. The opinion also cited the language in *Rochester* that seemed to be "inviting" the legislature to bring corporations within the statutory purview of corporate homicide. Even though the indictment was ultimately dismissed on other grounds, the *Ebasco* court concluded that the broader definition of "person" applied and that the revised New York Penal Code manifested a legislative intent to include corporations among those persons having the capability to commit homicide.[60]

A survey of cases at the time of the Indiana prosecution thus did not provide a single operative principle regarding the application of homicide statutes to corporations. As one commentator observed:

> Given the ubiquitous nature of corporations in our society, economic and social considerations have preempted the importance of anachronistic theories and conceptual consistency. This does not, however, resolve the issue completely since a definitive rule has yet to be produced. The absence of both judicial consideration and legislative guidance in many states suggests that uniform treatment regarding the compatibility of criminal homicide and the corporate entity must await further development.[61]

Notably, the pretrial battles waged in the Pinto case, accompanied by their broad economic and social implications, revived many of the conceptual and definitional issues just discussed. The following section analyzes the adversaries' arguments and the Indiana court's resolution of these issues.

The Interpretation of Reckless Homicide in the Pinto Case

As the preceding survey indicates, the success of previous corporate homicide indictments has turned largely upon judicial interpretation of relevant statutory language. The court's approach to the conceptual questions raised by Ford was no exception. Significantly, the fact that Indiana's Penal Code had been rewritten completely and had become effective less than a year before Ford's indictment meant that almost no case law existed that interpreted anything about the new reckless homicide statute, much less anything about its application to corporations. Indeed, Ford's attorneys had used adjectives like "novel" and "bizarre" in their briefs to describe Cosentino's indictment for corporate homicide. Not surprisingly, the prosecution in a reply brief reacted strongly to the choice of labels attached to the prosecution: "It is not the prosecutor's legal theory which is 'novel' or 'bizarre.' The novel element instead is Ford's alleged conduct of deliberately placing on the nation's highways over one million vehicles, known by it to possess an intolerably unsafe design, which would predictably and unnecessarily take human life."[62] In any event it was, as lawyers say, clearly a case of first impression; the stage had been set for a lengthy battle over the interpretation of Indiana's new law.

Building upon conceptual arguments that were similar to those made by corporate defendants in *Rochester* and *Pacific Power*, Ford's motion to dismiss attacked vigorously the prosecution's interpretation of Indiana's reckless homicide statute and concluded that corporations simply were not covered under the law. This contention elicited an equally vigorous response from the prosecution. Cosentino and the law professors were well aware of American judges' predilection for weighing questions concerning any new or unusual application of criminal statutes in favor of the accused, a tendency that reflects our society's deep distrust of discretionary power in the hands of law enforcement officials. Accordingly, Berner, Kiely, and their students increased their already hectic pace (because the fall term was in session, the students and professors had regular class schedules) to prepare what they hoped would be a clear and convincing line of argument showing the applicability of the reckless homicide statute to Ford. The following discussion presents summaries of the conceptual challenge made by Ford in its memoranda supporting the motion to dismiss. (The Indiana court's resolution of the conceptual issue will be analyzed in the final section of this chapter.)

Ford's first argument was grounded in its construction of Indiana's definition of reckless homicide, which reads: "A *person* who recklessly kills another *human being* commits reckless homicide."[63] Asserting that any uncertainties or ambiguities must be construed in favor of the defendant, Ford contended that the plain meaning of "another" in the statutory context was "one of the same kind." Hence, because the victim was referred to as "another human being," it followed that the perpetrator of the crime must also be human.[64]

Ford's second argument employed analogy in an attempt to persuade the court that a corporation could not conceptually be a "homicidal person" under Indiana law. Conceding for the sake of argument that "person" as defined in the Penal Code might include corporations for some purposes, Ford argued that certain uses of the term within the Code led to a logical exclusion of corporations by virtue of physical— and thus legal—impossibility:

> There are numerous examples in the Criminal Code where the legislature has used the word "person" to refer exclusively to a human being. See, e.g., the section prohibiting rape. . . . ("A person who knowingly or intentionally has sexual intercourse . . ."). Thus, although corporations may generally be covered by the definition of "persons," there are clearly crimes—essentially crimes of violence against other human beings—where it is irrational to read the statutes as applying to corporations.[65]

Ford's attorneys thus concluded that just as it would be impossible for a corporation to commit rape, neither could it commit the violent physical crime of homicide.

Knowing that the conceptual obstacle set before them was central to their adversary's pretrial attack, the professors quickly assigned their best students to work with them to validate Cosentino's application of the reckless homicide statute against a corporate being. Personal conferences led to assignments of preliminary research, the completion of which led to more brainstorming and further research. After several weeks and numerous drafts, the finished product was finally turned over to Cosentino for review.

In the resulting memorandum filed in opposition to the motion to dismiss, which Cosentino called "the finest body of legal research I have ever been associated with," the professors-turned-prosecutors responded to Ford's initial line of argument by citing two relevant sections of the Penal Code. First, they pointed out that "person" and "human being" were distinguished clearly in the Penal Code definitional section:

> "person" means a human being, corporation, partnership, unincorporated association or governmental entity.

> "human being" means an individual who is born and is alive.[66]

Second, in perhaps its clearest statement on the matter, a separate section of the Indiana Penal Code provided that:

> A corporation, partnership, or unincorporated association may be prosecuted for any offense; it may be convicted of any offense only if it is proved that the offense was committed by its agent acting within the scope of his authority.[67]

The memorandum then explained that the use of "another" reflected a legislative intent to negate liability for suicide or its attempt, and it was noted that previous judicial interpretations supported this contention.[68] The prosecution thus concluded that Ford's argument was unfounded and that a corporation could be convicted of any crime in Indiana, providing that (1) the crime was committed by a corporate agent and (2) the agent was, at the time, acting within the scope of his or her authority.

The prosecutors then proceeded to dismiss summarily Ford's second line of argument, based on its rape analogy, by recalling the basic characteristics of the corporation as legal fiction. Labeling as "simply incorrect" the defendant's premise that "person," in the context of the rape statute, could not include a corporation, the memorandum began by reciting the elementary notion that a corporation was merely a legal fiction created by law. Then, in one of the most memorable passages contained in any of the numerous pretrial briefs, Berner and Kiely demonstrated succinctly how Ford's rape analogy distorted and exploited the "fictional person" concept of the corporation as actor:

> Of course, a corporation cannot itself engage in sexual intercourse; a corporation cannot itself do anything. As it is a fictional person, it can act only through its natural-person agents. A corporation has no genitals, to be sure, but neither does it have a trigger finger, a hand to forge a check, an arm to extend a bribe nor mind to form an intent or to "consciously disregard" the safety of others. Nevertheless, a corporation is liable for all crimes of its agents acting within their authority. The unlikelihood of corporate rape liability is because sexual intercourse by its agents will almost always be

outside the scope of their authority—not because the crime is definitionally ridiculous (emphasis added by prosecution).[69]

CONSTITUTIONAL OBSTACLES

That a large corporation may have more substantial financial resources is no more valid ground for depriving it of its constitutional rights than is possession of greater wealth by an individual.

—excerpt from *U.S. v. Security National Bank*[70]

One thing very interesting about the Pinto case, which was also very frustrating, is that the criminal process is designed on the assumption that the comparative economic advantage is with the prosecution. When this is untrue in a given case, the prosecution is twice cursed—once for having fewer resources and once for playing by rules that assume it has more. In connection with one of their motions, Ford attorneys were citing *Gideon v. Wainwright* and other Warren court decisions extending rights to defendants, and I was struck by the irony of it.

—Bruce Berner, Special Deputy Prosecutor[71]

Henry Ford II, who personally reviewed many of the legal documents before the lawyers submitted them to the court, reportedly preferred the development of constitutionally based challenges over the kind of conceptual argument discussed above. Certainly he held this preference because a dismissal based on well-recognized constitutional principles might appear more legitimate in the public eye than one based on mere "legal technicalities."[72] As a result, Ford attorneys put forward several constitutional arguments in their motion to dismiss. Any one of them, if not counteracted by Cosentino and his staff, would have been sufficient to stop the prosecution in its tracks and allow Ford to avoid being brought to trial. Of these arguments, two merit special attention:[73]

1. Indiana's reckless homicide statute, as applied against automakers, was preempted by the National Traffic and Motor Vehicle Safety Act of 1966, and thus the prosecution violated the supremacy clause of the U.S. Constitution.

2. Indiana's reckless homicide statute, which did not become effective until 1977–78, was being applied to conduct that predated it (the design, manufacture, and marketing of the 1973 Pinto), and thus the prosecution violated the *ex post facto* clauses of the Indiana and U.S. Constitutions.

We have chosen to examine these arguments in detail for two reasons. First, they were considered by most observers to represent the strongest of all the pretrial arguments made by Ford and thus were subjected to comprehensive and rigorous analyses by the adversaries (and, in time, by the Indiana court). Second, even though the court ultimately dismissed each of Ford's pretrial objections, these two particular arguments resurfaced during the trial and presented Cosentino again with serious legal obstacles, as we shall see in Chapter 6. The following two sections present summaries of these constitutional challenges and the prosecution's rebuttal argument.[74] (The Indiana court's resolution of the constitutional issues will be analyzed in the final section of this chapter.)

The Supremacy Clause: The Power to Regulate

The first argument developed by Ford's legal counsel was grounded in the supremacy clause of the U.S. Constitution, Article VI, clause 2, which provides:

> This Constitution, and the Laws of the United States which shall be made in pursuance thereof . . . shall be the supreme law of the Land; and the Judges in every State shall be bound thereby, anything in the Constitution or Laws of any State to the Contrary notwithstanding.

Ford argued that by passing the National Traffic and Motor Vehicle Safety Act (referred to hereinafter as The Safety Act), which established a federal system to regulate safety in automotive design, manufacture, and modification, Congress intended to preempt any application of state criminal laws in the same field.[75] Ford asserted that the principles of preemption under the supremacy clause prevailed not only when there was an express conflict between a federal statute and a state law but whenever Congress had chosen to regulate any field comprehensively. U.S. Supreme Court cases old and new (a landmark 1824 decision, *Gibbons v. Ogden*,[76] and an influential 1977 case, *Jones v. Rath Packing Co.*[77]) were cited to support the conclusion that even when state law shares a common policy with a federal statute, prohibits conduct similar to that enjoined by federal law, or is not preempted completely by federal legislation, it must give way "whenever Congress has comprehensively occupied a field, as it has in the area of safety-related regulation of automotive design and manufacture."[78]

After reviewing several provisions of the Safety Act, Ford contended that "Congress not only devised a network of mechanisms to develop, implement, and enforce safety standards, but it also specified the appropriate penalties if the provisions are violated: *civil* penalties only."[79] An extensive review of the legislative history behind the Safety Act, Ford continued, indicated that Congress had intended to preserve only state civil actions based on product liability theory and not state criminal action.[80] Under our system of federalism, Ford seemed to be saying, the buck must stop somewhere; Congress, under the authority of the supremacy clause, had decided that the responsibility for regulating auto safety must both begin and end at the federal level.

Ford concluded its preemption argument by warning of the potentially dire consequences should a state criminal jury be allowed to judge the safety of an automobile:

> An automobile manufacturer cannot, as a practical matter, produce an automobile according to two sets of standards, one established by the federal agency, and the other constructed by a state criminal jury. Even more clearly, any automobile manufacturer cannot be forced to confront 51 different sets of standards—since Indiana has no greater power in this field than any of the other 49 states.[81]

This first constitutional obstacle initially caused significant concern among the prosecution staff. Had the balance of power under our system of federalism shifted so as to eliminate the possibility that an individual state might use its criminal justice resources to prosecute a wayward corporation? After conducting their own research, however, Berner and Kiely were convinced that Ford's preemption arguments were not nearly as problematic as they had appeared initially. The prosecution's first response to Ford was that the indictment represented a constitutionally sound example of a state's broad police powers to enact criminal laws protecting the health, safety, and welfare of its citizens. While asserting that such authority vested by the police powers is reserved to the states under the Tenth Amendment and is fundamental to our system of federalism, the prosecution emphasized that the reckless homicide statute was *not* a regulatory measure but simply a traditional part of Indiana's criminal statutory scheme. No conflict existed between the statute and the Safety Act because no precedent could be found for the proposition that Congress had *ever* intended to preempt a state's prerogative under its police powers to enact and enforce a general statutory system of criminal law.

Like Ford's attorneys, Berner and Kiely drew upon old and new precedents to support their propositions. Citing, as Ford had, *Gibbons v. Ogden,* the prosecution argued that the 1824 landmark could be read to suggest that the preemption doctrine applies *only* when the federal regulatory scheme is so pervasive that it is reasonable to assume that Congress intended to leave no room for state regulation. A more recent case, which confirmed this interpretation for the prosecution, was *Raymond Motors v. Rice,*[82] a 1978 Supreme Court decision that considered a preemption challenge to a state highway regulation. A particularly salient part of this decision, quoted by the prosecution, stated that

> the Court has been most reluctant to invalidate . . . "state legislation in the field of safety where the propriety of local regulation has been long recognized." . . . In no field has this deference to state regulation been greater than that of highway safety regulation. . . . Thus, those who would challenge state regulations said to promote highway safety must overcome a "strong presumption of validity."[83]

The prosecution's memorandum then noted that Ford had been unable to cite even a single case in which a traditional, general criminal statute was found to have been preempted by a federal regulatory scheme.[84] After several cases were cited to support the view that the courts have long been reluctant to preempt a state's general criminal law, this line of reasoning concluded with an analogy based on federal labor laws:

> If the State of Indiana enacted a criminal law which made it an offense for employees to engage in violence on a strike site so as to interfere with the right to picket, such a statute may be considered to be in direct conflict with federal labor laws and be deemed preempted. However, if the State chose to prosecute such individuals under State assault and battery provisions, clearly there would be authority to do so without reference to the federal regulatory scheme. The State's right to prosecute the Ford Motor Company for its reckless behavior resulting in the death of three persons within its borders is equally obvious, regardless of the provisions of the federal regulatory scheme created by the Traffic Safety Act.[85]

The prosecution responded to Ford's other argument, the undesirability of the "multiple standards" that might result from allowing criminal juries to consider automotive safety, by noting how that issue had been addressed in civil product liability cases. After observing that the federal guidelines in the Safety Act were intended to establish *minimum* standards only, the prosecution tersely cited the following passage from *Turner v. General Motors*,[86] a 1974 civil case that rejected essentially the same argument when raised by another automaker:

> The danger that juries will arrive at conflicting conclusions is a hazard every manufacturer who distributes nationally runs. The complex, technical questions facing juries, aided by expert testimony, cannot be more difficult than the question in such fields as medical malpractice. *Finally, the argument that a single jury verdict may have profound consequences disrupting an essential industry has been characterized as contending that the desirability of immunity from liability is directly proportional to the magnitude of the risk created.* (emphasis added by prosecution).[87]

In a subsequent brief, which perhaps showed the "battle-readiness" they had developed, the prosecution chided Ford for what they termed its "Chicken Little" arguments pertaining to the potential negative consequences of a corporate homicide trial to manufacturers generally:

> If this prosecution proceeds, the national economy will not crumble, international trade will not collapse, and the sky will not fall. What will happen—and Ford knows it—is that a jury may find it guilty of the reckless homicide of Judy, Donna and Lyn Ulrich.[88]

The *Ex Post Facto Clause*: A Question of Timing

In what Cosentino and his legal team considered the strongest challenge to the indictment, Ford's motion to dismiss charged that the reckless homicide statute as applied to the facts of this case violated the *ex post facto* clauses of the Indiana and United States Constitutions.[89] In the words of the U.S. Supreme Court, this Fifth Amendment provision was designed to protect against "imposed punishment for past conduct [which was] lawful at the time it was engaged in."[90] Similarly, Ford noted, in a 1931 case the Indiana Supreme Court had given clear expression to this prohibition when it wrote:

> An ex post facto law is a legislative act relating to criminal matters retroactive in its operation, which alters the situation of an accused to his disadvantage, or deprives him of some

lawful protection to which he is entitled, as a law which imposes a punishment for an act which was not punishable when it was committed.[91]

In contrast to Ford's preemption argument, which was based on the supremacy clause's limitation of "states' rights" under our federalist system, the second challenge was rooted in the Bill of Rights, which protects against potential abuses of state and federal criminal laws. Ford's factual basis for this argument centered on a comparison of two crucial dates: first, the date when the reckless homicide statute became effective and, second, the date when the alleged criminal conduct actually occurred. Regarding the first date, it should be recalled that Indiana's Criminal Code had been rewritten recently. As a result, liability for homicide caused by reckless acts did not take effect under the new Code until October 1, 1977. Not until 10 months later, on July 1, 1978, was the statute amended to impose liability for homicides caused by reckless *omissions* as well. Ford directed the court's attention to language in the indictment that charged that the defendant had recklessly designed and manufactured the 1973 Pinto in which the girls died on August 10, 1978; the company pointed out that its conduct concerning these business operations must have occurred before late 1972, when the car was first marketed. Hence, more than four years had elapsed between Ford's designing and manufacturing of the 1973 Pinto and the Indiana legislature's passage of the reckless homicide statute. Ford concluded that even if the prosecution *could* prove recklessness on the part of the company, the retroactive application of the reckless homicide statute was barred by *ex post facto* principles. For this reason, Ford concluded confidently, "the entire indictment must be dismissed."

Again, for Cosentino and his research staff of professors and students, no other pretrial obstacle created as much concern as Ford's *ex post facto* challenge. There was certainly no question that the design, manufacture, and marketing of 1973 Pintos had occurred years before 1977, when the revised reckless homicide statute had taken effect. Yet the accident and the deaths had not occurred until *after* the effective date of the law: Might this fact be taken into account in order to resolve the *ex post facto* dilemma?

After spending considerable time on this crucial issue, Professor Berner devised two lines of attack for the prosecution. The first concerned establishing the date of the offense. The prosecution disagreed with the premise that the criminal conduct occurred before 1973. Berner contended that the date of the *completion* of the offense—*not* the date of the initial steps in the commission of a crime—determine whether *ex post facto* provisions have been violated.[92] Maintaining that homicide in Indiana is committed as of the date of the victim's death, the prosecution cited passages from two Indiana cases to illustrate this point:

> A homicide consists not only of striking the final blow which produced the death, but is not complete until the victim has died [sic].[93]

> * * *

> The crime we are talking about [homicide] is a composite one. The stroke does not make the crime. The death does not make the crime. It is the composition of the two.[94]

To lend further support to this proposition, it was noted that the statute of limitations for homicides in Indiana begins to run on the date of death, *not* at the time the causative act was committed. Hence, because Ford could not possibly have been prosecuted for homicide until after the girls died, the prosecution concluded that no *ex post facto* violation had occurred.[95]

Berner introduced his second line of attack by drawing attention to the language used in the indictment. As noted previously, Ford had been charged specifically in the indictment with both reckless acts *and omissions*. Whereas Ford in its argument had emphasized the affirmative acts of designing and manufacturing the 1973 Pinto, the prosecution reminded the court that the defendant's omissions—regarding its duty either to repair the vehicle or to warn its owners—constituted important elements of the offense. Although the reckless homicide statute was amended later to include omissions as well as acts, the deaths of the Ulrich girls occurred even after the amended statute took effect—albeit by only 41 days (July 1 to August 10). The prosecution then followed the citation of numerous cases with the statement, "It is universally recognized that when a defendant acts over a period of time, a relevant criminal statute enacted or amended to the defendant's detriment presents no *ex post facto* problem."[96] (To provide further support, it was noted that Indiana courts had followed this same line of reasoning only recently in rejecting *ex post facto* challenges to its new habitual offender law.) The prosecution thus concluded that once any actionable act or omission was shown to have postdated a criminal statute, all of the defendant's prior acts and omissions could be considered by the court without offending either the Indiana or the United States Constitution.

Before presenting how the Indiana court resolved the conceptual and Constitutional issues discussed above, we examine in the following section another, somewhat broader, issue that was debated during the pretrial stage by lawyers and nonlawyers alike: Were there any other features of Indiana law that encouraged Ford's prosecution?

CORPORATE HOMICIDE AND THE DISTRIBUTIVE AND REDUCTIVE FUNCTIONS OF LAW

Traditionally, the social control of corporations has been primarily a function of civil cases and administrative action, not of the criminal law. According to Christopher Stone, although the first question asked about measures to control operations is often "How well do the measures work?," a more functional inquiry would be "What are the measures trying to accomplish?" As Stone has observed (and as noted earlier in this chapter), the law generally seeks to accomplish one or both of two divergent but not mutually exclusive goals:

> One goal is fundamentally distributive. When losses occur in society, the law aims to distribute them fairly and reasonably. . . . [I]f a car does not perform as adequately as the purchaser was given fair reason to believe it would, the law, as an ideal, aims to place the unanticipated repair bills on the company's doorstep, rather than the purchaser's.

> But while making a corporation pay damages to persons it has injured is an important goal of the law, it is, in one sense, a secondary goal. A person who has received a cash settlement for the loss of his vision or his limbs has not really been, as the law is fond of saying, "made whole."

> Thus, what we should expect of law, as a more primary goal, is that it reduce . . . the incidence of harmful behavior in the first place. This is what we might call its reductive goal.[97]

What Stone terms the distributive goal is furthered through the application of civil law and its remedies, particularly compensatory damages. Except in states that provide for compensation to victims of crime in narrowly defined circumstances, the criminal justice system is simply not designed to accomplish the distributive goal of law.[98] The reductive goal, on the other hand, may be promoted by either criminal or civil sanctions. In the criminal justice system this goal is furthered through the deterrent effect of criminal penalties. On the civil side, a primary means by which to reduce or deter egregiously harmful corporate behavior in the future is through court-awarded punitive damages.[99] Although punitive damages are imposed far less frequently than compensatory damages, the years leading up to the Indiana prosecution saw a marked increase in the use of punitive damages to serve the quasi-criminal function of deterrence.[100] Indeed, many of the numerous Pinto civil cases brought in various states involved claims for both compensatory and punitive damages. As observed previously in this chapter and in Chapter 4, *Grimshaw* was the most notable of these cases.[101]

Criminal penalties, which normally take the form of monetary fines when applied to corporations,[102] and punitive damages, imposed in civil cases only when a defendant's behavior is alleged to have been "reckless" or "willful and wanton," serve a similar function in furthering the reductive goal. What then is the essential difference between civil and criminal law in terms of application? An increasing number of legal scholars perceive the distinction as primarily economic.[103] An important aspect of this school of thought has recently been summarized as follows:

> The cost of criminal litigation is borne by the state; that of civil litigation by the private citizen. Thus, the "morality or immorality of proscribed conduct has little to do with whether the law labels the conduct criminal or leaves enforcement in private hands. . . ." In some instances, the potential award to the litigant is assumed incentive enough to motivate civil action against an offender; in others, the benefits of private litigation are outweighed by the cost of such proceedings. In order to ensure punitive action against rule violators, these latter instances have been "socialized" through the use of criminal law. From this perspective, then, the application of criminal codes to corporate misconduct is largely a matter of administrative efficiency.[104]

This viewpoint is presented here because it relates directly to one of the most critical and most common questions that was raised in the aftermath of the indictment: Would corporate criminal prosecutions of this type, funded by tax dollars, contribute anything to the public interest when better-developed and less burdensome theories are available on the civil side in the form of product liability suits? Putting aside for the moment all consideration of the moral nature of the case, the economic pragmatists must answer "yes." The reasoning is as follows. Normally, when a person dies or is injured as a result of a defective product, the civil law provides incentive for private litigation, and the law is set in motion toward its distributive goals (via compensatory damages) or, if flagrant misbehavior is involved, toward its distributive and reductive goals (via compensatory and punitive damages). These results, however, assume that legally recognized causes of action and appropriate remedies are readily available to facilitate each goal. But, what happens if the law effectively denies the plaintiff access to an appropriate civil remedy? This is exactly what occurred in the Pinto case. Because a just and adequate legal remedy was unavailable under state law, the criminal prosecution represented the only meaningful legal response. For reasons that will be discussed below, Indiana law essentially foreclosed the civil alternatives that one would expect to be available to product liability plaintiffs, namely, compensatory and punitive damages.

As a result, the burden of "seeking justice" shifted to state authorities because there was no practical way for the surviving parents to pursue either the distributive or the reductive goals through civil remedies.[105] The absence of civil remedies, then, along with the willingness of a resolute state prosecutor to take on the case, distinguish the legal response to the accident in Indiana from the preceding responses to Pinto cases elsewhere, including *Grimshaw*.[106] Paradoxically, the fact that the three girls were killed rather than injured created the barrier to civil remedies. Under Indiana's wrongful death statutes,[107] surviving parents may recover damages only for the pecuniary interest in their child's life, which is measured by "the value of the child's services from the time of [death] until he would have attained his majority, less his support and maintenance."[108] Because the Ulrich girls were 18 or nearly 18 (the age of majority in Indiana), any compensatory damages awarded would have been speculative and nominal. In addition, a long line of Indiana cases has held that neither the pain and suffering of the deceased, nor the mental anguish, grief, sorrow, or loss of happiness suffered by the next of kin are recoverable.[109]

Finally, and most important, a 1978 Indiana decision had reaffirmed an early policy decision by the Indiana Supreme Court and made it clear that Ford could not have been subjected to punitive damages for the wrongful deaths of the girls.[110] This is a crucial point, because it is through the imposition of punitive damages that reckless business behavior has been increasingly sanctioned and deterred.[111] In the light of such firmly entrenched limitations on civil remedies—especially the fact that Ford would not have had to pay the Ulrichs any punitive damages—Cosentino remarked that "the criminal prosecution truly serve[d] as the sole opportunity for the people of Indiana to express their outrage, to punish the defendant for the death[s] of these girls and to deter this defendant and others from like recklessness in the future."[112] Notably, this gap in Indiana's civil remedies was used by the prosecutors in their legal brief to develop a powerful justification—based on sound social policy principles—for taking Ford to trial.

Thus, the legal gap afforded virtual civil immunity to defendants who may have recklessly caused the death of persons who were young, unmarried, and without careers. This situation recalls the period in nineteenth-century America when tort actions were considered "personal"; any right to file suit died along with the victim. Because the damages caused by a wrongful death were difficult to measure and because courts were reluctant to impose a "pensioner role" upon businesses, especially railroads, during their growth years, it practically became "more profitable for the defendant to kill the plaintiff than to scratch him."[113]

Although the law has progressed far enough to eliminate this type of injustice in most instances, exceptions remain in which private civil actions are rendered virtually impotent, as in the Pinto case. If the severe restrictions discussed above were limited to the State of Indiana, perhaps because of quirks or loopholes in its statutory and case law, the mobilization of the Elkhart County prosecutor's forces might be viewed simply as an isolated attempt to fill an unusual void left by one state's legal legacy. Yet a review of the law at the state and federal levels indicated that at the time of Ford's prosecution there were no meaningful legal alternatives to the kind of response elicited from Indiana authorities by the perceived recklessness of Ford's behavior: the application of the state's general criminal laws to a corporate entity.

Viewed in this light, the corporate homicide prosecution led by Cosentino served to provide a striking example of one state's response to the conflict created by the law's desire to achieve its reductive goal and the inability of the existing civil process to carry it out.[114] Cosentino once said that a criminal prosecution would probably be appropriate in "no more than one percent" of all cases where corporations caused harm and only when other sanctions proved ineffective. It was clear, however, that he and his staff could not have been any more convinced of its appropriateness than they were in the Pinto case.

One final observation: In the context of this dichotomy between the civil and the criminal law, the reactions and motivations of the Ulrich girls' families were not overlooked. According to Berner, "The Ulrichs immediately and unreservedly supported Mike Cosentino's effort to bring the criminal prosecution. One could make all sorts of guesses as to what would lead them to do that; my own personal feeling is that they were extremely decent people with a very powerful sense of right and wrong and were persuaded Ford was wrong."[115] With this comment in mind, as the Indiana court continued to examine the legal arguments for and against holding the trial and as a final decision drew near, it is clear that the status of insurance, punitive damages, and other economic legislation in Indiana did not tell the whole story. Cosentino knew that he was not only responding to the systemic limitations of civil law in Indiana; he was also representing the moral conscience of the Ulrich families and their communities.

CONCLUSION: CLOSING THE DEBATE

Nearly five months had passed since the tragedy on U.S. Highway 33; nearly four months since the grand jury's indictment of Ford. In the meantime, amid the flurry of research and the proliferation of memoranda, 1978 had passed into history. With the new year came the retirement of Judge Charles E. Hughes, the nearly 70-year-old Elkhart Superior Court judge who had had the responsibility for handling the Pinto case from the beginning. After having convened the grand jury, issued the warrant, and allowed the parties a generous period in which to prepare their pretrial arguments, Hughes was due to retire on January 1, a date that had been set before his involvement in the case. Slated to succeed the highly respected Hughes was Donald W. Jones, a former Elkhart Court judge who had been elected to the Superior Court judgeship in November 1978. The youthful Jones, who had launched his legal career as a public defender, took over with a reputation as a thorough researcher and an excellent communicator. Because the adversaries' final memoranda in support of their positions had just been filed in the Superior Court, Jones would have no grace period in which to cut his new judicial teeth on less exceptional and lower-profile legal disputes. Instead he would be faced immediately with making a pretrial decision that would be reported across the country by the news correspondents who were now standing vigil at the Elkhart County courthouse.

Judge Jones heard two hours of oral arguments, during which Ford (represented primarily by Roger Barrett of Mayer, Brown, and Platt) and the prosecution (represented by Cosentino, Berner, and Kiely) summarized the legal positions stated in their briefs. The judge spent the remainder of January 1979 studying the many issues that had been raised by the motion to dismiss. Meanwhile, the adversaries waited eagerly for some sign that a decision had been reached. The members of the prosecution team felt highly vulnerable because they knew that Judge Jones could throw the case out of court at any time if he was persuaded by any one of Ford's numerous arguments.[116] Considering the thousands of hours that had been donated to the cause over the past four months, the lawyers, professors, and students found this possibility too painful even to consider.

On the other hand, the Ford staff was disconcerted by the idea that the multinational company might actually be forced to stand trial for three counts of reckless homicide. The possibility of a trial must have appeared significantly more real than it had several months earlier. Before the indictment, according to both Cosentino and Berner, Ford representatives privately seemed "amused" by the prosecution's corporate homicide theory, although they were by no means unconcerned that it had been brought to bear against their company.[117] Nonetheless, the legal staff that the company had amassed in preparing its full-scale attack on the indictment made it perfectly clear that the case was no longer "amusing" to Ford management, if indeed it ever had been.

On Friday afternoon, February 2, 1979, the main courtroom in the Elkhart County courthouse was alive with nervous, speculative conversation from the standing-room-only crowd of lawyers, reporters, students, business people, and other spectators. When Judge Jones made his entrance at 1:00 P.M., the conversational din was replaced by a tense, anticipatory silence. Almost six months had passed since the Ulrich girls' deaths, and the fate of Ford's motion to dismiss and Cosentino's prosecutorial response would be revealed at last by the newly elected Superior Court judge.

Jones did not prolong the tension. "There are substantial factors in this case for which there are no precedents in law," he began, giving no clue as to how he planned to rule. Shortly after, with an abruptness that surprised those in attendance, Jones looked up from his prepared text and tersely announced his decision: "The indictment is sufficient; I therefore deny the motion to dismiss."

The sense of relief could be both seen and heard throughout the courtroom as Cosentino and his staff congratulated one another, reporters raced toward the prosecution's table or the lobby telephones, and spectators renewed their animated conversations. Only the attorneys for Ford and the company representatives from Detroit failed to exhibit signs of any relief as they picked up copies of Jones's 20-page written opinion, packed their briefcases, and prepared to leave.

Just outside the courtroom doors, television reporters were prepared to obtain statements from the principals. Cosentino, glowing in the aftermath of the decision, was brief but enthusiastic: "The court has justified our position. As far as the law is concerned, a corporation can be indicted for homicide. . . . We're over our major hurdle."

Earl and Mattie Ulrich, whose privacy prosecution staff members had guarded closely at their request, agreed reluctantly to give the press a short statement. "There comes a day of reckoning," the father of Judy and Lyn told the hushed crowd quietly but dramatically, "and I think that day of reckoning is here."

Roger Barrett, showing obvious concern and frustration at his failure to thwart the prosecution's case before trial, would only state the obvious—"I'm disappointed, naturally"—before he hurried to lead the phalanx of lawyers from Ford and from Mayer, Brown, and Platt out of the building.[118]

In light of his written opinion, Judge Jones had little difficulty in disposing of Ford's contention that conceptually it was impossible for a corporation to commit reckless homicide under Indiana law. In rejecting this argument, Jones paid particular attention to three factors. First, he acknowledged that in Indiana the traditional doctrine of corporate criminal immunity had eroded gradually; this legal development, the prosecution had argued, was consistent with the historical trend nationwide. Second, the judge relied on the New York court's reasoning in *People v. Ebasco Services,*[119] the country's most recent precedent on corporate homicide. After reviewing the similarities between New York's and Indiana's reckless homicide statutes, Jones drew support from the *Ebasco* court's opinion for his own conclusion that a business corporation could be considered capable of committing homicide: "In construing whether the corporation could be charged with criminal liability the [New York] Court, by way of dicta, stated that while a corporation could not be a victim of a homicide, there was no manifest impropriety in applying the broader definition of person to a corporation with regard to the commission of a homicide."[120] Third, and most important, Jones was persuaded by the clear expression of legislative intent in the Indiana Criminal Code section that stated, "A corporation, partnership or unincorporated association may be prosecuted for *any* offense" (emphasis added).[121] Although he reminded the parties that a corporate conviction could be obtained "only if it is proved that the offense was committed by its agents acting within the scope of [their] authority," Jones concluded that the Indiana legislature had never intended to grant corporations blanket immunity from criminal prosecution, even for reckless homicide.[122] As a result, the conceptual foundation of the prosecution—that a corporation could be punished for the violent crime of reckless homicide—had received new life after a long burial in a handful of all-but-forgotten cases.

By contrast, the constitutional challenges raised by Ford were not as easily dismissed by Jones. No fewer than 16 of the 20 pages in his opinion were dedicated to the constitutional matters so thoroughly researched and argued by the adversaries. In the following discussion of Judge Jones's resolution of Ford's preemption and *ex post facto* challenges, it is clear that although Cosentino had been given the right to proceed to trial, his victory was not absolute. Although Jones concluded unequivocally that the prosecution was standing on firm theoretical ground, his opinion also showed that a handful of obstacles remained, which Ford could use to restrict Cosentino's options at trial.

In ruling that the application of Indiana's reckless homicide law was not preempted by federal auto safety laws, Jones relied on guidelines established in *Perez v. Campbell,*[123] a 1971 U.S. Supreme Court decision. In that case, the Court indicated that questions concerning potentially overlapping state and federal laws were to be resolved through the use of a two-tier inquiry: Did a review of the construction and operation of the two statutes indicate that they served substantially common purposes? If so, did there appear in the federal law a "clear and manifest" intent by Congress to supersede the state's police powers?[124] Only if the answer to both inquiries was "yes" could a state law be considered to have been preempted by federal law and thus declared unconstitutional.

In reviewing the purposes of the two laws alleged by Ford to be conflicting, Jones followed the guidelines laid out in *Perez*. After noting that the law places the burden of proving any constitutional conflicts on the party that makes the challenge (Ford), Jones described the essential purpose of the National Highway Traffic and Motor Vehicle Safety Act by citing a concise statement from *Chrysler Corporation v. Tofany*,[125] an influential 1969 precedent that had considered another preemption challenge involving the Safety Act: "The express purpose of the [Safety Act] . . . is the reduction of traffic accidents."[126] Jones then agreed with the prosecution that the case was preceding under the general criminal code of Indiana and *not* under any automobile regulatory scheme. In contrast to the purpose of the Safety Act, which was to reduce the number and seriousness of traffic accidents by regulating auto safety standards (as well as other traffic-related factors), Indiana's reckless homicide laws were designed to serve the traditional goals of virtually any homicide statute: deterrence and retribution. The fact that the alleged criminal behavior in this case happened to involve auto safety, Jones concluded, did not prevent the State of Indiana from enforcing its criminal laws in order to achieve these ends.

The negative answer to the first inquiry in *Perez*'s two-tier test made the second inquiry moot. Jones's opinion, however, went on to note that historically the courts have given a strong presumption of constitutional validity to the exercise of a state's police power (the authority that is granted to each state under our system of federalism to protect the general health, safety, and welfare of its citizens). Without proof of a "clear and manifest" supercession of this authority by Congress—something that appeared to be absent from the Safety Act—Jones concluded that in this case the application of the reckless homicide statute represented a valid exercise of Indiana's police powers and thus had not been preempted by federal law.

Even so, certain aspects of the federal regulatory issues raised by Ford remained unresolved. For the prosecution, perhaps the most crucial issue concerned the possible impact of federal auto safety standards on the trial itself. If Ford could introduce evidence, for example, that its Pinto complied with or even surpassed any federal rear-end crash standards, what effect would this evidence have? Would such evidence establish that Ford, by meeting government-established standards, could not possibly have been guilty of recklessness? Might Ford divert the jury's attention from the moral issues at hand by making what already promised to be a lengthy, complex trial even more so through the introduction of a maze of federal regulatory laws? As Ford's attorneys considered their strategy for the upcoming trial, Cosentino and his staff had a strong feeling that this was not their last encounter with obstacles related to the federal regulation of automobiles.

In another section of his opinion, Jones cited his reasons for ruling in addition that Indiana's newly revised reckless homicide statute was not being applied retroactively and thus did not violate *ex post facto* principles. Jones was apparently persuaded by the "continuation theory" advanced by the prosecution: although Ford's design and marketing of the 1973 Pinto preceded Indiana's adoption of its revised criminal code in 1977 and 1978, both the company's continuing refusal to recall and repair its Pintos and the Ulrich girls' deaths postdated the adoption. Several precedents were cited to lend support to this interpretation, but Jones appeared to be influenced especially by *U.S. v. Reed*,[127] a federal prosecution in which the defendant was convicted of violating a statute that prohibited possession of instruments used for wiretapping. Jones explained its relevance to the Pinto prosecution as follows:

> The defendant in [*U.S. v. Reed*] purchased the equipment before the statute was effective. In affirming the conviction, the court noted that there were many cases which had dealt with and rejected an *ex post facto* argument of some element of a crime where the element "but not the prohibited act" had come into being or taken place prior to the passage of the criminal statute.

> An examination of the [Pinto] indictment shows an allegation of the continuation of acts and essentially alleges that the reckless design and manufacture was simply an antecedent fact to the defendant's alleged reckless act of failure to repair after the new code took effect. . . . Since the alleged reckless act of failing to repair occurred after the passage of the present penal code, no *ex post facto* consideration is applicable and the statements referring to the design and manufacture were just to show the factual basis for the duty to repair.

> Since it appears that at least part of the indictment is based entirely upon alleged reckless conduct occurring entirely after the passage of the reckless homicide statute [the failure to repair], the dismissal of the indictment on ex post facto grounds is not justified.[128]

This interpretation would have profound consequences for the forthcoming trial. Although he had ruled that the indictment was not constitutionally defective, Jones's approach meant that the prosecution's allegation of recklessness in the design, manufacture, and marketing of the 1973 Pinto could not remain the central issue of the case against Ford. Instead, because each of these business functions preceded the implementation of the new criminal code by several years, proof of Ford's recklessness at any of these stages could be offered *solely* for the purpose of demonstrating that the company had created for itself the duty to recall and repair any defective Pintos. In other words, proving beyond a reasonable doubt that Ford recklessly disregarded human safety in its design, manufacture, and/or marketing of the 1973 Pinto would *not* be enough to sustain a conviction: the prosecution would be forced to go one step further and also prove that the company's primary recklessness lay in its *failure to recall and repair* the Ulrich family's Pinto before August 10, 1978, the day of the accident.

For the forthcoming trial, then, the critical issue of recklessness had split into two parts: (1) Did Ford even have a legal duty to warn Pinto owners and repair any defects in the fuel tank system? (2) If so, was Ford's failure to warn the Ulrich family before the accident in reckless disregard of this duty? Cosentino now understood that the success of the prosecution's case would depend upon his ability to convince a jury beyond any reasonable doubt that the answer to both questions was "yes."

Yet another issue, potentially even more serious, troubled the prosecution. The amended provision of the reckless homicide statute, which permits prosecution of any person who caused a death by failing to perform a required duty (in addition to affirmatively acting in opposition to one), had gone into effect on July 1, 1978—*only 41 days before the Ulrich accident.* Jones's opinion made it clear that this 41-day period, or "window," would have a significant effect on the requirements of proof at the trial. In essence, the *ex post facto* considerations required the prosecution to show that during the 41 days between the implementation of the law and the Ulrichs' deaths on August 10, Ford had been reckless in its failure to recall and repair the Ulrich family's Pinto. As a result, Cosentino would need to determine exactly what Ford management's policies and operations were during this period and to prove that they constituted reckless disregard for the safety of Pinto owners. The practical problems related to the task of investigating and presenting these internal corporate matters loomed large.

Thus, Cosentino was troubled by the fact that in two recent appellate court decisions, Ford had been severely chastised for "misrepresenting" and "withholding" important information regarding internal safety records and reports.[129] His concern was not that Ford would be uncooperative—what criminal defendant ever willingly assists the prosecution?—but that even if other information relevant to the Pinto existed, it would never see the light of day. Facing problems such as this, Cosentino realized—as he had months before, after the grand jury's return of Ford's indictment—that he and his staff would have little time to savor their victory in advancing their case past the pretrial obstacles presented by Ford.

Although certain aspects of Judge Jones's decision posed practical problems for the prosecution at trial, it represented a major triumph for Cosentino's volunteer staff over the forces of Ford and its cadre of lawyers. There can be no doubt that it also served to legitimate the prosecution's corporate homicide theory in the eyes of the American public (not to mention the legal and business communities) in at least two ways. First, it demonstrated that it was indeed possible for a county prosecutor to proceed against a powerful and resourceful corporate defendant within the criminal justice system of at least one state. Second, it showed that a fundamental redefinition of corporate misbehavior—from a "bad business decision" to a "violent criminal act"—could be justified under the right circumstances. Although this was only one case, it had clear implications for American business. As Ralph Nader observed after the indictment was upheld, Ford's board of directors was not the only one that followed the case closely. Corporate boardrooms across the country, he asserted, were watching and thinking, "We could be next."[130]

Each side began its preparations for the upcoming trial with certain concerns. Realistically, Cosentino knew that the obstacles would continue. He wondered whether his small budget and staff would be able to hold out as the case shifted from a battle of legal memos, in which each side had more or less equal access to law libraries, to a battle in the courtroom, where, in Berner's words, the rules "twice curse the prosecution when the economic advantage is with the defendant."[131] Ford, on the other hand, finally had to face the fact that the final confrontation would take place where the company least wanted to do battle: inside an Indiana county courthouse, before a local jury and the national media.

NOTES

1   Excerpt from a keynote speech given by Cosentino in Honolulu at the 1980 American Bar Association's annual convention (co-authored with Berner).

2   Lee Patrick Strobel, *Reckless Homicide? Ford's Pinto Trial*. South Bend, IN: And Books, 1980, p. 39.

3   Andy Pasztor, "Ford Tries Low Prices to Revive the Pinto as Consumer Fears Still Nag the Small Car," *The Wall Street Journal* (September 12, 1978), p. 48; cited in Strobel, *Reckless Homicide?* p. 40.

4   Strobel, *Reckless Homicide?* p. 41.

5   Ford was quoted by Walter Guzzardi, Jr. in "Ford: The Road Ahead," *Fortune* (September 11, 1978), p. 42.

6   Strobel, *Reckless Homicide?* p. 41. Some commentators have criticized this account as too harsh. See, for example, Brent Fisse and John Braithwaite, *The Impact of Publicity on Corporate Offenders*. Albany: SUNY Press, 1983, pp. 50–51.

7   Fisse and Braithwaite, *The Impact of Publicity on Corporate Offenders*, p. 51.

8   *Ibid.*, p. 51.

9   *Ibid.*, p. 51.

10   In addition to gaining control of the first and often best information available in a case, a prosecutor generally possesses broad discretion and control over the indicting process, and many of the basic procedural protections available to the defendant at trial are not available at the grand jury hearing. Although the historical performance of the grand jury as a safeguard against unjust prosecution has been widely recognized, contemporary opponents have argued that "the grand jury usually degenerates into a rubber stamp wielded by the prosecuting officer according to the dictates of his own sense of property and justice." See Livingston Hall, Yale Kamisar, Wayne R. LaFave, and Jerold H. Israel, *Modern Criminal Procedure*. St. Paul, MN: West, 1969, pp. 791–794.

11   Virtually any study of criminology will include discussion of the relationship between crime and poverty and the reasons why indigents appear as defendants in such a high percentage of criminal prosecutions. See, for example, Sue Titus Reid, *Crime and Criminology*, 3rd ed. New York: Holt, Rinehart and Winston, 1982.

12   It can be said that the prosecutorial advantage of a "head start" existed in the early stages of the Pinto case as well; Cosentino, Shewmaker, and Graves commenced investigations within hours of the accident. Indeed, Ford attorneys later complained on several occasions that they felt disadvantaged because they had to interview certain individuals in the Elkhart community after those individuals had been in contact with someone from the prosecution.

13   Strobel, *Reckless Homicide?* p. 45.

14   Cosentino did not gain the cooperation of federal agencies easily, however. After "running into a brick wall" in trying to obtain certified copies of crucial documents, for example, Cosentino said he was forced to contact a state senator, who in turn contacted Ralph Nader's office in Washington, DC, before federal government employees would respond to his requests. Cosentino stated, however, that once the door was opened, agency cooperation was "excellent."

[15] The absence of pay for the long hours of work quickly became the focus of some good-natured gallows humor among the prosecutorial staff. Mock-strikes, for example, were sometimes staged by the student volunteers, who demanded that Cosentino provide "better pay, better hours."

[16] Taken from a letter written by Berner to W. J. Maakestad, dated July 16, 1981 (hereinafter cited as Berner's letter to author).

[17] Author William Maakestad became involved at this point in the case. Virtually the only other exception to the "local talent" commitment was an early consultation with Leonard Orland, a law professor at the University of Connecticut who had done some research in the field of corporate criminality.

[18] See our discussion in Chapter 4 pertaining to the background and character of Elkhart County State Prosecutor Cosentino.

[19] Defendant's Memorandum in Support of Motion to Dismiss (filed October 23, 1978), pp. 1–2, in *State v. Ford Motor Co.*, No. 5324 (Ind. Super. Ct.) (hereinafter cited as Ford's Memorandum).

[20] For a general introduction to the field of products liability see, for example, William Kimble and Robert Lesher, *Products Liability*. St. Paul: West, 1979.

[21] 10 M. & W. 109, 152 Eng.Rep. 402, 11 L.J.Ex. 415 (1842).

[22] 217 N.Y. 382, 11 N.E. 1050, 1916 L.R.A. 696, 1916C Ann.Cas. 440 (1916), affirming 160 App.Div. 35, 145 N.Y.S. 462 (1914).

[23] See generally Justice Cardozo's discussion of these precedents in the *MacPherson* case (see note 22).

[24] Cornelius W. Gillam, *Products Liability in the Automobile Industry: A Study in Strict Liability and Social Control*. Minneapolis: University of Minnesota Press, 1960, p. 47. See also C.A. Peairs, Jr., "The God in the Machine: A Study in Precedent," *Boston University Law Review* 29 (January 1949), pp. 37–78.

[25] Although in a few jurisdictions theories were developed judicially, which eased the plaintiffs burden under certain circumstances, the fact remained that in most cases negligence theory required specific proof of fault before liability could attach—even if it could be proved easily that the product was both defective and unsafe.

[26] Gillam, *Products Liability in the Automobile Industry*, pp. 6–9.

[27] This approach became known generally as the implied warranty theory, which was imposed judicially under limited circumstances before it was written into the Uniform Commercial Code in 1962.

[28] 32 N.J. 358, 161 A.2d 69 (1960).

[29] According to William Prosser, three main points make up the rationale for the development and acceptance of the strict liability theory as a supplement (and in many cases a replacement) for the negligence and warranty theories: "First, the public interest in human life and safety demands the maximum possible protection that the law can give against which they are helpless to protect themselves; and it justifies the imposition, upon all suppliers of such products, of full responsibility for the harm they cause, even though the supplier has done his best. Second, the maker, by placing the goods upon the market, represents to the public that they are safe and suitable for use; and by packaging, advertising or otherwise,

he does everything that he can do to induce that belief. Third, it is already possible to enforce strict liability by resort to a series of actions, in which the retailer is first held liable on a warranty to his purchaser, and indemnity on a warranty is then sought successively from other suppliers, until the manufacturer finally pays the damages, with the added costs of repeated litigation. This is an expensive, time-consuming, and wasteful process, and it may be interrupted by insolvency, lack of jurisdiction, disclaimers, or the statute of limitations, anywhere along the line." See William Prosser, *Handbook of the Law of Torts,* 4th ed. St. Paul, MN: West, 1971, p. 6.

30 59 Cal.2d 57, 377 P.2d 897 (1963).

31 Section 402A, Restatement, Torts 2d.

32 391 F.2d 495 (8th Cir. 1968).

33 *Huff v. White Motor Co.,* 565 F.2d 104 (7th Cir. 1977), cited in State's Memorandum, p. 15.

34 See generally David G. Owen, "Punitive Damages in Products Liability Litigation," *Michigan Law Review* 74 (June 1976), pp. 1258–1371.

35 This statement obviously represents the viewpoint of prosecuting attorneys, and does not take into account the possibility that a plea-bargaining agreement may have been considered, at least initially, in the best interest of the State for administrative or other reasons. From the viewpoint of defense attorneys, an acquittal (or, under certain circumstances, a conviction of a lesser included offense) would be the corresponding measure of success.

36 This observation, of course, does not mean that prosecutors are ever personally satisfied with less than a guilty verdict. Regardless of their pretrial successes, prosecutors, like athletic teams, are evaluated almost solely on the basis of "wins" and "losses."

37 Defendant's Memorandum, pp. 1–2.

38 Berner's letter to author. Law students from Valparaiso and DePaul who assisted Berner and Kiely included, among others, Don Seberger, Eugene Schoon, Cathy Schmidt, Donn Wray, Mary Lawton, Deidra Burgman, Dan Lane, and Mike Meyer.

39 See, for example, Wayne R. LaFave and Austin W. Scott, *Criminal Law.* St. Paul, MN: West, 1971, pp. 229–230.

40 Thomas J. Bernard, "The Historical Development of Corporate Criminal Liability," *Criminology* 22 (February 1984), p. 6.

41 212 U.S. 481 (1909).

42 *Ibid.,* pp. 494–495.

43 See generally Nancy Frank, "From Criminal to Civil Penalties in the History of Health and Safety Laws," *Social Problems* 30 (June 1983), pp. 532–544.

44 Lave and Scott, Criminal Law, pp. 229–230.

45 Glenn A. Clark, "Corporate Homicide: A New Assault on Corporate Decision Making," *Notre Dame Lawyer* 54 (June 1979), pp. 911–951.

[46]   For further discussion, see our analysis of this issue in Chapter 2.

[47]   32 N.H. 215 (1855).

[48]   For an excellent discussion of this issue, see Lawrence M. Friedman, *A History of American Law*. New York: Touchstone, 1973, pp. 409–427.

[49]   134 F. 592 (2d Cir. 1904).

[50]   *Ibid.*, p. 374.

[51]   90 N.J.L. 372, 103 A. 685 (1917).

[52]   *Ibid.*, p. 374.

[53]   195 N.Y. 102, 88 N.E. 22 (1909).

[54]   *Ibid.*, p. 107, 88 N.E. at p. 24.

[55]   226 Ore. 502, 360 P.2d 530 (1961).

[56]   77 Misc.2d 784, 354 N.Y.S.2d 807 (1974).

[57]   *Ibid.*, p. 786, 354 N.Y.S.2d at p. 810.

[58]   *Ibid.* (emphasis by the court).

[59]   *Ibid.*, p. 787, 354 N.Y.S.2d at p. 811.

[60]   The *Ebasco* indictment was dismissed on due process grounds, the court stating that the indictment's language "was not sufficiently precise so as to apprize each defendant individually as to the conduct which was the subject of the accusation against him or it individually."

[61]   Clark, "Corporate Homicide," p. 917. The failure of corporations to avoid prosecution for homicide on conceptual grounds since the Ford Pinto case (see our discussion of recent cases in Chapter 7) appears to indicate that the "further development" to which Clark refers has been favorable to prosecutors.

[62]   State's Memorandum in Opposition to Motion to Dismiss (filed December 1, 1978), p. 2, in State v. Ford Motor Co., No. 5324 (Ind. Super. Ct.) (hereinafter cited as State's Memorandum).

[63]   Indiana Code Sec. 35-42-1-5.

[64]   Ford's Memorandum, pp. 24–25.

[65]   *Ibid.*, pp. 25–26.

[66]   Indiana Code Sec. 35-41-1-2, cited in State's Memorandum, p. 8.

[67]   Indiana Code Sec. 35-41-213(a), cited in State's Memorandum, p. 8.

[68]   *State v. Lehigh Valley Railroad*, 90 N.J.L. 372, 103 A. 685 (1917); cited in State's Memorandum, p. 12.

[69]   State's Memorandum, p. 10.

[70]   546 F.2d 492, 494 (2d Cir. 1976).

[71]   Berner's letter to author.

[72]   See Strobel, *Reckless Homicide?* pp. 41–42.

73   The other two constitutional arguments presented by Ford in its memorandum were as follows: (1) The reckless homicide statute, applied in such a way as to attempt to regulate automobile safety, violated the commerce clause of the U.S. Constitution; and (2) The same statute, through its vague and untimely application under the facts of this case, violated defendant's due process rights, which are afforded by the Indiana and U.S. Constitutions.

      Note also that much of the substance of the constitutional arguments was developed by the Los Angeles law firm that Ford had also retained, Hughes Hubbard and Reed, and not by Mayer, Brown, and Platt of Chicago. See Strobel, *Reckless Homicide?* p. 42.

74   Note that our discussion of these issues is not intended as a treatise on the complicated interplay between constitutional law and corporate prosecutions, but merely as an analysis of the particular constitutional objections raised by Ford in the context of the Pinto case. For an excellent discussion of several constitutional issues that may arise when a corporation is a criminal defendant, see Howard Friedman, "Some Reflections on the Corporation as Criminal Defendant," *Notre Dame Lawyer* 55 (December 1979), pp. 173–202.

75   Ford's Memorandum, p. 48.

76   22 U.S. 1 (1824).

77   430 U.S. 519 (1977).

78   Ford's Memorandum, p. 43.

79   *Ibid.*, p. 45.

80   *Ibid.*, p. 48.

81   *Ibid.*, pp. 48–49. Ford used essentially the same reasoning to support another one of its constitutional arguments: that the prosecution represented an undue burden on interstate commerce and thus violated the commerce clause of the U.S. Constitution. See note 73.

82   434 U.S. 429 (1978).

83   *Ibid.*, pp. 443–444 (citations omitted).

84   State's Memorandum, p. 57.

85   *Ibid.*, p. 58.

86   514 S.W.2d 497 (Tex. Civ. App. 1974).

87   *Ibid.*, p. 506.

88   State's Supplemental Memorandum in Opposition to Motion to Dismiss (filed December 20, 1978), pp. 1–2, in State v. Ford Motor Co., No. 5324 (Ind. Super. Ct.).

89   Indiana Constitution Art. I, Sec. 24; U.S. Constitution Art. I, Sec. 10.

90   *Garner v. Los Angeles Board,* 341 U.S. 716, 721 (1951); cited in Ford's Memorandum, p. 32.

91   *In re Petition to Transfer Appeals,* 202 Ind. 365, 174 N.E. 812 (1931).

92   State's Memorandum, p. 46.

93 *Alderson v. State*, 196 Ind. 22, 25, 145 N.E. 572, 573 (1924); cited in State's Memorandum, p. 47.

94 *Carrier v. State*, 233 Ind. 456, 134 N.E.2d 688 (1956), quoting *Brockway v. State*, 192 Ind. 656, 138 N.E. 88 (1923); cited in State's Memorandum, p. 47.

95 State's Memorandum, p. 48.

96 State's Memorandum, p. 50. Fourteen cases were cited in support of this proposition.

97 Christopher D. Stone, *Where the Law Ends. The Social Control of Corporations.* New York: Harper and Row, 1975, p. 30.

98 By the time of Ford's prosecution, more than half the states had come to provide for victim compensation under statutorily determined circumstances. See, for example, William E. Hoelzel, "A Survey of 27 Victim Compensation Programs," *Judicature* 63 (May 1980), pp. 485–496.

99 The threat of statutorily prescribed civil penalties may also deter corporate misbehavior, but only in narrowly defined situations. Punitive damage awards are generally more widely available and have been used more frequently in civil cases involving reckless business decisionmaking. See note 100 and accompanying text.

100 See generally Vincent M. Igoe, "Punitive Damages: An Analytical Perspective," *Trial* (November 1978), pp. 48–53; Owen, "Punitive Damages in Products Liability Litigation," pp. 1258–1371; Comment, "Criminal Safeguards and the Punitive Damages Defendant," *University of Chicago Law Review* 34 (Winter 1967), pp. 408–435.

101 *Grimshaw v. Ford Motor Co.*, No. 197761 (Orange Cty. Super. Ct., filed Nov. 22, 1972). According to studies by NHTSA, at least 30 civil cases in addition to *Grimshaw* had been filed against Ford by May 1978 in connection with the Pinto's fuel tank design. There are no reliable estimates of the total number of Pinto suits that have been filed to date.

102 By the time of the Indiana prosecution, a wide range of articles were available that discussed the legal problems attendant upon the application of criminal sanctions, including fines, against corporations. Examples include Comment, "Criminal Sanctions for Corporate Illegality," *Journal of Criminal Law and Criminology* 69 (Spring 1978), pp. 40–58, and Note, "Corporate Crime: Regulating Corporate Behavior Through Criminal Sanctions," *Harvard Law Review* 92 (April 1979), pp. 1227–1394.

103 See, for example, Harry V. Ball and Lawrence M. Friedman, "The Use of Criminal Sanctions in the Enforcement of Economic Legislation: A Sociological View," *Stanford Law Review* 17 (January 1965), pp. 197–223, and Lawrence M. Friedman, "Two Faces of Law," *Wisconsin Law Review* 13 (No. 1 1984), pp. 13–35.

104 Victoria Swigert and Ronald Farrell, "Corporate Homicide: Definitional Processes in the Creation of Deviance," *Law & Society Review* 15 (No. 1, 1980-1981), pp. 161–182. See also Ball and Friedman, "The Use of Criminal Sanctions in the Enforcement of Economic Legislation: A Sociological View," p. 214.
    Ball and Friedman, proponents of the economic school of thought, make this interesting observation concerning the inefficiency of regulation through the criminal process: "The shift to administrative enforcement takes place partly because criminal sanctions drag with them all the traditional safeguards sur-

rounding the defendant. Proof beyond a reasonable doubt, trial by jury, and other forms of protection are required. The socialization of remedies thus has the dysfunctional result of making large-scale enforcement difficult for reasons irrelevant to the purpose of making the proscribed acts illegal."

[105]   Even if the legal restrictions concerning civil remedies were not present, the possibility exists that parents of children who suffered a premature, wrongful death would decline to pursue a monetary settlement on religious or moral grounds. In addition, certain families might suffer considerable psychological effects by accepting money from the individual or company responsible for the death of their child.

[106]   No. 197761 (Orange Cty. Super. Ct., filed Nov. 22, 1972). See note 101.

[107]   Ind. Code Ann. Sec. 34-1-1-8 (Burns 1973 & Supp.1982).

[108]   *Pennsylvania Co. v. Lilly,* 73 Ind. 252, 254 (1881). Although the Indiana civil code provides both a general wrongful death statute, Ind. Code. Ann. Sec. 34-1-1-2 (Burns 1973 and Supp. 1982), and a wrongful death statute for children (see note 107), the same result would have been produced under either alternative. Furthermore, the two statutory schemes are mutually exclusive and thus could not have been pursued simultaneously, according to *Vera Cruz v. Chesapeake & Ohio Ry. Co.,* 192 F. Supp. 958 (N.D. Ind. 1961).

[109]   See *Ohio & Miss. R.R. v. Tindall,*13 Ind. 366 (1859); *Estate of Pickens v. Pickens,* 264 N.E.2d 151 (Ind. 1970); *Hahn v. Moore,* 133 N.E.2d 900 (Ind. Ct. App. 1956). This line of cases reflects an early common-law tradition that, legally speaking, viewed the primary value of children as the amount of labor they contributed to the household.

[110]   The early Indiana Supreme Court decision was *Taber v. Hutson, Ind.* 322 (1854), with *Glissman v. Rutt* 372 N.E.2d 1188 (Ind. Ct. App. 1978) in accord.

[111]   See note 100.

[112]   Statement made in Elkhart by Michael Cosentino, explaining the State Indiana's position against *Ford's Motion to Dismiss* (December 23, 1978).

[113]   William Prosser, *Handbook of the Law of Torts.* 3rd edition. St. Paul, MN: West, 1964, p. 924. For a fascinating historical discussion of this issue, see Friedman, *A History of American Law,* pp. 409–427.

[114]   The prosecution also argued that in this case the general criminal law was a more appropriate vehicle by which to accomplish the same goals as punitive damages because of the possibility of financial overkill: where punitive damages are assessed in multiple cases against a corporation, the total societal loss that could occur following the financial devastation of that company must be considered. Ironically, by taking the position that it is necessary to balance the social costs and the benefits of repeated applications of punitive damages against corporations, the prosecution borrowed a line of reasoning normally employed by corporations seeking to avoid the burden of such damages. See State's Memorandum, pp. 25–27. For an extended discussion of this issue, see the opinion of Circuit Court Judge Friendly in *Roginsky v. Richardson-Merrell, Inc.,* 378 F.2d 832 (2d Cir. 1967).

[115]   Berner's letter to author.

[116]   Had Judge Jones decided, however, that the indictment was constitutionally or conceptually invalid, Cosentino could have appealed his decision.

117 From conversations with Cosentino and Berner, June 1983.

118 This account of Judge Jones's decision and its immediate aftermath was drawn partially from Strobel, *Reckless Homicide?* pp. 55–56.

119 See note 56.

120 *State v. Ford Motor Co.*, No. 5324, slip. op. at p. 8 (Ind. Super. Ct., Feb. 2, 1979).

121 Ind. Code Sec. 35-41-213(a); cited in State's Memorandum, p. 8.

122 See note 123, p. 9.

123 402 U.S. 637 (1971).

124 See note 123, p. 11.

125 419 F.2d 499 (2d Cir. 1969).

126 *Ibid.*, p. 511.

127 489 F.2d 917 (6th Cir. 1974).

128 See note 123, p. 14.

129 The two cases, both civil, were *Rozier v. Ford Motor Co.*, 573 F.2d 1332 (5th Cir. 1978), and *Buehler v. Whalen*, 374 N.E.2d 460 (1977).

   Both cases are unusual in terms of the strong language used by appellate court justices to condemn Ford and its attorneys for unethical practices. "Through its misconduct in this case," the federal court hearing Rozier concluded, "Ford completely sabotaged the federal trial court machinery, precluding the 'fair contest' which the Federal Rules of Civil Procedure are intended to assure. Instead of serving as a vehicle for ascertainment of the truth, the trial in this case accomplished little more than the adjudication of a hypothetical fact situation imposed by Ford's selective disclosure of information."

   In its Buehler decision, the Supreme Court of Illinois stated: "We cannot condemn too severely the conduct of the Ford Motor Corporation in the discovery procedures here. It gave false answers to interrogatories under oath. It secreted evidence damaging to its case. Under the circumstances, the trial court would have been justified in striking the answer of this defendant and submitting to the jury only the issue of damages."

130 Statement by Ralph Nader during appearance at Western Illinois University after the Ford indictment, Spring 1979.

131 Berner's letter to author; see especially text accompanying note 71.

6

Trying Ford

Bringing Ford to trial had not been an easy task. Since the days immediately after the deaths of the Ulrich girls, Cosentino had been confronted with a series of obstacles that had to be overcome before Ford's culpability could be weighed in a courtroom.

The initial barriers were largely personal and perceptual. Was Ford Motor Company really to blame for the tragic consequences of the accident? Should Cosentino bring criminal charges against a corporation? Would his community, as represented by a grand jury, support a prosecution? Once these uncertainties were resolved and his course of action determined, Cosentino faced the more concrete problem of assembling a prosecutorial team with the expertise to handle the complex legal issues raised by Ford's attorneys in their attempt to quash the indictment for reckless homicide against the corporation.

In their showdown with Ford, Cosentino and his colleagues had sacrificed much of themselves. The case consumed many hours of work, and they also felt the constant anxiety of knowing that all their efforts would be wasted if Judge Jones barred them from continuing with the prosecution. Yet now that they had secured the court's permission to take Ford to trial, the time seemed well spent and the corporation seemed less formidable than it had originally. In the battle of legal briefs, Cosentino's group had more than held its own. They were optimistic that the corporate Goliath could be beaten.[1]

Even so, Cosentino retained a healthy sense of caution. From the inception of the case, he had wondered when Ford was going to use its considerable resources and bring out its "big guns." Now that the reputation of Ford Motor Company was hanging precariously in the balance, Cosentino was not left to wonder very long. Realizing that there was no room left for mistakes, Ford executives moved quickly to acquire the services of the best legal talent available. Their search led to James Foster Neal, one of the nation's foremost criminal defense attorneys. Although short in stature at 5'7", the 49-year-old Neal was long in experience. He had burst into the national spotlight in the early 1960s, when he was appointed as an assistant to Attorney General Robert Kennedy. Although still in his early thirties at the time, he was given the task of prosecuting former Teamsters boss Jimmy Hoffa. His initial attempt to convict Hoffa on charges of accepting $1 million in illegal payments ended in a hung jury. His second crack at Hoffa, however, succeeded in winning a guilty verdict on the charge of jury tampering. After several attempts by other government attorneys, Neal was the first lawyer to secure Hoffa's conviction.

A decade later, the Watergate scandal provided Neal with another opportunity to participate in a trial of historical importance. As the government's chief trial lawyer, he prosecuted the main Watergate case, which resulted in the convictions of John Ehrlichman, H.R. Haldeman, and John Mitchell. His performance led Watergate judge John Sirica to conclude, "He's the best lawyer I ever heard in a courtroom." Leon Jaworski praised Neal by adding, "I am as much impressed with him as any trial lawyer I have ever seen. And I have seen many in fifty years of practicing law."

In the period between the Hoffa and Watergate cases, Neal returned to his home state of Tennessee, where he served as U.S. Attorney. In 1971, he joined with Aubrey B. Harwell, Jr., to establish a profitable private practice in Nashville, with a branch office in Washington. The firm's clients included such celebrities as Dolly Parton, Johnny Cash, and Roy Orbison. Neal and Harwell also gained valuable experience by representing corporations such as Volkswagen, GM, Subaru, and Union Carbide against product liability suits.

Much of Neal's effectiveness in the courtroom stemmed from his ability to mix a strong thirst for success with a genuine, folksy personal style. Since his boyhood days as the son of a tobacco and strawberry farmer, Neal's intense competitiveness had earned him a string of honors: a football scholarship to the University of Wyoming, the rank of captain in the Marine Corps during the Korean war, and the status of top student in his graduating class at Vanderbilt University School of Law. As a lawyer, he lost none of this desire to win. When he took a case, he would work endless hours preparing for trial; he would miss no detail and leave nothing to chance. As one Nashville prosecutor observed, "If there is a weakness in a case, he flat tears into it."

Yet Neal's country roots softened the hard-driving edge of his personality. Though he had rubbed shoulders with Washington's elite, he could still talk plainly with common folks. Neal's middle-Tennessee drawl has been characterized as "somewhere between Kentucky twang and Southern aristocrat." During a trial, as another Nashville attorney noted, "he cultivates that country-boy image a little, but very effectively. He'll have every juror thinking he's his long-lost friend before he's through." As Judge Sirica concluded after the Watergate affair, Neal was "able to convince jurors that he is not trying to hoodwink them . . . [he is] a master of the art of jury psychology."

Why should Neal want to use his considerable talents to defend a giant company that was accused of such insensitivity that it allowed three teenagers to perish in a burning Pinto? A monetary factor was present, of course. Neal commanded high fees, and Ford was clearly ready to meet his asking price. In this instance, no one, including company officials, disputed the strong rumor that Neal's firm received $1 million for taking on Ford's case and that the company spent another million on additional expenses related to the Pinto case.

Money, however, was not the whole story; indeed, it was probably not even the major part of the story. The financially secure Neal did not have to take on all paying customers. As he commented, "I pick and choose my cases pretty carefully these days." If not for reasons of profit, then, why did he pick the makers of the Pinto? It appears that two considerations influenced his decision.

First, the case involved fascinating and important legal issues. National attention would surely surround the criminal prosecution of a major corporation for reckless homicide, and the trial potentially would occupy a prominent place in American legal history. Such an opportunity was too good to pass up; it was Jim Neal's kind of case. As Neal commented two years after the case had been decided, he saw Ford's prosecution as "one of the ten or fifteen most important trials in this century" and "one of the one or two most important trials" in his career.

The second consideration was ideological. To be sure, Neal was no staunch conservative. He had worked under Robert Kennedy, prosecuted top Republican officials in Watergate, and would later head Walter Mondale's presidential campaign in the State of Tennessee. Jimmy Carter had considered him as a possible successor to Clarence M. Kelly as director of the FBI, and he was often mentioned as a possible Democratic gubernatorial candidate in his home state. Yet Neal had also come to believe that corporations, which were responsible for much of the good in society, had become an easy and fashionable legal target. "American industry," he noted, "is unable to keep up with all the federal regulations and restrictions. It's so easy to attack big companies." In Neal's view, the prevailing social context had put corporations like Ford on the defensive and turned them into underdogs. As for the Pinto, he did not believe that Ford officials had consciously built a dangerous car, and he opposed the idea that Ford could satisfy all federal regulations and still be prosecuted under Indiana state law. Viewed together, these factors made Neal comfortable in taking on an "unpopular cause. . . I believe in what I am doing. I believe what I'm doing is right. I don't think that this case should have ever been brought."[2]

These sentiments were shared by his partner, Aubrey Harwell. In general, Harwell did not believe that the criminal law was appropriate in manufacturing cases like the Pinto. His reasons for this view were both practical and legal. Practically, he felt that the nation's criminal courts were already overburdened with crowded dockets and backlogs. In a society as litigation-minded as ours, it would be troublesome to create a whole new area of criminal law. Pragmatic considerations aside, Harwell's primary reservation regarding corporate criminal liability was the legal issue of intent. He believed that malicious intent typically was lacking in corporate cases, although he would not go so far as to dismiss criminal liability altogether. "Where intent can be demonstrated," he commented, "the corporation should be subjected to criminal prosecution like any other person. All of us are responsible for our actions."

Yet, was not Ford culpable of consciously allowing potentially lethal products to remain in the hands of unsuspecting customers? Harwell was adamant that Ford was innocent; again, intent was the significant issue. According to Harwell, the Ford people were honorable; they did not have the malicious intent to manufacture a death trap. He was convinced that Ford did not believe the Pinto was an unusually dangerous automobile. Even so, Harwell admitted that he would not want his family to drive a Pinto or any other small model and that motorcycles were "absolutely off limits" to his sons. Aside from fuel economy concerns, small cars simply were not as safe as larger cars. Harwell believed, however, along with Ford, that the Pinto was no more dangerous than other small automobiles on the market.[3]

This general perspective was shared, if not embraced, by Malcolm E. Wheeler, a third key member of the defense team. Once again, the paradoxical features of the Pinto case were apparent. If corporate crime fighter Michael Cosentino had all the trappings of a law-and-order conservative, then corporate defender Wheeler seemed to be the classic liberal. A 1969 graduate of Stanford Law School, he had devoted a great deal of time to performing free legal work in the Haight-Ashbury section of San Francisco. In 1971, he joined the law faculty at the University of Kansas, where he taught a course on prisoner rights and took on cases defending Native Americans.

Yet the 35-year-old Wheeler had another side. Liberal causes aside, he was also an expert on antitrust legislation. In 1974, he was hired by the Los Angeles office of the prestigious Wall Street firm, Hughes, Hubbard, and Reed, whose clients included the Ford Motor Company. After Ford's devastating loss in the *Grimshaw* civil case, Wheeler was assigned the task of developing a new defense that would protect the company against similar defeats in future liability suits. As a graduate not only of Stanford Law School but also of the Massachusetts Institute of Technology, he had the expertise to grasp the technical complexities of the Pinto and to place them within a legal context. By the time of the Ulrichs' deaths, he understood well the many aspects of the Pinto controversy. He would prove to be a valuable addition to Ford's defense team.

As with Neal and Harwell, the appeal of the Pinto trial to Wheeler was twofold. First, he saw the legal significance of the case. It was, he admitted, "an opportunity I couldn't turn down. I think everyone agrees it's a real ground-breaking case." He also believed in a cause: the idea that the criminal law was an inappropriate sanction in product liability cases and that Ford was an inappropriate target of Cosentino's prosecution.[4]

Wheeler argued that it was easy to sensationalize the injuries suffered by consumers, to blame corporations for placing profits above safety, and to offer the criminal sanction as a panacea for the risks created by the manufacturing process. But these claims, he observed, were attractive precisely because they played on emotions and proposed simplistic solutions to complex problems. Indeed, Wheeler perceived real danger in campaigns against corporations—like the one being waged against Ford—that embraced the noble goal of protecting the public's interests but ultimately were based on misinformed good intentions rather than on thoughtful analysis.

Wheeler had no shortage of reasons for opposing the extension of the criminal law into the realm of product liability and for issuing a warning that this would be an imprudent reform. First, he could find little evidence that the current regulatory system did not function adequately to control corporate conduct. After all, manufacturers already faced the prospect of administrative recalls of faulty products, pressures from consumer groups, expensive losses in civil suits, and unfavorable publicity that threatened sales and profits when lawsuits were filed. "Such a broad array of noncriminal deterrent forces," he asserted, "attends few other activities engaged in by members of our society."

Second, Wheeler felt that much of the impetus behind the call to apply criminal sanctions stemmed from the perception that corporations placed a dollar value on human life and crassly ignored safety considerations when they did not prove cost-effective. In Wheeler's eyes, however, cost-benefit analysis was at the core of the manufacturing process. Executives had to balance safety against factors such as a product's price, durability, comfort, efficiency, style, and overall marketability. The alternative to the systematic assessment of costs and benefits was decisionmaking based not on careful evaluation but on intuition and idiosyncratic standards—clearly not an attractive option.

Third, Wheeler questioned whether the threat of criminal sanctions would in fact serve the public's interests. There was a risk, he cautioned, of too much deterrence. If companies feared the constant threat of criminal prosecution, they would be forced to place excessive emphasis on product safety. As a consequence, quality and cost levels in other product areas might suffer, even though the public had not shown that it wished to place safety above all other concerns. In particular, prices would inevitably rise and have the socially regressive effect of excluding many poorer consumers from purchasing new products. Disadvantaged citizens would be priced out of the new-car market and compelled to buy used vehicles, which threatened, ironically, to be less safe than those to which they currently had access.

As a fourth consideration, Wheeler wondered whether the criminal justice system was equipped to handle intricate corporate cases. He was concerned that the criminal sanction carried such a heavy stigma that even corporations found innocent in a trial would suffer damaged reputations. This sullied image could diminish consumer faith in the firm, jeopardize profits, and potentially cost workers their jobs. What provisions could the criminal justice system make for rectifying this harm? Further, Wheeler observed that juries were ill-prepared to weigh the complex factors involved in the production process. "Lay jurors," he asserted, "have neither common experience nor statutory guidance to assist them in judging the propriety of that conduct under general criminal statutes." Of course, this was also true in civil cases, in which decisions often were made on "gut feelings" rather than on expert assessment of all relevant facts. Even so, much more was at stake in labeling a company criminal. "Subjecting manufacturers to that irrational antipathy in a civil suit for compensation is bad enough," lamented Wheeler, but "doing it in a criminal proceeding is much worse." Finally, Wheeler contended that gearing up the criminal justice system to attack corporations either would lessen the system's capacity to deal with common-law offenses or would require substantial budgetary increases so that the state could hire the personnel required to undertake the fight against corporate illegality. "It is far from clear," he concluded, "that it is socially desirable to devote already scarce police, prosecutorial, and judicial resources to the criminal prosecution of product manufacturers."[5]

In the end, Neal, Harwell, and Wheeler saw their defense of Ford as morally correct because of their conception of the appropriate relationship between business and the criminal law. Cynics could portray this view, as well as their interpretation of Ford's criminal culpability, as mere justifications for taking a case that promised to bring a healthy fee and professional prestige, just as cynics could claim that in prosecuting Ford, Cosentino was seeking publicity and political reward. Nonetheless, the members of the defense were ready to articulate an ideology that could compete with the popular vision of "Pinto madness." Ford Motor Company, they argued forcefully, was not a sociopath that randomly victimized its customers, but a responsible citizen that obeyed federal regulations and carefully weighed all factors in manufacturing a product that the public wanted: a small, affordable American car.

Moreover, Ford had done well in hiring a talented legal team who would know how to use the many resources that the company placed at their disposal. Michael Cosentino had had to overcome a series of obstacles in bringing Ford to trial; this team would require him to negotiate a far more demanding obstacle course before he could convict Ford on charges of reckless homicide.

THE ROAD TO WINAMAC: A CHANGE OF VENUE

Ford's opening gambit was an attempt to move Cosentino off his home turf by arguing that the bias against the Pinto in Elkhart was strong enough to warrant a change of venue. This strategy was important to the defense because of the real possibility that the local community would regard the company with suspicion. Something else was at stake as well: even if Elkhart citizens were not consciously prejudiced against Ford, they were likely to be familiar with their popular prosecutor. To potential jurors, Cosentino would not be an outsider undertaking an unusual case against a well-known corporation but an elected official pursuing his duty for his constituents. In addition, Cosentino would be trying the case before a judge who knew him and respected his work. The home-court advantage was likely to give him the edge in close calls.

There were also pragmatic considerations. Ford lawyers bristled at the media portrayal of the prosecution as a David pitted in a battle with a corporate Goliath. After all, Cosentino not only drew upon the help of legal volunteers in his campaign against Ford, but also had the resources of the State of Indiana at his disposal: the highway patrol, the coroner's office, and criminal laboratories.[6] Yet, unlike the resources for a corporation-funded defense, the prosecution's resources were largely fixed, not liquid. Thus, Cosentino's team could rely upon volunteer time and expertise and could use existing state facilities and personnel, but could not transform these resources into cash that could be allocated for other, unanticipated purposes. This lack of flexibility was not a critical disadvantage as long as the trial was held in Elkhart, close to the homes of those involved in the prosecution and Cosentino's office. Should the trial be transferred to another jurisdiction, however, the dearth of cash reserves would prove more serious. The prosecution would have to bear the added expenses of food, lodging, travel, office space, and local legal assistance. With a $20,000 budget, this change of venue would place an additional strain on Cosentino. His opponent, of course, would not have to practice frugality.

Donald W. Jones, the judge who had permitted the case to reach the trial stage, presided over the hearing in which Ford argued its request for a change of venue. The defense came well-prepared. To prove bias against the Pinto, they commissioned a telephone survey of 600 homes in Elkhart and the surrounding five counties; the price of the poll reportedly matched Cosentino's entire $20,000 budget. The investment was wise, however, for the survey's results gave empirical support to Ford's claims. In Elkhart County, 37.6 percent of the "potential juror population" answered, "Ford is guilty of the criminal charges of reckless homicide." Another 18.7 percent responded that Ford was "probably guilty as charged," and another 12.6 percent said that they "could not give the State and Ford a fair trial." Thus, the total of "prejudiced jurors" in Elkhart was placed at 68.9 percent; for the five surrounding counties the figure was 50.8 percent.[7] The defense solidified its position further by calling Hans Zeisel, a nationally known legal scholar, to the stand. Zeisel, who would surface again as a Ford consultant during jury selection, testified that his content analysis of local news reports revealed that 86 percent of the stories were biased against the defense. A fair trial, he concluded, was not possible in the Elkhart area.

Cosentino countered by pointing out that there had been no change of venue in many highly publicized cases (e.g., the Watergate trials). He also observed that Ford's Pinto advertisements balanced any negativism that could have accumulated from pretrial media coverage, and he argued that according to Ford's data, nearly two-thirds of the Elkhart residents had yet to decide that the company was guilty. Perhaps the most convincing support for the prosecution's stance came from a letter sent to Ford by Joseph M. Webb, a professor of communications at the University of Evansville. The letter contained Webb's rationale for declining to testify on Ford's behalf: he did not believe that there was enough evidence to show that the corporation "has been prejudiced in the news media."[8]

On April 10, 1979, Judge Jones ended his deliberations and handed down his decision: the case would not be tried in Elkhart or in the five adjacent counties; Ford had won a change of venue. A critical question now emerged: where would the landmark trial be held? To resolve this matter, Judge Jones presented a list of five counties to which the case could be transferred. Ford was granted the right to make the first and third choices in eliminating a potential site; the prosecution would have the second veto and then make the final choice between the fourth and fifth counties. After alternating vetoes had been exercised, Cosentino was left to choose between Grant and Pulaski Counties.

With so much at stake, the decision was difficult. The scouting report on Harold P. Staffeldt, the circuit court judge in Pulaski County, was mixed. Cosentino's sources noted that he was "unbiased and fair, is especially good on evidence and runs a tight ship." Yet, in words that would later prove prophetic, the report also warned that Staffeldt was usually "pro-state but because of the nature of our case it would be hard to determine. . . . He is a strict construction of statute judge and does not care for 'screwball' arguments. . . . The main thing that the Judge does not want is to be reversed on appeal and he would take the most conservative approach." The potential jurors, however, were characterized in uniformly positive terms: "The jury would be fair and impartial. . . . [F]armers in this county do not like or trust big business."[9] The problem with Grant County was that many citizens were employed in the local Chrysler and Delco plants. Cosentino feared the risk of having a jury that was favorable, even if only unconsciously, to the automotive industry. This concern tipped the scales; the trial would be held in Pulaski County.

The Pulaski county seat was the small community of Winamac, located 55 miles southwest of Elkhart and described by one reporter as "a sleepy Tippecanoe River town in the soybean fields of central Indiana." The community had a population of 2,400, three luncheonettes, and one motel; penny parking meters lined its three-block business district. The trial would take place in the tallest structure in Winamac, a three-story limestone courthouse built in the late nineteenth century. The courtroom, located on the second floor, featured old woodwork lined with green and gold flocked wallpaper. The courtroom, refurbished with padded gold-colored seats, accommodated about 75 observers. The judge's bench rested below a picture of George Washington, flanked on one side by a copy of the Bill of Rights and on the other by a copy of Lincoln's Gettysburg address.[10]

Harold P. Staffeldt had been hearing cases here since his appointment as circuit court judge in 1969. Sixty years of age, white-haired, thin, and fond of bold polka-dot bow ties, Staffeldt was a lifelong resident of Winamac. He received his legal training at Tulane University and returned to his hometown in 1947 to establish a local practice. Though he was not experienced in homicide cases ("we don't have any murderers around here"), he had presided over product liability cases.

Most often in these cases, farmers sued feed companies "when their cattle don't grow plump."[11]

With the site of the trial determined, Ford quickly set up its defense operations. One of its first and shrewdest moves was to hire Lester Wilson as local counsel. For a number of years, Wilson had shared a law office and a secretary with Harold Staffeldt. In addition to Wilson, the defense team included more than 10 lawyers, a public relations executive from corporate headquarters, a professional jogger to rush materials from the courtroom to the defense's office, numerous typists and secretaries, and college students whose tasks included filling coffee cups and carting around boxes of files and evidence. Ford also imported word processors, copiers, a videotape recorder to monitor television network reports, and a machine to transmit paperwork between Winamac and the Ford offices in Dearborn, Michigan.

To accommodate the equipment and their small army, Ford rented a former restaurant and installed offices. Because Lester Wilson's law office was not large enough, they knocked down a wall and expanded into the barbershop next door. (The barber was amply compensated and was promised that the shop would be reconstructed once the trial had ended.) The Ford staff was housed in four rooms rented from the lone motel in town and in nine brand-new furnished apartments; the apartments reportedly cost $27,000 a month. Transportation did not prove problematic; the local Ford dealership supplied the cars.[12]

The defense also arranged to purchase one additional luxury: daily transcripts of the trial. This item was not inexpensive: nine dollars a page, for a total of more than $50,000 for the trial. The transcripts were a good investment, however; they gave Neal and his associates the opportunity to review testimony when preparing cross-examinations and challenges of previous prosecution contentions. In the face of his limited resources, Cosentino had to forego this advantage.[13]

Ford barely edged out Cosentino in the race for Lester Wilson's services. Cosentino called Wilson early one morning only to discover that Ford had hired him the previous evening. As a second choice for local counsel, the prosecutor selected David Tankersley, a young and capable Winamac attorney. Tankersley, however, did not have any special relationship with the judge.

The prosecution's team set up shop in Tankersley's office. The space was somewhat cramped but adequate for their needs. Lodging proved to be more of a problem, as there was little local housing and Ford had rented most of the units available. On a tip from an FBI agent, Cosentino discovered two cottages next to Bass Lake, 10 miles to the north of Winamac. Typically empty during the off-season, the cottages were not built to withstand the winter's cold. Still, the price was right: at $800 a month, they would do.

Despite this minimal cost, funds were short. To lessen the burden, Cosentino used his own money to pay most of the bills for rent, telephone, and utilities. Everyone else would chip in for groceries. No local dealership offered to supply free cars: Cosentino managed the daily trip to Winamac in his 1976 Chevrolet Blazer.[14]

THE ART AND SCIENCE OF SELECTING A JURY

Jury selection for the Pinto trial began on Monday morning, January 7, 1980. Almost a year and a half had passed since the Ulrich girls had perished; the time had come to choose the people who would assess whether Ford was to blame for the reckless endangerment and homicide of the three teenagers. The jurors would be drawn from a pool of nearly 250 Pulaski County citizens. Both the prosecution and the defense would have an opportunity to question each potential juror, and each side had 10 "peremptory challenges," which they could use to exclude any person from the jury without cause. Other citizens could be excused from jury duty by Judge Staffeldt, either because they were too prejudiced to render a fair decision or because of personal exigencies.

Both Neal and Cosentino came fully prepared to pick a jury sympathetic to their cases, in part because of their past experiences. Their previous records of repeated success in the courtroom indicated that each had mastered the art of jury selection. Nonetheless, the Pinto trial was a different game. The ideology surrounding the case was anomalous and seemingly contradictory; a conservative was fighting a "liberal" cause, and Ford was portraying itself as a victim of the overreach of the law. In such a context, it was riskier than usual to predict which way potential jurors would lean upon entering the case. The help of outside experts would be needed to minimize the possibility of misinterpretation and error.

James Neal used science to corroborate his "lawyer's sense" of what constitutes a good juror. Although he ultimately trusted his intuition in making jury selections, Neal valued empirical data because they furnished additional perspective and thus increased his confidence.[15] Once again, Ford settled for nothing less than the best consultant in the field: Hans Zeisel. The 74-year-old Zeisel had worked in marketing research when he immigrated to the United States; later he joined the law faculty at the University of Chicago. He achieved prominence as one of the foremost experts on juries when he collaborated with Harry Klaven on their celebrated book, *The American Jury*. His consulting fee was reportedly $1,000 a day.

To develop a profile of a juror favorable to the defense, Zeisel conducted an extensive survey of registered voters in four states. His study revealed that women in general, and young women in particular, would be the worst jurors for Ford, while older men would be the best. The only exceptions to this trend were females who drove trucks. Such a respondent, Zeisel concluded from his data analysis, "became a man for purposes of jury selection; she was a good juror for Ford." Zeisel not only provided a juror model, but also attended each day of the selection process and consulted with Neal during breaks. In general, there was little disagreement between his advice and the assessments Neal made based on his questioning of the potential jurors.[16]

In this regard, Neal used the voir dire process to probe the underlying ideology of the jurors. Thus, he did not confine his questions to eliciting only direct anti-Ford sentiments. Instead, he tried to learn the extent to which a prospective juror embraced liberal causes, supported government safety regulations, and mistrusted corporations. Those who felt positively about Ralph Nader and Common Cause (who thought that the government should mandate air bags, believed that a small car should be as safe as a luxury automobile, and were suspicious of corporate America) had little chance of surviving Neal's challenge.[17]

Unlike his opponent, Cosentino did not have the option of hiring an expensive consultant on jury selection. He did, however, hold valuable discussions with psychiatrist Otto Klassen, director of a community mental health center in Elkhart. As a result, Cosentino perceived that his chances would be improved if he could select jurors who were the exact opposite of the kind normally favorable to the state and, ironically, of the kind he normally chose to hear his cases. An older, male, conservative jury might be ideal for a typical homicide case, but it was unlikely that such a group would be inclined to view a corporation, like Ford, as a criminal capable of committing homicide.

With the help of his associates, Cosentino developed a series of more than 40 questions. These questions were aimed at unmasking biases that would make the juror "good" or "bad" for the prosecution. They ranged from whether a person owned a Ford vehicle or stock in Ford and believed that a "corporation is responsible for its conduct" to what magazines were read, what television shows were watched, and what health activities were pursued. Lifestyle questions were important, Cosentino believed, because they served as indicators of a person's political orientation and general attitude toward the centers of power in America. Thus, citizens who read *Mother Earth News* rather than *Time*, preferred PBS to CBS, were "into jogging" for their health, and avoided smoking because they believed the government's warnings about its dangers seemed more likely to be critical of Ford's handling of the Pinto. Unfortunately for the prosecution, however, this kind of prospective juror was in short supply in Pulaski County.[18]

Jury selection took four days and involved the tedious questioning of nearly 60 citizens, but by Thursday afternoon, the 12 jurors and three alternates had been chosen. Both sides were pleased with the results and felt that a "fair" jury had been seated.

The jury included seven men and five women, and were of an average age of 41. All the members were or had been married; all were parents. Although every juror had earned a high-school diploma, few had any higher education. They worked in varied occupations; the jury included two farmers, two housewives, several self-employed business people, a railroad employee, an X-ray technician, a telephone service worker, and a steelworker. One woman, Hans Zeisel was pleased to learn, drove a truck, and half the jury members owned Ford vehicles. Juror Raymond Schramm even had a Pinto, but he claimed this would not bias his views. After all, he noted, "I used to drive a Corvair."[19]

The jury selection process indicated clearly the kind of courtroom battles that would erupt in the weeks ahead. Reporter Lee Strobel observed that only 15 seconds after the start of the trial, Cosentino and Neal began a dispute over how close a lectern should be placed to the jury box.[20] The opening days also revealed the stylistic differences between the two lawyers. Because this was a homicide case, Cosentino adopted a serious demeanor. He spoke assertively and with an intensity meant to emphasize the gravity of the charges leveled at Ford. By contrast, Neal did not hesitate to use humorous quips to lighten the mood of the courtroom, and he often relied on folksy language to score points with prospective jurors. "From the Ford side of the courtroom," reporter Alan Lenhoff commented smartly during the first week, "the accepted way of addressing the jury seems to be 'you.'"[21]

Now that the jury was seated, the small community of Winamac, executives at Ford, corporate America, and legal scholars across the nation waited eagerly for testimony in the Pinto trial to begin. The preview of the "Mike and Jim show," as local residents came to call it, had ended; the curtain was about to rise on the main event.[22]

Preparing for Trial: Documenting Ford's Culpability

Before the trial, the prosecution spent considerable effort on neutralizing Ford's attempt to quash the indictment; they also faced the critical task of preparing their substantive case. In part, this preparation involved analyzing the details of the accident and establishing that a faulty car, not faulty driving, had caused the Ulrichs' deaths. Much more evidence would be required, however, to prove that Ford was guilty of recklessly manufacturing a lethal vehicle and of keeping it on the road despite its obvious dangers. Cosentino would have to penetrate Ford's corporate shield to acquire the documents that would reveal the company's inner workings and allow him to show how executives' decisions, informed by a profit ideology, had led to the marketing of a hazardous product.

As mentioned in Chapter 4, the general crusade against the Pinto made it feasible to secure internal Ford documents. In particular, Cosentino carefully tracked down the numerous lawyers who had civil cases against Ford; many were willing to share whatever damning information they had obtained. Over time, the prosecution became a clearinghouse for data on the Pinto.

Even so, the various threads of evidence still had to be interpreted in such a way that the complex history of the Pinto could be reconstructed and presented to a jury in a convincing fashion. Terry Kiely, the law professor from DePaul who had volunteered his services, assumed much of this burden. His task was to gain the technical expertise that would enable him to sift through the stack of "Pinto papers," as he called them,[23] and to craft the prosecution's account of what had happened nearly a decade earlier, when Ford went about the business of manufacturing "Lee's car."

In a sense, Kiely had plenty of material. The prosecution's digging had uncovered 101 documents, including 35 crash tests, 44 financial documents, and a number of correspondences between Ford and the National Highway Traffic Safety Administration (NHTSA).[24] Yet this was a "corporate crime"; therefore the method of establishing guilt was quite different and more intricate than required in a typical street crime. It would not be sufficient for Kiely to portray the Ulrichs as "homicide victims" and to equate their charred Pinto with the "smoking gun" found at the scene of a "normal" homicide. Instead, he would have to demonstrate that the origins of the teenagers' deaths rested not so much in the rapid sequence of events on Indiana's Highway 33 as in the cumulative effects of decisions by Ford executives, which caused the company to manufacture a vehicle that it had ample reason to believe was potentially lethal.

After months of poring over his Pinto papers, Kiely believed he had the documents to substantiate five broad observations that, taken together, painted a disquieting picture of Ford's conduct.[25] First, while the Pinto was still in the planning stages, Ford already had "state-of-the-art" technology that would have allowed it to build a safe fuel-injection system in a subcompact vehicle. Most notably, the company had produced the Capri, a modified version of which later became the Pinto. Ford engineers avoided the problems that would beset the Pinto's fuel system by placing the Capri's gas tank over the rear axle. In European advertisements, in fact, Ford emphasized that the Capri's tank was "safely cradled between the rear wheels and protected on all sides."[26] Despite this knowledge, Kiely concluded, Ford located the Pinto's "fuel tank behind the axle (3 inches from differential bolts and other hostile sources) and 6 inches from the rear ornamental bumper."[27]

Second, before the initial marketing date, Ford crash-tested four prototypes—a Toyota and three Capris—all modified to have the Pinto's fuel tank arrangement. In these tests, the prototypes were rammed into a wall at approximately 20 mph. In each instance the vehicles leaked fuel and failed the test. Although these results constituted an ominous warning, the company nonetheless "released the Pinto for sale on September 11, 1970 without any further testing of even one production Pinto."[28] Corporate memos indicate that the placement of the tank over the axle was scrapped because it consumed too much trunk space and hence would jeopardize sales. From Kiely's perspective, this decision was clear evidence—drawn from a time before the car was distributed to dealerships—that corporate profits were placed above consumer safety and that Ford had neglected its duty to alter the Pinto's design, even though the corporation knew of the car's inherent dangers.

Third, shortly after the release of the Pinto onto the open market, NHTSA informed Ford of its intention to promulgate standards mandating that all vehicles be able to withstand a 20-mph rear-end collision into a fixed barrier (wall) by January 1, 1972, and a 30-mph collision by January 1, 1973. This mandate led the company to analyze systematically the ability of its products, including the Pinto, to meet these standards. Crash tests confirmed that the Pinto was unable to meet the 20-mph standard, but the investigation also noted that the technology was available to satisfy the forthcoming regulations. Yet, despite continuing knowledge of the Pinto's dangers, the management decided that the costs of altering the fuel system were too great. "Safety," observed Kiely, "is never a consideration and the word does not even appear in the documents."

As an alternative to revamping the Pinto, Kiely continued, Ford's strategy was to lobby the government for a more lenient standard—one that was consistent with an internal company regulation stating that by 1973 all models, including the Pinto, must be able to withstand a 20-mph moving barrier crash. (In a moving-barrier test, a barrier is rammed into a car; in the more stringent fixed-barrier test, the car is towed rearward into a wall and sustains greater damage at a comparable speed.) Concretely, Ford's 20-mph moving-barrier standard meant that in an actual highway or car-to-car accident, a 1973 Pinto would risk fuel leakage if struck in the rear at a speed between 26 and 28 mph—a speed lower than the speed limit on most city streets. The proposed NHTSA standard mandating fuel-system integrity in a 20-mph fixed-barrier test would have boosted the Pinto's safety level approximately six miles per hour, while the 30-mph standard proposed for 1973 models—like the Ulrichs' Pinto—would have required fuel-leakage protection during rear-end collisions at speeds well above 40 mph. Of course, Kiely and the other prosecutors believed that the Ulrichs' car had burst into flames when hit at a speed much lower than 40 mph.[29]

Fourth, though Ford executives chose for the moment to "stand their ground" on the Pinto, they considered developing a solution to the growing prospect that NHTSA would eventually impose tougher safety standards. At that point they weighed the possibility of using a bladder to line the Pinto's fuel tank, and even secured cost estimates from Goodyear and Firestone. Ford management rejected this option, however, in order "to realize a design cost savings of $20.9 million."[30] A memo dated April 22, 1971, five days before Henry Ford II and Lee Iacocca spoke with Richard Nixon in the White House (see Chapter 4), instructed that the manufacturing process allocate space in which a bladder or another protective device could be inserted should NHTSA regulations be forthcoming. By October, however, these instructions were amended so that the Pinto would no longer even be "packaged" or designed for the possibility of an improved fuel system "until required by law."[31] The political climate apparently had become more sympathetic to Ford's corporate interests; therefore the need to make the Pinto more crashworthy was no longer a pressing concern.

Fifth, Ford continued its efforts over the next several years to stifle governmental regulation and to resist revamping the Pinto. In making its argument against more stringent standards, Ford developed its cost-benefit memo, which balanced human lives and injuries against profits—the memo popularized by Dowie in his "Pinto Madness" article (see Chapter 4). Because the analysis contained in this document did not focus on the Pinto, and was related to fuel leakage in a rollover test rather than a rear-end collision, it was not critical to the prosecution's case. Kiely found it relevant, however, because it displayed a mind-set that shaped the thinking of Ford executives and represented the kind of argument that the company made to NHTSA to avoid safety regulations. The memo, suspected Kiely, revealed why Ford did not recall its Pintos until NHTSA prompted it to do so in 1978.[32]

Kiely believed that these five observations, viewed together, demonstrated a pattern that consistently guided Ford's handling of the Pinto: knowledge of the dangers inherent in the fuel-injection system, possession of the technology to rectify the hazards of the tank location, conscious decisions not to improve the fuel system, and efforts to maximize profits by resisting governmental policies that would have mandated safety standards. In Kiely's view, these observations made a compelling case that Ford was reckless in its manufacturing and continued marketing of the Pinto, as well as in its failure to recall the 1.5

million vehicles it allowed to remain on the road. Therefore, the circumstances underlying the Ulrichs' deaths were years in the making and were tied up intimately with Ford's way of doing business.

Still, a sticky problem remained. Although the prosecution had numerous documents at its disposal, these were generally copies of originals supplied by lawyers with civil cases against Ford or by former Ford executives. As a result, Cosentino was confronted with the chore of "authenticating" the documents, that is, of proving that the documents in his possession were indeed Ford's and not forgeries. Until this was accomplished, none of the documents would be admissible as evidence.

The prosecution began to address this issue in the summer preceding the trial. Cosentino's opening gambit was to ask Judge Staffeldt to permit the prosecution to have the "right of discovery," that is, the right to compel the defendant—in this case, Ford—to turn over potentially relevant evidence. Cosentino's purpose was twofold. First, if Ford produced the requested documents from its files, it could be argued that they were authentic and thus admissible in the trial. Second, a discovery process would allow Cosentino to obtain copies of damaging reports that he did not currently possess.

Jim Neal moved quickly to neutralize this attack. In civil cases, he admitted, discovery rights were broad, and both sides had the obligation to surrender any evidence specifically requested by the opposition. But this was a criminal case, Neal reminded Staffeldt; therefore, Ford, as a defendant, enjoyed the Fifth Amendment right against self-incrimination. The State of Indiana could not legitimately expect Ford to help convict itself. Cosentino countered that unlike individual defendants, corporations did not have the right against self-incrimination. Discovery, he asserted, should be allowed in a corporate prosecution.

This would not be the last time in the case that Judge Staffeldt faced a fuzzy legal issue. The very novelty of prosecuting corporations on charges such as reckless homicide (the very point that would bring news reporters to Winamac) meant that Staffeldt would have few clear legal precedents on which to base his rulings. The small-town judge could seek to break new legal ground at the potential risk of having his decisions reversed on appeal by a higher court, or he could take a safer, more conservative approach and decide issues on narrower grounds. As would be seen, the judge was reluctant for the most part to stray too far from his conservative roots; he did not care to be a trendsetter.

In this instance, Staffeldt was not prepared to grant the prosecution broad discovery rights in a criminal case. He did, however, add one caveat: should Ford request evidence from the prosecution (such as autopsy or police reports), as defendants typically do in criminal cases, the company would have to disclose the materials designated by the prosecution.

Neal, who wished to keep tight control over corporate information, refused to initiate a process of mutual discovery. Instead, he relied on Aubrey Harwell, his law partner, to coordinate an exhaustive and costly pretrial investigation that used more informal means—most notably, extensive interviews—to accumulate information about the accident. In response, Cosentino appealed to the Indiana Supreme Court. Much to his chagrin, the Court voted 4–1 to uphold Staffeldt's ruling.

Despite this setback, Cosentino did not lack hope or alternatives. He felt that he had enough evidence to win a conviction; thus, Ford's disclosure of new materials was not critical. Discovery was primarily a way of authenticating the documents already in his possession; now he would have to employ different means. His first attempt was to subpoena Henry Ford II and 29 Ford executives, asking them to appear in court with the relevant documents. Again, authentication would be achieved by the fact that the documents were produced by Ford officials from company files. This effort was derailed, however, when Wayne County, Michigan, Judge Richard D. Dunn rejected the prosecution's bid to have the executives testify at the trial. Cosentino, unwilling to be denied, then served a subpoena on the CT Corporation, a Ford subsidiary designated to represent the corporation in the State of Indiana.

Neal's hand was finally forced, and he offered to provide the requested documents, but only on two conditions. First, any original documents not accepted into evidence must be returned uncopied. Because Ford was facing civil suits, the company did not want any evidence to find its way into the hands of potential plaintiffs. Second, although Neal produced the documents from company files, he refused to admit that this act substantiated for legal purposes that the documents were in fact Ford's.

On Monday, January 7, Neal turned over two hefty cartons of Ford materials, but the issue of the documents' authenticity would not be settled until well into the trial, after much wrangling between the defense and the prosecution. Judge Staffeldt was reluctant to resolve the continuing dispute; when he did rule, he leaned toward Ford. "The party offering the evidence," he concluded, "must prove its authenticity." Undeterred, Cosentino—reportedly at his own expense— arranged for civil lawyers to travel to Winamac; each lawyer would testify that in previous cases Ford had relinquished a specific document and had not challenged its authenticity. Cosentino also knew former Ford executives who could substantiate that they had seen the documents when in Ford's employment and could state that they recognized the signatures on these materials.[33]

Eventually Neal relented on the authentication issue, in part because Ford feared that public opinion might turn against the company for claiming that obviously genuine documents might have been forged. In the end, at any rate, the prosecution lawyers did not believe that the hassle over authenticating documents had a major bearing on the case's outcome.[34] Nonetheless, this issue quickly taught Cosentino that Jim Neal would use every legal maneuver to frustrate the prosecution and to drain their limited budget and energies. As Aubrey Harwell commented later, the firm of Neal and Harwell was a "legal machine" that knew how to use its immense resources to wear down the opposition.[35]

Indeed, Neal wasted little time at the trial before making a concerted effort to cripple Cosentino's case. He filed more than 15 motions *in limine,* that is, motions that attempt to restrict severely the kind of evidence that a prosecutor can introduce. Now that jury selection was completed, Judge Staffeldt announced that he would hear evidentiary arguments at 9:30 on Monday morning, January 14. Opening statements to the jury would begin the next day.

Among Ford's many motions, two had the potential to constrain the prosecution so severely that the corporation's acquittal would virtually be assured. First, Neal noted, NHTSA had mandated that all 1977 model cars meet the standard of minimal fuel leakage in a 30-mph rear-end crash. In turn, Neal reasoned, this mandate suggested that in deciding whether Ford had constructed the Ulrichs' Pinto recklessly, the jury should consider only this federal standard. After all, as a national company, what would be more reasonable than to use uniform federal criteria to evaluate Ford's conduct? "One would think," Neal asserted, "if we met these standards we would not be subject to prosecution."

Cosentino realized that the entire prosecution was hanging in the balance. He believed that he had enough evidence to show that when Robert Duggar's van hit the Ulrichs' Pinto, it was moving about 35 mph faster than the Pinto, yet if NHTSA's 30-mph standard was used to define "recklessness," then Ford was clearly off the hook. Neal's argument, however, was not new to the prosecution. In its attempt to quash the initial indictments, Ford had previously contended, though unsuccessfully, that the company could not be held accountable to individual state standards (see Chapter 5). The stakes were high, but at least the territory was familiar.

Bruce Berner, one of Cosentino's volunteer law professors, was assigned the task of arguing this critical issue. Federal regulations, he asserted, were not operative when the Ulrichs' 1973 Pinto was manufactured; they also served merely as minimum standards of acceptable conduct. The prosecution was prepared to show that during the Pinto's production a higher standard for fuel-system integrity—one that Ford chose to ignore—was technologically and economically feasible. More broadly, Berner contended that a federal regulation did not preempt a criminal statute in the State of Indiana. A jury of Indiana citizens, not Washington bureaucrats, should decide what constituted reckless homicide in the Hoosier State.

The prosecution was relieved when Staffeldt announced that he would permit the jury to set its own standards for determining whether Ford was reckless. To James Neal, the decision meant that the fight would continue. "If we had won that one," he observed, "we all could have gone home."[36]

A second critical motion remained to be resolved, however. Neal argued that the prosecution should be prohibited from introducing any evidence, including internal Ford memos and crash tests, that did not pertain specifically to the 1973 Pinto, the type of car involved in the Ulrichs' deaths. If Staffeldt accepted this reasoning, the prosecution would have only a shadow of its case. Cosentino did not possess data for relevant crash tests on the 1973 model, and his budget prevented him from having these tests conducted. More important, a ruling in Ford's favor would indicate that Staffeldt did not embrace, or perhaps even understand, the theory informing this corporate prosecution.

In a "normal" homicide, the specific characteristics of the murder weapon may be of special significance in establishing the guilt of the defendant: Did the weapon found at the scene of the crime belong to the defendant? Did it carry his or her fingerprints? Did anyone witness a smoking gun in the defendant's hands? In a case like the one against Ford, however, the key evidence was not simply the characteristics of the Pinto that the Ulrichs were driving or what Ford did in 1973 when it manufactured the vehicle. Equally salient, in the prosecution's view, was what the evidence revealed about the nature of Ford's conduct in designing and manufacturing its whole Pinto line and in failing subsequently to recall products—such as the Ulrichs' car—that the company knew were potentially dangerous. In this context, internal corporate documents and crash tests relating to 1971 and 1972 models, as well as to later models, were relevant, because they demonstrated the process by which the lethal defects in the 1973 Pinto's fuel system were created and then not repaired. In short, this material showed why Ford was reckless and could be blamed for the three teenagers' deaths.

To the prosecution's dismay, Judge Staffeldt ruled to exclude all documents that did not deal directly with the 1973 Pinto. "If I can't get that evidence admitted," Cosentino lamented, "I'll have a lot of problems." Yet not all was bleak; some hope was drawn from the judge's qualification that if Cosentino "could lay the proper foundation," evidence on other models might be admitted during the trial. Further, to the surprise and confusion of both the prosecution and defense,

Staffeldt added that on all the day's rulings, he was "subject to chang-ing [his] mind. . . . We'll just take it a day at a time and a motion at a time."[37]

Thus, as Cosentino was about to bring his landmark case before the jury, he and his colleagues faced an uncertain future. After months of preparation, they had accumulated and analyzed numerous Ford memos and Pinto crash tests, and they were confident that with some effort they could authenticate these materials. Indeed, they felt that their case was compelling and that Ford's culpability in the Ulrichs' deaths could be documented amply. As the trial progressed, however, would Judge Staffeldt prove flexible and admit the prosecution's evidence? Would Cosentino have an opportunity to tell the jury the full Pinto story?[38]

PROSECUTING FORD: PROFITS OVER LIVES

Although engaged in a complex corporate prosecution, Mike Cosentino felt that his case hinged on a simple but powerful truth: because Ford Motor Company had decided that fixing the Pinto was not cost-effective, three teenage girls had suffered needless, horrible deaths. The pictures of the Ulrichs' incinerated bodies had left an indelible mark on the consciousness of every member of the prosecu-tion; they called them the "car wars photos." Despite all the talk of set-ting legal precedents and the constant media attention (Jim Neal said, "I've not seen anything like this since Watergate"), no one who had viewed the pictures could forget what this case was really about. Cosentino was fully prepared to have the jury face this reality; they, too, would be shown the "car wars photos."[39]

Neal, who knew how damaging the photos could be to Ford, took the offensive with a bold tactic to prevent the jury from seeing any pho-tographs of the victims, living or dead. The defense would stipulate that the Ulrichs died from burns and not from injuries sustained in the crash (as might be expected in a high-speed collision). In light of this conces-sion, Neal reasoned, there was no need for Cosentino to introduce any information about the girls' identities or to show gruesome photographs of incinerated bodies. Such evidence lacked probative value; indeed, its only purpose would be to prejudice the jury. So Neal entered a motion to prohibit the prosecution from making "any mention of any and all oral, documentary, physical and photographic evidence of the identities of the victims, their manner of death or the condition of the victims and their belongings during or after the accident."[40]

Learning of this motion on Monday, January 14, Cosentino had only until the next morning to develop a rationale for its denial. Bruce Berner quickly placed a call to his volunteer law students at Valparaiso University, and their research helped to uncover two cases that seemed to put the prosecution on firm legal ground. In one case, over which Judge Staffeldt had actually presided, an appeals court affirmed the judge's admission of gory autopsy pictures as prosecution evidence. A second court decision, handed down just two months before the start of the Pinto trial, was even more encouraging: a mother accused of child abuse stipulated that she had beaten her son, and her lawyer used this admission to claim that four photographs of the boy's battered body, taken at a hospital emergency room, should be excluded as prejudicial evidence. The mother then said that she would contest only the issue of her sanity. On appeal, the defense argued that the trial judge had erred in permitting the jury to view the four photographs. The appeals court, however, did not accept this logic, in part because it believed that evidence on all aspects of the case should be heard "where [the] State in prosecution . . . did not agree to [the] stipulation that [the] defendant would only contest [the] issue of her sanity."[41] This recent Indiana precedent suggested that unless the prosecution agreed, a defendant could not stipulate facts to prevent a jury from viewing photographs of a victim's injuries; armed with such a precedent, Cosentino seemed well prepared for the next day's skirmish.

In Tuesday morning's oral arguments, Bruce Berner contended that the "State has an obligation and right to prove every material element of the crime. . . . In a criminal case, a defendant has two choices. He can plead guilty or not guilty. He cannot plead partially guilty." Citing the legal precedents uncovered in the prosecution's research, Berner added that regardless of Ford's stipulation, the obligation remained to present evidence on the cause of the Ulrichs' deaths. Staffeldt was unconvinced, however, embracing instead Jim Neal's position that the information on the girls would distract from "genuine issues," create a "melodramatic spectacle," and inflame the jury. Indeed, the judge accepted Ford's motion nearly intact, excluding not only the "car wars photos" but also all other pictures of and information about the girls.

After this session, an angry Cosentino commented to the media that "Ford has sanitized the State's case. We cannot show that they [the Ulrichs] were alive, and we can not show that they died. We can't show what they looked like before; we can't show what they looked like after. We can't prove anything about the victims themselves and the victims are what this case is all about."

Yet Cosentino could not afford to dwell on this stinging defeat or, for that matter, on Staffeldt's previous ruling, which potentially excluded documents on non-1973 Pintos. A more pressing matter was at hand: in the afternoon session, he would present his opening arguments. This would be his first crack at the jury, and he faced the critical task of setting the proper tone and foundation for the prosecution's case.

In a presentation lasting almost an hour, Cosentino sent a clear message to the jury. "Ford management," he maintained, "deliberately chose profit over human life," and the Ulrich girls "needlessly died as a result of the callous, indifferent, and reckless acts and omissions of the defendant." Although they knew that the Pinto's gas tank was defective and "susceptible to an explosion equivalent to 250 sticks of dynamite," the company decided to market the car and to resist warning owners of the Pinto's inherent and potentially lethal dangers. Indeed, the Pinto "was designed with one thing in mind: profit, not safety."

Jim Neal then rose to unveil, in reporter Lee Strobel's words, "Ford's million dollar defense."[42] He began his 75-minute address by assertively challenging Cosentino's characterization of Ford. Although he admitted that Ford may have made mistakes or may have been wrong in some instances, he denied that "we are reckless killers." Neal then outlined nine considerations that would form the core of Ford's case. Once the defense had elaborated and substantiated these "facts," he declared confidently, the company's innocence would be beyond dispute:

1. The curbs on Highway 33 were badly designed, prevented the Ulrichs from pulling off the road, and thus contributed to the accident. Yet those who planned and approved the road's construction were not being held accountable for their negligence.

2. Robert Duggar, the driver of the van, was the primary cause of the accident, but he, too, was escaping trial.

3. Ford's 1973 Pinto met every government fuel safety standard.

4. For the 1973 model, Ford was the only automaker to have an internal company standard requiring fuel-system integrity for a rear-end crash (20-mph moving-barrier test).

5. The Pinto was comparable in design to other 1973 subcompacts.

6. As an indicator of the Pinto's safety, Ford engineering executives involved in the development of the car furnished Pintos for their wives and children.

7. Government statistics revealed that the Pinto was no more likely than other subcompacts to suffer from fires, and fared as well in collisions.

8. During the 41-day period in which Cosentino had to prove that Ford was reckless in not warning the Ulrichs of the Pinto's dangers, the company was undertaking a vigorous recall campaign.

9. Given the speed difference between the Ulrichs' subcompact Pinto and Duggar's heavy van—which was 50 mph, and not under 35 mph as the prosecution claimed—other subcompacts and many larger automobiles would also have suffered ruptured fuel systems.[43]

In closing his remarks, Neal asserted, carefully emphasizing each word, "We are not reckless killers."

After the opening arguments were ended, Cosentino launched his case against Ford; his evidence would take longer than a month to present. He intended to prove Ford's guilt by establishing four broad points that, when taken together, revealed how the corporation's recklessness led to the Ulrichs' deaths.

First, Cosentino wanted to show that during the collision on Highway 33, the fuel system of the Ulrichs' Pinto had displayed a disquieting lack of structural integrity. Called to the stand as the State's lead witness, Trooper Neil Graves described how he had found a mixture of gas and water (from the fire hoses) in the front passenger compartment. Apparently, he testified, the fuel gushed into this area through a split in a seam connecting the wheel housing to the floor. The question of origins remained, however: where did the gasoline come from? Graves provided the obvious answer: the Pinto's fuel tank had ruptured. Although it had been filled only minutes before the accident, the 11-gallon tank was almost empty. Clearly, the fuel had escaped through the "large gaping hole in the left side of the fuel tank." In a dramatic demonstration, Graves illustrated just how large this breach was. With the Pinto's scorched and mangled tank resting on a table before the jury, Graves placed his hand and then his forearm through the hole. After the accident, he said, this was how he determined the amount of gasoline left in the tank.

Mattie Ulrich, the mother of Judy and Lyn, was the prosecution's next witness. Her testimony would corroborate Cosentino's second point: before her daughters perished, the family had not been warned of the Pinto's hazards. Her presence meant more than this, however. For the most part, Neal had indeed succeeded in "sanitizing" the prosecution's case, but with Mattie Ulrich in the courtroom, the jurors would be reminded—concretely and vividly—of the enormous loss suffered in the accident.

"Yes, sir," she replied softly, when asked if she had ever received a Pinto recall notice from Ford. Then, revealing a tragic irony that shocked the courtroom's packed audience, she noted quietly that the company's letter arrived in February 1979, six months after the fiery crash that took her daughters' lives. And if the warning about the Pinto's dangers had come earlier? "I would have gotten rid of it," she answered dramatically. "I would not have let the girls drive it that evening." Her words left the courtroom hushed and filled with tension.

Cosentino moved next to support the prosecution's third major contention: the difference in speed between the Ulrichs' Pinto and Duggar's van was no more than 30 to 35 mph. This empirical issue was critical to the prosecution's case. If it could be established that a rear-end crash at this relatively low speed had transformed the teenagers' Pinto into a flaming death trap, then a compelling argument could be made that the car's fuel system was designed recklessly and did not meet acceptable safety standards. By contrast, if the speed difference between the Pinto and the van had approached 50 mph—as Neal contended—then the fire could be attributed to the force of the impact and not to the fuel system's lack of integrity. Any subcompact hit by a heavy van at that speed, Ford could argue persuasively, would have suffered the same fate.

Cosentino was confident, however, that the prosecution's assessment of the speed difference would be sustained; after all, he had six eyewitnesses to the crash as well as other convincing evidence.

Albert Clark was the first of his eyewitnesses to take the stand. "It was—I'm an ex-GI—like a large napalm bomb," he said, "It just blew up." But what was the crash like? Although the windows were down in Clark's mini motor home, the impact "was not that terrific. I heard no noise. . . . I thought it was going to be a fender-bender." Clark then estimated that Duggar's van was traveling 40 to 45 mph, and the girls' Pinto 30 to 35 mph—a difference of only 5 to 15 mph. "Will you ever forget that day?" asked Cosentino. Remembering the sight of Judy Ulrich as he tried to pull her free of the Pinto, Clark answered softly, struggling to hold back tears, "No . . . no."

One by one, the other eyewitnesses confirmed Clark's version of the accident. They agreed that the van's speed did not exceed 50 mph. The Pinto's exact velocity was less clear; but everyone agreed that the car was moving at a minimum of 15 mph. The calculations were clear: the maximum speed difference was 35 mph. In addressing the other issue—the horror of the accident—each witness relived that moment, often at an emotional cost. It was "like a bomb blowing up," recalled teenager Yolanda Ihrig. College Professor William Martin told a similar story. "I could look directly into the front windshield area of the Pinto," he commented. "I saw a solid mass of orange flames. There was absolutely no air space in the passenger compartment." Later, with the jury dismissed from the courtroom, he told about seeing Judy Ulrich on the ground, "supporting herself on her arms." Visibly upset, Martin added, "It shocked me that a person could be so incredibly burned and be alive."

The prosecution was optimistic; the eyewitnesses were persuasive and unshaken by Neal's cross-examination. The evidence indicated that the Ulrichs' Pinto had been moving when hit and had exploded "like a bomb" at a speed difference that was unacceptably low.

Cosentino wished to maintain the prosecution's advantage by solidifying this image in the jurors' minds. Robert Duggar, he believed, would help him do so. Now 22 and a freshman at a small Michigan college, Duggar testified that he had been driving at 50 mph; he had checked his speed after passing a police car equipped with radar. After recounting the moments before the crash—how he had glanced toward the van's floor to locate a fallen cigarette pack, only to look up and find "the Pinto ten feet in front of me"—he estimated the Pinto's speed at 15 to 20 mph. "I hit the Pinto and smelled gasoline," he said. And then what happened? "Before I could think, there was a fire. The whole car was on fire."

Cosentino had one final piece of evidence to support the prosecution's version of the difference in speed between the two vehicles. Thus far, he had based his proof on the subjective assessments of the witnesses to the crash; now he would provide some hard scientific data. When asked to describe the nature and origin of the bodily trauma suffered by the Ulrichs, Goshen radiologist Sean Gunderson testified that no life-threatening physical damage could be traced to the impact of the crash. This conclusion was corroborated by Dr. Robert J. Stein and Dr. James A. Benz, who presented the dramatic findings of the autopsies they had conducted on the exhumed bodies of Judy and Lyn Ulrich. Stein, who conducted Judy Ulrich's autopsy, testified that she had sustained no internal injuries; Benz revealed that Lyn, who had sat in the back seat of the Pinto, suffered only a few minor broken bones and did not show the kind of spinal-cord damage that typically occurs in a high-speed rear-end accident. Thus, Cosentino's scientific experts were in agreement that if not for the girls' burns, the girls would be alive. Again, the point was clear: because the force of the collision did not cause serious physical injuries, the crash must have occurred at a relatively low speed.

After two weeks of testimony, Cosentino was satisfied that he had established three key points: (1) during the accident, the fuel system of the Ulrichs' Pinto lacked structural integrity; (2) Ford Motor Company did not warn Mattie Ulrich of the Pinto's inherent dangers until after her daughters' deaths; and (3) the maximum speed difference between the van and the Pinto was approximately 35 mph. Yet, as Cosentino understood, "the meat—the heart of the State's case" remained. In order to make a convincing case, the prosecution had to support a fourth point: Ford knew of the Pinto's safety hazards and had economically feasible technology to prevent and rectify the fuel system's defects. Byron Bloch and Harley Copp, both of whom had testified in previous civil cases against Ford, could be counted on to lend credence to this contention. Yet the critical evidence—the crash tests and the internal Ford documents that Terry Kiely had analyzed diligently and arranged to tell the "Pinto story"—had yet to be admitted as evidence. Although Cosentino felt that he could fulfill Judge Staffeldt's requirement that he lay a "proper foundation" for these materials, he had also learned that little was certain in a precedent-setting corporate prosecution.

Byron Bloch, a safety consultant based in West Los Angeles, was a veteran not only of past Pinto cases but also of an array of product liability suits. Cosentino intended to use Bloch as an auto safety "expert" who could verify the nature of the Pinto's defects; in his week-long testimony, Bloch undertook this task vigorously. With the help of a rear section of a 1973 Pinto that Cosentino purchased for $100 and brought into the courtroom, Bloch showed the jurors the "hostile environment" that surrounded the car's gas tank and made it excessively vulnerable to punctures, rips, and tears. He also used color slides of the Ulrichs' Pinto to explain how the tank had ruptured and how the "filler tube definitely pulled out of the gas tank," allowing fuel to "whoosh out." Then Bloch asserted that the Pinto's hazards were avoidable. Backing Cosentino's claim that Ford's use of "state-of-the-art" technology would have created a much safer fuel system, he listed a number of models that located the gas tank above or forward of the axle rather than (as in the Pinto) behind the axle and close to the bumper. Most revealing, he observed, Ford itself had used an above-axle or forward-of-the-axle design in its late-1950s Skyliner, its pre-Pinto Capri, and its more recent Fiesta. In light of these considerations, did Ford "deviate substantially from acceptable standards of conduct" in designing and marketing the Pinto? Bloch's conclusion was clear: "Yes. Ford Motor Company did deviate."

Although he educated the jurors about the technical aspects of the Pinto and fuel-system safety, Bloch proved ultimately to be a disappointing prosecution witness.[44] The defense had systematically investigated Bloch's background and testimony in previous product liability cases, and now Neal was well equipped to discredit his "expert" opinions. One strategy was to force Bloch to admit that "95 percent of all American cars had the gas tank flat behind the axle as it was in the 1973 Pinto." If the Pinto was comparable to other 1973 models, Neal reasoned, then how could Bloch claim that it "deviated" from the automotive industry's standards? "They were all bad" was the best answer Bloch could muster, though Cosentino offered a more compelling response: "It's a typical tactic of defendants to say that 'Everybody else did it, so we can do it too.'"

Neal's second line of attack was even more damaging. The defense's research into Bloch's past revealed inconsistencies between the academic credentials listed on his résumé and those he had actually earned. Neal also noted that Bloch had testified as a safety "expert" on a wide range of products (e.g., coffee percolators, garbage trucks, hospital tables, train accidents) and in 1976 had advertised a combination cocktail party and seminar with the promise of showing lawyers "how to expand accident cases into product liability cases." As reporters James Warren and Brian Kelly observed, this evidence succeeded in portraying Bloch as a "mercenary consultant."[45] After all, Neal remarked, "if a man advertises how he can expand accidents into product liability cases, it seems obvious to me he's got an axe to grind."

Heading into the final stages of his case, Cosentino realized that much would hinge on the effectiveness of his next witness, former Ford executive Harley Copp. Now that Bloch's testimony was tainted, Copp would have to convince the jury that Ford knew about and could have restricted the Pinto's defects. Further, Cosentino was counting on Copp's expert testimony to lay the foundation for the admission into evidence of non-1973 Pinto documents.

As mentioned, Cosentino had been thwarted substantially in his attempts to show the jury why the prosecution blamed Ford's recklessness for the Ulrichs' deaths. Until this point in the case, Cosentino's tenacity regarding the evidence had resulted in only one major breakthrough. Over Neal's strong objections, Judge Staffeldt had admitted NHTSA's letter of May 1978 to Lee Iacocca, which informed Ford that it would hold hearings on recalling the Pinto because "when impacted by a full-sized vehicle from the rear, the 1971-1976 Pinto demonstrates a 'fire threshold' at closing speeds between 30 and 35 miles per hour." More controversial, however, was Staffeldt's permitting the jury to see the technical "investigation report" attached to the letter. As noted in Chapter 4, this report contained the crash test data—10 tests conducted on 1971, 1972, 1974, and 1976 Pintos—that led NHTSA to "its initial determination of the existence of a safety related defect." Although apparently he had not read the report, the judge said that he would "take a chance on this one" and let the jury view the letter and report; according to his rationale, the NHTSA material revealed Ford's knowledge that the government believed the Pinto was defective before the Ulrichs' accident. Given the grounds for this decision, Staffeldt also instructed the jury not to assume that the technical information in the report was necessarily accurate.

To be sure, the crash test data were an immeasurable help to the prosecution's case, but these data were only suggestive. In themselves they did not establish the extent of Ford's awareness of the Pinto's dangers, nor did they confirm that its executives had made a conscious decision to place profits over human safety. To prove Ford's motives, Cosentino knew that he would still have to convince Staffeldt to let the jury see the company's internal documents. Moreover, Cosentino wanted the judge to approve his showing the jury movies of rear-end crash tests, in which 1971 and 1972 Pintos exploded into raging infernos when struck at 35 mph. These vivid sights, he believed, would be far more powerful than sterile reports in forcing the jurors to consider why the Ulrichs' Pinto had burst into flames.

Thus, as Harley Copp took the stand, both sides were aware that he held the key to the prosecution's case. Cosentino began by establishing Copp's credentials: he had been employed by Ford since the 1940s, had risen to the number-six position in the company as an executive testing engineer, and had been forced into retirement at age 55, four years earlier, after giving safety lectures critical of the automotive industry. (Ford cited "excessive and unauthorized absences" as the reason for his dismissal.) Clearly, Copp had the engineering expertise and the first-hand knowledge to tell the Pinto story.

Now came the crucial point in Copp's testimony. Asked how new models were developed, Copp explained that automakers use a "cycle plan," in which the car's structure remained the same throughout the model's existence. Apart from cosmetic or stylistic changes, as the cycle progressed, only minor structural changes were made based on the car's performance in its earliest years.

Cosentino had the opening he needed: How long was the Pinto's cycle? How long did Ford plan to keep the same fuel system? "I believe it was for the life of the vehicle," Copp responded, "ten years." Copp then discussed the obvious implication of this remark, noting that all Pinto models were essentially the same car. A left-side frame rail was added to the 1973 make; even so, he observed, this rail increased the crashworthiness of the fuel system only from 21 to 25 mph

Cosentino believed that he had succeeded at last in laying the foundation that would enable the bulk of his documents to be admitted as evidence. After all, it seemed irrefutable that if the Pinto's structure and fuel system remained unchanged, materials on non-1973 Pintos should be admitted as evidence. In particular, crash tests and company memoranda related to pre-1973 models should be relevant because the structure of the Ulrichs' 1973 Pinto had been determined during these years.

Judge Staffeldt, however, remained unconvinced. "I don't know what more knowledge you want [to show the jury] than that they [Ford] produced that [the Ulrichs' 1973] automobile. I don't think that these things should be admitted because they allow the jury to speculate. The only thing important here is if what they failed to warn [about] caused the deaths."

"How can you lay a better foundation than we did with Copp?," Cosentino challenged. "[Ford] built a bomb in '71 and '72 and they know it. That's why they don't want it known." Refusing to budge, Staffeldt countered, "This is a criminal case, not a product liability case. Strict construction should be involved here."

Neal moved to reinforce the judge's view. As news reporters noted, Neal had developed a special rapport with Staffeldt. Whether because of the defense attorney's charm, his reputation, or his ideology, Staffeldt had "become unusually aware of Neal," even to the point of "openly anticipating objections from Neal as Cosentino presented his case." As one reporter quipped, "You'd think we were at an art auction. Maybe the judge and Neal have a set of secret signals." Most important, Staffeldt appeared to defer to Neal and to give him wide latitude in shaping the direction of the trial. "All this," observed reporters James Warren and Brian Kelly, "allowed Neal to define the case almost as he wanted."[46]

Thus, Neal bolstered Staffeldt's strict constructionist interpretation of what constituted relevant evidence. "I am concerned this will turn into a broad general examination of how a car is made or should be made," he said. "This is a criminal case." The prosecution, Neal warned, was trying to use criminal charges against Ford as a "Trojan horse" in their effort to criminalize the whole realm of product design. He concluded, "that's why I thought this case never should have been brought."

With so much at stake, the prosecution persisted. Terry Kiely took his turn: "Mr. Neal, Your Honor, would have you believe that they can make this car over the weekend. Ford had this knowledge [about the Pinto's fuel system] for years. They kept it from the public and tried to keep it from the federal government until they were pressured to recall the Pinto." As usual, Neal responded by narrowing the focus of the case. "The issue," he reasserted, "is did we recklessly fail to warn how this car [the Ulrichs' Pinto] was built. . . . We are charged with what this car is, and was—not what might have been. This car might have been a horse." Kiely replied, "Yes, it might have been a horse. But it could also have been a car that didn't incinerate three girls. The issue is what are acceptable standards of conduct."

The prosecution's arguments, however, were ineffective. Staffeldt even remarked "that there has been a lot of [prosecutorial] evidence admitted that probably should not have been admitted." A despondent Cosentino could only comment, "I don't know what I'll do now." Later he complained to the press that out of the plethora of documents, government reports, and internal Ford memos that the prosecution had compiled by the start of the trial—including the materials analyzed by

Terry Kiely—only 10 or 12 had been admitted. "We are not getting our story told," he continued. "We have a case, but we are being handicapped. It's like fighting a battle with one hand tied behind your back."

Sensing that his opponent was ready for a knockout, Jim Neal was quick to capitalize on the situation. Walking by Cosentino in the hallway of the courthouse, he taunted in a sing-song voice, "Don't lose your cool. Don't lose your cool." Still Cosentino and his crew of volunteers had come too far to throw in the towel. At first, they contemplated requesting a mistrial based on Staffeldt's rulings. This was dismissed as unfeasible; even if it succeeded, the resources simply were not available to support another trial. Instead, they would rely on Harley Copp to tell the Pinto's history. Without the documents, the story would be less compelling, but as a former Ford executive, Copp might have enough credibility to convince the jury of the company's recklessness. After all, Copp had been a devastating witness in Ford's loss of the Grimshaw civil case.

Copp did not disappoint. Following Cosentino's lead, he substantiated the prosecution's key accusations against Ford: because of intense foreign competition and at Lee Iacocca's urgings, the Pinto's parameters were set at an upper limit of $2,000 and 2,000 pounds, and subsequently the car was rushed into production without proper testing. Ford officials knew about the problems of the fuel system, and for $6.65 per car could have increased the Pinto's ability to withstand rear-end-crash fuel leakage from 20 mph to 30 mph. This proposal was rejected on the basis of "cost and the effect on profitability." In short, to enhance company profits, Ford executives allowed an "unreasonably dangerous" Pinto to be manufactured and to remain on the road.

With the help of Copp's testimony, Cosentino had been able to tell the jury the Pinto's story, but once again, this account lacked the depth and force he had anticipated. It remained uncertain how many jurors were convinced of Ford's recklessness and how their inclinations would be shaped by Neal's upcoming defense. Despite these misgivings, however, the prosecution remained optimistic. They had overcome many obstacles before the trial, and now had survived Neal's best attempts to prevent them from portraying Ford as a reckless killer. They hoped the jury might have heard enough to blame the automaker for the Ulrichs' deaths. Indeed, even Judge Staffeldt agreed that the issue of Ford's guilt should be left in the jury's hands; he rejected Neal's motion for a directed verdict of not guilty on the grounds that the prosecution had not proven its case. Ford Motor Company would still have to defend itself against charges of reckless homicide.

DEFENDING FORD: THE LEGAL MACHINE RESPONDS

As Aubrey Harwell observed, Mike Cosentino was pitted against a "legal machine." He was not only facing one of the nation's best trial lawyers in Jim Neal; he also had to confront a firm with the skill and experience to keep constant pressure on an adversary by using the vast resources at its disposal. Already, Neal and Harwell had shrewdly deployed their assets to defend Ford and keep the prosecution off balance. They had wisely hired consultant Hans Zeisel, who provided testimony that helped to win a change of venue and who assisted in the critical task of jury selection. They retained Lester Wilson, Judge Staffeldt's former office mate, to give Ford a respected local representative. Further, before coming to Winamac, Neal and Harwell's research staff had become a "brief factory," producing the legal reasoning and written documents that later persuaded Staffeldt to limit the evidence that Cosentino could present to the jury.[47] Indeed, though Cosentino was able to fend off several of these attacks, the defense's meticulously planned legal maneuvers had severely constrained his case. As he often lamented, he could not tell the jurors the full Pinto story.

Neal and Harwell would continue to benefit by their demand that nothing be overlooked or left to chance. In the preceding months, the defense's preparation had ranged from costly crash tests to an exhaustive investigation of everyone even remotely associated with the accident. The result was a formidable defense, bolstered at key points by surprising testimony.

On Wednesday, February 13, Neal opened Ford's defense with a dramatic witness, Levi Woodard. Now employed in a Michigan hospital, Woodard had been working as an orderly at Elkhart General Hospital the night of the Ulrichs' accident. Unknown to Cosentino, he had been called to Judy's side when she asked, "Does anyone know Jesus? Can anyone here say Bible verses?" As a Seventh Day Adventist, Woodard comforted her; he also talked with her about the events on Highway 33.

Until this point, no one had explained why the Ulrichs were driving away from rather than toward Goshen, where their church volleyball game was scheduled. Woodard unraveled this mystery. Judy explained that after they had stopped at a self-service gas station, they had left the cap to the gas tank on the roof. Seeing it fly off the roof and roll across the highway, she had made a U-turn to retrieve the cap and had put on her emergency flashers. Then Woodard offered a shocking revelation: Judy said that when hit by Duggar's van, her Pinto was "stopped beside the cap to get it." Neal argued that this was why the gas cap was found near the place where the van first struck the Pinto rather than down the road, where the car eventually came to rest. Moreover, Neal reasoned, Woodard's testimony exonerated Ford: any small compact car stopped on the road and hit by a 4,000-pound van traveling at 50 mph would have exploded.

Cosentino felt that Woodard's story could be disproved by the testimony of his six eyewitnesses, all of whom had said that the Pinto was moving when struck by the van. Yet he was concerned that doubts may have been raised in the jurors' minds and that the prosecution's credibility had been shaken by its obvious failure to interview Woodard during its investigation. A lesser opponent, however, would never have produced Woodard. Indeed, he was discovered only after an arduous search. Operating on a tip that someone named "Levi" had talked with Judy Ulrich, Harwell learned Woodard's full identity only after calling a former Elkhart nurse doing missionary work in Costa Rica; she gave him the name of another person who knew Woodard's name. Because Woodard was not listed in any telephone directory, Harwell dispatched two investigators—Thomas Dundon and former Dallas Cowboy Richmond Flowers—to find their potential witness. As Neal commented, "We traced him to a cabin in the woods near Levering on the first day of the Michigan deer hunting season. Have you ever heard what it's like walking through the woods when Michigan opens its deer season? The guys all wore big red hats. But they, finally found Levi—and Aubrey came in with the evidence."[48]

Having started his case with a bang, Neal wanted to establish a key technical point: Ford was not a reckless manufacturer, because the Pinto's fuel system was comparable to that of other 1973 compacts. To substantiate this claim, Neal convinced Staffeldt to allow the jury to view the rear ends of four cars (a Dodge Colt, a Chevy Vega, a Toyota Corolla, and an AMC Gremlin) that he had brought into the basement of the courthouse. Douglas W. Toms, the director of NHTSA from 1969 to 1973, was then called in to show the jurors that all the vehicles' gas tanks were located in the same general place as the Pinto's: behind the rear axle. On the stand, Toms testified further that he was "amazed" that the Pinto had been recalled, because it "did not substantially deviate" from acceptable industry standards. "It would be my opinion," he concluded, "that it was a very conventional automobile."

Reinforcing this line of reasoning, Tom Sneva, the first driver to break the 200-mph barrier at the Indianapolis 500, argued that it was safer to place a car's gas tank behind the axle. An over-the-axle design, he claimed, redistributed a car's weight and made handling more hazardous. Moreover, fuel-tank bladders, which the prosecution contended were an inexpensive means of preventing gas leakage, were costly: the one in his racing car cost $3,700.

Ford's next witness, though less famous, was also prepared to defend the company's decision not to fortify the Pinto's fuel system. Donald Huelke, a University of Michigan anatomy professor and a Ford consultant from 1964 to 1973, observed that deaths from rear-end collisions were rare events and not a major safety hazard. As a result, in his advisory capacity, he did not warn Ford that "fires on rear-end impact were a problem in the real world."

Neal's witnesses had clearly scored points on the technical issues. If nothing else, they had shown that determining where to place a gas tank is a complex decision that requires considering a number of variables. Moreover, Toms had laid the groundwork for a key element of Ford's defense: the Pinto's design was not radically different from that of other subcompacts.

In cross-examination, however, the prosecution was able to minimize the potential damage of this testimony. One strategy, which Cosentino used throughout the trial, was to show that the witnesses had a conflict of interest because at one time or another they had financial ties to Ford. Huelke had been a consultant, Sneva had driven Ford cars, and Toms's recreational vehicle company currently did a "substantial" business with the automaker. In addition, deputy prosecutors Terry Kiely and Terry Shewmaker chipped away at the witnesses' substantive testimony. Toms, for instance, admitted that it was unusual for NHTSA to recommend a recall, that he was not "personally aware" that Ford's Capri could withstand a 44-mph rear-end crash, and that Ford (like other automakers) lobbied against safety standards. Sneva revealed that the use of a fuel tank bladder had limited leakage in one of his racing accidents, and that the Indianapolis 500 Technical Committee had required drivers to insert bladders as a protective measure. Huelke conceded that he had conducted his research on rear-end fires before the production of the 1973 Pinto; furthermore, he did not know that more people died each year from such fires than from airplane accidents.

At this point, Neal decided to call to the stand Ford executives involved in the Pinto's production. He understood well the risks of this maneuver: it would give Cosentino an opportunity to question the executives in an open court before the nation's media. A misstatement or a fumbled answer could lead the jurors to impute culpability to the entire corporation and could result in news reports damaging Ford's reputation. Yet Neal also realized that much could be won if a confident and unapologetic Ford representative came willingly before the court. On the one hand, such an appearance would counteract the jurors' tendency to see Ford as an impersonal corporation; now they would have to ask themselves if the respectable person before them was a reckless killer. On the other hand, Neal feared that if he did not call someone directly associated with the Pinto to testify, Cosentino would ask why "Ford" was afraid to take the stand. Did they have something to hide? The implication would be clear: only guilty defendants remain silent and "seated at the side" of their high-priced attorneys.

Fortunately for Neal, he had the ideal candidate for Ford's corporate representative: Harold C. MacDonald, vice president of engineering and research. A 62-year-old grandfather of five and church deacon, MacDonald was Ford's engineer in charge of all passenger cars—including the Pinto—built in the United States from 1965 to 1975. In an obvious attempt to counter Cosentino's depiction of the Pinto as Lee Iacocca's car, Neal referred to MacDonald as the "father of the Pinto." He also told reporters that "big companies are made up of people like Mr. MacDonald—good decent people, people doing the best they can in a difficult world."[49] Decent people may make mistakes, but they do not recklessly endanger the lives of teenagers in the crass pursuit of profits.

Showing the human dimension of the automaking industry, MacDonald explained why he had a "great personal concern about the placement of the fuel tank in the 1973 Pinto." In 1932, his father had been burned to death when his Model A Ford hit a tree. The gas tank, located between the engine and the passenger compartment—almost in his "father's lap"—had exploded upon impact. This event convinced MacDonald that the fuel system should be placed "as far from the passenger compartment as possible"; the Pinto, with its tank behind the rear axle, met this criterion.

Personal history aside, MacDonald was proud of the Pinto and ready to defend its record. First, he denied Harley Copp's charge that the Pinto was ever "locked into" the $2,000 and 2,000-pound limits— the rigid standards reportedly dictated by Lee Iacocca. Second, he felt that the car's fuel system was "reasonably safe." After all, the Pinto in question met all 1973 federal regulations, and even satisfied a voluntary internal Ford standard that the car be able to withstand a 20-mph rear-end collision from a moving barrier—a standard that no other American automaker had in force. Moreover, objective statistical data confirmed his assessment of the Pinto's safety. A 1975-1976 federal study indicated that Pintos constituted 1.9 percent of all cars on the nation's highways and were involved in 1.9 percent of all fatal accidents involving fire. Clearly, a recklessly designed car would have been overrepresented rather than represented proportionately in its share of such fatalities. Third, from an engineering perspective, MacDonald believed that placing the tank above the axle was not desirable. The danger of this design, he claimed, was that during a collision, the tank was more vulnerable to puncture by unsecured items inside the trunk. Fourth, and what was perhaps MacDonald's most convincing testimony that he believed in the Pinto's safety, he drove a 1973 Pinto and had bought one for his son.

Cosentino quickly launched a vigorous cross-examination. He began by demonstrating MacDonald's personal stake in Ford's well-being. In the previous year, he had been paid $195,000 in salary and another $200,000 in bonuses; he also owned nearly $450,000 in company stocks. Cosentino then disputed the Pinto's safety record by introducing statistics indicating that the Pinto was not represented proportionately in fatal rear-end accidents in which a fire occurred—as Ford claimed—but rather was involved in such accidents two times more often than would normally be expected. The data showed that by 1976, Pintos comprised 3.5 percent of all automobiles on U.S. roads, yet were involved in 7 percent of these fatal fire crashes. MacDonald responded weakly, "I am not familiar with those statistics." He also admitted that he did not know the Pinto was the only 1973 subcompact recalled by the government. Cosentino continued to score points for the prosecution when MacDonald said that he did not believe Ford could have built a 1973 Pinto that would be able to withstand a rear-end collision at 43 or 44 mph. This statement presented Cosentino with the opportunity to show the jury a 1969 advertisement in which Ford stated that its Capri, manufactured in Great Britain, could indeed safely withstand impact at this speed. Finally, Cosentino made an observation about Ford's internal standard requiring the Pinto's fuel system to have integrity in a 20-mph moving-barrier rear-end crash test: in an equivalent highway crash, the car would begin to leak fuel if hit at a speed greater than 26 to 28 mph.[50] "But," Cosentino asked, "didn't this mean that it could not withstand a collision at the 30-mph speed limit on most residential streets?" And when Ford recalled the Pinto, did they ever warn consumers, such as the Ulrichs, that their vehicles were "subject to fire on rear-end impact" if hit at a speed greater than 28 mph?

In response, Jim Neal called a series of witnesses to repair the damage done by Cosentino's cross-examination. Two Ford engineering executives came forward to testify that they allowed family members to drive Pintos. Particularly effective was James G. Olson, who had bought a 1973 Pinto for his 18-year-old daughter, the same age as Judy and Donna Ulrich. "Would you have purchased it if you didn't think it was safe?" asked Neal. "Most certainly not," replied Olson.

James J. Schultz, a 24-year Chrysler employee, who at the time of the trial was employed by a California engineering firm, reiterated that the Pinto was "certainly comparable, and in some respects was superior" to other subcompacts. He also contended that his analysis of the evidence led him to conclude that the Ulrichs' Pinto was stopped and hit at a speed of 60 mph. The car's structure, he added, "did quite well in light of the speeds involved." Cosentino succeeded, however, in diminishing Schultz's credibility. He showed not only that Schultz was being paid $41 an hour for his testimony (and that another $24 was going to the firm he represented), but also that Ford's "expert" witness did not know at what speed the Pinto experienced hazardous gas leakages. Further, Schultz claimed that when a 1973 Pinto was hit from behind by a moving barrier at a test speed of 21 mph, the welds on the floor-pan would not split and make it possible for fuel to spill into the passenger compartment. This claim contradicted earlier testimony by Harold MacDonald, "the father of the Pinto," who had admitted that such splits were possible. An elated Cosentino announced to reporters, "I think the state's case against Ford is getting better with every witness Ford produces."

Engineering vice-president Thomas J. Feaheny was brought forward to explain why Ford recalled the Pinto. He asserted that the company did not recall the car because it was dangerous, but only because adverse publicity about the Pinto's alleged fuel-system defects had become "a critical problem—damaging our corporate reputation." By reaching an agreement with NHTSA on how to modify the Pinto, he continued, Ford felt "it would reassure our owners and the public of the company's good intentions on the matter." To substantiate this claim, Feaheny produced 1975-1976 data revealing that the Pinto had a similar if not a lower incidence of fire-related crashes during that time than five other subcompacts. He also testified that this information was compiled because of escalating public concern, and was presented to Ford's Board of Directors in March 1978. In light of the data, the corporation's "state of mind" was that the Pinto was as safe as comparable subcompacts.

Again, Cosentino was able to blunt the effectiveness of the prosecution's witness. He forced Feaheny to state that he was unaware of government statistics indicating that the Pinto's fuel system was more fire-prone in rear-end collisions than other models in its class. More important, Feaheny conceded that he did not inform the company's directors about Ford's own crash tests, which showed that a 1973 Pinto would suffer fuel leakage at relatively low speeds.

Neal now embarked on a second line of attack against the prosecution's case. Thus far, he had attempted to show that the Ulrich teenagers did not die because Ford had designed their Pinto's fuel system recklessly. The testimony, he hoped, had established three major conclusions: (1) the speed difference between Duggar's van and the Ulrichs' Pinto was so great that any car would have exploded in flames; (2) Ford had complied with all federal regulations and the Pinto was comparable to other subcompacts; and (3) the good people at Ford, including engineers directly involved in the Pinto's production, believed so strongly in the car's safety that they purchased Pintos for their spouses and children. Yet, even if the jurors were unconvinced of these points, Ford's conviction on charges of reckless homicide did not necessarily follow. According to pretrial rulings (as discussed in Chapter 5), the prosecution had to demonstrate that Ford had not only built a dangerous vehicle but also had been reckless in its failure to recall the Pinto during the 41 days between the implementation of Indiana's reckless homicide statute and the Ulrichs' deaths on August 10, 1978.

Fortuitous circumstances made this side of the prosecution's case especially vulnerable to attack. On June 9, 1978, three weeks before the Indiana statute took effect, Ford had agreed with NHTSA to recall the Pinto. As a result, a full recall effort was under way throughout the 41-day period in which the company's recklessness was in question. Furthermore, Neal was prepared to show that Ford had done "everything possible" to contact Pinto owners, including the Ulrichs.

Ronald Hoffman, a 32-year-old supervisor with Ford's parts and services division, testified that once the decision to recall the Pinto had been made, he was told to "drop what I was doing and work on this as quickly as possible. . . . We did everything we could, with no cost constraints and no time constraints, in order to get this done as quickly as possible." Although the company worked around the clock and even hired planes to rush parts to dealers, Hoffman noted, the recall was a complicated task that required time to complete. Not only did the addresses of Pinto owners have to be traced, but the kits used to modify the Pinto had to be manufactured. These kits contained 16 pieces, including a longer filler tube and a plastic shield to prevent tank punctures. These items were not ready to be shipped until August 9, one day before the Ulrichs' deaths. Recall notices were not distributed until later that month. The first person to own the Ulrichs' Pinto was sent a letter on August 22.

Neal's advantage dissipated quickly, however. In a surprise move, Cosentino attempted to introduce evidence that in February 1973 Ford was convicted of 350 criminal counts of filing false reports to the Environmental Protection Agency and was fined a total of $7 million ($3.5 million in criminal penalties and $3.5 million in civil damages). This crime occurred in 1972, when Ford performed unauthorized maintenance on test vehicles and submitted falsified data certifying that the emission levels of its 1973-model-year cars (including the Pinto) met the standards prescribed by the 1968 Clean Air Act.

This evidence should be admitted, the prosecution argued, for three reasons. First, although prior convictions normally could not be used in court because they would bias a jury unduly against a defendant, Indiana law stated that such convictions were admissible when they were related to a defendant's reputation for truthfulness, and that a court had no discretion to exclude "anything having to do with false and fictitious representations" by a defendant. Clearly, Ford's attempt to deceive the Environmental Protection Agency (EPA) fell into this category. Second, the convictions were related directly to 1973 models and thus met Staffeldt's demand that the prosecution restrict evidence to the year in which the Ulrichs' Pinto was manufactured. Third, because Ford executives were testifying on behalf of the company—and were portrayed as "churchgoers" and "family men"—the prosecution had the right to impeach their testimony by introducing evidence regarding Ford's corporate character. "The jury," Bruce Berner told Staffeldt, "has the right to know that Ford has not been truthful in the past." By contrast, Neal argued that it was inappropriate to use information about a corporation to cast suspicion on the testimony of an individual.

After hearing legal arguments for more than an hour, Staffeldt announced that although this was "a novel question of law," he would admit the evidence on Ford's convictions because it tended to show "the poor reputation of the defendant for truth and veracity." The jurors were then allowed to read the details of Ford's earlier brush with the law.

Neal immediately took steps to reaffirm the integrity of Ford's corporate character. Herbert Misch, a company vice president, was called to explain what had transpired. He stated that only lower-echelon employees had falsified records, and no one who had testified in the current case was involved. More instructive, after the matter was brought to his attention, Misch met with Henry Ford II, who told him "to investigate this and make it right." In turn, the company notified EPA of the misinformation and eventually pleaded "no contest" to the criminal charges.

Outside the courtroom, the usually restrained Neal was "openly distressed" about Staffeldt's ruling. In a "booming voice" he vigorously defended Ford's handling of the EPA situation. Noting that his client "blew the whistle" on itself, he claimed that this was "not only Ford Motor Company's but American industry's finest hour. . . . All these people [who] go around talking about immorality should applaud, not condemn us." Privately, however, Neal was worried that even though Ford admitted its EPA transgressions, the evidence might prove "devastating." As one of his associates commented, "You can imagine what this will do to the jury—to continually hear how we were convicted for lying about our 1973 cars."

Indeed, the second week of the defense's case had not gone well. Although Hoffman's testimony on Ford's recall efforts was persuasive, Cosentino had effectively cross-examined several witnesses—most notably Harold MacDonald, proclaimed by Neal himself to be "the Pinto's father"—and had won a rare legal victory on the EPA convictions. Cosentino had reason to tell reporters that "our case gets stronger and stronger as the defense continues. The longer this trial goes, the better I feel."

Over the weekend, however, Neal worked to halt the prosecution's momentum. He captured the attention of the press by promising to close his defense the following week with a "bomb." Headlines were no longer reporting, "Week's Testimony Shakes Ford's Pinto Defense" or "Ford Lawyer Becomes Upset." Instead, everyone was waiting to learn "how he would produce a document this week which would devastate the prosecution's case like a 'bomb.'"[51] Jim Neal had a history of fulfilling his promises.

On Monday, February 25, Herbert Misch continued his testimony. Building on Hoffman's earlier description of Ford's recall efforts, Misch noted not only that everything possible was being done to notify Pinto owners but also that the whole recall effort was being regulated by NHTSA. Furthermore, if Ford had followed all conditions set down by NHTSA, how could the company have been reckless during the 41 days in which they had a legal responsibility to Pinto owners?

Cosentino, however, contended that Ford did not simply have an obligation to repair the vehicles but also had a duty to warn people like the Ulrichs as soon as possible that they were driving a potentially lethal car. Thus, he asked Misch whether Ford's June 9 press release announcing the Pinto's recall told owners not to drive their cars until the defect in the fuel tank could be fixed, or whether the company subsequently had taken television or newspaper advertisements cautioning its customers of the full extent of the Pinto's dangers. In response, Misch asserted that because the Pinto was recalled merely to protect Ford's corporate reputation and not because of any alleged hazards, it would have been "ridiculous" to ask "one and a half million or more people not to drive their vehicles . . . and the one they'd be getting into would be no more safe than the Pinto." It remained to be determined whether the jury believed that Ford had fulfilled its duty to the Ulrichs by feverishly embarking on a recall effort, or whether the company was reckless because it did not warn owners immediately and publicly that their Pintos might explode when struck from the rear at less than 30 mph.

Now Neal was ready to launch his "bomb" at the prosecution: he had crash-test data indicating that the Ulrichs' Pinto was hit at a speed of 50 to 55 mph. John D. Habberstad, a Spokane, Washington, mechanical engineer and accident reconstruction expert, had been hired to conduct a series of tests in which a Pinto and comparable 1973 subcompacts were struck by a 1972 Chevy van identical to Robert Duggar's. The price of conducting this experiment was substantial: Habberstad was paid a consultant's fee of approximately $22,000, and each of the nine crash tests cost between $8,000 and $9,000. Nonetheless, winning, not money, was the prime consideration of Neal's legal machine.

Over the prosecution's strenuous objections, Judge Staffeldt ruled that the jury could see films of the crash tests because "any scientific demonstration of the evidence is encouraged by the court." In the key test, a 1973 Pinto sedan was hit by the van at 50.3 mph. Red stoddard solvent, used as a substitute for fuel so that no fires would occur, gushed from the Pinto's gas tank. Moreover, the rear end of the test Pinto was "crushed a little bit less than the actual accident vehicle," suggesting that the Ulrichs' car had been struck by a vehicle traveling above the 50.3 mph test speed; Habberstad estimated the speed difference at 55 mph. The implication was clear: the teenagers' Pinto must have been stopped when hit by Duggar's van.

The jury was shown the films of five other tests that involved four subcompacts—a Vega, a Colt, a Gremlin, and a Corolla—and a full-sized Chevrolet Impala. In each instance, stoddard solvent leaked from the cars' fuel tanks. These data, Habberstad concluded, indicated that virtually any car would be a fire hazard if hit at 50 mph. Further, he claimed that a protective device or plastic shield, such as that contained in the recall modification kit, would not have prevented a fire in the Ulrichs' Pinto. In a high-speed rear-end collision, fuel does not leak because external objects puncture the gas tank, but because the buildup of liquid pressure inside the tank causes a rupture. "A plastic shield," Habberstad remarked, "will not prevent a hydrostatic burst."

As reporter Lee Strobel observed, the defense had presented its "most dramatic evidence" that the Ulrichs' fiery crash "involved an impact more powerful than eyewitnesses reported."[52] Cosentino scrambled to recoup the losses inflicted by Habberstad's engrossing crash-test films and expert "scientific" testimony. To prepare the next day's cross-examination strategy, he worked far into the night with his staff. He would launch a counterattack on several fronts.

First, Cosentino noted not only that Habberstad was paid a hefty consultant's fee by Ford, but also that he had conducted his supposedly "independent" experiments at the company's own testing grounds in Dearborn, Michigan. Second, he asked Habberstad if the testimony of numerous eyewitnesses who saw the Ulrichs' Pinto moving would cause him to change his assessment. The point, of course, was that it was difficult to reconcile the test results with the accounts of those who had actually witnessed the accident. Third, he forced Habberstad to admit that the dummies used to represent drivers or passengers in a crash test "would be thrown around quite violently" in a high-speed collision. The Ulrichs, however, had not been "thrown around" in their Pinto, and they had not sustained the kind of serious bodily harm one would expect in a 50-mph crash. Indeed, medical testimony had established that they would have survived the accident if their Pinto had not burst into flames. In the same vein, why hadn't Habberstad's tests included cameras that filmed what happened to the dummies inside the crash vehicles? Didn't he "want the jury to see that people are seriously injured, maybe killed, without fire at those speeds"? Fourth, Cosentino noted that if the Pinto had been stopped when hit by Duggar's van, glass and underbody debris would have fallen to the ground at the point of the impact; after all, this is what had occurred in Habberstad's Pinto crash test. Yet the debris found on Highway 33 was scattered 24 to 113 feet down the road, thus indicating that the Ulrichs' Pinto must have been moving. Fifth, Cosentino questioned Habberstad about a four-page report on "vehicle fires" that he had presented at a 1971 accident seminar in Portland, Oregon. Hadn't he written that "fuel tanks located near the perimeter of a vehicle"—like the Pinto's—were "particularly susceptible to damage during an impact between two vehicles"?

Despite Cosentino's inventive and unrelenting cross-examination, Habberstad was not an easy witness to shake.[53] He claimed, for example, that the Ulrichs may not have suffered serious injuries because "the back end of the Pinto was forced forward 38 inches, which gives you a big sponge, the big cushion that allows the riders to adjust to the change in velocity." Similarly, he disputed the contention that no debris was found at the point of impact between the van and the Pinto. A close examination of the photograph of the accident scene revealed fragments of debris at the contact point; the rest of the glass and underbody pieces could have been propelled down the road by Duggar's moving vehicle. Moreover, Habberstad offered, his examination of the Ulrichs' Pinto indicated that the damage sustained by one of the support posts meant that the car door was open at the time of impact. This fact also explained, he continued, why the gas cap was discovered close to where the Pinto was initially struck and not down the road, where it eventually came to a halt: the car was stopped and someone was opening the door to retrieve the cap.

To be sure, Habberstad did not counter all of Cosentino's attacks. Yet, when taken in conjunction with Levi Woodard's claim that the Pinto was stopped, his testimony might have raised enough uncertainty about the speed difference between the Pinto and the van to create a "reasonable doubt" in the jurors' minds regarding Ford's guilt. Consequently, Cosentino knew that once the defense rested its case, he would have to make the most of his opportunity to introduce rebuttal witnesses and evidence.

Neal had planned to conclude his case with the "bomb" of the crash test films. A late development, however, changed his mind. Once again, his insistence that every possible lead be explored, regardless of cost, proved critical. After Levi Woodard's surprise testimony, Cosentino sent his investigators to Elkhart General Hospital to see if any evidence disputing Woodard's account could be discovered. In response, Neal arranged for a South Bend attorney to "hang around" the hospital in case this new inquiry produced information that supported the defense's case. His hunch was accurate: prompted by the prosecution's investigation, hospital employees started to discuss the accident, a topic that had faded from their daily conversations. Through the grapevine, Neal's representative learned that another person had talked with Judy Ulrich as she lay near death in the emergency room: Nancy E. Fogo, the hospital's nursing supervisor for the evening shift on August 10.

Fogo testified that after encountering Levi Woodard and hearing his explanation of the accident, she went to talk with Judy. "I told her. . . . 'I understand that it was really a bad situation out there on [Highway] 33.' She said, 'Yes.'" Fogo continued, "'I understand you stopped on 33. Did you have car troubles?' She said, 'Yes I stopped,' and then something about the gas cap."

A startled Cosentino desperately assaulted Fogo's story. Judy had been through a "holocaust" and was under "heavy sedation" from painkillers. How could she accurately recount, Cosentino asked, what had occurred on Highway 33? Fogo noted, however, that Judy was able to provide telephone numbers where her parents and an aunt might be reached to tell them about the accident. Refusing to lessen the pressure, Cosentino observed that Judy's lips had been burned off, and that it could not have been possible to understand fully what she was saying. How could she talk? "Using her teeth," Fogo replied. "I believe, sir, she said, 'Yes, I was stopped.'" Cosentino demanded that she try to say "stop" without using her lips. Holding her lips back and speaking through her teeth, Fogo's muffled response sounded something like "stot."[54]

Outside the courtroom, an elated Jim Neal announced to reporters, "Cosentino challenged us to stop that Pinto. Well, now we've stopped it twice." Meanwhile, Michael Cosentino knew that his case had been damaged, and that winning Ford's conviction would hinge on the effectiveness of his upcoming rebuttal. He was optimistic, however, that he had the witnesses to demonstrate that the Ulrichs' Pinto was moving and that the three teenagers should not have perished in a fiery crash.

THE VERDICT

Taken together, Habberstad's crash test and the testimony of Levi Woodard and Nancy Fogo presented a strong challenge to the prosecution's assertion that the speed difference between Duggar's van and the Ulrichs' Pinto was so low that only a defective vehicle would have exploded on impact. Clearly, Neal had succeeded in raising doubts about Ford's guilt. In a high-speed collision, deaths might be blamed on careless driving, on an unfortunate sequence of fateful events, or on a market economy that demanded affordable though less safe cars, but the blame could not be placed on corporate recklessness.

To combat this assessment of responsibility for the Ulrichs' deaths, Cosentino prepared a rebuttal case that he felt would show the jury that the speed difference between the van and the Pinto was not nearly as great as the defense claimed. He planned to use Fred Arndt, an accident reconstruction specialist, to counter Habberstad's testimony by demonstrating that the maximum speed of impact was approximately 40 mph. Robert Stein, the pathologist who had performed the autopsy on Judy Ulrich, could be relied upon to state that her injuries were inconsistent with those typically sustained in high-speed collisions. Neil Graves would also be called back to the stand. He would suggest that Habberstad's test results overestimated the speed difference because the wooden bumper on Duggar's van was smaller than the bumper on the van used in the crash experiments and because the rear end of Ulrichs' car was rusted and hence more susceptible to crushing than the test Pinto. Further, Graves's testimony would be used to show how particular features of the accident scene—for example, the distribution of debris on the highway and the pattern of fire inside the Pinto—supported the conclusion that a defective fuel system and not a high-velocity impact caused the Pinto to catch fire.

Most important, Cosentino had his own "bomb" to drop on the defense: Frank C. Camps, a 15-year Ford employee who had retired in 1978. A veteran of more than 200 crash tests on Ford vehicles, Camps was ready to reveal that company personnel had rigged or misreported a number of tests that failed to meet federal regulations, and would "do whatever was necessary to pass a test." The implication was clear: given the company's less than reputable history, could the jury trust crash tests that were conducted at Ford facilities by a highly paid consultant?

Jim Neal moved quickly to ensure that the jury would not hear any of Cosentino's potentially damaging rebuttal. Citing a 1959 decision, Neal argued that in no instance was the prosecution permitted to "split its case" by reserving evidence for its rebuttal that could have been presented earlier in the trial. Instead, the prosecution had an obligation to present all evidence on a specific point during its original "case-in-chief" so that the defense would have the full opportunity to dispute the allegation. In light of this ruling, Neal asserted forcefully, "we object to any further testimony as to closing speed" between the van and the Pinto. After all, Graves and Stein had already testified, while Arndt and Camps were available and could have been called to the stand when the prosecution made its case against the defendant.

Bruce Berner retorted for the prosecution that throughout the trial Ford had endeavored to steer the evidence "to the posture they want and then close off any additional testimony." Further, he contended, the Indiana Supreme Court had ruled that expert testimony at this phase of the trial could "explain, contradict, or disprove" evidence presented by the defense. Rebuttal evidence is not limited to new evidence. Therefore, although it is inappropriate to repeat testimony, the court may admit information that specifically rebuts evidence offered by the defense in its case. On the basis of this principle, Berner reasoned, it became clear why the prosecution should be allowed to call its witnesses: because Neal had introduced crash-test data related directly to the issue of "closing speeds," the jury should be allowed to hear the prosecution's rebuttal evidence on this point.

Both sides anxiously awaited Staffeldt's critical ruling. Calling the decision "probably one of the toughest issues in the trial," the judge stated that it would be "an abuse of discretion if the court permitted the prosecution to separate its case-in-chief and its rebuttal." Consequently, the prosecution would not be allowed to present any evidence that "could have been produced in the case-in-chief and was available at that time."

In effect, Staffeldt's decision scuttled Cosentino's rebuttal case. Once again, Neal had maneuvered to create a legal obstacle that the prosecution could not surmount; once again, the full "Pinto story" would not be told inside the Pulaski County courthouse. In the end, Arndt, Stein, and Camps were not allowed to testify; meanwhile, Neil Graves was forced to limit his comments to several minor points related only tangentially to the issue of the speed difference between the van and the Pinto.[55] Later, Cosentino decided not to place on the stand a statistical consultant who was prepared to dispute Ford's claim that the Pinto was as safe as other subcompacts. Not wanting to "end with a statistical argument," he chose instead to rest the prosecution's case.

After Staffeldt's ruling, a disquieted and frustrated Cosentino refused—for the first time—to attend the daily briefing with media representatives. As one reporter noted, the "state's case had reached its nadir"; indeed, an "angry depression" hung over the entire team of prosecution lawyers as the prospects for winning Ford's conviction seemed to be slipping away.[56]

Cosentino was not one to remain gloomy for long, however; he still had reason to be hopeful. For one thing, though Judge Staffeldt reserved the right to overrule the jury's decision, he had rejected Neal's request for a directed verdict that would acquit his client. "We will submit this case to the jury," Staffeldt commented. In addition, final arguments still lay ahead, and this stage of the trial would present Cosentino with another opportunity to convince the jury of Ford's culpability. "We haven't been able to tell our entire story," he noted, "but I think it will be sufficient when we tie it up in final argument." Outwardly, at least, Cosentino's confidence had returned.

On Monday morning, March 10, Cosentino rose to address the jury for the last time. His remarks were couched on two levels: a technical discussion of the evidence and a consideration of the moral issues at stake. There were sound evidentiary reasons, he claimed, for blaming Ford's recklessness for the Ulrichs' deaths. Even Ford executives had testified that the Pinto could not safely withstand a rear-end crash at the speed limit in effect on most city streets, including downtown Winamac. "Do you know what happens to a Pinto when it's hit at a speed between 26 and 28 mph?" he asked. "It blows up." Moreover, he asked, could the jury really believe Ford's contention that it recalled a car that had "nothing wrong with it?" After all, this company not only was convicted of 350 counts of lying to the government, but also made $1.5 billion in 1978 profits. Yet it would not invest another $6.65 per car to ensure that Pintos like the Ulrichs' were free from a lethal fuel-system defect. And what of the defendant's allegation that the Pinto was comparable to other 1973 subcompacts? Well, said Cosentino, "this is like an accused burglar defending his actions because other people burgled."

Most important, however, the impact of the collision on Highway 33 "did not kill Judy, Donna, and Lyn. Were it not for the Pinto, they would be with us today." Ford, Cosentino continued, wished to deflect blame by arguing that any car would have exploded into flames; but what was their evidence? Crash tests conducted by a paid consultant? Conversations with a dying girl who had just been through a "holocaust"? By contrast, the prosecution had offered two incontrovertible facts: a number of eyewitnesses all agreed that the Pinto was moving when struck, and the girls' injuries were consistent with a low-speed collision. "If the crash doesn't kill you," Cosentino asserted, "the car shouldn't kill you."

Yet larger moral issues were also at stake. Waving three death certificates before the jurors' eyes, Cosentino demanded that the jury "give meaning to these senseless deaths." A wrong had been committed, and now the scales of justice must be balanced. Nothing could bring the Ulrich girls back to life, of course; but the jury did have the power to prevent others from suffering tragic fates at the hands of socially irresponsible corporations. Indeed, by convicting Ford Motor Company on charges of reckless homicide, Cosentino reminded the jurors, they would be "planting the seeds of needed corporate moral responsibility. You can send a message that can be heard in all the large boardrooms in this country. . . . All America awaits your verdict."

Neal's final argument contested Cosentino's interpretation of the evidence and raised a different set of moral issues. On a moral level, he disputed Ford's portrayal as a big business blindly pursuing profits in disregard of potential human costs. To be sure, the company "may not be perfect, but it is not guilty of reckless homicide." The Pinto was not the creation of crass capitalists but of "honest men who honestly believed the 1973 Pinto was a reasonably safe car, so safe that they bought it for their wives and children." They followed all federal regulations in the car's construction and even went so far as to implement voluntarily their own standard for fuel leakage in rear-end crashes. What other automaker could make this claim? Further, once Ford executives agreed to recall the Pinto rather than lose the confidence of consumers, they acted vigorously. During the 41-day period in which the company was legally liable under Indiana's reckless homicide statute, what more could they have done to contact the Ulrichs and give them the opportunity to modify their Pinto?

Neal also warned the jury that their verdict would have profound implications for the future of American business. "If this country is to survive economically," he cautioned, "we've got to stop blaming industry and business for our own sins. No car is now or ever can be said to be safe with reckless drivers [like Duggar] on the road." Particularly dangerous, he continued, was the attempt to preempt federal regulations with the personal biases of local prosecutors—prosecutors like Michael Cosentino. "What chaos it would involve if the federal government set standards, but state prosecutors started saying, 'I'm not satisfied.' How can any company survive?" It was the jurors' moral duty, Neal concluded, to halt the increasingly dangerous practice of vilifying corporations and undermining the nation's economic strength.

Beyond this broader issue, the hard facts substantiated the claim that Duggar's van hit the girls' Pinto at such a high speed that it "made no difference what kind of car" had been involved in the collision. Neal claimed that any comparable subcompact—if not any larger car—would have suffered fuel leakage and a fire. Indeed, all evidence supported the defense's view that the Pinto was not moving. Thus, the car door was open and the gas cap was found close to the initial point of impact, "right where it would have been" if the girls had "stopped to retrieve the cap." Scientific crash tests and analysis corroborated this interpretation, showing that the speed difference was greater than 50 mph. Most important, both Levi Woodard and Nancy Fogo testified that Judy Ulrich had told them her Pinto was stopped.[57]

With final arguments concluded, Pulaski County's crowded courtroom began to disperse. The room had been filled by an odd mixture of people whose social circles touched infrequently—lawyers with small and large reputations, local and national news reporters of all sorts, corporate executives, and rural Hoosiers—all drawn together by historical circumstance and a celebrated trial. Meanwhile, the jury faced the task of making sense of 29 days of testimony that resulted in nearly 6,000 pages of transcripts, 22 prosecution and 19 defense witnesses, and 200 exhibits introduced as evidence.[58] It was Monday afternoon, but they would not reach consensus on a verdict until Thursday morning, after 25 ballots had been taken.

The first vote was eight for acquittal and four for conviction. The majority voted for acquittal for a variety of reasons. First, they "felt the state never presented enough evidence to convince us that Ford was guilty." They felt a "little shortchanged" at not seeing more of Cosentino's information on 1971 and 1972 Pintos, but they had to decide on the basis of what was presented to them. Second, although they believed that the Ulrichs' Pinto was moving when the collision occurred, they thought the prosecution had failed to establish the exact speed at impact. Some jurors doubted that any Pinto, even if equipped with a recall modification kit, could have withstood the force of Duggar's van. Third, many jurors felt that the Pinto "was not safe enough"; nonetheless, the lack of safety was inherent in small cars, and the Pinto was not that much worse than comparable subcompacts. Moreover, "the American public has the right to choose whether they want to purchase that product." Fourth, and perhaps most important, the jurors believed that during the 41 days in which Ford was legally liable, the company did everything in its power to recall the Pinto. Ronald Hoffman, the Ford employee who supervised the recall, had been a particularly effective witness. As one juror commented, Hoffman was "an average working guy—truthful, honest and straightforward, and he could prove everything he said. He left no doubt in my mind that Ford did all that it could between June and August 10."[59]

As the deliberations continued, support for Ford's conviction weakened. By Wednesday evening, the jury voted 10 to two for acquittal. The two jurors in the minority remained convinced of Ford's guilt, and talks continued far into the night. Shortly before midnight, Staffeldt called the jury into the courtroom. He was prepared to read them the special instructions that typically are given only when a judge anticipates a strong possibility of a mistrial. Staffeldt had begun to fear this possibility after learning from Arthur Selmer, the jury's foreman, that the existing deadlock seemed unlikely to be broken.

"If you fail to reach a verdict," stated Staffeldt, "this case will be open and unresolved. Another trial would be a burden on both parties." He added, "There is no reason to believe that the case can be tried any better than it has been . . . [or] that a more intelligent or competent jury would be selected."

Staffeldt's prompting had an effect. By 2:00 A.M., one juror had changed her mind, making the vote 11–1. James Yurgilas was the lone holdout, but he was steadfast in his opinion that Ford was responsible for the Ulrichs' deaths. At 3:00, Selmer told Staffeldt that he was "very doubtful" a verdict could be reached. Nonetheless, the judge ordered the jurors to return at 10:00. If no decision was reached by the end of Thursday, Staffeldt would accept the existence of a "hung jury." He would then have to choose whether to declare a mistrial or whether to issue a verdict himself.

After a sleepless night, James Yurgilas reluctantly changed his mind, although convinced that the Pinto "was a reckless automobile. . . . On the other point you couldn't actually prove they [Ford] didn't do everything in their power to recall it. . . . They got off on a loophole." After more than 25 hours of deliberations, suddenly the 10-week trial was over. In a courtroom filled to twice its 48-seat capacity, Arthur Selmer delivered three envelopes containing the jury's verdict, one for each of the three reckless homicide charges.

As Judge Staffeldt ripped open the first envelope, suspense gripped the courtroom. His announcement: "We, the jury, find the defendant not guilty." These words were repeated twice more.

In the presence of reporters from nearly every major newspaper and television network, a triumphant Jim Neal stated that he was "grateful, relieved, and proud, and I thought the verdict was fully justified." He added that "the Pinto has been maligned for years, but we were tried by a jury of twelve people in the heartland of America and all twelve found us not guilty. That says something." At corporate headquarters in Dearborn, Michigan, news of the verdict interrupted a board meeting. Sitting around a horseshoe-shaped table, 18 corporate directors cheered loudly. By coincidence, the directors had assembled that day to see Henry Ford II retire and relinquish control of Ford Motor Company to Philip Caldwell, the first non-Ford since 1906 to head the company.[60]

Judge Staffeldt was reluctant to comment on the case, only remarking, "I won't quarrel with the verdict. It was the right one." Later he admitted that he might have acquitted Ford if there had been a hung jury, but he would not have overruled the jurors if they had found Ford guilty.

In stark contrast to the jubilation expressed by the defense, Cosentino and his band of volunteers could not hide their bitter disappointment. Asked for his reaction, Cosentino interpreted the verdict as meaning "that manufacturers can make any kind of car they want and it's up to the public to decide if they want to buy it or not." Given some time to reflect, however, he added that the trial would have at least one positive result. "It will make large corporations understand they can be brought to trial with twelve citizens sitting in judgment on decisions of the corporation—that boardroom decisions can be scrutinized by a jury."[61]

Finally, two days after the end of the trial, the Ulrich family wrote to Cosentino to "express our feelings." They thanked him for "being very patient with us" and for "keeping us informed about what is going on." "When we think about all the things that have taken place in the last year and a half," they continued, "and what motivated you and your staff to spend endless hours on the investigation of the Pinto . . . we admit we ask why us?" They also noted that "God has allowed us to be here for a reason. We are involved if we want to be or not. We realize you were limited in the evidence you were allowed to present. You did very well and need not be ashamed in any of your actions." They concluded, "We also have a moral obligation in the future of other peoples' lives. Our prayers are with you and your staff and families."[62]

Epilogue

It was over. For more than a year and a half, Mike Cosentino and his fellow prosecutors had been enmeshed in a case that had earned continued national attention. Before the Ulrichs' tragic deaths on August 10, 1978, the members of the prosecution team could not have predicted that historical circumstance would present them with an opportunity to participate in a landmark criminal trial. Further, to a large extent, none of the prosecutors could have anticipated what this trial would have meant for their lives. Their families, their regular offices, and their normal routines were replaced by a pressure-filled, absorbing crusade in which lawyers, a rural courtroom, and media representatives became part of their everyday landscape.

Today the Pinto trial remains a vivid memory, but not a dominant part of their lives. Even today, Michael Cosentino continues to carry the label of the "Ford Pinto prosecutor," and the law professors still use the case as an example when teaching about such topics as product liability and corporate crime, and as a bridge to show where private and public meet to exert social control over corporations. Yet, after the flurry of attention immediately following the end of the trial on March 13, 1980 (Cosentino, for instance, appeared on ABC's "Good Morning America"), they largely resumed their former lives. Cosentino returned to Elkhart, where he served a total of seven terms as a popular conservative Republican prosecutor while he also maintained a thriving civil practice—including taking on numerous product liability and personal injury claims that drew upon his Pinto experience. Terry Shewmaker remained his chief assistant and law partner for several years after the trial until he left to become a judge in northern Indiana. Bruce Berner returned to Valparaiso University, where he still teaches law and serves in an administrative post, while Terry Kiely continued at DePaul. Though both Berner and Kiely had planned to write about the case, neither one ended up penning a single word. Both felt too exhausted after having invested so much of themselves in the case, and felt that any work product might contain more emotional than intellectual content.[63] Perhaps the largest change took place in Neil Graves's life. Although he continued to serve as an Indiana State Trooper, he became involved in a newly formed white-collar crime unit that investigated offenses such as the illegal dumping of toxic waste products and other environmental crimes.

The members of the prosecution also had to adjust emotionally. Not only had they experienced a draining trial; they also had to come to grips with a stinging defeat. At first, the bitterness of the loss and the frustration of not having told the "whole story" did not wane. They were plagued by a sense that justice had not been served. In time, however, they were consoled by the realization that while they had failed to prove Ford's recklessness, they had succeeded in bringing Ford to trial. This success was critical, they believed, because it showed that "corporations can be prosecuted for any crime, including homicide; that corporations can be prosecuted criminally for failing to warn the users of its products of dangers known to the corporation; and that corporations are criminally accountable for their actions, as any other citizen to the people of the State of Indiana sitting as a jury."[64]

When a number of Indiana legal publications ran feature stories on the twenty-fifth anniversary of the Pinto trial, interviews with the principals indicated that time had deepened many of their reflections, and caused them to take a longer view of the case. Cosentino, for example, thinks the legacy of the Pinto case exists primarily in what it did—in showing that the prosecution of a corporation is possible even for as serious a crime as homicide. Yet, true to his essentially conservative legal philosophy, he maintains that corporate criminal prosecutions should be used sparingly, and only when nothing else works to deter corporate misconduct. He also believes that "cars are much safer today than they ever were, and that that the Pinto case may have had at least a small part in that."[65] He notes too that the Pinto case—along with other corporate criminal prosecutions that followed—seems to have "revitalized the function of the criminal law with regard to corporations and their officers, which does help in at least some small way to deter corporate misconduct."[66] Berner, on the other hand, believes that the impact of the Pinto case on auto safety cannot really be measured because there was so much going on at the time: "Ralph Nader was all over them [the automakers]. It drove the notion of corporate responsibility into consumers' minds like it hadn't before."[67] As for the eight law students who provided the prosecution with so much invaluable research and other assistance in those pre-Internet days, interviews conducted 25 years later indicate that the experience of working on the case left each one with an indelible, lifelong impression and taught powerful lessons about "real life" lawyering. Though there is some disagreement today among the former-students-now-attorneys as to whether the state or federal government stands in a better position to handle such cases, "everyone realized that despite the trial's outcome, the prosecution won just by getting the case to trial."[68]

For Jim Neal and Aubrey Harwell, the aftermath of the trial took a different direction. To be sure, they too were accorded celebrity status, receiving numerous speaking invitations and giving many news interviews. Yet the importance of the Pinto case soon receded. Although it was significant in establishing their law firm as a leader in defending those accused of committing white-collar crimes, the case lost its importance as they became absorbed in other cases of national scope. Aubrey Harwell, for example, decided that he would make about 30

Pinto-related speeches. He did so quickly when the trial ended, and then largely forgot about the case. In an interview in 1983, it appeared that he had not thought about the details of the trial in years. At first, in fact, he did not remember Levi Woodard's name—the star witness whom he was instrumental in unearthing.[69]

Following his victory in Winamac, Jim Neal's reputation continued to grow; *Fortune* magazine once labeled him one of the top five "lawyers for companies in deep trouble."[70] When he defends a client, the mention of his name is always accompanied by a list of his accomplishments: the defendant will be represented by Nashville attorney James F. Neal, former Watergate and Jimmy Hoffa prosecutor, and defender of Ford in the Pinto case and of Elvis Presley's doctor. After the Pinto trial, Neal was appointed by the U.S. Senate Select Committee to examine the role of the FBI in the 1980s Abscam scandal and other undercover cases. Later, he acted as the chief counsel representing Louisiana Governor Edwin Edwards, who was acquitted of charges of racketeering and fraud. Later in the 1980s, he also defended director John Landis on involuntary manslaughter charges stemming from three deaths that occurred during the filming of *Twilight Zone: The Movie*. Neal was at various times rumored to be contemplating a political career; as noted, he chaired Walter Mondale's 1984 presidential campaign in Tennessee, and was frequently courted, though never successfully, as a gubernatorial candidate.

Aubrey B. Harwell, Jr.'s reputation as one of the nation's premier defense attorneys grew as well, as he took on highly visible cases and clients, ranging from one of Michael Milken's former bond traders in Drexel Burnham Lambert who was charged with fraud in the 1980s, to a former White House aide who was a target in Ken Starr's investigation of President Bill Clinton in the 1990s.

A few years after the case, Neal accepted Michael Cosentino's invitation to address the Elkhart Bar Association. Cosentino asked him to Elkhart "because he's one of the foremost defense counsels in the country." Neal accepted the invitation. (In a sign that the Elkhart State's Attorney had lost neither his sense of irony nor humor, Cosentino and others met Neal at the local airport with a Pinto.) Neal later stated he "found Cosentino extremely competent and a friend— wrong-headed, but a friend . . . I think we both agree it was a very fascinating trial . . . one of the 10 or 15 most important trials in this century. I think we both agree it arose out of very tragic circumstances. We would clearly disagree as to whether justice was done."[71]

Twenty-five years after representing Ford, Neal would confirm a comment he once made about Pinto being one of the top three cases in his stellar career. He also seemed to agree with Cosentino that despite the acquittal, the case did have an effect on American business: "I think it made manufacturers more concerned and more aware. It had an enormous impact on Ford and for the Pinto [though] it seemed to quiet the litigation about the Pinto. If convicted, it would have opened the floodgates for more litigation and more punitive damages."[72] By contrast, Aubrey Harwell, now managing partner at Neal and Harwell, staunchly believes that the case had "no significant impact . . . although that would have been different had the verdict been guilty. The entire automotive industry was extremely aware of this case. If convicted, there would have been absolute panic for them at the thought they could be criminally charged for acts done in good faith."[73] He also continues to believe that the Pinto case never should have been brought in criminal court, which he believes should be reserved for truly "evil, sinister acts."[74]

Judge Harold R. Staffeldt died at age 62 on August 30, 1981. He was diagnosed as having cancer during the Pinto case's pretrial hearings—ironically, "during the only time in his career that he was in the national spotlight"—and he suffered pain as he presided over the 10-week case. When reporters faulted him in the midst of the trial for not reading all relevant memoranda before rendering an evidentiary decision, Staffeldt said, "I have been criticized and rightly so. But some people don't understand all of the problems I have." After the trial, he said that if he were retrying the case, he would still decline to admit the prosecution's documents.[75]

Lee Iacocca's career since his stewardship at Ford can be described as a quintessential but somewhat ironic American success story. Fired as president of Ford by Henry Ford II in July 1978, a month after the decision to recall the Pinto, Iacocca became an American folk hero after he was named president of the Chrysler Corporation in November 1978 and rescued the company from bankruptcy, partly as a result of a series of television commercials in which he personally appeared. He led a highly publicized and successful fund-raising campaign to restore the Statue of Liberty, and although he denied any interest, he was mentioned frequently as a possible Democratic presidential candidate. His autobiography, titled simply *Iacocca*, was a bestseller; indeed, it was the top-selling autobiography in the history of American publishing. In the book, Iacocca wrote very little about the Pinto debacle. Stating that while he was president the company "resisted making any changes [in the Pinto], and that hurt us badly," he admitted that it was "the fault of Ford's management—including me." He concluded, "It is fair to hold management to a high standard, and to insist that they do what duty and common sense require, no matter what the pressures. . . . But there's absolutely no truth to the charge that we tried to save a few bucks and knowingly made an unsafe car."[76] After several years of retirement, in 2005 Iacocca made a limited return to the public arena as a sort of elder spokesman for Chrysler in a series of television commercials.

The difficulties of Ford Motor Company did not end with its victory in Winamac or with its phasing out of the Pinto. After manufacturing more than 2.9. million of these cars, Ford rolled the last Pinto off the assembly line on July 18, 1980, in Metuchen, New Jersey—the same plant that had produced the Ulrichs' 1973 yellow subcompact.[77] Yet the Pinto's demise did not leave the company free from legal entanglements. Ford reached an out-of-court settlement with the Ulrich family in August, reportedly paying $22,500 ($7,500 compensation in each girls' death).[78] (As noted in Chapter 5, Indiana law severely restricted the damages that surviving families could receive in civil suits.) In addition, the company was confronted with suits from other Pinto owners: Ford reportedly made a $2.1 million settlement to the families of two Fayette County, Pennsylvania, girls who died when their 1971 Pinto burst into flames in a rear-end collision. Another case was settled in Texas just one week after the Winamac trial.[79]

Ford also faced litigation over the allegedly negligent placement of the gas tank in its popular Mustang. A New Hampshire jury awarded a man $821,375 for burn injuries suffered when his 1972 Mustang was hit from behind by a Cadillac. In a 1984 case, a Texas jury went even further, awarding $106.8 million to the family of a girl who perished when a rear-end crash caused her Mustang II to be engulfed by flames; the presiding judge reduced this amount to $26.8 million.[80] Further, Ford came under increasing criticism when charged with the allegation that defective transmissions in its products had resulted in approximately 100 deaths and 1,700 injuries. Attorneys claimed that the vehicles lurched backward after drivers had placed them in park. In addition, they argued, corporate documents showed "that as long ago as the early 1970s the company was aware of a defect in the transmissions of millions of cars and light trucks and could have corrected it for three cents a vehicle." Ford reportedly paid approximately $20 million "as a result of settlements of court verdicts in about 125 cases."[81] In one case, moreover, the Center for Auto Safety, a consumer group based in Washington, DC, requested that Wisconsin authorities file criminal charges against Ford: a 15-month-old boy strapped into his child-restraint seat drowned when the 1977 Thunderbird in which he was sitting jumped from "park" into "reverse" gear while his mother was opening the garage door, and backed into a pond across the street.[82] The Wisconsin attorney general decided against criminal charges after a coroner's jury determined that even though "the major perpetrating cause of the accident resulting in the death of Michael Cannon was this faulty design and function and the Ford Motor Company's omission of its corrections," not enough facts were presented to establish criminal negligence.[83]

During the mid- to late 1980s, Ford seemed to rebound from its lingering post-Pinto image problems and experienced a period of modest if not spectacular growth, as the American auto industry as a whole struggled to maintain its market share against foreign automakers—especially the Japanese.[84] Since then, however, Ford has been plagued by a series of safety problems with a wide variety of its vehicles. Clearly the most nagging problem has concerned allegations during the past 20 years of high rollover propensity in a number of Ford vehicles, including: the Ranger, a pickup truck; the Bronco II, a modified Ranger/SUV prototype; the Explorer, a popular SUV; and the Econoline E350, a 15-passenger van.[85] The allegations have led to a variety of problems, from including cautionary warnings from NHTSA, investigations by state and federal officials and regulators, multiple recalls by Ford, and hundreds of civil lawsuits across the country. As we have noted previously (and will see again in Chapter 7), the rollover problem—and adverse publicity—reached its zenith in the mid- to late 1990s with the Ford Explorer, which came equipped with defective tires manufactured by Bridgestone/Firestone that exacerbated the problem.

Rollovers have not been the only safety problem Ford has faced in recent years. Ford has also recalled many of its auto, truck, and SUV models for a wide variety of other reasons, including the following: F-150 pickup, Expedition, Lincoln Navigator, and Bronco (1994-2002, not all models for all years)—cruise control switch suspected of causing engine fires; Explorer, Explorer Sport, Explorer Sport Trac, and Mercury Mountaineer (1998-2002)—driver's seat bolts susceptible to cracking; Taurus (2000-2001)—adjustable gas and brake pedals located too close together; and Lincoln Town Car, Crown Victoria, and Mercury Marquis (2005)—battery cable and fuel tank strap capable of wearing and breaking.[86] Though no criminal prosecutions were brought for any of the above, Ford again has had to regularly contend with numerous civil lawsuits. Ford has prevailed in certain cases and entered into confidential settlements in others, but the costs have unquestionably been high. In 2002, for instance, a Texas jury ordered Ford to pay $225 million to the families of an assistant high school football coach and a student who died after having been thrown from an F-150 pickup truck that had rolled over; the verdict, the first of its kind involving a defective roof and door latches, was reportedly the largest compensatory damages award in a personal injury or wrongful death claim against Ford.[87]

In 2004 Ford came under intense criticism for allegedly showing a pattern of stonewalling information during the discovery process of civil lawsuits. Though legal experts agree that plaintiffs' discovery request for information from corporate defendants can be extremely daunting and complex, one report concluded that in a striking number of auto safety cases, judges have reprimanded Ford for failing to abide by court rules:

- In March 2003, an Ohio probate court found Ford had committed fraud and vacated a 15-year-old personal injury settlement in a Bronco II rollover case. The court found that Ford had concealed a doctor's report concerning brain damage to a two-year-old child injured in the accident. The family accepted a $10,000 cash settlement.

- A California judge assigned to resolve discovery disputes in a lawsuit involving a seat-belt injury to a five-year-old boy penalized Ford for being uncooperative and withholding documents by instructing the jury to assume the back seat lap belt in a Windstar van was unsafe and that Ford had failed to warn the public about it.

- In February 2003, a federal judge in Illinois sanctioned Ford for concealing evidence in a 15-passenger van rollover case. The judge found the company's behavior to "border on criminal."

- The Michigan Supreme Court upheld a $547,000 fine imposed on Ford in 2001 for failing to turn over test data in a lawsuit that involved a seat belt failure.[88]

NOTES

[1] In researching this chapter, we accumulated several sorts of data. First, accounts were provided by author William Maakestad, who attended much of the trial and provided volunteer legal assistance to the prosecution. Second, we had access to nearly 1,000 news clippings on the case. These included reports by both the local and national media. Although we compiled many stories ourselves and received others from Brent Fisse and John Braithwaite, most of the clippings were provided by Michael Cosentino's office. It should be noted that not all the news reports given to us contain full bibliographic information; thus we are limited to listing only author and title in some references. Third, Lee Patrick Strobel's *Reckless Homicide: Ford's Pinto Trial* (South Bend, IN: And Books, 1980) contained useful descriptions of the personalities of the participants in the trial and of the trial itself. Fourth, in June 1983, Francis Cullen and William Maakestad traveled to Indiana and conducted interviews with Michael Cosentino, Terry Shewmaker, Bruce Berner, and Neil Graves. Maakestad also interviewed local reporter David Schreiber at that time. In November 1983, Cullen and Maakestad interviewed Terry Kiely in Chicago and received documents relevant to the prosecution's case. Additional telephone interviews with Michael Cosentino, Bruce Berner, and Terry Kiely were completed in late 1985 and early 1986. Finally, on July 28, 1983, Gray Cavender interviewed defense lawyer Aubrey B. Harwell, Jr. in the law office of Neal & Harwell, located in Nashville, Tennessee.

Much of this chapter involves reconstructing events and social interactions by weaving together many minor details drawn from a variety of sources. To avoid burdening the text with an inordinate number of footnotes, we have chosen not to provide a reference for each specific detail of the trial. Instead, we have furnished footnotes that list the major sources used to write distinct sections of this chapter. We made exceptions to this general rule when specific information in the text was sufficiently important to warrant a clear citation.

2   David Jones, "Lawyer James Neal Likes the Big Cases," *Lexington Leader* (February 16, 1981), p. A-1; James Warren and Brian J. Kelly, "Inside the Pinto Trial," *American Lawyer* (April 1980), pp. 28–29; Joyce Leviton, "A Local D.A. Charges the Pinto with Murder—and Watergate's James Neal Comes to Its Defense," *People* (February 4, 1980); "Pinto Attorney Neal Returns for 'Reunion,'" *South Bend Tribune* (May 21, 1982); "Neal Not Bothered by 'Heavy' Image," *Elkhart Truth*; Strobel, *Reckless Homicide?* pp. 59–62.

3   Interview with Aubrey B. Harwell, Jr., July 28, 1983.

4   David Schreiber, "Defense Attorney One More Pinto Trial Paradox," *Elkhart Truth*; Strobel, *Reckless Homicide?* p. 63.

5   Malcolm E. Wheeler, "Product Liability, Civil or Criminal—the Pinto Litigation," *The Forum* 57 (Fall 1981), pp. 250–265. See also Wheeler, "In Pinto's Wake, Criminal Trials Loom for More Manufacturers," *National Law Journal* (October 6, 1980), pp. 28–30; "The Public's Costly Mistrust of Cost-Benefit Safety Analysis," *National Law Journal* (October 13, 1980), pp. 26–27; "Cost-benefit Analysis on Trial: A Case of Delusion and Reality," *National Law Journal* (October 20, 1980), pp. 28–29, 31.

6   Wheeler, "Product Liability, Civil or Criminal—the Pinto Litigation," p. 252.

7   "Summary of Findings," Defendant's Exhibit 37A, p. 5; Strobel, *Reckless Homicide?* pp. 65–66.

8   Strobel, *Reckless Homicide?* pp. 66–67.

9   Information contained in document supplied by Michael Cosentino.

10   Alan S. Lenhoff, "Pinto: The Big Case in the Small Town," *Detroit Free Press* (January 5, 1980), p. 11-D; George Barker, "Neal Counsels Ford in Landmark Trial," *Nashville Banner* (January 7, 1980), p. 22; Jeffrey Hadden, "Pinto Trial Puts Town on Map," *Detroit News* (January 7, 1980); Reginald Stuart, "Indiana Town Astir Over Pinto Trial," *The New York Times* (January 7, 1980); Brian J. Kelly, "A Corporation on Trial: Ford Pinto Case Begins," *Chicago Sun-Times* (January 7, 1980), p. 6; Lee Strobel, "Winamac Citizens Find Pinto Trial Trying," *Chicago Tribune* (January 13, 1980), p. 4.

11   Alan S. Lenhoff, "Judge Is Calm Despite Big-Stakes Drama," *Detroit Free Press* (January 6, 1980), p. 11-D; James Wensits, "Ford Trial Not Rattling Judge," *South Bend Tribune* (January 7, 1980).

12   Lenhoff, "Pinto: The Big Case in the Small Town," p. 11-D; Strobel, *Reckless Homicide?* pp. 70–71.

13   Strobel, *Reckless Homicide?* p. 99.

14   Interview with Michael Cosentino; Fred D. Cavinder, "The Man Who Tried Ford for Homicide," *Indianapolis Star Sunday Magazine* (1980), pp. 6–10.

15   Interview with Aubrey B. Harwell, Jr., July 28, 1983.

16   Alan S. Lenhoff, "An Expert Helps Ford Select Pinto Jury," *Detroit Free Press* (January 9, 1980), p. 5-C; Bruce Mays, "Hans Zeisel: The Time of His Life," *Student*

Lawyer 8 (April 1980), pp. 23, 37–39; Nina Totenberg, "The Jury Pickers," *Parade* (May 9, 1982), p. 12.

17   Strobel, *Reckless Homicide?* pp. 105–106.

18   Interview with Michael Cosentino, June 1983. We also had access to the document containing the *voir dire* questions used by the prosecution.

19   Alan S. Lenhoff, "Seven Men, Five Women Form Pinto Jury," *Detroit Free Press* (January 11, 1980), p. 6-C; Dennis M. Royalty, "Jury Chosen in Pinto Death Trial," *Indianapolis Star* (January 11, 1980), p. 27; Jeffrey Hadden, "The Pinto Trial: 'Plain Folks' to Judge Ford," *Detroit News* (January 13, 1980), p. 10-A.

20   Strobel, *Reckless Homicide?* p. 101.

21   Alan S. Lenhoff, "Just Folks: Ford's Lawyer Playing the Hick for Rural Jurors," *Akron Beacon Journal* (January 10, 1980), p. B-1.

22   Lee Strobel, "'Mike and Jim Show' Keeps Pinto Trial Fans Coming Back," *Chicago Tribune* (February 17, 1980).

23   Strobel, *Reckless Homicide?* p. 75.

24   Terry Kiely, "Case-in-Chief: Overview of Exhibits-Phase III." (Document prepared for the prosecution.)

25   Interview with Terry Kiely, November, 1983; Terry Kiely, "Phase III-Overview (Nutshell)." (Document prepared for prosecution.) It must be emphasized that throughout this section, we are reporting Terry Kiely's interpretation of the evidence at his disposal. In the actual trial, Ford would dispute both his interpretation of the corporation's motives and, more generally, the prosecution's reconstruction of the Pinto's history.

26   Strobel, *Reckless Homicide?* p. 81.

27   Kiely, "Phase III-Overview (Nutshell)."

28   *Ibid.*

29   See *Ibid.* for Kiely's evaluation of Ford's response to the proposed NHTSA regulations. Kiely's "best recollections" are the basis for the figures on how a 20-mph moving—and fixed—barrier test translates into the speed and impact of an actual highway accident. Telephone interview with Terry Kiely, March 3, 1986. See also Strobel, *Reckless Homicide?* pp. 79, 83–84. Further, Ford would note later in the trial that it was the only company to have a rear-end fuel-leakage standard for its 1973 models. Similarly, the other automakers also lobbied NHTSA for regulatory relief. It was not until 1977 that NHTSA passed a regulation mandating that vehicles not suffer fuel leakage in a 30-mph moving-barrier rear-end crash. This regulation was much less stringent than that proposed earlier in the decade. See Strobel, *Reckless Homicide?* p. 89.

30   Terry Kiely, "Summary of Ford Memo, 4-22-71: 'Fuel System Integrity Program Financial Review (Confidential).'"

31   Kiely, "Phase III-Overview (Nutshell)."

32   Terry Kiely, "Summary of Ford Memo, 9-19-73: 'FMC-NHTSA letter requesting reconsideration of FMVSS 301.'"

33   The section on authenticating documents was based on the following sources: telephone interview with Bruce Berner, November 10, 1985; Wheeler, "Product Lia-

bility, Civil or Criminal—The Pinto Litigation," p. 254; "Ford Aides' Subpoena Quashed," *The New York Times* (December 8, 1979), p. 8; Strobel, *Reckless Homicide?* pp. 93–97, 139–140, 143–144, 159–161; Reginald Stuart, "Ford Turns Over Papers as the Pinto Trial Begins," *The New York Times* (January 8, 1980), p. A-14; David Schreiber, "Pinto Jury, Selection Snail-Slow Process," *Elkhart Truth* (January 8, 1980), p. 2; Alan Lenhoff, "Ford Avoids Release of Pinto Crash Data," *Detroit Free Press* (January 8, 1980), p. 4-C; "Legal Arguments Surfacing in Pinto Trial Jury Selection," *Logansport Pharos-Tribune* (January 8, 1980), p. 2.

[34] Telephone interview with Michael Cosentino, November 10, 1985. See also David Schreiber, "Documents Issue at Winamac Trial," *Elkhart Truth* (January 23, 1980), and Jeff Kurowski, "New Method for Evidence: Cosentino 'Confident' of Document Acceptance," *South Bend Tribune* (January 23, 1980).

[35] Interview with Aubrey B. Harwell, Jr., July 28, 1983.

[36] David Schreiber, "Jury Permitted Own Standards," *Elkhart Truth* (January 14, 1980); Alan Lenhoff, "Judge Splits Decisions on Pinto Motions," *Detroit Free Press* (January 15, 1980), p. 3-B; Reginald Stuart, "Court Turns Back Ford Attempt to Limit Evidence in Pinto Trial," *The New York Times* (January 15, 1980), p. A-16; Lee Strobel, "Ford Lied During Probe of Pinto: Prosecution," *Chicago Tribune* (January 15, 1980), p. 3; Strobel, *Reckless Homicide?* pp. 109–111; James Warren, "Ford Loses Key Point in Pinto Trial," *Chicago Sun-Times* (January 15, 1980), p. 20; "Judge: Pinto Trial Shall Proceed," *Elyria Chronicle Telegram* (January 15, 1980), p. A-4; "Judge Restricts Use of Key Documents in Case Against Ford," *Globe and Mail* (January 15, 1980), p. 12.

[37] Lenhoff, "Judge Splits Decisions on Pinto Motions," p. 3-B; Strobel, *Reckless Homicide?* pp. 107–108; Stuart, "Court Turns Back Ford Attempt to Limit Evidence in Pinto Trial," p. A-16; Warren, "Ford Loses Key Point in Pinto Trial," p. 20; Hugh McCann, "Pinto Trial Judge Restricts Prosecutor on Documents," *Detroit News* (January 15, 1980), p. 14-A; Andy Pasztor, "Ford Loses on Potentially Crucial Point in Pinto Suit But Wins Technical Rulings," *The Wall Street Journal* (January 15, 1980), p. 2; "Pinto Data Restricted in Trial," *Cincinnati Enquirer* (January 15, 1980), p. A-7; "Ruling on Evidence Jolts Ford Prosecutor," *Akron Beacon Journal* (January 15, 1980).

[38] As stated in note 1, we used a variety of news reports to reconstruct the events of the trial. Listing the individual citations for each fact or event would be a laborious exercise of minimal substantive value, but it seems appropriate to note the major reporters whose works we used in the upcoming sections: David Schreiber of the *Elkhart Truth,* Jeff Kurowski of the *South Bend Tribune,* Lee Patrick Strobel of the *Chicago Tribune,* Alan Lenhoff of the *Detroit Free Press,* Brian Kelly and James Warren of the *Chicago Sun-Times,* Lisa Levitt of the *Associated Press,* Reginald Stuart of *The New York Times,* and Dennis Royalty of the *Indianapolis Star.* Apart from the stories filed by these reporters, the most comprehensive summary of the trial is contained in Strobel's *Reckless Homicide?* Finally, when specific information is not drawn from these sources or when a contention appears to require special verification, we have provided the relevant citations.

[39] Letter from Bruce Berner to William Maakestad, July 16, 1981. See Chapter 5 for the text of this letter.

[40] Wheeler, "Product Liability, Civil or Criminal—The Pinto Litigation," pp. 255–256.

41   *Mingle v. State of Indiana* 396 N.E. 2d 399; Interview with Bruce Berner, November 10, 1985.

42   Strobel, *Reckless Homicide?* p. 117.

43   "Nine Key Points Outline Ford's Winamac Defense," *Ford World* (February 1980), pp. 3, 10; Wheeler, "Product Liability, Civil or Criminal—The Pinto Litigation," pp. 256–257; Strobel, *Reckless Homicide?* pp. 117–119.

44   Following the publication of the first edition of *Corporate Crime Under Attack*, Byron Bloch contacted the authors regarding this depiction of his testimony. Because this conversation was years past and we did not keep notes, we are limited in accurately capturing his concerns. To the best of our admittedly imperfect recollection, however, Bloch believed that he was not used effectively by the prosecution. In particular, it was his view that he had warned the prosecution that the course of testimony they were planning for him was problematic. Although he suggested an alternative approach, the prosecution stayed with the original plan, which in turn brought him under attack on cross-examination.

45   Warren and Kelly, "Inside the Pinto Trial," p. 29.

46   *Ibid.*, p. 29. See also James Warren and Brian Kelly, "Pinto Case Judge No Sirica? Some Rulings Baffle Observers," *Indianapolis News* (February 13, 1980), from the *Chicago Sun-Times*.

47   Interview with Aubrey B. Harwell, Jr., July 28, 1983. Harwell noted that the defense's legal briefs were about 75 percent complete before the start of the trial; the remaining 25 percent involved either revisions necessitated during the proceedings or specific responses to the prosecution.

48   George Barker, "Neal: Didn't Think We Could Win," (March 14, 1980); Warren and Kelly, "Inside the Pinto Trial," p. 29.

49   David Schreiber, "Neal Hopes Pinto Witness Typifies Ford 'Good People,'" *Elkhart Truth* (February 19, 1980); Dan Larson, "Father of Pinto Defends Fuel Tank Location," *Logansport Pharos-Tribune* (February 19, 1980), p. 1.

50   For an earlier discussion of Ford's 20-mph moving-barrier test standard, see note 29 and the accompanying passages in the text.

51   David Schreiber, "Week's Testimony Shakes Ford's Pinto Defense," *Elkhart Truth* (February 23–24, 1980), p. 2; Jeff Kurowski, "Ford Lawyer Becomes Upset," *South Bend Tribune* (February 22, 1980); Dan Larson, "Neal Planning to Close Defense with a Bomb," *Logansport Pharos-Tribune* (February 24, 1980), p. 11; "Neal May Introduce Pinto Case 'Bomb'," *Nashville Banner* (February 25, 1980).

52   Lee Strobel, "Pinto Jurors See Crash Films," *Chicago Tribune* (February 28, 1980).

53   David Schreiber, "Ford Witness Hard Man for Cosentino to Shake," *Elkhart Truth* (February 29, 1980); Alan Lenhoff, "State Only Budges Ford Expert," *Detroit Free Press* (February 29, 1980).

54   Dan Larson, "Witness Talked to Pinto Driver," *Logansport Pharos-Tribune* (March 4, 1980). In addition, in a closed-door hearing in Judge Staffeldt's chambers, Neal raised the issue of whether the prosecution had illegally concealed the identities of Nancy Fogo and Levi Woodard. Their names were listed in the prosecution's files, and it was the state's duty to give the defense access to any information that could prove its innocence. The charge was dropped, however, when

Neal accepted Cosentino's response that "we never checked them out." Our interviews confirmed the fact that the prosecution did not investigate either witness and was surprised by their testimony. See Alan S. Lenhoff, "Pinto Was Stopped, Dying Girl Said," *Detroit Free Press* (March 4, 1980), p. 3-C.

55 In addition to the rebuttal issue, the defense also opposed Camps's potential testimony because he was not in Ford's employment when Habberstad conducted his tests, and because his crash-testing experiences were related to windshield safety and thus did not qualify him as an expert witness on fuel-system integrity. Further, Ford lawyer Malcolm Wheeler denied that Ford had rigged any crash tests required by the government. Compare this view, however, with Strobel, *Reckless Homicide?* p. 249. For accounts of the issues surrounding Camps's relevance as a witness, see Alan Lenhoff, "State Rests Case in Indiana," *Detroit Free Press* (March 6, 1980), pp. 1, 10; Dennis Royalty, "Ford Hid Test Failure Information, Former Designer Says at Pinto Trial," *Indianapolis Star* (March 6, 1980); and David Schreiber, "Ex-Ford Worker Not Allowed to Testify," *Elkhart Truth* (March 5, 1980).

56 Jeff Kurowski, "Prosecution Nadir?" *South Bend Tribune* (March 5, 1980); Alan Lenhoff, "Rulings Deal a Blow to Pinto Prosecution," *Detroit Free Press* (March 5, 1980), p. 4-B.

57 For accounts of the final arguments, see Dennis Royalty, "Pinto Jury Begins Deliberations After Emotional Final Arguments," *Indianapolis Star* (March 11, 1980); David Schreiber, "Pinto Judge Anticipates Jury Report by Midweek," *Elkhart Truth* (March 10, 1980); Lee Strobel, "Pinto Jury Told: 'Send Message' to Business," *Chicago Tribune* (March 11, 1980); Jim Thompson, "Jury in Pinto Trial Begins Deliberations," *Louisville Courier-Journal* (1980); Reginald Stuart, "Indiana Jury Gets Homicide Case Involving 3 Deaths in Pinto Fire," *The New York Times* (March 11, 1980), p. A-16; James Warren, "Jury Hears Final Plea to Convict Ford Over Pinto," *Chicago Sun-Times* (March 11, 1980), p. 2.

58 Lenhoff, "State Rests Pinto Case in Indiana," p.10-A.

59 After the end of the trial, the entire jury held a press conference at which several members explained the reasoning underlying their votes. This section is based on this information. For accounts of the jury's reactions, see Robert Ankeny and George Bullard, "Pinto Jurors Acquit Ford," *Detroit News* (March 14, 1980); "Despite Verdict, Jurors Have Doubts About Pinto," *Bergen County Record* (March 14, 1980); Mary Rose Dougherty, "State Didn't Prove Case, Jurors Say," *Pulaski County Journal* (March 20, 1980); Jeff Kurowski, "The Jury Talks," *South Bend Tribune* (March 14, 1980), pp. 1,14; "Prosecution Failed to Give Ford Jury Enough Evidence," *Indianapolis News* (March 14, 1980); Dennis Royalty, "Jury Says Ford Is Not Guilty," *Indianapolis Star* (March 14, 1980); David Schreiber, "Pinto Verdict: Questions Remain," *Elkhart Truth* (March 14, 1980); "Some Jurors Still Uneasy About Pinto's Safety," *Columbus Dispatch* (1980); Lee Strobel, "Pinto Jury Acquits Ford," *Chicago Tribune* (March 14, 1980), p. 1; Reginald Stuart, "Jurors Clear Ford in Pinto Deaths," *The New York Times* (March 14, 1980), p. 1; James Warren, "Ford Wins Pinto Case: 'Heartland' Jury Clears Ford Co. in Pinto Case," *Chicago Sun-Times* (March 14, 1980); "Why Pinto Jury Found Ford Innocent," *Oakland Tribune* (March 14, 1980).

60 Jeff Kurowski, "Neal Sees Ford's Acquittal as 'Vindication,'" *South Bend Tribune* (March 14, 1980); Alan Lenhoff, "The Ford Story: Victory in the Pinto Case," *Detroit Free Press* (March 14, 1980); "Ford Jubilant Over Pinto Case," *Cleveland Press* (March 14, 1980), p. A-2; "Ford Acquitted in Pinto Case: Jury Clears Car

Firm of Homicide," *Washington Star* (March 13, 1980), p. 1; "Three Cheers in Dearborn," *Time* (March 24, 1980), p. 24; David T. Friendly with William D. Marbach and James Jones, "Ford's Pinto: Not Guilty," *Newsweek* (March 24, 1980).

61   Lisa Levitt, "'Buyer Beware' Emerges as Lesson of Pinto Trial," *Indianapolis News* (March 14, 1980), p. 1; David Schreiber, "'No Regrets'—Cosentino," *Elkhart Truth* (March 14, 1980); Lee Strobel, "Clear Ford on Pinto: Indiana Jury Ends Deadlock," *Chicago Tribune* (March 14, 1980); James Warren, "Ford Wins Pinto Case"; "Prosecutor Denounces Pinto Verdict," *Cincinnati Enquirer* (March 14, 1980), p. 1. In addition, Cosentino initially indicated that the prosecution might appeal several of Judge Staffeldt's rulings. Because this was a criminal as opposed to a civil case, however, the "not guilty" verdict could not have been reversed on appeal. In the end, the prosecution decided not to pursue any appeals. See "Statement of Elkhart County Prosecuting Attorney and Staff on Pinto Trial Appeal."

62   Letter to Michael Cosentino from Mattie, Earl, and Shawn Ulrich, March 14, 1980.

63   "Reflections on the Ford Pinto Trial," *Valpo Lawyer* (Summer 2005), p. 7.

64   "Statement of Elkhart Prosecuting Attorney and Staff on Pinto Trial Appeal, "Press Release by Elkhart County State's Attorney's Office (Fenruary 1981). See also Diane M. Balk, "Cosentino Claims Partial Pinto Win," *South Bend Tribune* (March 2, 1981), p. 5; Jeff Kurkowski, "'Errors Made in Trial': Views on the Pinto Case," and "Ford Prosecutor Seeks Re-election," *South Bend Tribune* (March 1980); David Heidorn, "Berner: The Pinto Case," *The Forum*, Valparaiso University (November 10, 1980), p. 5.

65   Elizabeth Brockett, "Ford Pinto Rides History," *Indiana Lawyer* (April 6-19, 2005), p. 23.

66   Letter from Michael A. Cosentino to author, April 20, 2005.

67   Brockett, "Ford Pinto Rides History," p. 23. Berner also noted that there were also a lot of large jury awards in civil cases during the same time period, which certainly had an impact.

68   "Reflections on the Ford Pinto Trial," p. 8.

69   Author interview with Aubrey B. Harwell, Jr., July 28, 1983, in Nashville.

70   Liz Roman Gallese, "Lawyers for Companies in Deep Trouble," *Fortune* (October 14, 1985), pp. 106–114.

71   Ken Bode, "The Trial of Edwin Edwards," *The New Republic* (January 27, 1986), pp. 19–21; Karen Garloch, "Warner Bolsters His Law Team: Prosecutor in Watergate Trial Lends Expertise," *Cincinnati Enquirer* (September 8, 1985), p. 1; "Where Are They Now" *Cincinnati Enquirer* (August 5, 1984), p. A-4; "Pinto Attorney Neal Returns for 'Reunion,'" *Elkhart Truth* (1982).

72   Brockett, "Ford Pinto Rides History," p. 23.

73   *Ibid.*

74   *Ibid.*

75   Jeff Kurkowski, "Cancer Claims 'Pinto' Judge: Winamac Mourns," *South Bend Tribune* (August 31, 1981); "Staffeldt Dead: Had Pinto Trial," *Elkhart Truth* (August 1, 1981).

[76]   Lee Iacocca, *Iacocca*. New York: Bantam, 1984, p. 162. One of the very few Ford officials who later provided detailed—and fascinating—commentary on the Pinto problems was Dennis Gioia, who as a young M.B.A. served as Ford's vehicle recall coordinator in the early 1970s. After leaving the company, he reflected on his decision to twice vote against recalling the Pinto and concluded that his personal ethics were not up to the task of resisting the expectations of the corporate culture: "[The] socialization processes and the overriding influence of organizational culture provide a strong, if generally subtle, context for defining appropriate ways of seeing and understanding. Because organizational culture can be viewed as a collection of scripts, scripted information processing relates even to organizational-level considerations. Scripts are context bound . . . Ford and the recall coordinator role provided a powerful context for developing scripts—scripts that were inevitably and undeniably oriented toward ways of making sense that were influenced by the corporate and industry structure." For a detailed, honest, and anguished reflection on what it was like on the "inside" of Ford during the Pinto years, see Dennis Gioia, "Pinto Fires and Personal Ethics: A Script Analysis of Missed Opportunities," *Journal of Business Ethics* 11 (May 1992), pp. 379–389.

[77]   John Holusha, "Ford Conversion to Small Cars: Jersey Plant in Changeover for Post-Pinto Era," *The New York Times* (July 28, 1980), p. D-1; Ralph Gray, "Putting the Pinto Out to Pasture After a Decade," *Advertising Age* (April 7, 1980). As Fisse and Braithwaite have observed, Ford officials claimed that "contrary to rumor . . . the production of the Pinto had not been stopped as a result of publicity about safety, but because the car had come to the end of its planned 10-year cycle." Brent Fisse and John Braithwaite, *The Impact of Publicity on Corporate Offenders*. Albany: SUNY Press, 1983, p. 48. See also David Schreiber, "Ford Feeling Pinch of Pinto Publicity," *Elkhart Truth* (March 4, 1980).

[78]   Thus, $15,000 was paid to the family of Judy and Lyn Ulrich, while $7,500 was paid to Donna Ulrich's family. The families never formally filed a civil suit. See Jeff Kurkowski and Marti Heline, "Ford Settles in Pinto Case," *South Bend Tribune* (1980); Marti Heline, "Parents of Three Girls Consider Pinto Case Closed," *South Bend Tribune* (1980); David Schreiber, "Pinto Settlement Reported," *Elkhart Truth* (1980); Lee Strobel, "Ford to Pay $22,500 in 3 Pinto Deaths," *Chicago Tribune* (August 6, 1980), p. 3.

[79]   "Ford Settles Texas Lawsuit Over Deaths in Pinto crash," *The New York Times* (March 19, 1980), p. 19. In addition, as another 1980 report stated, "the legal battle over the subcompact isn't over—similar Pinto crashes prompted suits against Ford, and as many as 50 are pending in various courts." See "2 Years Ago Explosion Shook Auto World," *Tampa Tribune* (August 1, 1980). In contrast, Fisse and Braithwaite have contended that after Ford's "acquittal in the criminal trial, the flow of civil claims dropped to a trickle and a case proceeding to trial in December 1980 was won by the company." Braithwaite and Fisse, *The Impact of Publicity on Corporate Offenders*, p. 49.

[80]   William F. Doherty, "Man Burned in Crash Wins $821,375 from Ford Motor," *Boston Globe* (April 15, 1980), p. 19; "Family Gets $27 Million from Mustang Crash Suit," *Cincinnati Enquirer* (September 8, 1984), p. A-6. We do not know, however, whether Ford appealed these decisions and, if so, whether the financial awards were sustained, reduced, or vacated.

[81]   Raymond Bonner, "Ford Quietly Settles Transmission Suits," *Cincinnati Enquirer* (February 15, 1983), p. B-5. See also James Warren and Brian J. Kelly, "Ford Recall

May Trigger Suits," *Chicago Sun-Times* (June 15, 1980), p. 3; "Ford Transmissions Still Pose Dangers Despite Warning Program, Coalition Says," *The Wall Street Journal* (November 30, 1981).

82   "Consumer Group Seeks New Homicide Prosecution of Ford Motor Company," *Product Safety and Liability Reporter* (April 25, 1980), pp. 297–298.

83   "Acting on Results of Inquiry, Wisconsin Will Not Prosecute Ford," *Product Safety and Liability Reporter* (May 23, 1980), p. 356.

84   See, for example, Anne B. Fisher, "Ford Is Back on Track," *Fortune* (December 23, 1985), pp. 18–22. However, from 1977-2002, Ford's U.S. sales market share dropped from 23.4 to 16.4 percent—a significant decline, but not as drastic as the other two major American automakers, GM (46.3% to 25.5%) and Chrysler (13.7% to 6.5%). During the same 25-year period, the total American automaker market share dropped from 83.4 to 48.4 percent, while the total Japanese automaker market share rose from 12.4 to 33.8 percent. (Figures are for U.S. passenger car sales.) *Ward's Automotive Yearbook*, American Automobile Manufacturer's Association, 2004.

85   The incidence and severity of Ford's rollover problems have led to a number of Internet sites that provide regular updates on the status of lawsuits, recalls, and other information. See, e.g., "Ford Ranger Rollover," "Ford Bronco Rollover Accidents," and "15 Passenger Rollover Accident Lawsuit," available at http://www.rolloverlawyer.com; "Ford Bronco Rollover Lawsuits-Update," available at http://www.vehicleinjuries.com; and "Ford Engineers Warned of Death Risk from SUVs, Documents Say," available at http://www.yourlawyer.com. See also generally the web sites of The Center for Auto Safety, an independent, nonprofit monitor, http://www.autosafety.org, and The National Highway Traffic Safety Administration, the federal regulatory agency, http://www.nhtsa.dot.gov.

86   See, e.g., "CAS Testimony Before NY Senate on Crown Victoria Fires" (March 11, 2003) and "CAS Recall Request to William Clay Ford" (June 25, 2002), available at http://www.autosafety.org; Ken Thomas, "Ford Recalls 3.8 Million Pickups, SUVs" (September 7, 2005) and "Ford Recalling Six Models on Cables, Straps" (November 16, 2005), available at http://www.yahoo.com; and "Ford Recalls Nearly 800,000 Pickups, SUVs" (January 27, 2005) and "Ford Recalls Minivans and Volvo Cars" (June 27, 2002), available at http://www.yourlawyer.com. See also generally the web site of The National Highway Traffic Safety Administration, http:// www.nhtsa.dot.gov.

87   Margaret Cronin Fisk, "Ford to Pay $225 Million to Families in Texas Truck Crash" (December 7, 2002), *Bloomberg News*, cited at http://www.yourlawyer.com/practice/printnews.htm?story_id=8214. Ford appealed the jury's verdict, and the current status of the award is unknown.

88   Jeff Plungis, "Ford Cited for Holding Key Evidence: Judges Warn Company About Failure to Provide Court Papers," *Detroit News* (Washington Bureau, 2004), cited at http://www.autosafety.org/article.php?scid=90&did=924.

Part III

The Fight to Criminalize Business Violence

7

Beyond the Ford Pinto Case:
The Legacy of Criminalization

> But it would be naive for Ford or any other corporation to assume that the Indiana case will be the last of its kind. Sooner or later there will be other trials, and if the prosecution makes a stronger case there may be convictions. The precedent has been set—the notion that a corporation can be made to answer criminal charges for endangering the lives or safety of consumers has been ingrained in law and public thinking. It's a healthy precedent, and we don't think it should be—or will be—discarded.
>
> —*San Jose Mercury*,
> March 14, 1980

After the trial ended, the editors of the *San Jose Mercury* were not alone in predicting that the Pinto prosecution would have significant and long-lasting effects on the legal system and the public. Many commentators thought that the Pinto case had created new possibilities for controlling corporate misbehavior through the use of the criminal law. Obviously, we were among those who thought so. Indeed, we undertook to tell the story of the Pinto trial precisely because we thought it would have far-reaching effects. At the time we wrote the first edition of this book, we thought that the prosecution of the Ford Motor Company represented an important moment in the long evolution of societal control over corporations and harmful corporate conduct. For us, the case was a "sign of the times," an event that both illustrated and fostered distrust of big business in American society—distrust that had been growing for decades.

Although we thought that the Pinto case would be a turning point in the social movement against white-collar crime, one that would be followed by growing numbers of criminal prosecutions of corporations, we recognized that change does not come easily. Many obstacles remained in the way of increased criminalization of corporate conduct. Nevertheless, we thought that the Pinto case would have a legacy. Indeed, in the first edition, we speculated at some length on what we thought the future would hold for corporate crime prosecutions. Twenty-five years have come and gone, and at least some of the future that we imagined so long ago has come to pass. It is time now to reflect on what we thought would be the legacy of the Pinto case and on what has actually happened. Hence, that is the subject of the next two chapters. What has happened in the past 25 years in the realm of corporate crime and corporate crime control?

The legacy of the Pinto case can be viewed from several different perspectives—empirical, legal, and sociological. The empirical legacy of the Pinto prosecution is found in the cases that have followed it. The legal legacy of Pinto refers to changes in the law regarding corporate conduct and in the changes in criminal justice and regulatory agency policies and practices regarding corporate crime enforcement. The sociological legacy of Pinto involves broader and more subtle changes in the attitudes and perspectives of politicians, law enforcement personnel, and the public regarding corporations, the executives who lead them, and the moral status of corporate misconduct. In all of these areas much has changed since the Pinto prosecution, and we suspect there will be more such changes in the future.

It would be presumptuous and wrong to claim that all of the changes that we will describe are a direct result of the Pinto case. We do not wish to imply that if the Pinto prosecution had not taken place everything would have remained the same. That is, we do not wish to use the term "legacy" in a causal sense. We do not view the Pinto case as being a direct cause of everything that followed. No one knows what would have happened had Michael Cosentino decided against prosecuting Ford. The history that didn't happen can never be known with certainty. Instead, we use the term "legacy" in a metaphorical sense to capture the idea that many things have changed since the Pinto prosecution, and it is reasonable to assume that that case played some role in promoting or setting the stage for these changes. In a loose sense, these changes are the legacy that American society inherited from the Pinto case. In this chapter, we focus on the empirical and legal legacy of the Pinto case.

How We Viewed the Case Then

In writing the first edition of the book, we had a particular view of the Pinto case. We thought that it provided a means of illustrating our main proposition that social and legal changes have combined to fuel an attack on corporate lawlessness and to make even the most powerful members of the business community vulnerable to criminal prosecution. We argued that the United States had been undergoing a general social movement regarding corporate crime. Even though the movement was at the time still diffuse, it had nevertheless resulted in greater concern about white-collar and corporate crime. We thought that lawyers, scholars, and private citizens were no longer surprised by revelations of managerial misconduct; people were beginning to show little hesitation in supporting the use of criminal sanctions against guilty parties, whether they are companies or individual executives. We argued that the growing movement against corporate illegality was rooted in wider social changes, particularly changes that had taken place in the two decades before the Pinto prosecution. These changes, we argued, called into question the legitimacy of existing institutions and, in the words of Seymour Martin Lipset and William Schneider, created a pervasive "confidence gap."[1]

In our view, this framework shed light on the origin of the Pinto prosecution. Hence, we argued that the Pinto case was a "sign of the times," an event produced by the general social movement against white-collar crime. The prevailing social climate provided fertile soil for the growth of a crusade against the Pinto, which resulted not only in civil suits but also in widespread allegations that Ford had marketed a car it knew to be dangerously defective. This crusade, we thought, raised consciousness about the Pinto and in the social climate of that time created a context in which Ford's criminal prosecution became feasible.

In this new context, the crash that claimed the lives of the three Ulrich teenagers could be viewed as a "corporate crime" rather than as an example of reckless driving, hazardous road design, or fate. Reporters, engineering experts, and lawyers who had filed civil suits after earlier Pinto tragedies told Michael Cosentino that Ford should be blamed for these deaths. Given the social context, the conservative prosecutor did not dismiss this interpretation. He also felt that his constituents would not consider it farfetched to indict a major corporation. Later, he would discover that he would not have to fight Ford by himself. Talented law professors would volunteer many months of service, because they, too, wished to join an attack on corporate crime.

We believed, however, that another circumstance was needed to make Ford's prosecution possible. We proposed that for some time the law had been edging toward holding corporations criminally culpable for socially harmful conduct. Thus, Cosentino could argue that Indiana's reckless homicide statute applied not only to individuals but also to corporations, including Ford. In addition, sufficient legal precedent existed to counter Ford's attempts to quash the indictment and to prevent a trial from taking place.

In short, in our view the Pinto prosecution reflected the social and legal changes that had placed corporations under attack. Of course, we recognized that the interaction of many unique factors—such as Cosentino's personality and the peculiarities of the accident—determined why Ford was indicted on reckless homicide charges in Elkhart, Indiana, and not in some other jurisdiction. Nonetheless, we were confident in our assessment that the Pinto trial—as well as many other recent corporate criminal prosecutions—would not have taken place a decade or two earlier.

In addition to using Ford's prosecution to illustrate the relationship among social context, law, and corporations, we originally chose to study the case for a second reason: it provided a starting point for considering what lay ahead regarding the use of the criminal law in the control of corporate conduct. The richness of the case, we believed, would allow us to draw lessons about the possibilities for and against future corporate criminal prosecutions. Accordingly, we made three broad predictions about what would follow the Pinto case.

- Our most general prediction was that the social movement against white-collar and corporate crime would continue. Specifically, we predicted that corporate criminal prosecutions would increase in frequency, that the general public would increase its support for such prosecutions, and that the law would evolve in such a way as to facilitate them.

- We thought that criminal prosecutions would increase in part because we predicted that the ideological obstacles to corporate prosecutions would diminish. We thought that politicians, law enforcement officials, and the general public would increasingly define corporate misconduct in criminal terms and be increasingly mistrustful of large corporations and their executives.

- Finally, we expected that corporations and their leaders would not sit idly by while the world changed around them. We expected that they would take steps to adapt to the threatening contingencies posed by the changing legal and social environments. We saw immediate evidence of this adaptation at Ford. Following the conclusion of the trial, Ford established a stronger system for recording the kind of information that it would need to defend itself if it were to wind up in court again. New procedures were instituted that required more detailed documentation of safety and engineering decisions. We expected that Ford would not be alone in making these sorts of changes. While developments such as these can be viewed cynically as the corporate version of self-defense, they may also have the unintended and beneficial side-effect of resulting in corporate decisions that promote public safety over profits.

WHAT HAS HAPPENED SINCE THE PROSECUTION?

In the 25 years since the Pinto trial concluded, history has witnessed a parade of corporate scandals followed by criminal indictments, prosecutions, and many convictions. Thus, in one sense, the prediction that we made in the first edition regarding the continued use of the criminal law against corporations has proved correct. However, in another sense, we were wrong. Although there have been many criminal prosecutions of corporations and their executives in the past two and a half decades, very few have involved the manufacture of unsafe products. As we will show below, to the extent that the criminal law has been used against corporate violence, it has been used primarily in cases involving the deaths or injuries of workers, violations of environmental laws, and, to a lesser degree, the unsafe operation of a business. And even for these types of cases, the overall level of prosecutorial activity, while growing, could not be described as vigorous or high. Rather, prosecutors have been much more active with respect to nonviolent, financially oriented corporate crimes. Nevertheless, as a result of the Pinto case and other serious scandals, the legal landscape surrounding the "quiet violence" perpetrated by corporations has changed in important ways.[2]

In exploring what has happened in the quarter-century since the Pinto prosecution, primary emphasis will be placed on *federal legislation* and the actions of federal law enforcement and regulatory agencies. Most corporate criminal prosecutions are brought under federal statutes. However, we will also highlight many important actions that have been taken by courts, regulatory agencies, the executive branch, and prosecutors at the state level. This chapter is divided into two sections. The first section—*Recent Developments in the Criminalization of Health and Safety Violations*—surveys developments regarding the safety of consumers and workers and the environmental health of communities. The second section—*Recent Developments in the Criminalization of Financial and Accounting Fraud*—surveys the most significant developments in recent years concerning a more typical white-collar crime: fraud—more specifically, criminal laws designed to deter economic harm to shareholders and other investors caused primarily by various types of financial (and, more recently, accounting) fraud.

RECENT DEVELOPMENTS IN THE CRIMINALIZATION OF HEALTH AND SAFETY VIOLATIONS

Product Liability: Protecting Consumers

> Manufacturers, like other businesses, need to recognize that American society is ready to hold them more accountable through criminal sanctions than ever before for their misdeeds.
> — Mark Stavsky[3]

As we noted in Chapter 2, American product liability law evolved during the twentieth century so as to allow civil plaintiffs multiple, alternative theories with which to pursue their cases against sellers and manufacturers of defective products. We also saw that legal doctrine "edged toward criminal culpability" by allowing civil plaintiffs to recover *punitive damages* in an increasing number of instances when the defendant's conduct was shown to be especially egregious. Seen in this historical light, the criminal prosecution of Ford Pinto took the next logical step by responding in a dramatic way to allegations that a dangerously defective product was recklessly manufactured, marketed, and allowed to remain on the market. And while criminal sanctions in cases of product safety have been sought almost exclusively by federal regulatory agencies—especially the Food and Drug Administration—there is no reason to believe that in a particularly egregious situation a state or federal prosecutor would not consider available criminal remedies to punish that corporate conduct.[4] In the meantime, however, private civil lawsuits remain the legal remedy of choice in nearly all cases in which a dangerously defective product causes death or serious injury—*despite* continuing lobbying by manufacturers and their trade associations, under the guise of tort reform, to curtail or dismantle the legal doctrines and remedies that have evolved and been available to plaintiffs for many years.[5] There is also no question that for today's automobiles—as well as most other consumer products—the safety threshold now established by the federal government's regulatory testing, standard-setting, and enforcement exists at a significantly higher level than it was at the time the Pinto was being developed. Indeed, the National Highway Traffic and Safety Administration has developed an effective, multifaceted approach to ensuring safety. In addition to establishing auto safety performance standards and routinely recommending recalls, the agency creates public education programs, publishes safety statistics, and administers the popular and influential New Car Assessment Program, which rates the frontal, side, and rollover resistance of hundreds of motor vehicles by make, model, and year.[6]

This is *not* to say that defective cars have completely disappeared from the road. Indeed, in 2004, NHTSA reported that since its inception, the bureau has recalled more than 300 million cars, trucks, buses, motorcycles, and other motor vehicle–related products due to safety defects, or for noncompliance with a Federal Motor Vehicle Safety Standard.[7] In recent years, serious automobile deficiencies have included: defective seat belts in some GM and Ford cars; faulty latches in Chrysler minivans; rollover problems in Ford and some foreign-model SUVs; and dangerous gas tanks located on the side of GM trucks.[8] Since the Ford Pinto's problems first came to light in the 1970s, no consumer product issue has created as much public outrage as the Bridgestone/Firestone tire debacle of the 1990s.[9] The problem concerned Firestone's defective Wilderness AT tires, which had tread with an unsettling tendency to separate or shred at high speeds and temperatures. This was not the first time Firestone had a problem with safety. In the late 1970s, the manufacturer recalled 10 million Firestone 500 steel-belted radial tires—a public relations and economic disaster that precipitated the merger with Bridgestone. Whereas eventually the failing Wilderness AT tires were found to be primarily the responsibility of their manufacturer, there were also allegations against Ford that the company advised owners of its Explorer SUV to inflate the tires to a level other than that recommended by Firestone. This led to Ford being named as a co-defendant in a large number of the lawsuits, a majority of which were settled out of court. For a time, senior executives at Ford and Firestone denied any wrongdoing, and each pointed the finger at the other—even though it was eventually revealed that because of problems, Firestone tires on Ford Explorers had been replaced in several other countries almost two years earlier than in the United States.[10]

Perhaps most shocking in the public mind was that internal documents showed that neither company was moved to reveal the nature and seriousness of the problems—even after dozens of deaths and serious injuries were known to have occurred as a direct result. To many people this smacked of a corporate cover-up of the worst sort—one that, like the Pinto, appeared to represent a callous decision to value profits over life. Before it was over, the companies' highly publicized problems led to responses on several fronts, including: major recalls by Firestone; free tire replacement by Ford; extensive investigations by NHTSA, at the request of the Department of Transportation; hundreds of individual and class-action civil lawsuits; and hearings before the U.S. Congress.[11]

Though both Democratic and Republican senators took turns castigating both companies and called upon the Justice Department to investigate the possibility of bringing criminal or civil charges, in the end no formal charges were ever brought—nonetheless, Ford spent nearly three billion dollars replacing some 30 million tires in 2000 and 2001, while Bridgestone/Firestone agreed to pay $240 million to Ford in 2005 in final settlement of liability over the defective tire recall.[12] However, the large human toll of a dangerously defective product, combined with allegations of a cover-up by two major corporations, finally created sufficient momentum for new federal legislation designed to address the perceived malfeasance.

The end result was that in 2000, 20 years after the Pinto trial, Congress finally passed a consumer product law providing for criminal penalties: the Transportation Recall Enhancement, Accountability, and Documentation Act.[13] Known as the TREAD Act—or, in some quarters, the Ford/Firestone Act—the new law imposes some new regulations upon motor vehicle and tire manufacturers, including the duty to report whenever a product found to be dangerously defective has been introduced into the marketplace.[14] Note that it is the *failure to report* that is criminalized, *not* placing dangerously defective products into the market in the first place:

> Section 30170. Criminal Penalties
>
> (a) CRIMINAL LIABILITY FOR FALSIFYING OR WITHHOLDING INFORMATION
>
> (1) GENERAL RULE – A person who violates section 1001 of Title 18 with respect to the reporting requirements . . . with the specific intention of misleading the Secretary [of Transportation] with respect to motor vehicle or motor vehicle safety related defects that have caused death or serious bodily injury to an individual . . . shall be subject to criminal penalties of a fine under Title 18, or imprisoned for not more than 15 years, or both.[15]

Despite the tough-sounding 15-year prison sentence, the highly touted legislation came under immediate criticism. For example, though acknowledging that the law did expand NHTSA's power to act in several consumer-friendly but noncontroversial areas, the independent consumer watchdog Public Citizen concluded that, overall, TREAD clearly shortchanged consumer safety, noting that the law: (1) offered many things the federal government already had the authority to do, while whittling away at regulators' authority to make new rules concerned with sharing safety information with the public;

(2) restricted early warning information by placing new limits on federal power to make rules about safety information handed over by auto manufacturers; (3) enacted a narrow, essentially "toothless" criminal penalty because of a safe harbor provision that provides immunity to offenders if they correct their deception within a "reasonable time"; and (4) demanded the obvious by instructing NHTSA to carry out tasks it had the power to do.[16]

It is especially interesting to note that the legislative vision embodied in the Senate's version of the TREAD bill was significantly different from the one developed in the House. In addition to dramatically increasing the government's authority to gather crucial safety information from manufacturers and get early warnings on deadly safety defects to the public, the original legislation sought to criminally punish the actual *sale* of defective vehicles that had caused death or serious injury:

> Senate Bill sponsored by John McCain [R-Arizona]:
>
> (a) DEFECTS THAT CAUSE GRIEVOUS BODILY HARM – It is unlawful for a manufacturer to introduce a motor vehicle or motor vehicle equipment into interstate commerce with a safety-related defect that causes grievous bodily harm to an individual if the manufacturer knows of the defect at the time [it] is introduced . . .
>
> (b) DEFECTS THAT CAUSE FATALITIES – It is unlawful for a manufacturer to introduce a vehicle or motor vehicle equipment into interstate commerce with a safety-related defect that causes the death of an individual if the manufacturer knows of the defect at the time [it] is introduced . . .
>
> (c) PENALTIES – Violation of subsection (a) is punishable by fine of not more than $10,000, imprisonment for not more than 5 years, or both. Violation of subsection (b) is punishable by a fine of not more than $50,000, imprisonment for not more than 15 years, or both.[17]

Nevertheless, the Senate ultimately decided to reject McCain's proposal and accept the watered-down House bill, which continues in effect today. As a result, regulation of auto safety—and consumer product safety generally—is done almost exclusively by plaintiff attorneys who seek compensatory and occasionally punitive damages in civil product liability lawsuits, and by regulatory agencies—such as NHTSA, CPSC (Consumer Product Safety Commission), and FDA—that establish consumer product safety standards, mandate recalls, publish safety research and statistics, and, if necessary, impose fines on less-than-safety-conscious companies. Note that this reliance on civil and administrative regulation—and aversion to serious criminal sanctions—exists even for products such as tobacco and asbestos, long after their massive public health costs have been documented and the conspiratorial silence of company executives revealed.[18]

Interestingly, there appears to have been greater willingness to apply criminal sanctions to manufacturers among some of our European counterparts. For example, in recent years tire and pharmaceutical makers in Germany have been prosecuted for negligent homicide for failure to warn consumers of known product defects or risks, while filing criminal charges in product liability cases is reportedly considered a "long-standing tradition" in France, Belgium, Italy, Spain, and Portugal.[19] In the United Kingdom, as a condition for membership in the European Economic Community, Parliament was required to adopt a consumer protection law that specifically provided for criminal as well as civil liability for producers and suppliers of defective products.[20]

Occupational Safety and Health: Protecting Workers

There was another interesting set of statistics that a person might have gathered in Packingtown—those of the various afflictions of the workers. . . . [E]ach one of these lesser industries was a separate little inferno, in its own way as horrible as the killing beds, the source and fountain of them all. The workers in each of them had their own peculiar diseases. And the wandering visitor might be skeptical about all the swindles, but he could not be skeptical about these, for the worker bore the evidence of them about on his own person—generally he had only to hold out his own hand.
—*The Jungle* (1906)[21]

The dozen or so meatpackers that prepare nearly three-fourths of the beef and pork served on America's tables have raised the production quotas of their workers over the past 15 years to increase profits and squeeze out smaller competitors. This pressure for speed has caused an unparalleled elevation in lost time to injuries . . . [and] subjected workers to what can be excruciatingly painful hand, wrist and arm injuries caused by the chopping, pulling and cutting motions they must repeat all day—for some workers as many as 10,000 times—every workday.
—*The Chicago Tribune* (1988)[22]

> Nobody who worked at Imperial Food Products plant in Ham-
> let, NC, had much love for the place. The job—cooking,
> weighing and packing fried chicken parts for fast-food restau-
> rants—was hot, greasy and poorly paid. . . . But in the sleepy
> town of 6,200 there was not much else in the way of work. So
> most of the plant's 200 employees, predominantly black and
> female, were thankful just to have the minimum-wage job. Until
> last week, that is. The morning shift had just started when an
> overhead hydraulic line ruptured, spilling its volatile fluid
> onto the floor. Gas burners under the frying vats ignited the
> vapors and turned the 30,000-sq.ft. plant into an inferno. . . .
> Panicked employees rushed for emergency exits only to find
> several of them locked. [Later] twenty-five . . . employees . . .
> were found clustered around the blocked doorways or trapped
> in the freezer, where workers had fled in vain from the fire's
> heat and smoke.
>
> —*Time* (1991)[23]

One of the notable literary events of 1988 was the publication of the
first annotated edition of *The Jungle*, Upton Sinclair's novel depicting
the dangerous, unsanitary, and deceitful practices carried on in turn-of-
the-century meatpacking houses. As we noted in Chapter 3, though it
was first published serially in newspapers during 1905 and in book form
in 1906, *The Jungle* remains a quintessential example of muckraking
journalism with historical as well as visceral impact, having sparked a
sensational public controversy that contributed to the passage of both
the Meat Inspection *and* Pure Food and Drug Acts of 1906, while
reducing meat consumption in the United States for several years.[24] Yet,
as the passages above indicate, when the twentieth century drew to a
close all would *still* not be well in the meatpacking industry.

Nonetheless, in the past 25 years the Occupational Safety and
Health Administration (OSHA) has responded to some instances of
severe worker abuse with citations backed by significant civil penalties. For example, in 1988 OSHA fined John Morrell & Co., a large
Cincinnati-based meatpacking firm, $4.3 million—the largest penalty
ever assessed in the federal agency's history. OSHA's four-month investigation found that nearly 40 percent of Morrell's workers sustained
"serious and sometimes disabling" hand and arm injuries, and that for
several years management had been aware of the causes and remedies
concerning the disorders. OSHA further alleged that instead of responding to its safety and health problems, the company pressured employees to continue working on the production line. In a scenario that recalls
The Jungle, 63 workers who had undergone surgery were returned to
the line only 1.1 days after they underwent surgery, on average.[25]

More typically, however, OSHA's regulation of workplace safety—not only in the meatpacking industry but in industries and businesses generally—remains the two-pronged approach the agency had taken ever since its inception in 1970: establishing safety and occupational guidelines, and conducting regular inspections to guarantee compliance to safety and health standards. There is no question that federal and state-run OSHA programs—despite mounting responsibilities, diminishing resources, and increasing political polarization over the agency—have played an integral and irreplaceable role in making American workplaces safer. Indeed, 50 years ago, the number of job-related deaths was estimated to be nearly triple the current rate in a work force that was half the size of today's. Mandated safety measures and educational programs—backed up by inspections and civil penalties—unquestionably have had a significant positive impact.[26]

Still, with 6,000 to 10,000 deaths each year, workplace accidents remain the leading cause of preventable death in this country, not stemming from individual choice, such as smoking.[27] Workers still die every year because their employers violate safety regulations. Unfortunately, OSHA's response to many of these deaths leaves much to be desired. In a very careful review of the evidence, reporters and investigators for *The New York Times* attempted to identify every workplace death that resulted from a willful violation of safety laws between 1982 and 2002. They identified 2,197 cases in which the federal OSHA office or state versions of OSHA concluded that a worker had died because of a willful violation. The deaths prompted 1,798 investigations, of which OSHA conducted 1,242. The rest were done by state offices. Slightly more than 10 percent (196) of the cases were referred to state or federal prosecutors, leading to 81 convictions and 16 jail sentences. Thus, of the 2,197 cases in which a worker died because of a willful violation of safety laws, less than 10 percent were referred for prosecution. Less than half of the prosecutions (41%) resulted in convictions, and only 20 percent of those convicted received a sentence of incarceration. Taken together, the data reviewed by the *Times* shows that the likelihood that anyone will go to jail when a worker dies as a result of a willful safety violation is less than one out of 100.[28]

Across the nation there is a general unwillingness to prosecute these cases. Over the 20-year period examined by the *Times*' investigators, federal and state workplace safety agencies annually cited about 100 companies for willful safety violations that resulted in the deaths of workers. Yet, year after year, criminal prosecutions have been sought in only a small percentage of these cases. The only exception is California. In California, prosecutors pursued criminal charges in 31 percent of the cases involving willful safety violations that killed workers. In the vast majority of other states, however, the prosecution rate for deaths caused by willful safety violations is well below 10 percent and often is effectively, if not literally, zero percent. Although the prosecution rate for the nation as a whole fluctuated over the 20-year period, it remained consistently below 10 percent and did not appear to be increasing. [29]

Even though the investigation by the *Times* found that for decades the most egregious workplace safety violations routinely escape prosecution, there are signs that this may be changing. In May 2005, the *Times* reported on a new initiative involving OSHA, EPA, and the U.S. Justice Department.[30] These agencies were working on forming a partnership to identify and pursue for prosecution the most flagrant workplace safety violators in the nation. The central premise of this new initiative is that workplace safety violations often are coupled with environmental violations. Ideally, by working together, OSHA and EPA could overcome a longstanding weakness of the regulatory system—the failure of agencies to share information and to develop coordinated responses to problem companies.

Although it remains to be seen how many resources and how much political capital will be devoted to this new initiative, at least one company appears to have been targeted. Foundries owned by McWane Inc., a major pipe manufacturer based in Birmingham, Alabama, were successfully prosecuted three times for violations of safety rules and environmental regulations.[31] The convictions applied only to the company and not to individual executives, but fines upward of $3 million dollars were levied in each case.

Periodic exposés of shockingly deadly sweatshops such as Imperial Food Products and McWane Inc. remind us that safety is still not a high priority in some American workplaces. Given that both the existence and quality of human life is at stake, it appears there could not be a clearer moral imperative to consider, implement, and enforce *all* appropriate legal mechanisms and sanctions—regulatory *and* nonregulatory, public *and* private, civil *and* criminal—in order to best approach the ideal of "job safety for everyone, with no one left out."[32] Indeed, an influential report by the Office of Technology Assessment identified six factors *other than* OSHA that serve to motivate businesses to adopt workplace safety and health controls: (1) workers' compensation and insurance; (2) tort liability; (3) information on workplace hazards and controls; (4) collective bargaining and individual rights; (5) financial and tax incentives; and (6) the employer's enlightened self-interest.[33]

Just as product liability lawsuits represent an integral part of the law's systemic approach to encouraging manufacturers to produce safer products, the first two factors listed by the OTA—workers' compensation and tort liability—provide supplemental, nonregulatory legal incentives to employers to provide safer workplaces. Though a detailed examination of these two factors is well beyond the scope of this chapter, we can provide a very brief summary of how each works. First, through the use of experience ratings, which link a firm's insurance premium payments to its safety record, *workers' compensation laws* (the history of which was introduced in Chapter 2) generally provide employers with an economic incentive to control safety and health hazards in the workplace. While studies have shown that the effectiveness of this simple model is difficult to measure in actual practice, varies from state to state, and is greater for industrial accidents than diseases, experience rating and the increased cost of workers' benefits clearly send the right signals to employers.[34] As one report concluded, "the basic argument favoring extension of experience rating is that *any* [employer] incentive promoting greater safety consciousness is desirable, even if the extent to which experience rating actually reduces accidents cannot here be specified."[35]

Second, an employer's *tort liability* for personal injury and wrongful death can encourage accident reduction and safer conditions in the workplace as well. However, the right of an employee to sue an employer over an accident is severely restricted. Indeed, the basic premise behind workers' compensation is the trade-off between employees getting prompt and certain compensation and their giving up the right to sue. The practical consequences of this *quid pro quo*, then, is that filing a workers' compensation claim is ordinarily the *exclusive* remedy available to employees or their survivors for injuries, illnesses, or deaths arising out of and in the course of employment.

The reason tort liability remains a factor in an employer's workplace safety calculus is that the exclusivity rule is not absolute. Most states now recognize a number of exceptions, each of which would allow a worker to seek compensatory and possibly punitive damages from his or her employer.[36] Just as the business community has become increasingly aggressive in lobbying for tort reform in other areas, it has also paid close attention to challenges to the status quo concerning the traditional workers' compensation exclusivity rule and tort liability. As a result, while some erosion of the traditional rule has occurred, freeing more employees to sue in civil court for damages, the exclusivity rule has by no means been swallowed up by the exceptions. The slight increase in workplace tort litigation has not been—and never will be—a panacea for the limitations of the workers' compensation system. But frequent litigation is often symptomatic of a dysfunctional system, and a small but growing number of state courts have determined that workers' access to the civil courts should be incrementally expanded—*especially* when it will serve the public interest by encouraging employers to be as sensitive to employee safety as they are to profits.[37]

As noted previously in Chapter 3, the most dramatic response to the significant deregulation of workplace safety began in the 1980s. Recall that during Reagan's presidency OSHA's inspection staff was cut by 25 percent, leaving about 1,000 inspectors to police nearly five million American workplaces. The increasingly obvious inadequacy of federal efforts to police workplace safety led to a small but slowly increasing number of highly visible state and local criminal prosecutions of corporations and their managerial agents for workplace deaths and injuries.[38] While prosecutions at both the state and federal level for environmental and especially financial crimes had become more common by the mid-1980s, it took the guilty verdicts in *Film Recovery Systems*, Illinois' celebrated "corporate murder" case, to raise the stakes with regard to crimes against worker safety.

The remainder of this section provides an overview of the current status of first federal and then state criminal laws with respect to workplace prosecutions. Despite the government's primary delegation of workplace safety regulation to OSHA and its administrative actions related to setting standards, conducting inspections, issuing citations, and imposing civil penalties, federal statutory law *does* recognize at least a limited role for criminal law and sanctions. This limited role must be seen in context of the Occupational Safety and Health (OSH) Act's legislative history, which reveals that from its inception, the primary mechanisms for enforcing OSHA standards were citations and civil penalties; a majority of legislators felt criminal convictions would be too difficult to secure and therefore inefficient.[39] Nonetheless, there are currently three federal laws with provisions that *specifically* impose criminal liability on employers for willfully violating safety standards and/or endangering workers. A fourth provision, contained in an environmental statute, has been held to apply to workers. In summary:

1. The Occupational Safety and Health Act (29 U.S.C. Sec. 651, *et seq.*) applies to any employer who willfully violates a specific OSHA standard that results in an employee's death.

2. The Federal Mine Safety and Health Act (30 U.S.C. Sec. 801, *et seq.*) applies to any mine operator who willfully violates a mandatory health or safety standard, or knowingly violates or refuses to comply with any FMSHA order.

3. The Longshoremen's and Harbor Workers' Compensation Act (33 U.S.C. Sec. 901, *et seq.*) applies to any marine employer covered by the act who willfully violates or fails to comply with any LHWCA provisions.

4. The Resource Conservation and Recovery Act's "Knowing Endangerment" provision (42 U.S.C. Sec. 6928e) applies to any person who knowingly transports, treats, stores, disposes of, or exports any hazardous waste . . . who knows at the time that he thereby places another person in imminent danger of death or serious bodily injury.[40]

Because a *far* greater variety and number of employers and workers are covered by the OSH Act's provisions than by the other three federal statutes, it makes sense to focus our discussion on its criminal provision.[41] With respect to the federal OSH Act's criminal provision, the most significant statutory development in the last 25 years is that in 1984, as part of a broader sentencing reform, the maximum penalty for a willful violation that kills a worker was raised from only $10,000 to $500,000.[42] Although the increase in the maximum fine would appear to represent a step in the right direction, the offense, nevertheless, remains a *misdemeanor,* with the maximum prison sentence just six months. As a result, there remains little incentive for federal prosecutors to take on workplace cases, which, as we have seen, frequently require a tremendous outlay of human and other resources. And though for years bills have been introduced to elevate the offense to a felony, expand coverage, and increase the maximum prison term—the most persistent bills coming from U.S. Senators Howard Metzenbaum (D-Ohio) and Edward Kennedy (D-Massachusetts) in the early 1990s,[43] and the most recent from Senator Jon Corzine (D-New Jersey) in 2004 [44]—none has ever really come close to passing. It is interesting to note that the criminal penalty provision in the OSH Act as originally introduced was stronger than what was actually passed, with sanctions ranging from $5,000-$10,000 and up to *life imprisonment.*[45]

In addition to its lowly status as a misdemeanor, there are other limitations of the current law that render it less attractive to prosecutors. First, the law requires proof that a particular OSHA standard was violated, even though *many* workplace hazards are not currently regulated by OSHA. A second limitation is that a worker must *die* as a result of the violation, which means that seriously bodily harm resulting from a willful, flagrant, and even repeated violation cannot be prosecuted. Third, the provision specifically requires proof of willfulness, which is left undefined; proof of other culpable mental states, such as a knowing or negligent act, which are found in many criminal provisions, are not recognized. Finally, even if it *were* made a felony by Congress, the statute as written allows only *employers* to be prosecuted—not *supervisors* or *managers.* As a result, according to a Department of Justice official, smaller companies in which the employer also supervises or manages the work will normally be targeted, while large corporations are passed over.[46] Given such legal limitations and practical obstacles, the dearth of actual federal workplace prosecutions revealed in *The New York Times* study should hardly seem surprising.[47]

Many reasons have been offered over the years to explain Congress' collective unwillingness—despite periodic attempts by a small number of senators—to strengthen federal criminal law in this area, but one commentator may have caught the essence of the political reality in concluding:

> Effective strategies designed to serve the often competing interests of the corporation, its workers, and the public are more likely to be found in persuasive techniques than in punishment. Nevertheless, inducements to compliance are usually ignored as policy alternatives in favor of unenforced laws passed as legislative show pieces and disguised as punishment.[48]

Whatever the explanation, it is clear that a regulatory vacuum has developed with respect to federal workplace prosecutions—one that has cut across Republican and Democratic administrations ever since the OSH Act became law, two years into Richard Nixon's first term in office. As a result, a number of *state* prosecutors—most notably and consistently in California—have stepped in to bring criminal charges in workplace cases.[49] Whereas federal law allows only prosecution for a willful violation of an OSHA standard that causes a worker's death, in the wake of the landmark 1985 *Film Recovery Systems* prosecution, state prosecutors in major cities across the country—including Los Angeles, New York, Milwaukee, Austin, and Chicago—have brought a wide range of charges against employers and supervisors for killing or injuring workers, including: assault, assault with a deadly weapon, reckless endangerment, battery, reckless homicide, and manslaughter.[50] Moreover, in recent years, a small but increasing number of states have legislated changes to their penal codes specifically related to crimes against workplace safety. For example, 11 states have increased their maximum prison sentence for such crimes *beyond* the six-month federal maximum.[51] Further, at least four states now *legally require* safety inspectors to notify prosecutors of any workplace deaths caused by safety violations, while in at least three states it is a crime to commit a safety violation that causes severe injury, as well as death.[52]

Regardless of the particular state or criminal statute involved, a common thread among workplace prosecutions appears to be the existence of each of the following elements:

1. The employer/company was under a legal duty to its employees to use reasonable care to keep its premises safe for their use in their employment;

2. The defendant was authorized by the employer/company to maintain, control, operate, construct, alter, supervise, and/or manage the work premises;

3. The defendant accepted this responsibility for the work premises;

4. The defendant failed to act, or acted in willful, wanton, and/or reckless disregard of his or her duty to each injured employee and of the probable harmful consequences to the employee(s); *and*

5. The defendant thereby caused the injury or death of the employee(s).[53]

In addition to the daunting evidentiary task of proving each of the above elements at trial, most state prosecutors face other significant obstacles in taking on corporate defendants in workplace cases, and it is highly unlikely that there will *ever* be an explosion of such cases.[54] Investigatory, political, and especially resource constraints naturally affect prosecutors, who must decide whether to commit the substantial human and economic resources most often needed to pursue such cases. Indeed, many of the early workplace laws passed by state legislatures in the early twentieth century fell into disuse because of such constraints.[55] Similar constraints exist today. For example, a National Institute of Justice study indicated that that while more than 80 percent of California district attorneys believed that workplace-related prosecutions were now within the proper scope of their office, the most significant factor in their decision whether to proceed on a corporate criminal case was the level of resources available to them.[56] Prosecutors face resource allocation issues every day, and such considerations serve the essential functions of screening out marginal cases and limiting abuse of prosecutorial discretion.

Some critics have questioned the wisdom of having the real threat of criminal sanctions—as currently exists in California, for example—as an incentive for employers by arguing that their increased use may cause safety- and health-related recordkeeping to suffer for fear of leaving a paper trail, may make businesses less cooperative with regulatory agencies for fear of revealing incriminating information, and may even create a disincentive to trying new workplace safety approaches for fear of exposing the company to criminal liability.[57] Clearly, it is neither practical nor advisable to view criminal prosecution of employers as a preferred approach to what could be more justly and efficiently addressed by private civil suits, workers' compensation claims, or OSHA regulation. Yet no other meaningful legal deterrent to egregious, employee-endangering misbehavior currently exists. It is doubtful that workers would be the primary beneficiaries of returning *de facto* prosecutorial immunity to employers. Criminal sanctions *can and must* play an important role in deterring irresponsible business decisions, especially because managers may be among the most deterrable individuals in society.[58]

Safety and the Environment: Would Workers Be Better Off as an Endangered Species?

[W]hen people go to jail for environmental crimes, the rest of the regulated community pays keen attention to the legal consequence of their actions. The deterrent effect of criminal enforcement is far greater than that of administrative and civil-judicial enforcement because prison cannot be passed on to consumers or otherwise rationalized as a cost of doing business.

—James Strock, Former Assistant
Administrator for Enforcement,
U.S. Environmental Protection Agency[59]

If there is one area in which there is some evidence that the criminalization of corporate violence has moved forward, it is the area of environmental violations. At all levels of government—federal, state, and local—criminal enforcement of environmental offenses has expanded over the past 25 years. For example, at the federal level, between 1982 and 1989, the Environmental Protection Agency (EPA) referred 318 cases to the U.S. Department of Justice for criminal prosecution, resulting in the conviction of 351 defendants.[60] Thus, on average, during this eight-year period, the EPA referred about 40 cases per year for criminal prosecution.

By the late 1990s and early 2000s, the number of criminal referrals had increased significantly.[61] As shown in Table 7.1, between 1998 and 2005, the EPA annually referred well over 200 cases per year for criminal prosecution. In most years, more than 300 individual defendants were charged. At least some of these defendants received sentences of incarceration. The total number of "years sentenced" each year ranged from 146 in 2003 to 212 in 2001; fines ranged from $62 million in 2002 to $122 million in 2000. In 2004, the EPA changed the way it reported data on its criminal enforcement program and did not report the number of cases referred for prosecution. However, as indicated in Table 7.1, the number of cases initiated in 2004 and 2005 (425 and 372, respectively), as well as the number of defendants charged, are in the same range as in earlier years. Overall, compared to the 1980s, the EPA's criminal enforcement program from the late 1990s and forward appears to be substantially more active. Rather than referring less than 50 cases per year, the EPA now typically refers more than five times as many.

Table 7.1

Environmental Protection Agency—Enforcement and Compliance Trends, 1998 to 2005*

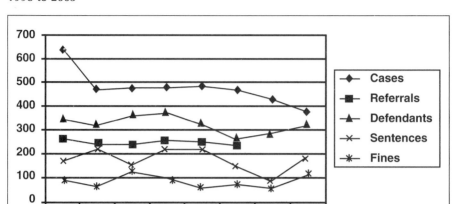

*For information on the source of the data presented in Table 7.1, see note 61.

The EPA's apparent increase in criminal enforcement activity must, however, not be exaggerated. Criminal enforcement remains primarily a reactive strategy, with the EPA responding after the fact to worst-case situations. The EPA is still primarily a regulatory agency, and the majority of its enforcement activity is administrative in nature and not criminal. For example, in 2004, as part of its civil enforcement program, the EPA conducted 21,000 inspections and evaluations, and the agency issued 1,807 administrative compliance orders.

The EPA is a large federal agency. It administers laws and regulations that are national in scope and that affect thousands of businesses and communities. Not surprisingly, its actions garner a great deal of attention from the news media. Because so much attention is focused on the EPA, the efforts of enforcement agencies at other levels of government often are overlooked. Yet, the EPA has not been alone in stepping up criminal enforcement of environmental laws. State and local regulatory and law enforcement agencies have also joined the battle against companies that pollute the environment.

The involvement of local prosecutors in environmental crime is a relatively new development. In 1978, in response to a raft of hazardous waste dumping incidents, officials in New Jersey established a state-wide Toxic Waste Investigation/Prosecution Unit, which was the first unit of its kind in the nation. Since then, evidence suggests that local prosecutors have begun to devote more resources to environmental crime.[62] A survey of local prosecutor's offices in large jurisdictions, which was sponsored by the National Institute of Justice, found that local environmental crime prosecutions rose steadily from 1990 to

1992. Criminal prosecutions of environmental offenses rose from 381 to 756 between 1990 and 1991. They increased even more rapidly during the first six months of 1992, in which 882 environmental prosecutions were reported, eclipsing those for all of 1991.[63] Environmental crime is one of the areas in which the limits of the law to control economic behavior are being redefined.[64]

In light of the increase in enforcement activity at the EPA, the lack of activity at OSHA is puzzling and deserves some consideration. Consider the following. In 2000, the EPA set a record for enforcement activity of all types: civil, administrative, and criminal. In that single year, it initiated 477 criminal cases and referred 236 of them to the Department of Justice (DOJ). The DOJ then filed criminal charges against 360 defendants, and eventually the defendants were collectively fined $122 million and sentenced to 146 years in prison. In contrast, in the previous 20 years—*from 1980 to 2000*—OSHA had collected a *total* of $106 million in civil fines and 30 years in prison sentences (20 of them in a single prosecution: North Carolina's Imperial Food Products case).[65] With respect to human resources, the EPA has at its disposal 200 criminal investigators, and at least 35 environmental prosecutors. OSHA, on the other hand, has no investigators who specialize in criminal cases, and a single workplace safety prosecutor.[66] Finally, with respect to penalties, the maximum penalty under environmental laws is at least *30 times* greater than the maximum penalty for OSH Act violations.[67]

As one commentator has observed, this presents a remarkable anomaly, given that OSHA and EPA laws were enacted in the same era; share many common goals and purposes, including protecting human health from harm; hold accountable companies that place workers or the public at risk; and regulate some of the very same toxic substances and dangerous processes.[68] Furthermore, both environmental and workplace laws may be enforced through administrative, civil, and criminal proceedings. Yet, improper handling of toxic waste is *far* more likely to result in criminal prosecution when it threatens the environment than when it threatens workers.[69]

This was not always the case. Though each of the major environmental regulatory laws—the Clean Air Act (and Amendments of 1990),[70] the Water Pollution Control Act (and Amendments of 1972),[71] the Clean Water Act,[72] the Resource Conservation and Recovery Act,[73] the Comprehensive Environmental Response, Compensation, and Liability Act,[74] and the Toxic Substances Control Act[75]—contain criminal penalty provisions, it is significant that criminal enforcement was virtually nonexistent in the early years. Further, the criminal penalties contained in the early environmental laws were modest, though still higher than the OSH Act. As environmental issues rose to the forefront of public awareness, however, the law developed apace. From specific instances of pollution such as the Exxon Valdez oil spill disaster and the Love Canal toxic waste debacle, to general concerns over global warming and the destruction of the ozone layer, environmental policy attracted a new level of public interest—and Congress eventually responded.[76] Both the penalties *and* the resources available to enforce them were greatly strengthened, eventually leading to the disparity laid out above. The key to these changes was a series of institutional developments, which gradually led to a highly coordinated criminal enforcement network nationwide:

> 1978:   EPA and DOJ form a Hazardous Waste Task Force, which begins bringing actions under the Resource Conservation and Recovery Act (RCRA)

> 1980:   DOJ creates an Environmental Enforcement Section within the Land and Natural Resources Division, which establishes as its top priority criminal enforcement of environmental laws

> 1981:   EPA creates an Office of Criminal Enforcement, which begins hiring criminal investigation specialists to work directly with U.S. Attorneys nationwide

> 1982:   DOJ establishes an Environmental Crimes unit within the Land and Natural Resources Division, which appoints first environmental prosecution specialists

> 1990:   Congress passes the Pollution Prosecution Act, which dramatically increases the EPA's criminal investigation staff[77]

Why have similar developments never occurred with respect to the enforcement of health and safety laws for workers? Is environmental protection simply viewed as a more important social value than worker protection? Recognizing the marked disparity between criminal environmental and OSH Act resources and provisions, commentators have posited different theories, including: (1) greater consensus by the public for environmental protection, due at least in part to a series of highly publicized disasters in the 1960s and 1970s, and the relative paucity of media coverage on workplace tragedies; (2) more willingness by Congress to address environmental concerns, due at least in part to the polarized nature of the debate that occurs on all labor legislation in this country; and (3) the common belief that regulating the workplace is "different," due in large part to free market theory assumptions that place less responsibility on government and more on the employer and employee to negotiate the terms, conditions, pay, and risk level of the job.[78] None of the theories and explanations seem to fully and satisfactorily justify the significant disparity between criminal enforcement of workplace safety and environmental standards, however, and the message it appears to send—that workers would be better protected if they were endangered species, in the words of one legal analyst—is one that deserves *far* more reform attention than it has received to date.[79]

RECENT DEVELOPMENTS IN THE CRIMINALIZATION OF FINANCIAL AND ACCOUNTING FRAUD

Until it was replaced by a memoir by feminist Gloria Steinem, the nation's number one nonfiction bestseller in 1992 was *Den of Thieves* by James B. Stewart, former front-page editor of *The Wall Street Journal*. It is the story of how Michael Milken, Ivan Boesky, and the firm of Drexel Burnham Lambert perverted American finance and industry through the unscrupulous use of junk bonds and secret, illegal deals—and how they and other Wall Street insiders were brought down in a wave of criminal prosecutions coordinated by Rudolph Giuliani, U.S. Attorney for the Southern District of New York.[80] Almost overnight, it seemed that prosecuting more traditional white-collar crimes such as securities fraud and other economic crimes became the highest calling of ambitious prosecutors everywhere. As a result, in the period from the mid-1980s to the early 1990s, three new journals appeared that were devoted *exclusively* to chronicling and analyzing corporate and white-collar crime issues: the *Corporate Criminal Liability Reporter*, a quarterly published in Los Angeles; the *White Collar Crime Reporter*, a monthly from New York; and the *Corporate Crime Reporter*, a *weekly* from Washington, DC. State and federal prosecutors began attending continuing education seminars on preparing white-collar cases, and in 1992 a new independent research center and think tank, the National White Collar Crime Center, was established with the mission of "provid[ing] a nationwide support system for agencies involved in the prevention, investigation, and prosecution of economic and high-tech crimes. . . ."[81] "Forensic accounting" developed into an integral tool in the detection and investigation of corporate crimes, and became a hot course offering for both undergraduate and graduate students.[82] Even tradition-bound curricula at America's law schools were affected. Whereas at the time of the Pinto prosecution not a single classroom textbook on white-collar or corporate crime was available, within a few years there were at least five being marketed by major publishers.[83]

As the 1980s with its insider trading scandal turned into the 1990s with its massive savings and loan scandal, a cottage industry of white-collar crime defense lawyers began to emerge, as evidenced by the mushrooming number of continuing legal education seminars and professional association sections dedicated to corporate criminal defense issues, as well as by the increased affiliation of criminal defense specialists with major law firms. And while television and popular culture may paint a different picture today, it must be remembered that in the real legal world's pecking order—both in the United States and in England—criminal defense attorneys had long wallowed at the muddy bottom, holding none of the status of a corporate counsel, patent attorney, or even personal injury lawyer. In other words, attorneys who specialized in any kind of criminal defense work were emphatically *not* the sort that major law firms would invite over for a glass of wine or cup of tea—let alone ask to join the firm as a partner or associate. However, by the onset of the 1990s, virtually every major law firm had one or more white-collar crime defense specialists on staff.

Recall that while the federal government had long had the statutory authority and legal means to prosecute corporations and their executives, historically most of these criminal statutes had actually been used against business only sporadically. Most corporate criminal statutes that *did* exist atrophied on the law library shelf, and ended up unenforced. Clearly, in the decade or so following the Pinto case, something had changed: the incidence and visibility of white-collar prosecutions for economic crimes were increasing dramatically. According to the American Bar Association, in 1970 the number of corporate and white-collar cases accounted for barely 8 percent of all federal criminal prosecutions; by 1985 it had risen to nearly a quarter of all federal prosecutions.[84] Convicted businessmen like Boesky and Milken became household names, their escapades not only depicted on television and in bestsellers, but also given major Hollywood exposure in such films as Oliver Stone's *Wall Street*, which won Michael Douglas an Oscar for best actor.

Though our book has as its primary focus corporate crimes against health and safety, we would be remiss if we failed to provide at least a brief overview of the most significant legal developments that have occurred since Ford Pinto in more traditional areas of corporate and white-collar crime: specifically, those pertaining to financial fraud and other economic crimes against shareholders, and other investors or potential investors. Indeed, the past 25 years have been witness to passage of the some of the most significant corporate criminal legislation—and prosecutorial activity—in American history. Kathleen Brickey, a top corporate crime expert, has observed that one convenient way of viewing these landmark developments is by identifying the wave of scandals that has marked each decade—the 1980s, 1990s, and 2000s—and the legacy of responsive corporate crime legislation each has left behind.[85] This "scandal-and-response" approach is consistent with the historical pattern, according to V.S. Khanna:

The normal pattern followed by corporate crime legislation is that it comes on the heels of a large public outcry for greater regulation following the revelation of a number of events of corporate wrongdoing usually during or around a weak economy. This was the case for the Federal Securities Laws [1933-34], the Foreign Corrupt Practices Act [1972] and other legislation surrounding Watergate, Insider Trading legislation during the mid-1980s, and the recent Sarbanes-Oxley Act [2002]. Against this backdrop of increased calls for regulation, Congress must, as a political matter, act and the issue is what will it do.[86]

A detailed analysis of the legacy of this very fertile quarter-century of corporate scandal legislation is beyond the scope of this chapter. Nevertheless, a brief summary of the quintessential white-collar crime of each decade since 1980 and the federal response to these scandals is in order. It reveals just how much more has been done to protect financial markets than workers or consumers.

The 1980s and the Insider Trading Scandals

This is not securities law litigation. This is basically cops and robbers.

The issue is, 'Did you get the information and did you trade on it?'

—Otto G. Obermaier,
former U.S. Attorney for the
Southern District of New York[87]

Securities fraud encompasses much more than illegal trading based upon inside information. However, the high-profile inside trading prosecutions of Wall Street icons Michael Milken and Ivan Boesky—combined with the successful guilty pleas and convictions of approximately 100 other prominent corporate insiders—became a powerful symbol for the "greed decade" and the dark side of American corporate culture.[88]

Insider trading—essentially the use of material, nonpublic information by corporate insiders to buy or sell securities—is considered a scheme to defraud under the Securities Exchange Act of 1934, which provides for both civil and criminal remedies.[89] Just as we have seen for virtually every other area of business regulation discussed in this book, most securities regulation is conducted *not* by criminal prosecutions, but through private civil suits by aggrieved investors and enforcement actions by the SEC. The aggressiveness of the criminal prosecutions during the 1980s, then, represented a departure from the norm. Further, there developed a certain amount of controversy over whether insider trading should even *be* a crime, with its proponents arguing that it should remain unregulated because it promotes market efficiency. In fact, one influential conservative think tank, the Heritage Foundation, issued a task force report in 1988 recommending that corporations be authorized to amend their charters to *permit* insider trading.[90] On the other hand, opponents of this view (including the SEC and DOJ) defended the criminalization of insider trading by making a "level playing field" argument that recalled an important goal of the original securities laws—namely, that insider trading must continue to be curbed if investors were ever to have confidence in the capital markets. In the end, Congress was not convinced that making allowances for insider trading was sound economic policy, and took no action to liberalize the practice.

Business groups also challenged the aggressive enforcement of insider trading laws on a second front. They argued that prosecutors were overstepping traditional boundaries of the criminal law and prosecuting cases that should have been addressed by civil or regulatory action. Because insider trading is neither specifically defined nor expressly forbidden by statute, prosecutors have significant discretion to apply, or not to apply, broadly worded securities, mail- and wire-fraud laws to "gray area" activities that have not previously been found to be illegal. As a result, the task of defining the parameters of insider trading has largely been left to the courts. Legal expert J. Kelly Strader believes this highlights three broader realities about the way many white-collar criminal statutes are written, interpreted, and enforced:

> First, the government typically has broad discretion in deciding whether to pursue administrative, civil, and/or criminal remedies. . . . Second, securities laws violations may [also] be charged as violations of other statutes, such as mail/wire fraud and conspiracy; prosecutors have broad discretion in deciding how many charges to bring based on a single criminal act. Third, the boundaries of many aspects of securities fraud, such as insider trading, are notoriously vague.[91]

During the late 1980s, a group of lawmakers, regulators, and defense attorneys attempted to come up with a firm statutory definition of insider trading, arguing that it was a matter of basic fairness to know clearly what kind of information is or is not proper to trade on. But the task was never successfully completed after opponents, including law enforcement officials, pointed out the downside: that innovative lawyers and creative traders would be able to work their way around any specific statutory prohibition and that *no* law could anticipate every kind of improper trading.[92]

The unprecedented number of successful insider trading prosecutions in the 1980s in turn led to numerous appeals by convicted defendants, thus giving the U.S. Supreme Court ample opportunity to address these issues, and to decide whether the relevant securities laws as written or applied were too broad to withstand constitutional scrutiny. Both federal prosecutors and Wall Street executives awaited each Supreme Court decision with great anticipation. At the risk of summarizing such complex litigation too neatly, the end result of this series of cases was that the Supreme Court curbed a few of the most expansive applications of the securities laws by prosecutors, but rejected the broad attacks on securities law enforcement; instead, the Court's decisions generally extended the reach of mail- and wire-fraud statutes *and* legitimized several new insider trading definitions, theories, and doctrines that would help guide federal prosecutors in their development of future cases.[93]

On the legislative front, not only did Congress refuse to water down the securities laws on insider trading, it responded to the wave of scandals by enacting two major laws—the first significant additions to federal securities laws in more than 50 years—that enhanced sanctions for securities violations. Signed by President Ronald Reagan in 1984, the Insider Trading Sanctions Act (ITSA) allowed the SEC to seek civil fines in federal court cases of up to "three times the profit gained or loss avoided."[94] The ITSA also increased the maximum criminal fine for *any* violation of the Securities Exchange Act *tenfold*.[95] Following its passage, the General Accounting Office (GAO) specifically noted the "punitive thrust" of the new law, and pointed out the inadequacy of incentives for compliance under the old statutory scheme.[96] It is also interesting to note that in its deliberations for the ITSA, Congress specifically rejected restricting insider trading to a single definition, and favored continuing to give the SEC the greatest flexibility possible in dealing with any new versions of insider trading.[97]

Four years later, in response to lingering public concern over whether convicted white-collar criminals had really gotten their due, Congress got even tougher and enacted the Insider Trading and Securities Fraud Enforcement Act of 1988, which raised the maximum prison sentence from five to 10 years, and the maximum fines for individuals from $100,000 to $1 million, and for corporations from $500,000 to $2.5 million. Just as important, the act also expanded coverage of the law by creating "controlling person" liability for persons who control others who engage in insider trading.[98] The provision was designed to serve a dual purpose: to close a loophole that had allowed some culpable supervisors to escape prosecution, and to provide an incentive for greater diligence in institutional supervisory policies. Finally, the important role of the SEC in working on securities fraud cases both independently and with federal prosecutors was recognized by Congress through higher budgets.

By the end of the decade, then, it was clear that business interests had convinced neither the Supreme Court nor Congress that insider trading was a concept that could or should be economically rationalized or legally justified. However, insider trading was not the *only* area of white-collar criminality that received attention during the 1980s. We have already noted the growth of environmental crime legislation and resource allocation during the same decade, and our brief analysis here has left unaddressed several other important developments that occurred during the decade, including (but not limited to) an explosion in the use of the Racketeer Influenced and Corrupt Organizations (RICO) Act, which originally targeted organized crime, against legitimate commercial businesses,[99] and the creation of the U.S. Sentencing Commission, which established federal sentencing guidelines that mandated more severe sanctions against both individuals and organizations than courts had typically imposed in white-collar crime cases.[100] Still, when future American business and legal historians look back upon white-collar crime in the 1980s, it will be best known for the courtroom battles that were fought over insider trading.

The 1990s and the Savings and Loan Scandals

The faults of the burglar are the qualities of the financier.
— George Bernard Shaw[101]

When President George H. Bush gave a primetime speech to the American public in February 1989 announcing the need to establish a program that would rescue the savings and loan (S&L) industry, it became clear just how severe the financial crisis, which had been bubbling under the surface since the mid-1980s, was. The estimates of a total cost of $30 to $50 billion, which shocked taxpayers at the time, turned out to be wildly optimistic. The savings and loan crisis abated in 1995, but the underwriting of U.S. thrifts ended up costing an extraordinary *$153 billion*—with taxpayers bearing $124 billion of the tab and the financial industry $29 billion. In purely economic terms, the disaster presented a major threat to the U.S. financial system, and was easily the most expensive financial-sector crisis the world had ever seen.[102]

The consequences of the savings and loan crisis were profound for the U.S. financial industry. By 1995, the number of savings and loan institutions had fallen by half, including nearly 1,000 of them closed by regulators—the most intense series of institutional failures since the 1930s.[103] It also led to an overhaul of the entire regulatory structure for American banking and thrift companies, a shake-up in the system of deposit insurance, changes in implied government guarantees, and the stiffening of criminal penalties for bank and financial crimes.[104] Last but not least, it generated a high-profile series of legal battles fought out in civil courts, regulatory hearings, and criminal prosecutions across the country—and, especially with the "Keating Five" scandal, charges of corruption that reached into the highest levels of American government. [105]

Just how significant the role of criminal conduct by savings and loan executives was in creating the crisis is a matter of controversy. Many analysts have made the case that the widespread collapse of the industry can be attributed primarily to a variety of external factors, including the rise of market rates beginning in the 1960s, the inflation of the 1980s, governmental regulatory failure, the decline of the real estate market in the 1980s, and the legal restrictions on the ability of savings and loan institutions to protect themselves against these events by diversifying their portfolios.[106] However, many other commentators—including federal regulators, legislators, and executive branch officials who investigated the scandals at the time—have just as convincingly made the case that criminal misconduct by insiders played a crucial role in the industry's downfall.[107]

Today, any historical analysis of the broad-based collapse would have to allow for the *interaction* of market, regulatory, and other external factors with multiple instances of individual and institutional wrongdoing.[108] The complexity involved in any causal analysis of the crisis is nicely summed up in the words of one commentator: "[the] savings and loan fraud is clearly white-collar crime on a grand scale, although it does not fit neatly into one of the categories of white-collar crime defined by sociologists and criminologists of state crime, corporate crime, and financial crime."[109] It is interesting to note that similar analytical complexities found their way into several massive, non-U.S. bank failures that became headline news in the 1990s, including England-based Barings Bank and the Bank of Credit and Commerce International (BCCI).[110]

Though structural factors most likely started savings and loans on a downward trend in the 1980s, many of the criminal prosecutions involved activity by executives that occurred on a sinking ship during the 1990s, both aggravating and accelerating the industry's demise.[111] In the words of one analyst, "With nothing to lose, careless risk-taking and looting permeated the institutions until they were finally, mercifully put out of their misery."[112] Indeed, a report by the Resolution Trust Corporation, which was set up specifically to liquidate hundreds of insolvent savings and loan institutions, concluded that "more than 60 percent of insolvent S&Ls were victimized by serious criminal activity."[113] When even top conservative Republican politicians started making comments such as "greed of . . . dishonest thrift insiders . . . was one of the primary causes of the collapse"[114] and "[i]t is no secret that fraud and other criminal conduct . . . have been major factors contributing to the massive financial mess,"[115] it was only a matter of time before Congressional action followed.

Even though the "varieties and possible permutations of criminal activity perpetrated by thrift operators [were] seemingly endless, . . . fraud in the savings and loan industry fell into three general categories, classified as unlawful risk taking, looting, and covering up."[116] Congress did not feel the need to focus primarily on creating "new" crimes for the thrift and banking industries as a result of the scandals, largely because existing, broadly written securities, mail and wire fraud statutes seemed adequate tools for most federal prosecutions. Instead, Congress responded on two other fronts: first, by allocating additional resources to U.S. Attorneys to be used for prosecuting the savings and loan cases, and second, by ensuring the availability of meaningful criminal penalties in a wide range of criminal misbehavior occurring in the thrift and banking industry.[117] With the credibility of both the private financial sector and a Republican administration once more under the gun, Congress enacted and the President signed into law a total of *six* new criminal statutes and provisions designed primarily to deter future transgressions in the bank and thrift industries. In summary:

1. The maximum penalty for mail and wire fraud was increased to 30 years in prison and a $1 million fine if the fraud affected a financial institution.[118]

2. A new bank fraud statute was enacted authorizing the same severe criminal sanctions as above (1).[119]

3. A new statute was enacted subjecting the obstruction of an examination or investigation of a financial institution to criminal sanctions.[120]

4. An existing law was amended to classify financial institution fraud a predicate crime under the Racketeer Influenced and Corrupt Organization (RICO) Act.[121]

5. A continuing financial crimes enterprise statute was enacted, based on the drug kingpin law.[122]

6. Civil and criminal forfeitures were authorized for selected financial institution crimes.[123]

Congress' enactment of these laws in the wake of the savings and loan scandals recalls the nation's "scandal-and-response" history noted previously. Once again, it took fraud on the scale of the S&L scandals to provoke the kind of moral outrage that is necessary to give rise to such a significant bundle of corporate criminal legislation in such a short time. Though the legislation was somewhat narrowly tailored and would be insufficient to prevent another tidal wave of financial and accounting fraud a decade later, it would be a mistake to conclude that Congress's response was insignificant—especially when it is viewed in conjunction with the passage of the Financial Institutions Reform, Recovery, and Enforcement Act of 1989, which substantially restructured the regulation of the entire U.S. financial industry. [124] The creation of new and enhanced criminal sanctions were designed to serve *not* as the exclusive or even primary means of addressing corporate misbehavior, but rather as an integral supplement to private civil remedies and enforcement action by the SEC. In short, the legal legacy of financial scandals of major proportion once again took the form of a mix of civil, regulatory, and criminal sanctions, the appropriateness of each to be determined on a case-by-case basis.

By most accounts, the savings and loan crisis reached its peak in 1992, and abated by 1995—though the $124 billion cost to American taxpayers would be felt for many years. The thrift scandals, though, hardly accounted for the entirety of white-collar crime for the decade. The prosecution of environmental crimes continued to grow significantly, boosted by the substantial legislative attention and institutional resources that the field had received in the 1980s. One measure of this is that in a list of the "top 100 corporate criminals of the 1990s," which ranked companies by severity of fines and prison sentences, *nearly 40 percent* were categorized as environmental offenders.[125] Another significant development was a resurgence in the federal prosecution of antitrust violations. In the above-mentioned list, antitrust offenders received six of the top 10 criminal fines (including first and second), and accounted for 20 of the top 100 overall—second only to environmental offenders.

A noteworthy white-collar crime development that followed in the footsteps of the insider trading scandals of the previous decade was the prosecution—by both federal and state authorities—of at least 10 major investment companies for securities fraud, most notably industry giant Salomon Smith Barney, which received the stiffest fines and was sanctioned as a corporate enterprise (in addition to having its individual executives punished).[126] One of the most interesting and lasting developments was the advent of something unprecedented in federal criminal law: the Organizational Sentencing Guidelines. Taking effect on November 1, 1991, these comprehensive guidelines were developed by the U.S. Sentencing Commission, which had established guidelines for sentencing individual offenders four years earlier. The guidelines completely changed the way federal law treated business organizations for criminal sanctioning purposes. We will discuss in the next chapter just how the guidelines, with the aim of changing the way American corporations do business, utilize a "carrot and stick" approach to corporate punishment;

that is, while the guidelines overall increase penalties for white-collar crimes (the "stick"), they authorize much lower penalties if the corporation did do something to avoid misconduct (the "carrot").[127]

The New Millennium and the Financial and Accounting Fraud Scandals of Enron, WorldCom, and Beyond

> Enron engendered these [hidden] partnerships with wild fecundity and in many variations; but some of the most important of them, to stay vital, depended on a high market price for Enron stock. Meanwhile, Arthur Andersen auditors were standing by reciting the only joke that makes accountants laugh:
>
> 'Q. What's two minus two? A. Whatever the client wants it to be.'
>
> —P.J. O'Rourke[128]

As we have just seen, the 1990s had its share of corporate fraud and deception, most notoriously the savings and loan scandals, but the tidal wave of white-collar criminality appeared to have receded by mid-decade. Though the business and popular press continued to report the occasional incident of corporate deceit—such as Sunbeam, Waste Management, and CUC International—the *real* story at the end of the last century was one of technological innovation, global dominance, and ever-rising stock prices.[129] As the new millennium approached, the popular press and broadcast media—not to mention the fledgling Internet—were filled with nothing but glowing economic news concerning innovative "dot coms," bottomless venture capital, endlessly rising markets, high-potential initial public offerings (IPOs), boundless global investment opportunities, and model businesses headed by America's newest celebrity heroes, corporate CEOs. Coming as it did on the heels of substantial financial deregulation by a newly elected Republican-majority Congress with a true believer's faith in unfettered markets, it led some to go so far as to ruminate on "the market as God."[130]

But on October 16, 2001—just over a month after the September 11 terrorist attacks—the Houston-based energy titan Enron announced a $618 million third quarter loss and a reduction of $1.2 billion in shareholder equity, and became "the first in a series of massive corporate frauds that caused billions of dollars in stockholder losses . . . cost tens of thousands of jobs . . . [and] resulted in record corporate bankruptcies, huge earnings restatements, and lost confidence in the integrity of the nation's financial markets."[131] Following Enron's implosion, described by corporate crime expert Kathleen Brickey as "a 10.0 on the Richter scale of financial frauds,"[132] several of America's best performing publicly traded corporations fell like dominoes in the wake of allegations of accounting fraud, including: WorldCom, Adelphia Communications, Rite Aid, Symbol Technologies, Qwest Communications, Dynegy, and HealthSouth. Between March 2002 and July 2004, federal prosecutors filed criminal charges relating to at least 19 major corporate fraud scandals, for a total of 69 actual prosecutions, and during the same time frame successfully concluded cases against two-thirds of the defendants[133] (see Table 7.2). For a time the endless stream of corporate crime reports seemed almost surreal, and made the front page of the business press resemble the police beat section. For example, *The Wall Street Journal* and *Forbes* each provided regular updates on the latest business crime developments in "The Scandal Scorecard" and "The Corporate Scandal Sheet," respectively; a *Fortune* cover story declared "It's Time to Stop Coddling White Collar Crooks: Send Them to Jail"; Random House published its first ever anthology of the *Best Business Crime Writing of the Year*; and, perhaps most representative, the national media produced a steady stream of headlines and updates on consumer-product maven Martha Stewart's indictments on insider trading and obstruction of justice charges.[134]

Table 7.2
Major Corporate Fraud Prosecutions Filed March, 2002–July, 2004

Investigation	Criminal Cases	Total Defendants	Total Dispositions
Adelphia	2	6	5
Cendant	4	5	3
Charter Communications	1	4	1
Credit Suisse First Boston	1	1	1
Dynegy	3	8	7
Enron	16	33	13
HealthSouth	16	20	17
Homestore	3	7	7
ImClone	4	5	4
Kmart	1	2	2
McKesson	4	7	4
NewCom	2	4	4
NextCard	2	2	1
Purchase Pro	2	2	2
Qwest	1	4	3
Rite Aid	3	6	6
Symbol Technologies	3	10	2
Tyco	1	1	0
WorldCom	5	6	5

Source: Brickey, Kathleen F., "Enron's Legacy." *Buffalo Criminal Law Review*, Vol. 8, No. 1, 2004. Reprinted by permission of Kathleen F. Brickey.

In the meantime, although the SEC does not have the authority to file criminal charges, its Enforcement Division frequently provides critical assistance to prosecutors in investigating and developing a criminal case, and it did so (and continues to do so) in many of the financial and accounting fraud cases of the early 2000s. Additionally, it is not uncommon for the SEC to conduct a parallel civil investigation and enforcement action at the same time the Justice Department is pursuing a criminal case against the same company and/or executive. For example, by the beginning of 2004 the SEC had brought enforcement actions that paralleled criminal investigations relating to such major corporations as Adelphia, Enron, WorldCom, Tyco, HealthSouth, Kmart, Dynegy, Qwest, Merrill Lynch, and many others[135] (see Table 7.3).

Table 7.3
SEC Enforcement Actions Filed Fiscal Years 2000-2003

Date of Filing	Financial Fraud and Issuer Reporting Actions	Total Enforcement Actions
FY 2000	103	503
FY 2001	112	484
FY 2002	163	598
FY 2003	199	679

Source: Brickey, Kathleen F., "Enron's Legacy." *Buffalo Criminal Law Review*, Vol. 8, No. 1, 2004. Reprinted by permission of Kathleen F. Brickey.

As the list of shamed and failed (or failing) companies continued to grow—along with the number of shareholder lawsuits, SEC enforcement actions, and federal and/or state prosecutions—it could not have become any clearer that "the narrative of productivity and boom [was] replaced by one of crime and bust."[136] Like the savings and loan scandals a decade earlier, the complexity of the wave of corporate collapses and massive investor losses that started with Enron makes it difficult to place blame entirely on criminal behavior by senior corporate executives. Indeed, what made Enron, WorldCom, and many other cases distinctive from previous financial scandals is the extent to which *accounting fraud* was found to be at the core of the problem. For example, white-collar crime authority John C. Coffee, Jr. has argued persuasively that Enron, "the private sector's Watergate," was less about failure in the boardroom than the failure of "gatekeepers"—that is, the reputational intermediaries, *especially independent auditors*, who provide verification and certification of investment information to the market.[137] (Along with the independent accounting firms that are supposed to testify to the accuracy of a firm's financial statements, other gatekeepers, or "independent knowers," include Wall Street securities analysts, who vet firm's financial prospects, and, since the 1930s, the SEC, which administers an elaborate system of securities regulation.[138]) With auditing failures leading the pack, Coffee presents evidence of a *systemic governance failure* that distinguished it from other spectacular securities frauds in recent years, such as insider trading during the 1980s. He concludes that it was the systemic nature of the problem that shook public trust, roiled the market, and created a widespread demand for reform, particularly with regard to greater transparency.[139]

Experts have offered many explanations for *why* the auditors and financial analysts—or other watchdogs, such as the SEC—did not "bark in the night" until it was too late as Enron and other companies built their financial houses of cards. Coffee has posited two theories, each having found support among other analysts. First, the *general deterrence theory* asserts that during the 1990s, the risk of legal liability to gatekeepers—again, *especially* auditors—was substantially lowered, largely as a result of legal changes brought by two cases decided by the U.S. Supreme Court in the early 1990s and two laws enacted by Congress as part of Republican House leader Newt Gingrich's conservative "Contract with America" agenda.[140] Nearly all of the changes served to prevent or restrict harmed investors from bringing private law suits for securities fraud. Hence, as the exposure to liability declined, the benefits of acquiescence to the client corporation's demands and expectations increased—leading to the widespread failure of the gatekeepers to carry out their watchdog function effectively. Note how this explanation highlights a theme that has run throughout this book: that efficient deterrence of corporate misbehavior requires not just the availability of criminal and administrative sanctions, but of private civil remedies as well.

Second, the *irrational market theory* explains the downfall of Enron as a consequence of a classic bubble that "overtook the equity markets in the late 1990s and produced a market euphoria in which gatekeepers became temporarily irrelevant." In other words, as stock prices continued to rise and reached unprecedented levels during the dot com boom, an atmosphere of euphoria—or, in Federal Chairman Alan Greenspan's famous words, "irrational exuberance"—ensued, and neither investors nor management were willing to listen to anything other than "the sky's the limit." As a result, Coffee concludes that reasonable predictions and long-term analyses offered during this bubble period by traditional gatekeepers—*especially* financial analysts—lost out to value-pumping, short-term focused investment gurus who had flooded the late 1990s scene.[141]

Other commentators have added that other factors that contributed to the wave of corporate frauds and failures were at work as well. For example, by the late 1990s the "Big Five" accounting firms were for the first time in history earning a greater percentage of their income from providing *consulting services* to their corporate clients than from *auditing* them. This created potential conflicts of interest and sometimes tempted auditors to "look the other way" or "soften" their reports. In addition, despite its enforcement successes during the 1980s and early 1990s, the SEC continually fought budget battles with Congress to allow its resources to keep pace with its increased responsibilities, given the exploding economy of the late 1990s. In our view, the collective influence of all these factors offers a better understanding of the context in which Enron's, WorldCom's, and other companies' crimes and scandals occurred than what popular commentary has offered: softer-edged concepts such as "infectious greed" and a general decline in morality. As Coffee has observed, "there is little evidence that 'greed' has ever declined; nor is it clear that there are relevant policy options for addressing it. In contrast, focusing on gatekeepers tells us that there are special actors in a system of private corporate governance whose incentives must be regulated."[142]

Kathleen Brickey has written that the true legacy of Enron and the many other financial and accounting frauds that followed can be found not only in the extensive record of criminal enforcement, but also in a broad array of federal legislative and regulatory responses, including: (1) enactment of the Sarbanes-Oxley Act; (2) amendments to the U.S. Sentencing Guidelines; (3) creation of the Corporate Fraud Task Force and Enron Task Force within the Justice Department; (4) revisions to the Justice Department's Corporate Prosecution Guidance; (5) publication of SEC enforcement criteria; and (6) significant increases in SEC funding.[143] Taken together, these six responses evidence the necessity of *structural reforms* to address the systemic failure of corporate governance mechanisms. A brief overview of each follows.

The Sarbanes-Oxley Act of 2002

Named after bipartisan sponsors Senator Paul Sarbanes (D-Maryland) and Representative Michael G. Oxley (R-Ohio), the Sarbanes-Oxley Act (SOX)[144] was widely heralded as the most important and comprehensive corporate reform measure since the stock market crash of 1929 led to the securities laws of 1933 and 1934.[145] The law followed by several months President George W. Bush's initial proposals, which he outlined in a 10-point plan during a public appearance on Wall Street. Despite the initial fanfare they received, the President's proposals promptly disappeared. Bipartisan criticism, based in part upon a consensus that an outraged public deemed the President's proposals inadequate, eventually led to near-unanimous approval of a very different—and tougher—law than originally called for by the President.[146] Among the most significant issues addressed by SOX are accounting oversight, auditor independence, insider trading, corporate responsibility, the transparency of financial statements, conflicts of interest among analysts, and the resource needs of the SEC.[147] SOX empowers regulators to address these corporate governance issues in a variety of ways, including (but not limited to): imposing new accountability rules on corporate executives, ensuring accuracy in financial reports issued by publicly held corporations, strengthening rules regarding auditor independence, and improving public accounting oversight mechanisms.[148]

The law's ambitious reform agenda is backed by substantial civil and criminal penalties. However, with respect to its criminal provisions, Congress was slow to reach consensus. Though the Sarbanes-Oxley bill was presented to the President on July 26, 2002, and signed into law on July 29, it was not until just two weeks beforehand that a package of five criminal amendments was offered and finally incorporated into the bill as the White Collar Crime Penalty Enhancement Act (WCCPA).[149] The amendments, when added to the limited criminal provisions of the original bill, essentially provide for the following substantive changes:

1. The very first securities fraud crime is actually codified in the federal criminal code.[150]

2. Premature destruction of corporate audit records is criminalized.[151]

3. Chief executive officers and chief financial officers are required to certify their company's financial records, under penalty of law.[152]

4. False certification of financial statements is severely punished.[153]

5. Retaliatory firing of whistleblowers who report criminal wrongdoing to federal authorities is punished.[154]

6. A new prohibition against document destruction is added to the panoply of obstruction of justice crimes.[155]

7. Criminal penalties for fraud and conspiracy to defraud are significantly increased.[156]

Though there have been complaints over the high costs of complying with the new law's provisions, the business community has generally acknowledged that, as John A. Thain, CEO of the New York Stock Exchange, stated, "There is no question that, broadly speaking, Sarbanes-Oxley was necessary."[157] Nonetheless, it should come as no surprise that SOX's criminal provisions have not been welcomed in all quarters. For example, they have been criticized for being needlessly redundant, relying too heavily on enhanced criminal penalties, and attaching too much significance to filling minor gaps in existing laws.[158] Some critics have argued more broadly that the new crimes and higher penalties are economically inefficient, while others dismiss SOX as representing "little more than political grandstanding."[159] Yet, some of the nation's leading corporate criminal law experts have rejected these claims and strongly defend the new law.[160] Brickey, for example, has carefully monitored the already substantial enforcement record under the Act, and concludes that there is already evidence that "the Act's criminal provisions make significant strides toward piercing the corporate veil of corporate silence [and] provide powerful incentives for targets of criminal fraud investigations to help prosecutors build cases against other participants in the fraud."[161] In sum, even as corporations complain about the high costs of complying with the law, most realize that noncompliance comes with an even higher cost in terms of stiffer penalties and jail sentences.

U.S. Sentencing Guidelines Amendments

The final provision in the WCCPA, the Amendment to Sentencing Guidelines Relating to Certain White-Collar Offenses, directed the United States Sentencing Commission "to amend the federal Sentencing Guidelines and related policy statements to implement" Sarbanes-Oxley.[162] Essentially, Congress was asking the Commission to review its existing guidelines in certain areas and adjust them if necessary to conform with the new priority and urgency given to white- collar crimes in Sarbanes-Oxley. Though most critics expected little from this directive, they were surprised when the Commission significantly increased prison time for individuals convicted of large-scale fraud (affecting 250 or more victims, up 25%), Enron-like fraud (endangering solvency or security of substantial number of victims or a publicly traded company, up 300%), and securities fraud (by corporate officers and directors, up 50%).[163] Further, after a two-year review, the Commission also approved the first amendments to the organizational sentencing guidelines since they took effect in 1991, adopting more rigorous criteria for corporate compliance programs that could affect the severity of criminal sanctions against corporations.[164] We will discuss in more detail the organizational sentencing guidelines debate in the next chapter.

Corporate Fraud / Enron Task Forces

One of the earliest responses to the corporate frauds was the establishment of two special task forces by President George W. Bush. Created by Executive Order in January 2002, the Enron Task Force was charged with the responsibility of investigating and prosecuting all criminal charges specifically related to the collapse of Enron.[165] Table 7.4 shows just how active this task force has been, and this does not include the recent trials and convictions of former Enron executives, Ken Lay and Jeffrey Skilling[166] (see Table 7.4). The far more broadly conceived Corporate Fraud Task Force (CFTF), created in July 2002, was charged with coordinating and directing the investigation and prosecution of major financial crimes, recommending how resources can best be allocated to combat major fraud, facilitating interagency cooperation in the investigation and prosecution of financial crimes, recommending regulatory and legislative reforms relating to financial fraud, and reviewing parallel civil enforcement actions brought by the SEC and other federal agencies.[167] The CFTF's members include some of the most influential law enforcement officials in the country, including the Deputy Attorney General (chair), the Director of the FBI, two Assistant Attorneys General, and seven U.S. Attorneys. Senior officials from several other executive departments, including the Securities and Exchange Commission (SEC) and the Treasury Department, also work with the Justice Department to promote interagency cooperation on the initiative. Whereas the creation of any task force might be initially perceived as a public relations move, one should recall the creation of the first environmental crime task force in 1978 and the crucial role it played in the eventual development of an institutional network that made prosecution of environmental offense a national priority. Indeed, the track record of the CFTF in its first year of operation was impressive, with more than 300 criminal fraud investigations, 350 criminal defendants charged, and 250 convictions or guilty pleas.[168] It is important to note that the federal government has not just been going after middle-management scapegoats and ignoring the higher-ups. In an analysis of cases that have actually gone to trial between 2002 and 2006, Kathleen Brickey found that

> Of the forty-six defendants who have gone to trial, twelve held the title of Chief Executive Officer, Chief Operating Officer, President, Chairman of the Board or, in the case of a partnership, Senior Partner. Defendants on trial also included five Chief Financial Officers, and an assortment of other financial and accounting executives. There were also seven Executive or Senior Vice presidents, five Investment Advisors, a Chief Legal Officer, and a Vice President for Legal Affairs.[169]

Justice Department Corporate Prosecution Guidance

Though we have seen that the law has long allowed corporations to be prosecuted criminally, in practice it remains the exception rather than the rule—with the Ford Pinto case being one of American legal history's most notable exceptions. In the wake of Enron, however, another notable exception occurred when the accounting firm of Arthur Andersen LLP—as venerable in its field as Ford was in the auto industry—was found guilty of a felony charge of obstructing justice in the SEC's investigation of Enron. At the time of its conviction, Andersen was one of the five largest accounting firms in the world.[170] Among other things, the case stands for the proposition that the federal government *can and will* criminally prosecute an entire corporate organization instead of (or in addition to) individual corporate officials, given the right set of facts.

Table 7.4
Enron-Related Parallel Civil and Criminal Proceedings

Defendant	Civil Filing	Civil Settlement	Criminal Filing	Guilty Plea
Lay	July 8, 2004		July 8, 2004	
Rieker	May 19, 2004	May 19, 2004	May 19, 2004	May 19, 2004
Skilling	Feb. 19, 2004		Feb. 19, 2004	
Causey	Jan. 22, 2004		Jan. 22, 2004	
Fastow	Oct. 2, 2002	Jan. 14, 2004	Oct. 1, 2002	Jan. 14, 2004
Delainey	Oct. 30, 2003		Oct. 29, 2003	
Colwell	Oct. 9, 2003		None	
Glisan	Sept. 10, 2003	Sept. 10, 2003	April 30, 2003	Sept. 10, 2003
Rice	May 1, 2003		April 29, 2003	
Hirko	May 1, 2003		April 29, 2003	
Hannon	May 1, 2003		April 29, 2003	
Shelby	May 1, 2003		April 29, 2003	
Yeager	May 1, 2003		April 29, 2003	
Howard	May 1, 2003		April 29, 2003	
Krautz	May 1, 2003		April 29, 2003	
Merrill Lynch	Mar. 17, 2003	Mar. 17, 2003	None	
Furst	Mar. 17, 2003		Oct. 14, 2003	
Tilney	Mar. 17, 2003		None	
Bayly	Mar. 17, 2003		Oct. 14, 2003	
Davis	Mar. 17, 2003		None	
Gordon	Dec. 19, 2003	Dec. 19, 2003	Dec. 19, 2003	Dec. 19, 2003
CIBC	Dec. 22, 2003	Dec. 22, 2003	Dec. 22, 2003	Dec. 22, 2003

Source: Brickey, Kathleen F., "Enron's Legacy." *Buffalo Criminal Law Review*, Vol. 8, No. 1, 2004. Reprinted by permission of Kathleen F. Brickey.

But what actually constitutes the right set of facts? In January 1999, the Justice Department addressed just this issue by establishing guidelines for federal prosecution of corporations, which identified eight major factors to be considered by federal prosecutors when charges against a corporation were being contemplated:

1. The nature and seriousness of the crime, including potential harm to the public;

2. the pervasiveness of wrongdoing within the company;

3. the company's prior history of similar wrongdoing;

4. the company's timely and voluntary disclosure of the wrongdoing and the degree of its cooperation in identifying individuals and providing evidence;

5. the effectiveness of the company's compliance program in preventing and detecting wrongdoing;

6. remedial measures the company took upon discovery of the wrongdoing;

7. potential collateral consequences of a corporate conviction, including adverse effects on third parties; and

8. the adequacy of available non-criminal remedies as an alternative to criminal prosecution.[171]

Following the first wave of criminal charges related to the corporate fraud crisis, the Justice Department issued revised guidelines, now called Principles of Federal Prosecution of Business Organizations, in order to provide even more guidance to federal prosecutors who may be considering charges against an organizational defendant. In the following chapter, we will discuss in greater detail the influence that the current guidelines—and the landmark Arthur Andersen prosecution—may have on the government's present and future policies concerning corporations themselves being charged as criminals.

SEC Enforcement Criteria

While the SEC wields a variety of civil and administrative tools with which to combat fraud, the agency does not possess criminal enforcement authority; in most cases its staff decides whether criminal prosecution is appropriate and, if so, refers the case to the Justice Department, which has the ultimate discretion to accept or decline the case.[172] Nonetheless, in deciding whether to refer the case, the SEC does consider criteria very similar to those followed by the Justice Department, and with a similar focus on the nature and degree of the company's "self-policing, self-reporting, remediation and cooperation."[173] In light of the recent accounting frauds at Enron and other firms, however, note the SEC criteria's more specific references to the company's auditors:

1. The nature of the misconduct, including the level of cul-pability and whether the company's auditors were misled;

2. why the misconduct occurred (e.g., pressure from senior management), what compliance measures were in place, and how and why they failed;

3. the organizational level where the misconduct occurred, the duration of the wrongdoing, and whether the behavior was systemic;

4. the degree of harm to investors and other outside parties;

5. the length of time between the discovery of the wrongdoing and an effective organizational response—including disciplining wrongdoers, prompt disclosure to regulators and the public, and full cooperation with law enforcement authorities;

6. whether the company conducted a thorough review, who conducted it, and whether the audit committee and the board were fully informed;

7. the degree of the company's cooperation, including whether it voluntarily disclosed the results of its review to the SEC and whether it made its employees available to assist in the investigation; and

8. the likelihood that the wrongdoing will recur.[174]

Considering the Arthur Andersen prosecution and the accounting frauds at Enron and so many other firms, it is interesting to note the specific references that the SEC's criteria make to a company's auditors. The next chapter will discuss in greater detail the prosecution of criminal corporations, but suffice it to say that each set of guidelines makes it clear that "in the eyes of both the Justice Department and the SEC, criminal and civil enforcement actions against business entities are legitimate tools of corporate governance reform."[175]

SEC Funding

In the mid- to late 1970s, the SEC was beginning to be seen as retreating from its role as protector of investors. As we have seen, however, in the 1980s the SEC regained respect for its vigorous pursuit of insider trading through its own enforcement activities and cooperation with federal prosecutors. In the 1990s, it further strengthened its enforcement record, both during and after the savings and loan scandals. But by the 2000s, the growing volume of enforcement actions was putting the SEC in a resource bind, as it did not have the staff to keep up with its volume of cases.[176] In a scenario that recalls the inspector shortages at OSHA previously discussed, between 1995 and 2002, the number of mutual funds subject to SEC inspection rose from just over 5,700 to more than 8,200, but the number of SEC inspectors remained the same. Additionally, between 1991 and 2001, the number of cases opened by the SEC's Enforcement Division rose 65 percent, while the Division's staff grew by just 27 percent.[177] To make matters worse, in a series of proposals reflecting the prevailing spirit of government deregulation (if not demolition) during the mid- to late 1990s, Congress planned "to further hobble the SEC by freezing its budget for five years, reducing the number of Commissioners from five to three, and requiring the SEC to justify the cost of any change in its regulatory requirements [and] while these onerous initiatives never became law, Congress imposed a freeze on SEC staff positions for four consecutive years."[178]

Even after passage of the 2002 Sarbanes-Oxley Act, the Republican Congress and President sent mixed signals about their commitment to providing the SEC with the budget it needed to do its job effectively. Finally, after an intense political and very public tug of war that lasted two years, the President proposed to increase the SEC budget by a full 10 percent for the 2005 fiscal year.[179] At least for the short term, the political momentum for adequately funding the country's most critical financial regulatory agency appears to have finally turned in its favor; if it continues, a strengthened SEC will represent the final piece in a very significant legacy left by Enron, WorldCom, and other financial and accounting scandals.

The passage of the landmark Sarbanes-Oxley Act, the prosecution of the greatest number of senior business executives in modern history, the creation of a national corporate fraud task force, and the other legal legacies of the early twenty-first century's financial disasters all took place at the federal level, and collectively they have involved each branch of government: legislative, judicial, and executive. Yet all has not been quiet at the *state* level, at which defrauded investors have filed hundreds (if not thousands) of civil suits for damages and state regulators have launched their own investigations of the massive frauds. However, taking center stage in state responses against the financial scandals is one state's chief law enforcement officer: New York Attorney General Eliot Spitzer. Since Enron, Spitzer—sometimes in collaboration with Manhattan District Attorney Robert Morgenthau—has made frequent use of New York's 1921 Martin Act, a state law that previously had been applied mostly to low-grade stock frauds or high-pressure "boiler room" operations.[180] Just as Michael Cosentino made history with his unorthodox application of Indiana's reckless homicide statute against an automaker, Spitzer has made unprecedented use of the dormant 80-year-old law against a wide variety of firms within the financial industry, including Merrill Lynch, Tyco, WorldCom, Qwest, Citicorp, and several of New York's leading brokerage houses.[181] Kathleen Brickey has observed that Spitzer has also broken new ground in his "M.O."—that is, the way that he both perceives and responds to corporate malfeasance. She notes that he often sees corporate crime as arising not just from within an individual company, but throughout *entire industries*, such as investment banking, mutual funds, and insurance. In such instances, he may then employ the broad anti-fraud provisions of the Martin Act against two, three, or four target companies within that industry—a strategy that has been used to achieve industry-wide reform with remarkable efficiency.[182]

CONCLUSION

At the beginning of this chapter we quoted from an editorial that appeared in the *San Jose Mercury* shortly after the conclusion of the Pinto trial. The *Mercury*'s editors asserted that "the notion that a corporation can be made to answer criminal charges for endangering the lives or safety of consumers has been ingrained in law and public thinking." We agreed with the editors of the *Mercury* at the time. Now with the advantage of hindsight it is difficult to avoid the conclusion that they and we were at least partially wrong. In the years following the Pinto trial, there were no criminal prosecutions for the manufacture or sale of dangerous products. No corporation has been made to answer criminal charges for endangering consumers through the marketing of an unsafe product, although some probably have come close.

Nevertheless, we believe that to view the Pinto case as a one-of-a-kind event that will never be repeated and hence of little lasting influence is shortsighted. Such a view ignores the broader significance of the Pinto trial as an indicator of continuing changes in social attitudes, enforcement practices, and law regarding corporations. Although it is true that there have been no prosecutions for dangerous products, there have been plenty of prosecutions and convictions for other types of corporate crimes. As demonstrated in this chapter, every year employers are brought to trial for killing or injuring workers as a result of maintaining unsafe workplaces. True, it is not many, but it is also not zero. Criminal enforcement of environmental laws is now imposed on hundreds of businesses annually. In recent years, prosecutions of corporate executives for financially related crimes have become, if not exactly commonplace, certainly no longer unusual. In addition, the law has changed. Consider the TREAD act and the Sarbanes-Oxley legislation. New enforcement mechanisms have been established to take advantage of these legal changes. Consider the Corporate Fraud and Enron Task Forces. Taken together, these developments and the others addressed in this chapter suggest that the social control of corporations has been expanding since the Pinto trial concluded—perhaps not as quickly as we had imagined 25 years ago, but expanding nevertheless.

If we were wrong in our predictions about the legacy of the Pinto case, we think that our mistakes were mainly in regard to some of the details, not the general thrust of legal and social change. Clearly, the criminal law has not been used as a means of controlling the manufacture and marketing of dangerous products, but just as clearly there has been an expansion in regulatory controls on automobile safety and product safety generally. In addition, to be fair, in the first edition we noted that many obstacles remained in the way of greater use of the criminal law to control corporate conduct. These obstacles remain and work against the expansion of criminal controls on harmful corporate behavior. In the final chapter of this book, we address these obstacles and argue that they have become less daunting because of a series of broad social and legal changes of which the Pinto case is but one example.

Notes

[1]   Seymour Martin Lipset and William Schneider, *The Confidence Gap. Business, Labor, and Government in the Public Mind.* New York: The Free Press, 1983.

[2]   The term "quiet violence" was coined by Nancy Frank in her book *Crimes Against Health and Safety.* New York: Harrow and Heston, 1985.

[3]   Mark Stavsky, "Manufacturers' Liability," Chapter 35 in Frumer and Friedman, *Products Liability.* Newark, NJ: Matthew Bender/LexisNexis, 2003, vol. 4, p. 2. [Hereinafter cited as Stavsky, "Manufacturers' Liability."] Nonetheless, even with the dearth of such prosecutions since Pinto, it is noteworthy that in the Matthew Bender treatise *Product Liability*, a leading resource book for practicing attorneys, an entire chapter is dedicated to the topic of potential *criminal* liability of manufacturers for unsafe products.

[4]   *Ibid.* It should be noted that in its listing of the Top 100 Corporate Criminals of the [1990s] Decade, the *Corporate Crime Reporter* included six manufacturers convicted of Food and Drug Act–related crimes: C.R Bard, Inc.; Genentech Inc.; Copley Pharmaceutical, Inc.; Warner-Lambert Co.; Odwalla Inc.; and Andrew and Williamson Sales Co. *Corporate Crime Reporter*, vol. 13, no. 34 (September 6, 1999), pp. 11–16. Also on the receiving end of serious civil and potential criminal attention in recent years have been manufacturers of some defective heart-related products. See, for example, Meier, "Repeated Defect in Heart Devices Exposes a History of Problems," available at http://www.newyorktimes.com (October 20, 2005).

5   For a discussion of some of the ways in which plaintiffs' access to compensatory and/or punitive damages in tort cases may be limited, see generally Bonner and Forman, "Bridging the Deterrence Gap," pp. 14–19. By 2005, about half the states had enacted some form of tort reform legislation. See Sean Purdy, "Product Liability," in Lawrence Salinger (ed.), *Encyclopedia of White-Collar and Corporate Crime*. Thousand Oaks, CA: Sage, 2005, vol. 2, pp. 637–640. (Hereinafter cited as *Encyclopedia of WCC*.)

6   See Kevin Golson, "National Highway Traffic [Safety] Administration," in *Encyclopedia of WCC*, p. 556. See also the official NHTSA web site at http://www.nhtsa.dot.gov.

7   *Ibid.*

8   Matthew Robinson, "Defective Products," in *Encyclopedia of WCC*, p. 249.

9   One possible exception might be the Food and Drug–related prosecutions.

10   Elizabeth Purdy, "Firestone Tires," and Robinson, "Defective Products," in *Encyclopedia of WCC*, pp. 322–323 and p. 249.

11   *Ibid.*

12   See "Ford Ordered to Pay $61 Million to Crash Victim Family," available at http://www.yahoonews.com (November 17, 2005). Though no prosecutions were ever brought, for a time serious consideration was given to criminal charges in the United States. See Voris, "Tire Deaths: Criminal Acts?" *National Law Journal* (September 18, 2000), p. 1. It is also interesting to note that in Venezuela, where Ford Explorers equipped with Firestone tires allegedly caused a significant number of fatal accidents, that country's consumer protection agency (Indecu) recommended that its attorney general investigate whether to bring criminal charges against Ford or Firestone. No prosecution was ever brought. See Stavsky, "Manufacturers' Liability," p. 3.

13   The TREAD Act—49 U.S.C. 30101, *et seq.*—took legal effect on November 1, 2000.

14   The law follows the trend in some other countries to criminalize the failure to report dangerous products. See Stavsky, "Manufacturers' Liability," p. 14. Japan, in particular, has actively prosecuted such violations in recent years, including some high profile cases. See, for example, Hijino, "Mitsubishi Motors Indicted in Tokyo," *Financial Times* (April 26, 2001), p. 13.

15   See Stavsky, "Manufacturers' Liability," p. 4

16   *Ibid.*, p. 5. See also "The Ford/Firestone T.R.E.A.D. Bill (H.R. 5164) Reduces Public Access to Crucial Safety Defect Information," available at http://www.publiccitizen.org (October 18, 2000), pp. 1–3.

17   For more details on the original, tougher bill sponsored by Senator McCain, see Stavsky, "Manufacturers' Liability," pp. 4–5.

18   For a detailed analysis of the tobacco industry and litigation see, for example, Larry C. White, *Merchants of Death: The American Tobacco Industry*. New York: Beech Tree Books, 1988. For a similarly detailed analysis of the asbestos industry and litigation see, for example, Paul Brodeur, *Outrageous Misconduct: The Asbestos Industry on Trial*. New York: Pantheon, 1985. See also Brodeur's periodically updated website on the asbestos tragedy at http://www.bumc.bu.edu.

19   See Stavsky, "Manufacturers' Liability," p. 14. See also A. Aldred, "Executives Growing Liability to Force Tighter Risk Control," *Business Insurance* (November 18, 1988), pp. 31–32.

20   *Ibid.*

21   Upton Sinclair, *The Jungle*. Urbana, IL: University of Illinois Press, 1988, annotated edition.

22   Drew, "Meat Packers Pay the Price," *Chicago Tribune* (October 23, 1988), Sec. 1, p. 1. This article was the first in a series on health and safety hazards in the meatpacking industry. The series ran daily from Oct. 23-26, and concluded on Oct. 30.

23   Richard Lacayo, "Death on the Shop Floor," *Time* (September 16, 1991), p. 28.

24   Gary Green, "Upton Sinclair," in *Encyclopedia of WCC*, pp. 746–748.

25   Drew, "Meat Packers," pp. 1, 12. The OSHA report also noted that from 1973 to 1986, the number of workers decreased while the average number of lost workdays rose from 136.6 to 238.4 per 100 workers. Also cited were other federal statistics indicating that approximately one in three production line slaughterhouse workers suffer work-related injuries each year.

26   L. Scott Harshbarger, "Criminal Prosecution of Workplace Violence," *Trial* (October 1997), p. 18.

27   Brian Payne, "Workplace Deaths," in *Encyclopedia of WCC*, pp. 866–868.

28   David Barstow, "When Workers Die" (Parts I–III), *The New York Times* (December 21-23, 2003). This series includes the most extensive statistics yet compiled concerning workplace prosecutions at both the state and federal level.

29   *Ibid.*

30   David Barstow and Lowell Bergman, "With Little Fanfare, a New Effort to Prosecute Employers that Flout Safety Laws," *The New York Times* (May 2, 2005), p. 17.

31   David Barstow, "Pipe Maker Will Admit to Violations of Safety Laws," *The New York Times* (August 30, 2005), p. 16.

32   "Job safety for everyone, with no one left out" was a signature phrase of the National Safe Workplace Institute (NSWI), which became one of the most influential independent health and safety monitoring organizations in the United States beginning in the 1980s. The Chicago-based NSWI issued periodic reports on an unusually wide range of workplace safety–related matters before closing its doors in 1998.

33   Office of Technology Assessment, *Preventing Illness and Injury in the Workplace*, Summary 99th Congress (U.S. Government Printing Office, April 1985), p. 19.

34   See, for example, James Chelius, "The Control of Industrial Accidents: Economic Theory and Empirical Evidence," *Law and Contemporary Problems* 38 (1974), pp. 700–729; James Chelius, "The Influence of Workers' Compensation on Safety Incentives," *Industrial and Labor Relations Journal* 35 (1982), pp. 235–242; and Ronald G. Ehrenberg, "Workers' Compensation, Wages, and the Risk of Injury," in J. Burton (ed.), *New Perspectives in Workers' Compensation*. Ithaca, NY: ILR Press, pp. 71–96.

35   Ronald Conley and John Noble, *Workers' Compensation Reform: Research Report of the Interdepartmental Workers' Compensation Task Force*, 1979, vol. 1, p. 136. (Commissioned report for the Department of Labor.) For further discussion of this issue, see Linda Darling-Hammond and Thomas J. Kniesner, *The Law and Economics of Workers' Compensation*, Santa Monica, CA: RAND, 1980.

36   Darling-Hammond and Kniesner, pp. 39–40. It should be noted that these exceptions relate to allowing tort claims against employers only. For example, while there have been many developments in the area of third-party liability (especially for product liability), a discussion of them is well beyond the scope of this book. For a thorough discussion of third-party liability in the workplace, see generally Jonathan M. Weisgall, "Product Liability in the Workplace: The Effect of Workers' Compensation on the Rights and Liabilities of Third Parties, *Wisconsin Law Review* 19 (1977), p. 135.

37   This brief discussion has focused almost exclusively on the *reductive* function of workers' compensation as it currently applies to intentional torts. Workers' compensation may also have significant shortcomings in efficiently serving its *distributive* goals—especially with regard to occupational illness and disease, as opposed to workplace injury. Thus, it appears likely that any reform movement seeking greater access to the civil courts will need to respond to both the distributive *and* reductive failures of workers' compensation. Additionally, the massive asbestos-related litigation in recent decades has brought several of these issues forward for public debate.

38   Kenneth B. Noble, "The Long Tug-of-War Over What Is How Hazardous: For OSHA, Balance Is Hard to Find," *The New York Times* (January 10, 1988), sec. E, p. 5.

39   Lynn Reinhart, "Would Workers Be Better Protected if They Were Declared an Endangered Species? A Comparison of Criminal Enforcement Under the Federal Workplace Safety and Environmental Protection Laws," *American Criminal Law Review* 31 (1993), p. 355. See, for example, Subcommittee on Labor, Senate Committee on Labor and Public Welfare, 92nd Congress, 1st Session, *Legislative History of the Occupational Safety and Health Act of 1970* (Washington, DC: Committee Print), p. 300. See also Steven Bokat, "Criminal Enforcement of OSHA: Employers' Rights at Risk," *Kentucky Law Review* 17 (1989), pp. 135, 138.

40   *Ibid.* It should be noted that there are significant exclusions and inconsistencies in the application of these statutes. For instance, the Clean Air Act specifically excludes in-plant workplace exposures from the knowing endangerment provisions because it limits those provisions to releases into the air *outside* facilities. See Robert Schwartz, Jr., "Criminalizing Occupational Safety Violations: The Use of 'Knowing Endangerment' Statutes to Punish Employers Who Maintain Toxic Working Conditions," *Harvard Environmental Law Review* 14 (1990), p. 487. Critics have also noted inconsistencies in court decisions interpreting knowing endangerment provisions. As a prime example, in *U.S. v. Protex Industries, Inc.*, 974 F.2d 740 (1989), the Tenth Circuit upheld the conviction of an employer for knowingly endangering ihis employees in violation of the Resource Conservation and Recovery Act. But in *U.S. v. Borowski*, 977 F.2d 27 (1992), the First Circuit reversed the conviction of an employer for knowing endangerment of employees in violation of the Clean Water Act. The courts reached opposite conclusions *even though they were applying nearly identical statutory language*. See Reinhart, "Endangered Species," pp. 371–373.

41   Research revealed no reliable statistics on prosecutions under the Federal Mine Safety and Health Act or Longshoremen's and Harbor Workers' Compensation Act, and only a small number of prosecutions under the Resource Conservation and Recovery Act.

42   See generally David Barstow, "When Workers Die" (Part I), *The New York Times* (December 21, 2003), sec. 1, p. 1. This article was the first in an excellent and extensive three-part series on the underutilization of criminal law in deterring serious employer misconduct leading to employee deaths. The series included the most extensive statistics yet compiled concerning workplace prosecutions at both the state and federal level. Parts II and III of the series continued on page 1 of the *Times* on December 22 and December 23. The article noted that the maximum criminal fine for knowingly causing a worker's death under the OSH Act was finally raised from $10,000 to $500,000 (its current level) in 1984.

43   Reinhart, "Endangered Species," p. 385.

44   James L. Nash, "Justice Department Drops Most Criminal OSHA Referrals," *Occupational Hazards* (February 25, 2004), p. 1, available at http://www.occupationalhazards.com.

45   Reinhart, "Endangered Species," p. 355. See also Senate Subcommittee, *Legislative History of OSHA*, p. 425. A summary of the Senate Bill noted that "for the most part [the bill] rel[ies] on civil monetary penalties rather than criminal sanctions as the means of assuring compliance with the act's requirements."

46   Nash, "Justice Department," p. 1. Senator Metzenbaum (D-Ohio) also introduced a bill that made a number of changes designed to increase the level of penalties in existing law as well as expand the situations under which criminal prosecutions are authorized. See Reinhart, "Endangered Species," p. 385 and accompanying footnotes.

47   There have been some indications that OSHA may be considering an increase in the use of more severe sanctions against employers who flout the law and cause worker injury or death. In March 2003, for example, OSHA announced a new "enhanced enforcement policy" on workplace safety, designed to strengthen its ability to act against companies who receive "high-gravity" citations. Additionally, the Justice Department and EPA launched a criminal investigation of the McWane Corporation in January 2003, the same month the *The New York Times* and PBS/Frontline reported on the long record of serious safety and health violations that have occurred at several of that company's plants. See PBS, "Frontline: An Update on 'A Dangerous Business,'" (May 15, 2003), available at http://www.pbs.org/wgbh/pages/frontline/shows/workplace/etc/update.html. Also, in 2005, one of the nation's oldest electrical contractors, L.E. Myers Co., was convicted in federal court of violating workplace safety rules in the 1999 death of an employee. See Tom Rybarczyk, "Company Guilty in '99 Death," *Chicago Tribune* (May 20, 2005), sec. 1, p. 7.

48   Jay Albanese, Book Review, *Journal of Criminal Law and Criminology* 77 (1986), pp. 1186–1187.

49   In instances in which a worker died as a result of a "willful" safety violation under OSHA, California has criminally prosecuted 36.2 percent of such cases, compared to under 5 percent at both the federal level and in other states. See Barstow, "When Workers Die" (Part II), (December 22, 2003), sec. 1, p. 1—especially the statistical charts and graphs.

50   See William Maakestad and Charles Helm, "Promoting Workplace Safety and Health in the Post-Regulatory Era: A Primer on Non-OSHA Legal Incentives that Influence Employer Decisions to Control Occupational Hazards," *Northern Kentucky Law Review* 17 (1989), pp. 37–42

51   See Barstow, "When Workers Die" (Parts I-III). Note that the maximum criminal penalties in California are far stricter: three years in prison and $1.5 million in fines.

52   *Ibid.*

53   Harshbarger, "Criminal Prosecution of Workplace Violence," pp. 18–20. The author also emphasizes that in addition to common law crime theories, *state* occupational safety and environmental statutes can provide a basis for redressing hazardous workplace practices.

54   As was the case when the first edition of this book was published, the constitutional question of whether the federal OSH Act preempts individual states from bringing criminal charges against corporations and their managerial agents remains unresolved. There are no federal precedents that directly address the matter, and only two state appellate courts have decided the matter—both holding that states are *not* preempted from conducting workplace prosecutions. *People v. Chicago Magnet Wire Corp.*, 126 Ill.2d 356, 534 N.E. 2d 962, cert. denied sub nom. *ASTA v. Illinois*, 58 U.S.L.W. 3202 (1989), and *People v. Hegedus*, 432 Mich. 598, 443 N.W.2d 127 (1989).

55   See generally William Maakestad, "States' Attorneys Stalk Corporate Murderers," *Business and Society Review* 56 (Winter 1986), pp. 21–25; and Nancy Frank, "From Criminal to Civil Penalties in the History of Health and Safety Laws," *Social Problems* 30 (1983), pp. 532–534.

56   See Michael L. Benson, William Maakestad, Francis T. Cullen, and Gilbert Geis, "District Attorneys and Corporate Crime: Surveying the Prosecutorial Gatekeepers," *Criminology* 26 (August 1988), pp. 505–518. In 1989, the National Institute of Justice commissioned the same authors to conduct a national study of the same type, the results of which were analyzed in Michael L. Benson and Francis T. Cullen, *Combating Corporate Crime: Local Prosecutors at Work*. Boston: Northeastern University Press, 1998.

57   See, for example, T. Dunmire, "A Misguided Approach to Worker Safety," *Criminal Justice* (Summer 1988), p. 44.

58   See, for example, John Braithwaite and Gilbert Geis, "On Theory and Action for Corporate Crime Control," *Crime & Delinquency* 28 (April 1982), especially pp. 300–305. The authors argue that business offenders are far more deterrable than "street" criminals for two reasons: They are not committed to crime as a way of life, and their offenses are quintessentially rational rater than expressive or impulsive. For a classic compilation of case studies testing the hypothesis, see generally Brent Fisse and John Braithwaite, *The Impact of Publicity on Corporate Offenders*. Albany: SUNY Press, 1983.

59   Reinhart, "Endangered Species," p. 389. In addition, the title of this section of our book is a paraphrased abbreviation of that article's full title.

60   Theodore M. Hammett and Joel Epstein, *Local Prosecution of Environmental Crime*. Washington, DC: National Institute of Justice, 1993.

61   The material in Table 7.1 and the statistics cited in the text come from the EPA's annual compliance and enforcement reports and are available online. Data for the years 1998-2002 can be found online at http://www.epa.gov/compliance/data/ results/annual/fy2003.html. Click on the tab for "Five Year Trends." For 2004, visit http://www.epa.gov/compliance/data/results/annual/fy2004.html. Again, click on the tab for "Five Year Trends." Finally, for 2005, see http://www. epa.gov/compliance/data/results/annual/fy2005.html and click on the tab for "Numbers at a Glance." In general, for information on EPA enforcement activities, go to the EPA Enforcement and Compliance Home page.

62   Hammett and Epstein, *Local Prosecution of Environmental Crime*, p. 14.

63   Donald J. Rebovich and Richard T. Nixon, *Environmental Crime Prosecution: Results from a National Survey*, Research in Brief. Washington, DC: National Institute of Justice, 1994.

64   Jay Magnuson and Gareth Leviton, "Policy Considerations in Corporate Criminal Prosecutions after *People v. Film Recovery Systems, Inc.*," *Notre Dame Law Review* 62 (1987), pp. 913–939.

65   See Barstow, "When Workers Die" (Part II), especially the statistical charts and graphs.

66   *Ibid*. In response to the lack of preparation of OSHA inspectors, it was recently announced that a new criminal investigation training program was being developed at the agency's training institute. Nash, "OSHA Will Train Inspectors to Do Criminal Investigations," *Occupational Hazards* (February 27, 2004), p. 1, available at http://www.occupationalhazards.com.

67   The six-month maximum prison sentence under the OSH Act is in stark contrast with the maximum 15-year sentence under the Clean Water Act Reinhart, "Endangered Species," p. 353, footnote 15.

68   *Ibid.*, pp. 353–354. The author notes, for example, that both OSHA nd the EPA regulate hazards such as lead, asbestos, and other toxic substances. Yet the EPA's health-based regulations for protecting public health are frequently many times stricter than OSHA's parallel provisions.

69   *Ibid.*, p. 354.

70   42 U.S.C. Sec. 7413.

71   33 U.S.C. Sec. 1155.

72   33 U.S.C. Sec. 1251–1376.

73   42 U.S.C. Sec. 6901–6987.

74   42 U.S.C. Sec. 9601–9675.

75   15 U.S.C. Sec. 2601–2629.

76   For very brief historical sketches with references to other works addressing these watershed environmental events, see generally Chapter 7 ("Environmental Crimes") in J. Kelly Strader, *Understanding White Collar Crime*. Newark, NJ: LexisNexis Matthew Bender, 2006.

77   Robert McMurry and Stephen Ramsey, "Environmental Crime: The Use of Criminal Sanctions in Enforcing Environmental Laws," *Loyola of Los Angeles Law Review* 19 (1986), pp. 1133, 1137–1140.

78   Reinhart, "Endangered Species," pp. 373–380.

79   *Ibid.*

80   James B. Stewart, *Den of Thieves*. New York: Simon and Schuster, 1991.

81   Headquartered in Richmond, Virginia, the National White Collar Crime Center was created by the Leviticus Project Association, which is comprised of law enforcement agencies from several states. See Debra Ross, "National White Collar Crime Center," in *Encyclopedia of WCC*, pp. 558–559.

82   For an excellent summary of how this discipline helps uncover certain white-collar offenses, see Patrick Walsh, "Forensic Accounting," in *Encyclopedia of WCC*, pp. 330–332.

83   Jerold Israel, Ellen Podgor, Paul Borman, and Peter Henning, *White Collar Crime: Law and Practice*, 2nd ed. St. Paul, MN: Thomson/West, 2003; Pamela Bucy, *White Collar Crime: Cases and Materials*, 2nd ed. St. Paul, MN: West Group, 1998; Julie R. O'Sullivan, *Federal White Collar Crime: Cases and Materials*, 2nd ed. St. Paul, MN: Thomson/West, 2003; Kathleen F. Brickey, *Corporate and White Collar Crime: Cases and Materials*, 3rd ed. New York: Aspen Law and Business, 2002; and Harry First, *Business Crime: Cases and Materials*. Westbury, NY: Foundation Press, 1990. Supplemental materials are also available to law students in at least two forms: J. Kelly Strader, *Understanding White Collar Crime*. Newark, NJ: LexisNexis Matthew Bender, 2006, and Ellen Podgor and Jerold Israel, *White Collar Crime in a Nutshell*, 3rd ed. St. Paul, MN: West, 2004. A second edition of Strader's *Understanding White Collar Crime* was released by LexisNexis Matthew Bender in 2006. A fourth edition of Brickey's *Corporate and White Collar Crime: Cases and Materials* was released by Aspen in 2006.

84   Gary Hengstler, "Corporations Under the Gun," *ABA Journal* 73 (June 1987), pp. 32–33. However, this statistic reflects a very broad definition of what constitutes white collar crime.

85   Brickey interview with author (Maakestad), November 23, 2004.

86   V.S. Khanna, "Corporate Crime Legislation: A Political Economy Analysis," Olin Center for Law and Economics (University of Michigan) Paper #03-012 (2003), pp. 10–11, available at http://www.lawumich.edu/centersandprograms/olin/papers/html. The author later published a condensed version of this fascinating paper; see V.S. Vhanna, "Politics and Corporate Crime Legislation," *Regulation* (Spring 2004), pp. 30–35.

87   Quote appears in Stephen Labaton and David Leonhardt, "Whispers Inside. Thunder Outside," in James Surowiecki (ed.), *Best Business Crime Writing of the Year*. New York: Anchor Books, 2002, p. 187. The article originally appeared in the *The New York Times* (June 30, 2002).

88   Strader, *Understanding White Collar Crime*, p. 85. See also Brickey, *Corporate and White Collar Crime*, Chapter 5, pp. 261–275 for a list of 98 defendants prosecuted for insider trading and related violations in the Southern District of New York and, when known, the disposition of their cases.

89   Section 10(b) of the Securities Exchange Act of 1934 prohibits use of a manipulative or deceptive device in connection with the purchase or sale of securities, while Rule 10(b)(5) specifically proscribes the following: (1) employ[ing] a device, scheme, or artifice to defraud; (2) employ[ing] any untrue statement of a material fact or omit[ting] any such fact necessary to make the statement not misleading;

or (3) engag[ing] in a transaction, practice or course of business that would operate as a fraud or deceit. See, for example, Brickey, *Corporate and White Collar Crime*, pp. 225–261.

90   "Conservative Group Urges Easing of Restrictions, Narrower Definition," *Corporate Counsel Weekly*/BNA (December 14, 1988), p. 2. Cited in Brickey, *Corporate and White Collar Crime*, p. 225, footnote 11. The "debate" over the costs and benefits of insider trading laws has since abated, and one sign of this has been the widespread adoption of insider trading laws—frequently modeled after U.S. laws—throughout Europe, east Asia, and in other countries around the world. See Hongming Cheng, "Insider Trading," in *Encyclopedia of WCC*, pp. 430–431.

91   Strader, *Understanding White Collar Crime*, p. 82. For further discussion, see also Julian Friedman and Charles Stillman, "Securities Fraud," in *White Collar Crime: Business and Regulatory Offenses*, vol. 2 (Obermeier and Morvillo, eds.), sec. 12.01[1], p. 2.

92   Labaton and Leonhardt, "Whispers Inside," in *Best Business Crime Writing*, p. 188.

93   The seminal cases in the evolution of the doctrinal rules of insider trading are presented and discussed in Brickey, *Corporate and White Collar Crime*, pp. 226–261. For further discussion, see also Strader, *Understanding White Collar Crime*, pp. 96–106. It should be noted that insider trading prosecutions did *not* end at the end of the 1980s decade. See, for example, *U.S. v. O'Hagan*, 521 U.S. 642 (1997), a landmark in which the Supreme Court dramatically expanded the boundaries of fiduciary duties by approving the misappropriation theory.

94   Pub. L. No. 98-376, Sec 2, 98 Stat. 1264 (1984). Cited in Strader, *Understanding White Collar Crime*, pp. 93–94.

95   The law initially increased the maximum fine to $100,000, which was later increased to $250,000. S. Gunkel, "Insider Trading Sanctions Act," in *Encyclopedia of WCC*, pp. 432–433.

96   *Ibid.*

97   *Ibid.*

98   Pub. L. No. 100-704, Sec. 3-4, 102 Stat. 4677-4678 (1988). The Act's legislative history quotes the following statement made by Wall Street entrepreneur Ivan Boesky to business students in 1985: "Greed is all right, by the way. I want you to know that. I think greed is healthy. You can be greedy and still feel good about yourself." Cited and quoted in Strader, *Understanding White Collar Crime*, p. 94.

99   The RICO law was enacted as Title IX of the Omnibus Crime Control Act of 1970, but lay dormant for several years before its full potential (including its forfeiture provision) was seized upon by federal prosecutors and then (mostly) approved by a series of court decisions. See, for example, *Sedima, S.P.R.L. v. Imrex Co.*, 473 U.S. 479 (1985). For an extended discussion of RICO in practice, see Chapter 10 in Brickey, *Corporate and White Collar Crime*, pp. 527–643.

100   For an extended discussion of the Federal Sentencing Guidelines in practice, see, for example, Chapter 14 in Brickey, *Corporate and White Collar Crime*, especially pp. 849–914; Chapter 19 in Strader, *Understanding White Collar Crime*, pp. 313–326. As noted previously in the book, the Guidelines were established by the U.S. Sentencing Commission, which had been created by the Sentencing Reform

Act of 1984 (Title II of the Comprehensive Crime Control Act of 1984). For a brief history, see Gary Green, "Sentencing Guidelines," in *Encyclopedia of WCC*, pp. 732–737.

[101]   George Bernard Shaw, *Major Barbara*. New York: Penguin, 1957.

[102]   Rob Jameson, "Case Study: U.S. Savings and Loan Crisis," available at http://www. Erisk.com (July 8, 2005).

[103]   Timothy Curry and Lynn Shibut, "The Cost of the Savings and Loan Crisis: Truth and Consequences," *FDIC Banking Review* 13, no. 2 (December 2000), p. 26. Cited in Jameson, "Case Study," p. 5.

[104]   Jameson, "Case Study: U.S. Savings and Loan Crisis," p. 5.

[105]   In 1990, the U.S. Senate Select Committee on Ethics investigated charges that five U.S. Senators had improperly interfered with government investigators on behalf of Charles Keating, who had become embroiled in one of the largest savings and loan scandals. Only one of the senators, Alan Cranston (D-California), ended up being formally rebuked by the Senate. For a brief summary of this scandal, see Elizabeth Purdy, "Keating Five," in *Encyclopedia of WCC*, pp. 476–478.

[106]   Bruce Green, "After the Fall: The Criminal Law Enforcement Response to the S&L Crisis," *Fordham Law Review* 59 (May 1991), p. 1–2. See also A. Scott, "Never Again: The S&L Bailout Bill," *Business Lawyer* 45 (1990), pp. 1885–1889.

[107]   *Ibid.*

[108]   *See*, for example, Paul Pilzer with Robert Dietz, *Other People's Money: The Inside Story of the S&L Mess.* New York: Simon and Schuster, 1989; Stephen Pizzo, Mary Fricker, and Paul Muolo, *Inside Job: The Looting of America's Savings and Loans.* New York: McGraw-Hill, 1989; Martin Mayer, *The Greatest-Ever Bank Robbery.* New York: C. Scribner's Sons, 1990; Michael Waldman, *Who Robbed America?* New York: Random House, 1990.

[109]   Michael McGregor, "Savings and Loan Scandal," in *Encyclopedia of WCC*, p. 712.

[110]   See Mark Roodhouse, "Barings Bank" and "Bank of Credit and Commerce International," both in *Encyclopedia of WCC*, pp. 83–85, 79–80.

[111]   For example, one of the earliest and most blatant frauds in the thrift industry— Centennial Savings and Loan—led to its collapse back in 1985. See Michael Siegfried, "Centennial Savings and Loan," in *Encyclopedia of WCC*, pp. 148–149. See also *72nd Report of the Committee on Government Operations*, House Report 100-1088 (U.S. Government Printing Office).

[112]   McGregor, "Savings and Loan Scandal," p. 716.

[113]   See 136 *Congressional Record* S9478 (July 11, 1990), cited in Green, "After the Fall," p. 2, footnote 5.

[114]   Statement by U.S. Senator and presidential candidate Robert Dole (R-Kansas), quoted in Green, "After the Fall," p. 2, footnote 6.

[115]   Statement by U.S. Senator Charles Grassley (R-Iowa). *Ibid.*

[116]   McGregor, "Savings and Loan Scandal," p. 712.

[117]   It is interesting to note that the very first criminal provision incorporated into a comprehensive legislative package regulating business practices appears to have been related to financial institutions: The National Bank Act, 12 Stat. 665, 675 (1863).

Green, "After the Fall," p. 2, footnote 19. It predates by more than 20 years Section 10 of the Interstate Commerce Act of 1887, which is commonly thought to include the first "business crime." See, for example, First, *Business Crime*, pp. 1–2.

118 18 U.S.C.A. Sec. 1341, 1343 (West. Supp. 2003). Cited in Brickey, "From Enron to Worldcom and Beyond: Life and Crime After Sarbanes-Oxley," *Washington University Law Quarterly* 81 (2003), p. 377, footnote 86. Also see generally Kathleen F. Brickey, *Corporate Criminal Liability: A Treatise on the Criminal Liability of Corporations, Their Officers, and Agents*, 2nd ed., Chapter 8A. Deerfield, IL: Clark Boardman Callaghan, 1992.

119 18 U.S.C.A., Sec 1344 (West 2000). *Ibid.*

120 18 U.S.C.A., Sec. 1510(b)(1) (West 2000) and 18 U.S.C.A. Sec. 1517 (West 2000). *Ibid.*

121 18 U.S.C.A., Sec. 1961 (West 2000 & Supp. 2003). *Ibid.*

122 Compare 18 U.S.C.A. Sec. 225 (West 2000) with 21 U.S.C.A. Sec. 848(c) (West 1999). *Ibid.*

123 18 U.S.C.A. Sec. 981(a)(1)(C)-(E) (West Supp. 2003). *Ibid.*

124 12 U.S.C. Sec. 3331, *et seq.* See also Baxter Dunaway and Deon Dunaway, *FIRREA: Law and Practice*. Deerfield, IL: Clark Boardman Callaghan, 1992.

125 The number of environmental criminals was 38, to be exact. See *Corporate Crime Reporter*, vol 13., no. 34 (September 6, 1999), pp. 1, 11–16.

126 Elizabeth Purdy, "Salomon Smith Barney," in *Encyclopedia of WCC*, pp. 709–710.

127 Dan Webb, Steven Molo, and James Hurst, "Understanding and Avoiding Corporate and Executive Criminal Liability," *Business Lawyer* 49 (February 1994), p. 619.

128 P.J. O'Rourke, "How to Stuff a Wild Enron," in *Best Business Crime Writing*, p. 220. The article originally appeared in *Atlantic Monthly* (April 2002).

129 James Surowiecki, "Introduction," in *Best Business Crime Writing*, p. ix.

130 Harvey Cox, "The Market as God," *Atlantic Monthly* (March 1999), pp. 18–23.

131 Kathleen F. Brickey, "Enron's Legacy," *Buffalo Criminal Law Review* 8 (2004), p. 222, footnotes 2–4 and accompanying text.

132 2004 Brickey interview with author.

133 Brickey, "Enron's Legacy," p. 246. It must also be noted that like most complex corporate and white-collar crime prosecutions, these cases are not easy cases for the prosecution to prove. For a fascinating discussion by legal experts regarding the kinds of hurdles faced by prosecutors in "Enron-era" cases, see "Analysis: White Collar Convictions," National Public Radio's Talk of the Nation (June 8, 2005), available at http://nl.newsbank.com/nl-search/we/Archives?p_action=doc&p_docid=10A9E11159333. See also Burns, "Enron Trial Turns on Truth, Intent," *Chicago Tribune* (February 19, 2006), sec. 5, p. 1. Nonetheless, some of the prosecutions have led to unprecedented prison sentences for criminal fraud, including potential 25-year terms for former CEOs of major companies. See Ken Belson, "WorldCom Chief is Given 25 Years for Huge Fraud," http://www.nytimes.com (July 14, 2005), and Andrew Ross Sorkin, "Ex-Tyco Executives Get 8 to 25 Years in Prison," available at http://www.nytimes.com (September 20, 2005).

134 "Scandal Scorecard," *The Wall Street Journal* (November 18, 2003), sec. C, p. 1; Clifton Leaf, "It's Time to Stop Coddling White-Collar Crooks. Send Them to Jail," *Fortune* (March 18, 2002), pp. 60–64, 68–76; Penelope Patsuris, "The Corporate Scandal Sheet," *Forbes* (August 26, 2002), available at http://www.Forbes.com; Surowiecki, *Best Business Crime*; and, for an excellent analysis of the celebrated Martha Stewart prosecution, see Kathleen F. Brickey, "Mostly Martha," *Washburn Law Journal* 44 (Spring 2005).

135 Brickey, "Enron's Legacy," p. 252. As of August 29, 2005, the Corporate Fraud Task Force secured more than 700 corporate fraud convictions; convicted more than 100 CEOs and presidents, more than 80 vice-presidents, and more than 30 CFOs; charged more than 1,300 defendants; and collected more than $266 million in restitution, fines, and forfeitures. At the same time, the Enron Task Force obtained charges against 33 Enron defendants; convicted 11 Enron defendants (including its former CFO and treasurer); and seized more than $162 million for victims of fraud. "Fact Sheet: Corporate Fraud Task Force," U.S. Department of Justice (August 29, 2005), # 05-434, available at http://www.USDOJ.gov.

136 Surowiecki, "Introduction," in *Best Business Crime Writing*, p. ix.

137 John C. Coffee, "Understanding Enron: It's the Gatekeepers, Stupid," *Business Lawyer* 57 (August 2002), pp. 1–2.

138 Surowiecki, "Introduction," in *Best Business Crime Writing*, pp. xii–xiii.

139 Coffee, "Understanding Enron," p. 1. For perhaps the best books on the Enron scandal, see Bethany McLean and Peter Elkind, *The Smartest Guys in the Room: The Amazing Rise and Scandalous Fall of Enron.* New York: Portfolio, 2003; and Kurt Eichenwald, *Conspiracy of Fools: A True Story.* New York: Broadway Books, 2005. *The Smartest Guys in the Room* was also made into a feature film and released in early 2005.

140 *Ibid.*, pp. 3–4.

141 *Ibid.*, p. 5.

142 *Ibid.*, p. 8.

143 Brickey, "Enron's Legacy," pp. 228–229.

144 Sarbanes-Oxley Act, Pub. L. 107-204, 116 Stat. 804 (2002).

145 David Stout, "Bush Signs Broad Changes in Business Law," *The New York Times* (July 30, 2002), available at http://www.nytimes.com/2002/07/30/business/30 CND-BUSH.html. Cited in Jennifer Recine, "Note: Examination of the White Collar Penalty Enhancements in the Sarbanes-Oxley Act," *American Criminal Law Review* 39 (Fall 2002), p. 1535, footnote 2.

146 Sarbanes-Oxley passed by a vote of 423–3 in the House, and 99–0 in the Senate.

147 Recine, "Penalty Enhancements in Sarbanes-Oxley," p. 1. These issues are listed in Sarbanes-Oxley's table of contents, Sec. 1(b).

148 Brickey, "Enron's Legacy," p. 231, footnotes 40–43 and accompanying text.

149 Recine, "Penalty Enhancements in Sarbanes-Oxley," p. 1547.

150 18 U.S.C.A. Sec. 1348 (West Supp. 2003). Cited in Brickey, "Enron's Legacy," p.231, footnote 44.

151 18 U.S.C.A. Sec 1519 (West Supp. 2003). *Ibid.*, footnote 45.

152 18 U.S.C.A. Sec. 1350(a), (b) (West Supp. 2003). *Ibid.*, footnote 46.

153 18 U.S.C.A. Sec. 1350(c) (West Supp. 2003). *Ibid.*, footnote 47.

154 18 U.S.C.A. Sec. 1513(e) (West 2000 & Supp. 2003). *Ibid.*, footnote 48.

155 18 U.S.C.A. Sec. 1512(c) (West 2000 & Supp. 2003). *Ibid.*, footnote 49.

156 See, for example, 15 U.S.C.A. Sec. 78ff(a) (West 1997 & Supp. 2003), which increases penalties for securities fraud, and 18 U.S.C.A. Sec. 1341 (West 2000 & Supp. 2003), which increases penalties for mail fraud. *Ibid.*, footnote 50.

157 Jonathan Glater, "Here It Comes: The Sarbanes-Oxley Backlash," *The New York Times* (April 17, 2005), p. 5. A survey by Financial Executives International indicated that the average cost of compliance would be $4.36 million for firms with revenues of at least $5 billion— 39 percent higher than initial estimates.

158 See Michael Perino, "Enron's Legislative Aftermath: Some Reflections on the Deterrence Aspects of the Sarbanes-Oxley Act of 2002," *St. John's Law Review* 76 (2002), pp. 676–689. Cited in Brickey, "From Enron to WorldCom and Beyond," p. 359, footnote 6.

159 See, for example, Brickey, "From Enron to WorldCom and Beyond," p. 359, footnotes 7–8 and accompanying text. See also Recine, "Penalty Enhancements in Sarbanes-Oxley," pp. 1155–1163. It is interesting to note that Sarbanes-Oxley and other recent legal changes created first a market and then a cottage industry for software aimed at corporate compliance. See Bulkeley and Forelle, "How Corporate Scandals Gave Tech Firms a New Business Line," *The Wall Street Journal* (December 9, 2005), sec. 1, p. 1.

160 See generally, for example, Brickey, "Enron's Legacy" and "From Enron to WorldCom and Beyond"; and Recine, "Penalty Enhancements in Sarbanes-Oxley."

161 Brickey, "From Enron to WorldCom and Beyond," pp. 359–360.

162 Recine, "Penalty Enhancements in Sarbanes-Oxley," p. 11, footnote 184. This language is found in Sec. 905(a) of Sarbanes-Oxley.

163 Brickey, "Enron's Legacy," p. 232, footnotes 53–55 and accompanying text.

164 *Ibid.*, p. 233.

165 *Ibid.*, p. 230, footnote 37.

166 *Ibid.*, p. 253.

167 *Ibid.*, pp. 229–230, footnotes 30, 36.

168 *Ibid.*, footnote 36.

169 Kathleen F. Brickey, "In Enron's Wake: Corporate Executive on Trial," *Journal of Criminal Law and Criminology* 96 (Winter, 2006), pp. 406–407.

170 See, for example, Susan E. Squires et al., *Inside Arthur Andersen: Shifting Values, Unexpected Consequences.* Upper Saddle River, NJ: Financial Times/Prentice Hall (2003). See also McLean and Elkind, *The Smartest Guys in the Room.* On May 31, 2005, the U.S. Supreme Court reversed the conviction of Arthur Andersen. *Arthur Andersen LLP v. U.S.*, 374 F.2d 281 (2005).

171 Brickey, "Enron's Legacy," p. 234, footnote 63.

172 *Ibid.*, pp. 251–252.

173 *Ibid.*, p. 240, footnote 85.

174 *Ibid.*, p. 241, footnotes 86–93.

175 *Ibid.*, p. 242, footnote 95.

176 For a brief, accessible description of the most common types of securities frauds, see generally Patrick Walsh, "Securities Fraud," in *Encyclopedia of WCC*, pp. 725–729.

177 Brickey, "Enron's Legacy," p. 242, footnote 97.

178 *Ibid.*, p. 243, footnotes 100–101.

179 *Ibid.*, p. 245, footnote 112.

180 The Martin Act, N.Y. Gen.Bus.Law, Art. 23-A, sec. 352 *et seq.* (McKinney 1996), is considered a Progressive-era "Blue Sky" law previously thought to have limited potential outside extreme securities frauds and "boiler room" operations. Whereas Depression-era federal securities laws have generally supplanted the use of the older state laws everywhere else, Spitzer has used the Martin Act as a tool to bring reform to the investment banking, mutual fund, and insurance industries in New York. See, for example, Robert McTamaney, "New York's Martin Act: Expanding Enforcement in an Era of Federal Securities Regulation," *Washington Legal Foundation Legal Backgrounder* 18 (February 28, 2003), p. 1.

181 *Ibid.*, p. 2.

182 2004 Brickey interview with author.

8

Prosecuting Corporate Crime in the Twenty-First Century

Near the end of the first edition of this book, we observed that despite the great notoriety and significance of the Pinto case, corporate prosecutions were still rare, and when they did occur they often did not succeed. In one sense, the situation today is not greatly different from what it was then. Compared to ordinary street crimes, corporate prosecutions still are rare events. However, as we demonstrated in the preceding chapter, they are neither as rare nor as likely to fail as they used to be. Although there still are formidable ideological, legal, and structural obstacles to corporate prosecutions, these obstacles are not quite as forbidding as they were in the past. Times have changed. In this final chapter, we address what has and what has not changed regarding the use of the criminal law against corporations. We begin by acknowledging and describing the obstacles that prosecutors must consider when deciding whether to take on corporate cases. Then, we conclude by describing broad changes in legal doctrines and social perceptions regarding corporate wrongdoing. We believe these changes have made it increasingly likely that prosecutors will decide, despite the obstacles, that it is legally feasible and morally necessary for them to take on corporate prosecutions.

THE PRAGMATICS OF ENFORCEMENT

There is no getting around the fact that the very structure of corporations coupled with the types of crimes they commit make prosecutions difficult and costly. Indeed, at each stage of the criminal justice system, circumstances exist that limit the practicality of using the criminal law to control corporate wrongdoing—even when a prosecutor might wish to launch a case and would be permitted to do so by existing legal statutes. These circumstances often place the greatest burden on county prosecutors such as Michael Cosentino, but they can be formidable obstacles to successful corporate criminal cases even for federal prosecutors, who may possess more resources and experience in trying white-collar offenders.

Detecting Crime

To begin with, corporate offenses are difficult to detect, and detection is a precondition for any prosecution. Although it is usually obvious when a traditional crime has taken place, corporate crimes are almost always less apparent. The difference in visibility is tied directly to the nature of the crimes involved in each offense category. Missing property, a mugging, or an assault are forced upon a victim's attention. By contrast, the very structure of most corporate acts insulates workers or citizens from knowledge of their victimization.[1] Typically, corporate offenders are not present physically at the scene of the crime, and the effects of their victimization are diffused over time (as when toxic agents are released into the workplace or the environment) and over populations (as when prices are fixed on consumer products). The offender–victim relationship is distant, if not fully abrogated. In addition, corporate offenders typically go to great lengths to hide the illegal nature of their activities. They use deception and deceit to conceal the fact that a crime has occurred.[2] These factors militate against people blaming corporations for lost income or impaired health.

The loosely linked nature of the victim–offender relationship and the mechanics of the offenses necessarily limit the detection of corporate lawlessness. Law enforcement is primarily a reactive process: investigations begin only after citizens report that a crime has taken place. Because many victims of corporate illegality lack the awareness to file a crime report, no state response is forthcoming. Of course, police do employ proactive methods to detect certain ongoing criminal activities—for example, "undercover agents" and "sting operations" when investigating vice-, drug-, and "Mafia"-related enterprises—and these could be used to unmask corporate malfeasance. In most jurisdictions, however, this remains a moot point: criminal justice agencies have neither the inclination nor the expertise to undertake proactive operations in hopes of discovering unlawful corporate practices.[3] In addition, even when proactive strategies are used, they are typically employed against small businesses, such as auto or appliance repair shops, not major corporations.[4]

Deciding to Prosecute

In corporate cases the decision to prosecute often is ambiguous and complex. It is ambiguous because prosecutors must first decide whether a crime has indeed occurred. As we have tried to demonstrate throughout this book, establishing this fundamental fact may not be easy. The decision to prosecute is complex because prosecutors must balance their desire to enforce the law against the reality of limited resources. "Desirable as it may be to punish the wicked," John Coffee has observed, "one cannot ignore that the supply of such persons vastly exceeds available prosecutorial resources."[5] Necessarily, then, prosecutors must exercise discretion in deciding which cases to pursue and which cases to ignore or refer to other control agencies (e.g., state or federal regulatory agencies). Certainly, prosecutors face powerful disincentives for embarking on a campaign to maintain law and order in the business community.

To understand why prosecutors decide to proceed against some instances of corporate illegality and not others, it is helpful to first understand what purposes they hope to serve in conducting a prosecution. In regard to ordinary street crimes, the primary goals of prosecution are special deterrence and incapacitation. Prosecutors want to get the bad guys off the street. In corporate cases, however, the primary goal is more likely to be general deterrence. Prosecutors see these cases as important opportunities to get a message out to the business community. General deterrence is the purpose that is uppermost in the mind of prosecutors of corporate cases.[6] A prosecutor involved in the famous *Film Recovery Systems* case summed up his view in this way.

> There's only one advantage to these prosecutions. One of these prosecutions is worth five hundred as far as deterrent value is concerned. I've prosecuted maybe fifty murderers, and I've never deterred the street murderer once. I've probably prosecuted one industrial murderer and I think we've deterred a whole lot of people, at least woke them up and some people are trying to do the right thing. So even with a lack of resources, one [of these] prosecutions is much more valuable than one streetwise, or what they call traditional, street crime prosecution.[7]

Another closely related rationale, the desire to educate both the business community and the general public, also guides prosecutorial decisionmaking. Hauling a corporate offender into court makes it explicit just where the boundary line is drawn between acceptable and unacceptable conduct in business. In the opinion of prosecutors, the educational potential of corporate prosecutions also extends to the general public. It sends a message that the system is fair and that no one, not even powerful corporate executives, is above the law. A prosecutor interviewed as part of a national study of how local prosecutors respond to corporate crime put it this way, "I believe that we need to send the signal that crime in the suites is just as important as crime in the streets."[8]

Finally, it is important to note that Michael Cosentino is not alone in having a moral and emotional response to corporate violence. Other prosecutors and other officials in the criminal justice system share his view that corporate violence deserves to be punished. They do not view these crimes in morally neutral terms. Rather, they are morally outraged by the callous indifference with which some business decisions are made. As a result of this outrage, they believe that it is important to punish corporate offenders and to make sure that they get their just deserts.[9]

Nevertheless, despite their desire to achieve general deterrence, educate the business community, and punish corporate misbehavior, prosecutors often decide not to file charges. A variety of circumstances may prove influential in persuading prosecutors that the costs of pursuing a corporate case outweigh the benefits. Investigating and prosecuting corporate cases make considerable demands on investigatory and prosecutorial resources. Before deciding to prosecute, prosecutors must weigh the feasibility of winning a complex case against a powerful corporation and decide whether it is prudent to devote their limited economic and human resources to a case with an unpredictable outcome, particularly in light of their constituents' potential reaction and the simultaneous need for resources to process street-crime offenders.[10] We may recall that in the Pinto prosecution, Cosentino tried to overcome these obstacles by requesting a special budget allocation of $20,000, securing a volunteer staff, and keeping a close eye on community sentiments. Other prosecutors, less adventurous or more cautious, have often chosen to bypass the disruption of routines, political risk, and personal cost entailed in attacking a corporation.

Another consideration concerns the relationship between district attorneys' offices and other governmental agencies. Because most allegations of corporate crime involve activities supervised at least partially by regulatory agencies, the path of least resistance for many prosecutors has been to refer any irregularities to an administrative agency. The availability of alternative remedies in the form of regulatory actions is a significant factor that limits the willingness of local prosecutors to take on corporate cases.[11] Even when prosecutors do decide to try a corporate offender, they still must take into account the interests and priorities of other governmental agencies. Officials in regulatory agencies may react as though their "turf" has been violated and may become uncooperative—as did officials from NHTSA and OSHA during the early stages of the Pinto case and *Film Recovery Systems* case, respectively. Though such problems may be overcome (both NHTSA and OSHA eventually provided assistance in the Ford and Film Recovery Systems prosecutions), a prosecutor cannot risk alienating a potentially helpful regulatory agency: in corporate cases, a prosecutorial staff often is overwhelmed by technical documents and jargon, and hence can ill-afford to forfeit the expertise and resources an agency has to offer.[12]

Prosecutors also face the difficult decision of whether to indict individual executives and/or the corporate entity. Legal scholars still dispute this issue on a number of philosophical and policy grounds: Can a corporation form criminal intent? Will the harm incurred by a corporate sanction fall on innocent parties, such as shareholders and employees? Do chief executives create pressures that induce mid-level managers to violate the law, but remain insulated against criminal culpability by their organizational position? Are individual executives or corporations more deterrable?[13]

We suspect, however, that the key issue for many prosecutors is less esoteric and more narrowly pragmatic: whom do they have a reasonable chance of convicting? The presence or absence of obstacles, then, will not only determine whether a prosecution is initiated, it will also pinpoint the target of any indictment that might be secured. Certainly this was true in the Pinto case, in which Cosentino determined quickly that he had little chance of extraditing and convicting individual Ford officials. In the *Film Recovery Systems* case, by contrast, the size of the firm and the nature of the offense made it feasible to attempt to convict both the corporation and individual executives.

Building a Case

Once the initial decision is made to move ahead with a prosecution, the very nature of corporate illegality creates special barriers. In processing street crimes, prosecutors often can rely on witnesses to furnish damning testimony; they saw who mugged them or can identify stolen property found in a suspect's possession. This situation occurs only occasionally in white-collar cases, especially those that take place within large corporations, as when current or former employees—like

Harley Copp in the Pinto dispute—become "whistleblowers" and reveal what took place behind the closed doors of a corporation. More often, however, organizational secrecy means that the only witnesses to a corporate crime are the offenders themselves.[14]

Like other defendants, corporate offenders are reluctant to cooperate with their accusers. However, in contrast to street criminals, who have little control over the evidence that comes to the attention of enforcement officials, the organizational position of corporate executives gives them the opportunity to obfuscate evidence or to reveal it selectively. As a result, they exert considerable control over both the degree and the kind of information that prosecutors will be able to ferret out.[15]

Moreover, their attorneys help them to deflect prosecutorial attempts to secure incriminating evidence. In his study of white-collar crime defense attorneys, Kenneth Mann discovered that the main strategy of these lawyers is "information control"—keeping "evidence out of government reach by controlling access to information"—rather than "the conventional advocacy task of substantive argument in which the defense attorney analyzes a set of facts and argues that a crime is not proved."[16] These attorneys use two approaches to ensure that items such as company records, reports, internal memoranda, and test results escape the prosecutor's grasp. First, in "adversarial information control," they invoke legal rules and precedents to argue that prosecutors should not have access to certain corporate documents. Second, in "managerial information control," they instruct clients "holding inculpatory information how to refrain from disclosing it to the government and, if necessary, to persuade or force him to refrain."[17] The adversarial approach to information control is inherent in our system and can be used by counsel for traditional as well as corporate defendants. The managerial approach, however, is particularly well suited to corporate defendants: they often have considerable control over the very information—technical documents, internal memoranda, knowledge of how decisions were made—that prosecutors require to develop a plausible case against them.

Corporations do not always succeed, however, in maintaining complete control over potentially incriminating evidence. As we saw in the Pinto case, Ford's "corporate closet" was opened over the course of a decade by Harley Copp's revelations, by lawyers in civil cases, by investigative reports (such as Dowie's article in *Mother Jones* and the "60 Minutes" segment), and by NHTSA's testing and inquiries. Even so, building a case against Ford was not a simple task. Once company documents were compiled, it was necessary to decide how this information could be used to convince a jury to convict Ford of reckless homicide. As discussed in Chapter 6, Terry Kiely spent several months developing the necessary expertise to make sense of Ford's reports, reconstructing the Pinto's history, and preparing the prosecution's case for trial.

Similar difficulties are likely to face prosecutors who succeed in neutralizing a corporation's attempts to control information. Because illegalities are embedded within the corporation's decision-making structure and economic function, prosecutors must often devote considerable time to learning about the corporation and about how the criminal enterprise was carried out.[18] Moreover, the skills required to analyze evidence are quite different from those normally employed to build a case against a street criminal. Many corporate documents are couched in highly specialized or technical language, making the necessary research academic, tedious, and dull. Further, reviewing company files and reports can be a formidable assignment; even small corporations can produce a staggering volume of paperwork, particularly if several years' records must be studied. Without a staff of experienced investigators and researchers, deciphering what is salient and what can be ignored safely may not be accomplished quickly or accurately enough.[19]

Thus, prosecutors face a double-edged sword. On the one hand, successful information control by a corporation means that too little evidence will be available to win a conviction. On the other hand, access to a wealth of corporate documents may prove a Pyrrhic victory because there may be too much evidence to process. Whether the information is insufficient or overwhelming, it could lead a state's attorney to the same conclusion: a convincing case cannot be built and thus the prosecution should be terminated.[20]

Bringing the Defendant to Trial

As the chronicle of the Pinto saga reveals, the time between a corporation's indictment and the trial can determine the character and perhaps the very survival of a case. We noted previously that the defense will raise legal arguments to have the indictment quashed or critical evidence suppressed. Apart from the legal merit of these arguments, practical considerations also apply.

First, does the prosecution have the legal expertise to counteract the defense's efforts to scuttle the case or to limit it severely? Cosentino was able to counteract Ford's briefs with the assistance of law professors Bruce Berner and Terry Kiely, but not all district attorneys will have the good fortune to secure such expert services free of charge.

Second, how many prosecutors have the tenacity for this kind of fight? A corporation's legal maneuverings will consume a great deal of time and exhaust much of the prosecutor's emotional reserve. Many corporations have the resources to absorb the costs of filing legal brief after legal brief and of stretching out the pretrial phase over several years. By contrast, the organizational strength of most prosecutorial offices is limited, and the comparative organizational costs of a prolonged legal battle are potentially much greater. Moreover, the brunt of these burdens is likely to fall most heavily on the shoulders of a few individuals—like Cosentino and his small staff—who must sustain a high level of personal involvement and risk in the face of a corporate opponent.

Winning the Trial

As the Pinto case illustrates poignantly, success in bringing a corporation to trial does not mean that the most serious obstacles to winning a conviction have been surmounted. With so much at stake, corporate defendants have a large incentive to retain prestigious law firms—like Neal and Harwell—and give them the resources to formulate a vigorous counterattack. These resources allow such attorneys to conduct investigations that "leave nothing to chance" and to purchase the expert testimony needed to dispute the substantive points of the prosecution's case. Yet, if the Pinto case is representative, corporate defense lawyers are also apt to use their legal expertise and staff resources to make continued efforts at information control. At the very beginning of Ford's trial, James Neal filed numerous motions *in limine* to restrict severely the kind of evidence that Cosentino could introduce (such as pictures of the victims and documents on pre-1973 Pintos). As recalled from Chapter 6, these briefs were prepared in the months before the trial and played a crucial role in thwarting the prosecution's case.

Prosecutors must also overcome the problems inherent in presenting a complex corporate crime case to a jury of laypersons, particularly if the defense has used experts (such as Hans Zeisel) to assist in selecting jurors sympathetic to its interests. Unlike specialized corporate criminal defense attorneys who have had significant trial experience, prosecutors often are on unfamiliar ground as they use corporate documents and technical testimony to convince jurors that an intricate sequence of bureaucratic decisions over a number of years culminated in a criminal offense rather than in unforeseeable harm.[21] This task is complicated further for prosecutors, who must rely on scientific data (for example, test crashes or measures of toxicity of a work environment) to prove "guilt beyond a reasonable doubt." As John Braithwaite and Gilbert Geis have commented:

Pollution, product safety, and occupational safety and health prosecutions typically turn on scientific evidence that the corporation caused certain consequences. In cases that involve scientific dispute, proof beyond a reasonable doubt is rarely, if ever, possible. Science deals in probabilities, not certainties. The superstructure of science is erected on a foundation of mathematical statistics which estimate a probability that inferences are true or false. Logically, proof beyond a reasonable doubt that a "causes" b is impossible. It is always possible that an observed correlation between a and b is explained by an unknown third variable c. The scientist can never eliminate all the possible third variables.[22]

Beyond these constraints, prosecutors must deal at times with judges—such as Harold Staffeldt—who seem uncomfortable if not antagonistic to the prospect of bringing into their courtroom a corporation and its executives. Part of this reluctance may be ideological. As Leonard Orland has contended, "many judges perceive corporate crime as victimless. . . . Corporate crime is seen as nothing more than aggressive capitalism—a virtue, not a vice, in a capitalistic system which espouses profit maximization as morally sound."[23] We are not certain that Orland's insight is empirically accurate—we suspect that the tendency, even among judges, to view harmful corporate conduct as morally neutral has declined in recent times—but his point is well taken.[24]

There are other reasons, however, why prosecutors may not fare as well with judges as they do normally. Unlike typical street crimes, which are readily understood, judges must come to grips with the complexities of a corporate offense. Because not all judges succeed at this task, they may hesitate to view a corporation as clearly criminally culpable.[25] Judges also may find themselves in unfamiliar legal territory; prosecutors may ask them to embrace innovative applications of law, which the defense counters by filing lengthy briefs claiming rights traditionally afforded to individual defendants. As seen in the Pinto case, at least some judges seek to resolve this ambiguity by relying on narrow or strict constructionist readings of the criminal law that do not allow the prosecution, in Michael Cosentino's words, "to tell the whole story."

Finally, it should be mentioned that a prosecutor's work does not end with a guilty verdict. Corporate convictions can lead to lengthy appeals that involve intricate legal arguments and threaten to consume additional resources. The prosecution may not have the expertise and sustained commitment to win in the appeals court.

We do not wish to claim that we have presented an exhaustive list of the obstacles that limit the initiation and success of corporate criminal prosecutions. Nonetheless, we hope our analysis is sufficient to furnish a sense of the formidable barriers that prosecutors may encounter. At the same time, we do not intend to imply—as some commentators have done—that the obstacles are so great as to preclude or undermine all attempts to sanction corporations criminally. This viewpoint, we believe, leads to two errors.

First, such a perspective ignores the reality that the obstacles vary from one corporate crime case to another, and that prosecutors have varying incentives to launch a case despite the promise of a difficult struggle. Rather than assuming that barriers will deter all but the irrational or the ideological from seeking a corporate indictment, it is more profitable to explore the conditions under which prosecutions are likely to take place.

It is apparent, for example, that the capacity to punish corporations varies across jurisdictions; U.S. Attorneys and state prosecutors in large urban counties (like Cook County) are more likely to have the staff, funds, and expertise to undertake and win corporate cases.[26] This is true particularly when special units have been created to investigate and prosecute white-collar offenders, as in Los Angeles County. In addition, corporate defenders are not equally able to fend off attempts to criminalize them. Not all businesses possess the resources and the stature to attract expert legal counsel, and even when a quality defense attorney is retained, it will be difficult to avoid prosecution if existing evidence clearly establishes the corporation's culpability (as in the E.F. Hutton case). Research also indicates that the seriousness of an illegality is important in determining whether an indictment will be sought.[27] Prosecutors have a compelling reason to give a corporate case high priority when huge sums of money have been obtained fraudulently or, for that matter, when three teenagers perish in a flaming crash.[28] Further, as a number of commentators have observed, attempts to sanction corporations criminally are more likely when regulatory or civil controls either are not available or have proven ineffective. Thus, a study of the Securities and Exchange Commission enforcement process concluded that "criminal prosecution is often invoked as a residual response when other options cannot be pursued."[29] As observed earlier, prosecutors have pointed to the absence or failure of OSHA controls as a reason for indicting corporate offenders for harm in the workplace; again, Jay Magnuson, the prosecutor in the *Film Recovery Systems* corporate murder case in Chicago, stated that he "stepped in because nobody else would do it."[30] We also recall from the Pinto case that one of Michael Cosentino's justifications for prosecuting Ford was his feeling that neither NHTSA nor previous civil judgments had moved the company to fix the Ulrichs' Pinto, and that under Indiana law, the teenagers' parents could have received only limited financial compensation for their tragic loss.

The second pitfall of assuming that the obstacles to corporate prosecution are prohibitive is that this perspective ignores that the social and legal context changes over time. In the next section, we discuss how the context has changed in ways that will sustain a continued movement against corporate and white-collar crime and support attempts to bring business organizations within the reach of the criminal law.

CORPORATE CRIMINALS OR CRIMINAL CORPORATIONS? THE RISE OF ORGANIZATIONAL LIABILITY

> Corporation, *n*. An ingenious device for obtaining individual profit without individual responsibility.
> — Ambrose Bierce[31]

On June 16, 2002, a Chicago jury declared the accounting firm of Arthur Andersen guilty of a felony charge of obstructing justice for destroying more than a ton of documents and deleting more than 30,000 e-mails and computer files related to one of its most important clients: Enron. At the time of the conviction, Andersen was one of the five largest accounting firms in the world, with nearly 85,000 employees worldwide. Within a year of the conviction, employees of Andersen numbered less than 300.[32] The Arthur Andersen trial marked the most publicized criminal prosecution of a business organization since the Ford Pinto case. And, though the firm's conviction was later overturned by the U.S. Supreme Court on technical grounds, the Andersen case highlighted a core issue identical to one that had been raised in Ford Pinto more than 20 years before: Can a corporation—or any other form of business enterprise—commit a crime?[33]

While the very idea of holding a business enterprise criminally responsible was attacked on several legal fronts during the pretrial stage of the Ford Pinto prosecution, by the time of the Andersen prosecution, corporate criminal liability presented far fewer legal and conceptual obstacles. As Kathleen Brickey has observed, the Pinto case served as an important catalyst for getting us to think more broadly about the spectrum of liability for business crimes. In short, viewed after a quarter-century, Ford Pinto has left "less a product liability legacy, and more an enterprise liability legacy."[34] This legacy continues today, and can be found not only in statutory law and court cases, but also in the work of such leading legal scholars as Brickey and Pamela Bucy, whose writing has strengthened the philosophical underpinning of corporate criminal liability.[35] Thus, as we saw in the chapters on the pretrial and trial processes, despite Ford's acquittal, the Pinto case was one of the first modern cases that hinted at the possibilities for enterprise or organizational liability; what the Arthur Andersen case represents is a dramatic, contemporary example of its applied potential. Indeed, the Andersen precedent has already had a major impact. In August 2005, to spare itself from a potentially lethal criminal indictment like that which devastated Arthur Andersen, KPMG, the nation's fourth largest accounting firm, chose to admit in open court that a number of its executives had engaged in unlawful and fraudulent tax shelter scams, and agreed to pay nearly a half billion dollar penalty. KPMG, which like Andersen is set up as a limited liability partnership rather than a corporation, thus will be allowed to continue serving its roughly 1,000 corporate clients, but it will in effect be required to assist government prosecutors develop their cases against the individual partners.[36]

Commentators on corporate social control have long debated whether it is better for individual executives or business organizations to be the target of criminal sanctions. That is, is it best to apply the law to "corporate criminals" or "criminal corporations"? The most common answer—and one that is embedded in prevailing American law—is that the preferred statutory scheme should generally provide for both individual and enterprise liability, with the appropriateness of each to be determined case by case through the exercise of sound prosecutorial discretion.[37] Current legal rules concerning enterprise liability came into being after many years of discussion over such foundational issues as whether an organization could even possess the requisite mental state (*mens rea*, or guilty mind) to commit a crime.[38] Indeed, though criminal intent was first laid upon a corporation in the United States in 1908,[39] and nine years later in England,[40] it was not until 1956 that the influential American Law Institute (ALI) put its formal imprimatur on the doctrine of corporate criminal liability by incorporating it into the Model Penal Code (MPC).[41] Though the MPC's "dauntingly complex rule of corporate liability" was hardly met with universal acclaim, over the next 50 years the concept of corporations as criminals has been drafted into state and federal codes, and supported by legal decisions—though hardly in the orderly and rational way that the drafters of the MPC had envisioned.[42] One interesting note: The reader may recall how Indiana's adoption of the MPC's provisions allowed the prosecution to proceed against Ford in 1979-80, yet it was not until 1987 that Texas became the last state in the United States to recognize that business entities could be held criminally responsible.[43]

At the time the MPC and its corporate criminal provisions debuted in 1956, there was deeply rooted overseas resistance to the concept.[44] Since then, John Coffee has observed, an "incipient consensus" has developed around the world that the criminalization of corporate crime is a requirement for satisfactory control of organizational lawlessness.[45] For example, in Japan, where there has never been a general provision for corporate criminal responsibility, there is now a statutory exception for acts of environmental pollution.[46] In England, a 1987 ferry disaster that caused the death of 193 passengers stoked extensive debate on the concept of corporate manslaughter, both by the judiciary and a special-appointed Law Commission.[47] From 1994 to 1999, the first three successful prosecutions for corporate manslaughter in English history were carried out, while in 1996 the government published a draft proposal to create the new offense of "corporate killing."[48] In 1988, the Council of Europe recommended that member states give consideration to changing their criminal codes, if necessary, to include corporate criminal liability with the following four provisions:

1. The offender's act should be related to his or her employment, even if the offense is alien to the corporation's purposes;

2. liability should attach regardless of whether a natural person who committed the act can be identified;

3. the enterprise can be exonerated if "all necessary steps" had been taken to inhibit the behavior; and

4. corporate liability should be imposed in addition to individual liability.[49]

Some scholars—most notably Gilbert Geis and Sally Simpson—have argued persuasively that the doctrine of corporate criminal liability may have developed more as a result of expedience rather than any empirical evidence of its effectiveness.[50] And clearly, more and better empirical research is needed.[51] Nevertheless, there is no question that the legal concept has never been more settled than it is today. Accordingly, widely ranging methods, apart from the traditional practice of fining businesses, have been proposed or implemented to penalize corporate and other business enterprises, including: restitution, corporate community service, managerial intervention, government contract proscription, equity fines, mandatory adverse publicity, and even, in very rare cases, forced dissolution (the "corporate death penalty").[52]

A host of legal and institutional developments specifically related to corporate, organizational, and enterprise criminal liability have occurred in the 25 years since the Pinto case vitalized the concept. A brief survey follows of three of the most interesting and influential changes: (1) the federal Organizational Sentencing Guidelines; (2) the U.S. Justice Department Corporate Prosecution Guidance; and (3) the "collective knowledge" doctrine of *U.S. v. Bank of New England.*

Organizational Sentencing Guidelines

On November 1, 1991, a set of sentencing guidelines applicable only to organizational defendants in federal criminal courts became the law of the United States. As noted in Chapter 3, the U.S. Sentencing Commission was created in 1984 to review the federal enforcement system and develop concrete and equitable guidelines, and by 1987, it had established a separate set of guidelines for individual defendants.[53] With the adoption of the organizational guidelines, at least two messages seemed loud and clear in 1991. First, for law professors and white-collar crime defense attorneys, the message was that any lingering debate over such matters as whether corporations were legally capable of committing crimes or being criminally sanctioned was simply no longer relevant; under the new guidelines, there was no question that they were capable of both. Second, for senior executives and corporate counsel, the message was that continued reliance on the time-honored rogue employee (or "bad apple") scapegoat defense for corporate crimes was now a risky proposition; under the new guidelines, not only could the corporation be punished, it could be punished severely if it did not take steps to anticipate and prevent wrongdoing by individual employees.

The organizational guidelines mainly determine the offense levels in the same way as the individual guidelines, but the method for setting fines is much more complex. Employing what is commonly termed a "carrot and stick" approach, the guidelines provide for substantial increases in potential fines (through high baseline levels and certain "aggravating factor" multipliers), but offer significant fine reductions for two "mitigating factors": (a) corporate compliance in having implemented programs designed to prevent and detect corporate crimes, and/or (b) corporate cooperation in having voluntarily disclosed wrongdoing to the government.[54] The incentives for corporate compliance and cooperation go right to the heart of the organizational guidelines, which emphasize that the larger an organization, the more stringent the expectations for effective compliance programming. Consequently, the guidelines are also quite sensitive and explicit about what sentencing courts should look for. For instance, the guidelines require due diligence in designing, implementing, and enforcing an effective compliance program, and specify criteria that have become widely known as the "Seven Steps":

1. The establishment of compliance standards and procedures;

2. the designation of high-level personnel as having responsibility to oversee the program;

3. the avoidance of delegating authority to persons known to have a propensity to engage in illegalities;

4. taking steps to communicate effectively the standards and procedures;

5. the establishment of monitoring and auditing systems to detect violations and of a reporting system by which employees can report criminal conduct of others within the organization without fear of reprisals;

6. consistent enforcement of standards through disciplinary mechanisms, including the discipline of individuals responsible for overseeing compliance structures when there is a failure to detect an offense; and

7. the organization taking all reasonable steps to respond appropriately to an offense that has occurred and to prevent further similar offenses, including any necessary modifications to its programs.[55]

As noted in our discussion of Enron's legacy earlier, the Sarbanes-Oxley Act of 2002 directed the U.S. Sentencing Commission to review the organizational guidelines to make sure institutional wrongdoing was adequately addressed following the wave of scandals. In the first changes to the organizational guidelines since they became law in 1991, the Commission adopted amendments designed to foster a culture of compliance by adopting even more rigorous criteria for evaluating an effective compliance program. In sum, the amended guidelines: (1) provide incentives for a demonstrated commitment to ethical conduct as well as legal compliance, and establish minimum standards to this end; (2) broaden the role of senior management and the board of directors with respect to compliance programs; and (3) require periodic risk assessments as part of any effective compliance program.[56] Working in combination with Sarbanes-Oxley's ethics provisions, the amended organizational guidelines' heightened emphasis on ethical behavior has transformed what was a limited, esoteric market for business ethics consultants into a bustling cottage industry intent on servicing corporations' insatiable demand for experts to assist them in offering company-wide ethics education programs, creating ethics codes, hiring and training ethics officers, establishing ethics hotlines, and so on. Many of the nation's business schools have also responded, with required rather than recommended courses in business ethics—often with case studies of both Ford Pinto and Enron as assigned reading. It is too soon to tell whether this new focus on ethics education will make a difference in the way corporations do business, though research for the U.S. Sentencing Commission has found that most employees believe the organizational guidelines have had limited, insignificant, or negative effect on their companies' compliance efforts.[57]

In practice, prosecutions of corporations and other business organizations still constitute a very small minority of federal criminal cases, even though the number of federal criminal offenses for which a corporation could be convicted has been estimated to be more than 300,000.[58] For those organizations actually sentenced under the guidelines, a 1995 study indicated that well over 90 percent were "closely held" companies controlled by a small number of owners, and all but a few had been in business for 10 years or less. The vast majority, nearly 80 percent, had fewer than 50 employees, and about one in 10 was a recidivist.[59] It has even been suggested that with less than 5 percent of convicted and sentenced organizations being larger, publicly traded corporations, politically powerful companies may actually prefer the passage of the largely symbolic corporate criminal liability statutes to other alternatives.[60] Commenting on the available statistical data, Gilbert Geis concluded that "[i]t may be that the debate on corporate criminal liability, which tends to visualize the culprits as being the large and powerful Fortune 500 organizations, is dealing with an issue that is far from the reality of what actually happens . . . [yet] the recent outbreak of cases involving giant corporate business, exemplified by the Enron and Arthur Andersen scandals, may herald a shift in enforcement priorities."[61] And despite the relative rarity of corporate criminal prosecutions, Kathleen Brickey firmly believes that legal threat of enterprise liability is clearly the "300-pound gorilla in the room—especially after the Arthur Andersen case."[62]

Principles of Federal Prosecution of Business Organizations

As discussed previously, both the SEC and Justice Department adopted guidelines in the late 1990s to help prosecutors determine when corporations should be charged in addition to, or instead of, individuals when corporate crimes occur. Since then, as a direct result of the Enron, WorldCom, and other scandals, the Justice Department has issued revised guidelines that essentially call for increased emphasis on the authenticity of a corporation's level of cooperation with the investigation and the effectiveness of its compliance program.[63] The heightened priority the revisions give to corporate criminal prosecutions was made clear in an infamous internal memo sent by a senior Justice official to every U.S. Attorney's office in the country, a part of which reads: "Too often business organizations, while purporting to cooperate with a [Justice] Department investigation, in fact take steps to impede the quick and effective exposure of the complete scope of wrongdoing.

The revisions make clear that such conduct should weigh in favor of a corporate prosecution."[64]

The revisions, which offer details far beyond the scope of our discussion here, complement the broader reforms and objectives of the Sarbanes-Oxley Act, and in some ways mirror the organizational guidelines' use of a "carrot and stick" approach to cooperation and compliance. Yet, the heightened sense of urgency embodied in the revised guidelines, along with the increased scrutiny of corporate policies and practices, "send a clear message that the Justice Department believes the threat of [corporate] criminal prosecution can serve as a catalyst for positive change in a corporation's culture."[65] While the threat has not yet been transformed into a noticeable increase in the frequency of organizational prosecutions, it is equally clear that both legal doctrine and institutional policy are currently poised to support any federal prosecutor who may choose to exercise the "nuclear option" of corporate criminal liability.

U.S. v. Bank of New England

Given the often complex and decentralized nature of corporate decisionmaking, it is often difficult, if not impossible, to prove that any single corporate agent acted with the requisite intent or knowledge to commit a crime. However, under the judicially created "collective knowledge" doctrine, this will not prevent a corporation or other business organization from being convicted. The doctrine essentially considers an organization's knowledge to include the combined knowledge and intent of all of its employees.[66] Though the doctrine had been hinted at in previous court decisions, in 1987 *U.S. v. Bank of New England* expressly adopted the doctrine and became the leading case applying collective knowledge principles to corporate criminality.[67] To summarize the facts of the case, banks are required by law to file reports of any customer currency transactions involving $10,000 or more within 15 days, under penalty of law. Though the window tellers in this case took the deposits, different bank employees had the responsibility of filing the currency transaction reports (CTRs), which they failed to do. The bank was prosecuted. The jury convicted it after being instructed that the bank had to be viewed as an institution, and that the bank's knowledge is the sum of the knowledge of all the employees. The Bank argued on appeal that the prosecution had to show that the employees who failed to file the CTRs had actual knowledge of the transactions. The appellate court rejected the argument, concluding that in light of the realities of modern corporate organizational structure, collective knowledge instructions were "not only proper but necessary."[68]

Since the *Bank of New England* case was decided, the collective knowledge doctrine has been applied mainly to regulatory offenses rather than specific intent crimes, and has not given rise to the flood of corporate criminal prosecutions some had feared. Nevertheless, its approach to linking the two fundamental requirements of proof for nearly every crime—an act accompanied by a mental state, usually knowledge or intent—in complex corporate organizations has become accepted legal doctrine. Collective knowledge principles were utilized expressly in several institutional savings and loan cases during the 1990s, and implicitly in the recent landmark prosecution of Arthur Andersen.[69]

Despite these developments and the relatively small number of corporate prosecutions, the concept of organizational crime remains controversial, and some critics continue to argue against the application of criminal sanctions to corporate and other business enterprises, primarily on three grounds. First, they challenge the deterrent effect of the sanction, essentially because "corporations don't commit crimes, people do."[70] Second, they question the retributive function because corporate criminal sanctions may actually end up punishing innocent shareholders (by reducing the value of their shares) and consumers (by increasing the costs of goods and services).[71] Third, they contest the efficiency of organizational liability, arguing that economic analysis shows that, on the whole, civil liability may deter unlawful corporate conduct at less cost than criminal liability.[72] Although a detailed analysis of each objection is beyond the scope of this chapter, a few comments are in order, particularly because the Pinto prosecution—along with other important cases like the Arthur Andersen prosecution—involved organizational rather than individual defendants. We suggest that, in many instances, sanctioning the organization is the most prudent and equitable policy, and thus prosecutors' options should not be confined to imposing individual criminal liability.

The critics' first objection—that people, not corporations, commit crimes—ignores the reality that the labyrinthian structure of many modern corporations often makes it extremely difficult to pinpoint individual responsibility for specific decisions. Even in cases in which employees who carried out criminal activities can be identified, controversial questions remain. John S. Martin, a former U.S. Attorney who actively prosecuted corporate and white-collar crime cases, comments that when individual offenders can be identified they "often turn out to be lower-level corporate employees who never made a lot of money, who never benefited personally from the transaction, and who acted with either the real or mistaken belief that if they did not commit the acts in question their jobs might be in jeopardy." Further, says Martin, "they may have believed that their superior was aware and approved of the crime, but could not honestly testify to a specific conversation or other act of the superior that would support an indictment of the superior."[73] Thus, a thorough investigation may well lead a prosecutor to conclude that indictments against individuals simply cannot be justified, even though the corporation benefited from a clear violation of a criminal statute. Such a result would disserve the deterrent function.

The existence of corporate criminal liability also provides a powerful incentive for top officers to supervise middle- and lower-level management more closely. Individual liability, in the absence of corporate liability, encourages just the opposite: top executives may take the attitude of "don't tell me, I don't want to know." In the words of Peter Jones, former chief legal counsel at Levi Strauss, "a fundamental law of organizational physics is that bad news does not flow upstream." Only when directives come from the upper echelon of the corporation "will busy executives feel enough pressure to prevent activities that seriously threaten public health and safety."[74] For a similar reason, proponents of the conservative "Chicago School" of law and economic thought advocate corporate rather than individual sanctioning: a firm's control mechanisms will be more efficient than the state's in deterring misconduct by its agents and will bring about adequate compliance with legal standards as long as the costs of punishment outweigh the potential benefits.[75]

The second objection—that the cost of corporate criminal fines is actually borne by innocent shareholders and consumers—also seems unfounded. With regard to shareholders, whether individual or institutional, incidents of corporate criminal behavior may give the owners the right to redress the diminution of their interest by filing a derivative suit against individual officers and/or members of the board of directors. Although the cost and the uncertainty of winning such a suit may be high, shareholders must regard this cost as one of the risks incurred when they invest in securities. Just as shareholders may occasionally be enriched unjustly through undetected misbehavior by their company, it is only fair to expect them to bear a part of the burden on those occasions when illegality is discovered and duly sanctioned.

Next, it is simplistic, if not untenable, to argue that corporate criminal fines will simply be passed on to the consuming public through higher prices. Stephen Yoder, among others, notes that in such instances our economic system allows consumers to exert a type of indirect, collective control. If we assume that competition exists in the offending corporation's industry, the firm cannot simply decide to raise its prices to absorb the fine or the costs related to the litigation. If it does so, it risks becoming less competitive and suffering such concomitant problems as decreased profits, difficulty in securing debt and equity financing, curtailed expansion, and the loss of investors to more law-abiding corporations.[76]

The final objection—that civil remedies may be a cheaper and hence more efficient deterrent of unlawful conduct than criminal sanctions—also misses the mark. First, as we have seen throughout the book, it is common for corporate wrongdoing to be met by both criminal and civil responses, each seeking different moral and instrumental ends. Second, as Lawrence Friedman reminds us, deterrence and efficiency are not the only interests in play. Deterrence has never been regarded as the sole justification for criminal liability, and efficiency is but one basis for social policy. The pursuit of justice and the imposition of just deserts are also traditional and worthwhile considerations. Civil and criminal liabilities have distinct social meanings, and in the real world findings of civil and criminal liability are not transmutable for purposes of moral condemnation.[77]

Recalling a theme we explored earlier in discussing why criminal rather than civil sanctions were sought against Ford in the Pinto case, Dan Kahan concludes his broad investigation of social meaning in the context of corporate wrongdoing with a passage that emphasizes the civil-criminal distinction:

> Just as crimes by natural persons denigrate social values, so do corporate crimes. Members of the public show that they feel this way, for example, when they complain that corporations put profits ahead of the interests of workers, consumers, or the environment. Punishing corporations, just like punishing natural persons, is also understood to be the right way for society to repudiate the false valuations that their crimes express. Criminal liability "sends the message" that people matter more than profits and reaffirms the value of those who were sacrificed to "corporate greed."[78]

CONCLUDING THOUGHTS ON THE CRIMINAL LAW AND CORPORATE VIOLENCE

In 1947, two years before he wrote *Death of a Salesman*, Arthur Miller's play *All My Sons* appeared on Broadway.[79] During the course of the play, Joe Keller, a successful small manufacturer, is forced to accept individual responsibility and ultimately personal guilt for having knowingly sold, on one occasion during World War II, defective airplane engines to the government. Of course, the worst possible consequence follows: 22 pilots crash and are killed. The theater audience learns that while Keller was spared any legal punishment, his business partner was sent to jail for the fatal decision to sell the engines—even though it was made under severe business pressures. We realize that we are not doing Miller's play justice by focusing on a legal matter rather than the social psychological aspects of the play (it is perhaps like saying that *Crime and Punishment* is a murder mystery and *Les Miserables* is a story about the consequences of stealing bread), but the point we would like to make is that even though there were absolutely no legal precedents in 1947 for prosecuting a manufacturer for homicide, neither critics nor audiences had any problem recognizing that an important moral boundary had been violated and that a legal response as drastic as criminal prosecution was appropriate—even though, as Miller makes perfectly clear, perfect justice could never be achieved.

It was not until more than 30 years after *All My Sons* was first performed that life imitated art in a sleepy, rural Indiana community when, on September 13, 1978, an Elkhart County grand jury indicted the Ford Motor Company on three counts of reckless homicide. One of the 10 largest corporations in the world had been called to stand trial not for a regulatory offense but for recklessly causing the death of three human beings. As we have seen, Indiana prosecutor Michael Cosentino—who personified Andrew Jackson's adage that "one man with courage makes a majority"—led the fight against Ford with a volunteer staff and a $20,000 supplemental budget. Though he lost the battle by falling short of overcoming Ford's brigade of lawyers and virtually unlimited expense account, it may now be said that he won the war. By successfully negotiating significant legal, political, and resource obstacles to get the case to trial, he established an important moral, if not legal, precedent by relabeling what traditionally had been considered an instance of poor business judgment as a violent criminal act. Although a jury ultimately acquitted Ford, the real significance of the case was undiminished: a local community had expressed its outrage by requiring a corporation, which is legally considered a separate person cloaked with many Bill of Rights protections, to submit to the same legal mechanisms through which other actors in our society are from time to time judged.

Joseph Gusfield observed that governmental actions such as criminal prosecutions can be seen as ceremonial and ritual performances that designate the content of public morality and symbolize the public affirmation of social ideals and norms. Over time, these ideals and norms can—and inevitably do—change. In the 1930s, when it was first suggested to him that safety glass be installed, General Motors President Alfred P. Sloan refused, saying "accidents or no accidents, my concern in this matter is simply a matter of profit and loss." During the development of the Pinto 40 years later, Lee Iacocca, then president of Ford, was allegedly fond of saying "safety doesn't sell." One need not be an expert in organizational behavior or culture to interpret the signal that these kinds of comments send to line managers, design and safety engineers, and other employees on down the corporate ladder.

We are not suggesting that the Ford Pinto prosecution created a model for regulating auto safety; indeed, as indicated in the preceding chapter, no other criminal prosecutions of product liability cases on the scale of Pinto have occurred in the quarter-century since the trial. Rather, we believe the prosecution stood—and continues to stand—for something much broader: a symbolic declaration of the public's changed notions of what constitutes acceptable risk. In retrospect, this declaration appears to have had at least some practical impact. In the aftermath of the Pinto case came heightened business as well as consumer interest in crashworthiness and much improved government auto safety standards. We believe it is highly unlikely that we will ever again hear the kind of callous statements voiced by Sloan and Iacocca. Nonetheless, just as we will never know for certain whether Hester Prynne was truly chastened or not at the end of Nathaniel Hawthorne's *The Scarlet Letter*, we cannot say for certain whether Ford executives learned their lesson or were repentant following the Pinto debacle—especially given their continuing safety problems over the years with the Bronco II, Ranger, and Firestone-equipped SUVs.

Previously, we suggested that there may have been significance in the Pinto case having been prosecuted in Indiana rather than in a bellwether state such as California or New York: that even though Indiana was not (and is not) a state that signals what social trends are on the horizon, it may just be a place that tells us what has already arrived, and has penetrated into the American social fabric. This was, of course, not the first time that the Midwest has played host to a morality play or social movement involving sharp conflict between elementary business and social values. The Granger movement, farm belt populism, and La Follette progressivism all took root in the heartland—not among Marxist revolutionaries or student radicals, but among farmers, laborers, small-town merchants, and independent professionals. Biographers of two of the most influential white-collar crime scholars of the twentieth century—E.A. Ross and Edwin Sutherland—came to the conclusion that their solid Midwestern upbringing and values strongly influenced the direction of their life's work against wayward capitalists. In 1907, Ross, born in rural Iowa and raised in downstate Illinois, wrote *Sin and Society*—one of the earliest and most widely read progressive tracts on the wrongs of unfettered big business.[80] Interestingly, that book's Foreword was written by President Theodore Roosevelt, who expressed heartfelt support for Ross's attack on corporate greed; needless to say, times have changed. Further, it is Edwin Sutherland, a native Nebraskan who taught in Indiana, who is rightfully acknowledged as having laid the foundation for the modern study of corporate crime with his classic 1949 study, *White Collar Crime*, and who actually coined the term "white-collar crime" in 1939.[81]

While Upton Sinclair was not a Midwesterner, *The Jungle*, his gritty exposé of workplace conditions in the meatpacking industry, was researched and set in Chicago, as viewed through the life of a Lithuanian immigrant named Jurgis Rudkus.[82] Sinclair wrote in the urban tradition of Charles Dickens and Victor Hugo, and his work was serialized in newspapers much like his muckraking contemporaries Ida Tarbell and Lincoln Steffens. Sinclair employed gruesome detail to sensitize America to the hidden social and physical costs borne by its unorganized, exploitable urban immigrants. Yet, while *The Jungle* was a decisive force behind the passage in 1906 of both the Food and Drug Act and the Meat Inspection Act, it failed to generate reform in actual workplace conditions. Instead, its depiction of horrific turn-of-the-century packinghouse conditions and sausage-making processes lowered meat consumption in the United States for decades. As Sinclair himself lamented, he had aimed at the public's heart, but by accident hit its stomach instead.

A tragedy that did not miss America's heart was the Triangle Shirtwaist fire of 1911. In New York's garment district, 146 workers—most of them young immigrant women—died when a fire swept through the top three floors of a nine-story building where the fire escape doors were locked. While the fire gave rise to a failed criminal prosecution of the owners, a short-term boost to union organizing, and a few new safety laws around the country, the reform that received the greatest impetus from the tragedy (and represented its most lasting legacy) was the establishment of state workers' compensation laws. Without workers' compensation, employees who were hurt on the job were forced to file individual court claims. Long delays, absence of counsel, the inability of many urban workers to speak English, and lingering legal doctrines favoring employers often meant meager settlements for injured workers and their families—if they were fortunate enough to receive anything at all. For example, as we saw in Chapter 2, some states flatly denied wrongful death claims in workplace cases, holding that any legal claim a worker may have had was personal, and so expired with his or her last breath. In Lawrence Friedman's memorable phrase, for a time it was actually cheaper in some states for an employer to kill a worker than to scratch him.[83] However, the winds of progressive reform continued, kept alive in part by such tragedies as the Triangle Shirtwaist fire. Between 1911 and 1917 nearly every state legislature struck a compromise between business and worker interests, and adopted some form of workers' compensation—most of them modeled after the German system, which had been in place for at least 30 years.[84] In contrast, it is sad to note that there was no meaningful political response when in 1993 an inferno at the Kader Industrial Toy Factory in Thailand surpassed Triangle as the worst industrial fire in history. Neither did it receive much notice in the West, even though most of the stuffed toys and plastic dolls manufactured there were sold to the United States and other developed countries. Among other things, this demonstrates that in our globalized economy, the international community has not yet determined how best to respond to such tragedies.[85]

The law frequently seeks to accomplish one or both of two distinct, but not mutually exclusive, goals: whereas the law's distributive function seeks to allocate losses fairly when they occur in society, the reductive function seeks to reduce the incidence of harm in the first place. With respect to workplace harm, for example, the distributive function—making fair compensation to workers and their families— is approached primarily through the operation of workers' compensation laws. Fair determination and distribution of benefits is indispensable to any sense of workplace justice, of course, but in many instances the distributive goal should be secondary to the reductive goal; efficiently lowering the number of workplace deaths is obviously preferable to efficiently paying death benefits. There is no evidence, though, that our workers' compensation laws have ever provided employers with strong, effective incentives to reduce workplace accidents. With a patchwork quilt of state regulatory laws left to do the job, few states were willing to put local businesses at a competitive disadvantage by enacting and enforcing rigorous safety standards that would be ignored across state lines.

There were virtually no comprehensive federal laws designed to reduce workplace deaths and injuries across the country until 1970, when unions gained a long-sought-after objective by persuading Congress to pass OSHA. Labor's celebration was muted, however, when it became apparent that the agency's authority, resources, and standards would be politically compromised from the start. Even so, though gains in worker safety during the 1970s were agonizingly slow, inconsistent, and incremental, at least the curve was moving in the right direction. Thus, many within the ranks of government, labor, and business were stunned when the Bureau of Labor Statistics reported at the end of Ronald Reagan's first term as president that the number of occupational deaths in the United States had jumped 21 percent and injuries 13 percent. Following up on this report, *The Wall Street Journal* agreed with safety advocates that there was simply no other explanation for the higher rate of serious workplace accidents other than cost-cutting and less stress on safe practices—both of which were tolerated by an administration dedicated to government deregulation of business at virtually any cost.[86]

Yet, when our federalist system is working properly, the law will eventually compensate for such regulatory vacuums. Consequently, one dramatic response to the emasculation of workplace safety regulation that occurred in the 1980s was an increase in the number of states that were willing to prosecute corporations and their executives for workplace deaths and injuries. While prosecutions of environmental and financial crimes at both state and federal levels had become fairly common by the mid-1980s, it took three guilty verdicts in the celebrated 1985 corporate murder case from Illinois—*People v. Film Recovery Systems*—to raise the stakes with respect to crimes against worker safety.[87] Once again, the Midwest played host to a precedent-setting criminal trial that had corporate America tuned in.

The *Film Recovery Systems (FRS)* case shifted the consumer safety context of the Pinto case to the workplace, but its underlying proposition was similar: creating substantial and unnecessary workplace risks, previously considered an unfortunate but inevitable cost of doing business, should be disfavored by the threat of a criminal prosecution. *FRS* had an immediate impact on the scope, if not the exercise, of prosecutorial discretion nationwide. Except in California, workplace homicide prosecutions remain relatively rare, yet there is no question that the absolute sense of prosecutorial immunity that may have provided comfort to sweatshop employers for many years prior to *FRS* is gone forever. One needs only to recall the fate of the owner of Imperial Food Products, who in 1992 was sentenced to 20 years in prison for being responsible for the deaths of 25 of his workers.[88]

To further understand the change in legal consciousness underpinning workplace safety prosecutions, consider an analogy to homicide prosecutions of drivers who have recklessly caused a fatal accident. Owning and operating a business, like owning and operating a motor vehicle, is generally a socially encouraged and beneficial act. Likewise, running most businesses today, like driving cars and trucks, is regulated primarily by a set of administrative rules and fines. In either case, no moral stigma is risked: if you violate a rule, you normally pay a fine or, if you cause harm by your negligence, you are assessed damages. Yet when a reckless driver deviates so far from acceptable standards of driving that it takes a life and shocks the conscience of the community, we now see it as quite proper for a criminal prosecution to take place—simply issuing a traffic ticket and asking that the victim's family be paid something will not ordinarily be viewed as an adequate response. Moral stigma needs to attach in some way, whether it be through a court ordering the convicted defendant to pay a substantial criminal fine, suffer public humiliation, and/or spend time in jail. What cases such as *Film Recovery Systems*—and the Ford Pinto case—really stand for is this: There are certain ways of doing business that are just too objectionable to allow them to be bought and paid for, and recklessly exposing workers or consumers to substantial and unnecessary risks is one of them.

There were a number of other parallels between the *Film Recovery Systems* and Ford Pinto cases, five of which merit brief comment. First, each generated extensive publicity and debate nationwide.

Through the popular press, law reviews, and business journals, the public, the legal profession, and business management communities were educated as to the changing alliance between corporations and the criminal law. Second, each was conceived as a response to a conflict between outdated corporate values and the public's notions of acceptable risk. Third, each sought to use the criminal law to achieve both moral and instrumental ends—that is, to symbolize changed moral boundaries and to deter future transgressions. Fourth, each added something to our conception of corporate crime in that the costs were not financial and remote, but violent and personal. Finally, neither prosecution was intended to represent a preferred approach to traditional civil or regulatory responses; the unique and extreme circumstances surrounding each case led them to be borne of necessity, in the exercise of sound prosecutorial discretion.

Further comment on the last point is in order. As we have seen, criminal prosecution is just one of several legal mechanisms available to hold corporations accountable for their misbehavior. Virtually every experienced prosecutor we have met views criminal prosecution of businesses as appropriate only in a limited number of especially egregious cases. The criminal law is just one of many tools that can serve to reduce death and injury in the workplace. Workers need better equipment, more education, and the increased confidence and right to participate in their own workplace environment. We need workers' compensation insurance premiums that more substantially reflect a firm's experience-rating, and a way of awarding government contracts that factors in a company's safety record. And we need more responsive and better-funded federal safety regulation. Though funding for OSHA has fluctuated—sometimes wildly—during the past several administrations (both Republican and Democrat), overall some positive changes have been made at the agency, including greatly increased civil penalties and markedly improved response to worker complaints. While there remains much room for improvement, it may just be that we have begun to learn from our own nation's historical mistakes, the educational efforts of independent safety researchers, and dramatic landmarks such as *Film Recovery Systems*.

Criminal prosecutions, though, represent society's severest reprimand, a legal option of last resort. As such, they should not expand into unexplored territory too easily. Thus, a fundamental question may be raised: Is it even appropriate to use the criminal law to change what is considered morally blameworthy, rather than to simply reassert traditional social and legal norms? In other words, is it justifiable for the criminal law to intrude into the traditionally civil realm of workplace safety—or product liability, or environmental health—if not only business, but government and society as well, have traditionally accommodated a relatively high trade-off between safety and profit?

We believe this is a problem only if we ignore the reciprocal relationship between the criminal law and the public's perception of what counts as morally blameworthy. Evaluations of criminal laws usually focus on whether they offer adequate punishment and deterrence to both actual and potential wrongdoers. However, as many legal commentators over the years have observed, perhaps what most distinguishes the criminal law is its operation as a system of moral education. The public often learns what conduct is blameworthy largely from what gets punished. For example, consider the insider trading scandals on Wall Street previously discussed. How many people ever even thought about insider trading before a federal prosecutor exposed the massive securities frauds, with briefcases stuffed with money moving between New York investment bankers much like drug money moves in Miami?

Our point is that the criminal law, like society, does not remain static; it not only can but must create new traditions. As John Coffee has noted, the first and most significant modern white-collar crimes to be criminally prosecuted on a national scale—price-fixing, bribery, and securities fraud—were regulatory offenses in the sense of not being "Ten Commandment" crimes listed on the two tablets Moses brought down from the mountain.[89] The quieter, less theatrical nature of civil law limits its ability to socialize such behavior. It is the criminal law's more dramatic nature that is better suited to morally condemn and stigmatize—and thus deter—business behavior that is in direct conflict with fundamental values of society. And though most prosecutors continue to be more likely to seek criminal charges for financial rather than health and safety crimes, the recent increase in environmental crime prosecutions indicates that dramatic change in both consciousness and policy is possible.

With respect to traditional crimes of violence—what many call "street crimes" today—early English law was largely oriented toward private compensation for crime victims and their families. Guilt for most offenses—including many homicides—could be discharged simply by making cash or property payments. While the concept of blood money may have made perfect economic sense then, the law has a moral face as well—one that maintains that human health and safety should be considered no less sacrosanct when denied by corporations, which should be prohibited from purchasing exemption from moral condemnation.[90] We believe there is increasing evidence that our legal system is evolving, however slowly, into one that reflects a very different moral perspective—one insisting that a similar price be paid for true crimes of violence, whether inflicted in city streets or from corporate suites. In this new context, the obstacles to corporate criminal prosecutions, though still formidable, are not quite as intimidating as they used to be.

NOTES

1.   John Braithwaite and Gilbert Geis, "On Theory and Action for Corporate Crime Control," *Crime & Delinquency* 28 (April 1982), pp. 294–295. See also John E. Conklin, *"Illegal But Not Criminal": Business Crime in America*. Englewood Cliffs, NJ: Prentice Hall, 1977, pp. 109–110.

2.   Michael L. Benson and Tamara D. Madensen, "Situational Crime Prevention and White-Collar Crime," in Henry N. Pontell and Gilbert Geis (eds.), *International Handbook of White-Collar Crime*. New York: Kluwer Scientific, forthcoming.

3.   Braithwaite and Geis, "On Theory and Action for Corporate Crime Control," pp. 295–296. This does not mean that there are no efforts to detect corporate illegalities. A central task of regulatory agencies is to determine when corporations violate legal standards. However, the relationship between the control efforts of these agencies and subsequent criminal prosecutions is problematic and subject to a variety of contingencies.

4.   Michael L. Benson and Francis T. Cullen, *Combating Corporate Crime: Local Prosecutors at Work*. Boston: Northeastern University Press, 1998, pp. 172–194.

5.   John C. Coffee, Jr., "The Metastasis of Mail Fraud: The Continuing Story of the 'Evolution' of a White-collar Crime," *American Criminal Law Review* 21 (No.1, 1983), p. 19. Henry Pontell has observed that the criminal justice system has a limited "capacity to punish," but the system's capacity is particularly circumscribed in the domain of white-collar crime control. See Henry N. Pontell, "System Capacity and Criminal Justice: Theoretical and Substantive Considerations," in Harold E. Pepinsky (ed.), *Rethinking Criminology*. Beverly Hills, CA: Sage, 1982, pp. 137–138. More generally, see his *A Capacity to Punish: The Ecology of Crime and Punishment*. Bloomington: Indiana University Press, 1984.

6.   Benson and Cullen, *Combating Corporate Crime: Local Prosecutors at Work*, pp. 148–150.

7.   *Ibid.*, p. 148.

8.   *Ibid.*, pp. 151–152.

9.   Benson and Cullen, *Combating Corporate Crime: Local Prosecutors at Work*, pp. 152–153.

10.   William J. Maakestad, "States' Attorneys Stalk Corporate Murderers," *Business and Society Review* 56 (Winter 1986), p. 23; Charles B. Schudson, Ashton P. Onellion, and Ellen Hochstedler, "Nailing an Omelet to the Wall: Prosecuting Nursing Home Homicide," in Ellen Hochstedler (ed.), *Corporations as Criminals*. Bevery Hills, CA: Sage, p. 139. See generally, Benson and Cullen, *Combating Corporate Crime: Local Prosecutors at Work*.

11.   Benson and Cullen, *Combating Corporate Crime: Local Prosecutors at Work*, pp. 88–89.

12.   Maakestad, "States' Attorneys Stalk Corporate Murderers," pp. 23–24. By contrast, as noted in our discussion of the possible relationship between weakening OSHA controls and recent work-related prosecutions, the absence of a regulatory option may precipitate attempts to sanction corporations criminally. This issue receives additional comment later in this section.

13.   As indicated in the introduction to this chapter, we will comment on these issues in later sections. For relevant literature, see John Braithwaite, *Corporate Crime*

in the Pharmaceutical Industry. London: Routledge and Kegan Paul, 1984, pp. 308, 319–328; Eliezer Lederman, "Criminal Law, Perpetrator and Corporation: Rethinking a Complex Triangle," *Journal of Criminal Law and Criminology* 76 (Summer 1985), pp. 285–340; Brent Fisse, "The Duality of Corporate and Individual Criminal Liability," in Hochstedler (ed.), *Corporations as Criminals,* pp. 69–84; Benson and Cullen, *Combating Corporate Crime: Local Prosecutors at Work;* see also Clinard and Yeager, *Corporate Crime.*

14   Braithwaite and Geis, "On Theory and Action for Corporate Crime Control," p. 295; Diane Vaughan, *Controlling Unlawful Organizational Behavior: Social Structure and Corporate Misconduct.* Chicago: University of Chicago Press, 1983, p. 89.

15   Maakestad, "States' Attorneys Stalk Corporate Murderers," p. 23; Vaughan, *Controlling Unlawful Organizational Behavior,* pp. 98–99; John Hagan, Ilene H. Nagel (Bernstein), and Celesta Albonetti, "The Differential Sentencing of White-Collar Offenders in Ten Federal District Courts," *American Sociological Review* 45 (October 1980), p. 818. See also Jack Katz, "Concerted Ignorance: The Social Construction of Cover-up," *Urban Life* 8 (October 1979), pp. 295–316.

16   Kenneth Mann, *Defending White-collar Crime: A Portrait of Attorneys at Work.* New Haven: Yale University Press, 1985, p. 7.

17   *Ibid.,* pp. 7–8.

18   Vaughan, *Controlling Unlawful Organizational Behavior,* pp. 92–93.

19   Maakestad, "States' Attorneys Stalk Corporate Murderers," pp. 22–23.

20   *Ibid.,* p. 23. More generally, see Robert C. Holland, "Problems in the Investigation of White Collar Crime: A Case Study," *International Journal of Comparative and Applied Criminal Justice* 8 (Spring 1984), pp. 21–41.

21   Schudson et al., "Nailing an Omelet to the Wall: Prosecuting Nursing Home Homicide," p. 138.

22   Braithwaite and Geis, "On Theory and Action for Corporate Crime Control," p. 299. See also Braithwaite, *Corporate Crime in the Pharmaceutical Industry,* p. 342.

23   Leonard Orland, "Reflections on Corporate Crime: Law in Search of Theory and Scholarship," *American Criminal Law Review* 17 (1980), p. 511.

24   There is little empirical research that has systematically assessed judicial attitudes toward the use of criminal sanctions in instances of illegal corporate behavior. As noted in Chapter 2, however, public surveys provide little support for the view that corporate lawlessness is defined as morally neutral. In light of these data, we suspect that while his assessment is accurate for some judges, Orland has overstated the extent to which jurists see "corporate crime as nothing more than aggressive capitalism." Compare this view with the more complex portrait of judges' attitudes toward "white-collar" criminality found in Kenneth Mann, Stanton Wheeler, and Austin Sarat, "Sentencing the White-collar Offender," *American Criminal Law Review* 17 (1980), pp. 479–500.

25   John Hagan and Patricia Parker, "White-Collar Crime and Punishment: The Class Structure and Legal Sanctioning of Securities Violations," *American Sociological Review* 50 (June 1985), p. 313.

26   Jack Katz, "The Social Movement Against White-Collar Crime," in Egon Bittner and Sheldon L. Messinger (eds.), *Criminology Review Yearbook,* vol. 2. Beverly Hills, CA: Sage, 1980, pp. 161–184; Donald I. Baker, "To Indict or Not to

Indict: Prosecutorial Discretion in *Sherman Act* Enforcement," in Sheldon L. Messinger and Egon Bittner (eds.), *Criminology Review Yearbook*. vol. 1. Beverly Hills, CA: Sage, 1979, pp. 409–410; Schudson et al., "Nailing an Omelet to the Wall: Prosecuting Nursing Home Homicide," p. 138; Bruce L. Ottley, "Criminal Liability for Defective Products: New Problems in Corporate Responsibility and Sanctioning," *Revue Internationale de Droit Penal*, vol. 53, p. 151.

27   Benson and Cullen, *Combating Corporate Crime: Local Prosecutors at Work*, pp. 138–172.

28   Susan P. Shapiro, "The Road Not Taken: The Elusive Path to Criminal Prosecution for White-collar Offenders," *Law & Society Review* 19 (No. 2, 1985), pp. 193–198; Jed S. Rakoff, "The Exercise of Prosecutorial Discretion in Federal Business Fraud Prosecutions," in Brent Fisse and Peter A. French (eds.), *Corrigible Corporations and Unruly Law*. San Antonio: Trinity University Press, 1985, p. 182.

29   Shapiro, "The Road Not Taken: The Elusive Path to Criminal Prosecution for White-collar Offenders," p. 199. See also Nancy Frank, *Crimes Against Health and Safety*. New York: Harrow and Heston, 1985, p. 63; Coffee, "The Metastasis of Mail Fraud: The Continuing Story of the 'Evolution' of a White-collar Crime," p. 20; Schudson et al., "Nailing an Omelet to the Wall: Prosecuting Nursing Home Homicide," p. 138.

30   Magnuson was quoted in Gibson, "Corporate Crimes: Criminal Prosecutions Gaining More Favor," p. 6.

31   Ambrose Bierce, *The Unabridged Devil's Dictionary* (David E. Schultz and S.T. Joshi, eds.). Athens: University of Georgia Press, 2000. Thanks and a tip of the hat to Kathleen Brickey, who unearthed Bierce's wonderfully cynical definition and cites it in her introduction to "Enron's Legacy," p. 222.

32   Kristen Rouse, "Arthur Andersen," in *Encyclopedia of WCC*, pp. 57–58.

33   The giant Arthur Andersen accounting firm was actually organized as a limited liability partnership rather than a corporation, though it is treated similarly as a separate entity under the law and can be prosecuted separately from its officers and owners. Six months after the U.S. Supreme Court reversed the accounting firm's conviction, the Justice Department announced that it would not re-prosecute the case.

34   2004 Brickey interview with author.

35   Both Brickey and Bucy have published textbooks on corporate and white-collar crime that are widely used in law schools. Brickey, whose work has been cited extensively in this chapter, is widely considered the most influential legal scholar in the field of corporate criminal liability and is the author of a three-volume treatise on corporate criminal liability. See Brickey, *Corporate Criminal Liability: A Treatise on the Criminal Liability of Corporations, Their Officers, and Agents*, 2nd ed. Deerfield, IL: Clark Boardman Callaghan, 1992. Bucy has developed a systems or culture approach to corporate personhood, arguing that corporations possess an "ethos" that distinguishes them from the specific individuals who control or work for the organization. Her work has helped lay a theoretical foundation for expansion of the use of corporate criminal liability. See generally Bucy, "Corporate Ethos: A Standard for Imposing Corporate Criminal Liability," *Minnesota Law Review* 75 (1991). Another notable scholar is Peter French, a philosopher whose work on collective moral responsibility has been influential in justifying, on a theoretical level, collective (including corporate) criminal culpability. See Peter A. French, *Collective and Corporate Responsibility*. New York: Columbia University Press, 1984.

[36] Leon Lazaroff and Andrew Zajac, "KPMG Admits to $2.5 Billion Tax Fraud," *Chicago Tribune* (August 30, 2005), sec. 1, pp. 1–2. Less than two months after KPMG's guilty plea, federal prosecutors significantly widened the criminal cases against individual executives. See Glater, "Indictment Broadens in Shelters at KPMG," *The New York Times* (October 18, 2005), p. 1.

[37] Indeed, Brickey has stated that broad prosecutorial discretion is clearly both "necessary and proper in corporate and white collar criminal cases, in order to conserve resources, exercise judgment, and reserve enterprise liability for those truly egregious violations." 2004 Brickey interview with author.

[38] For example, in criminology, the major intellectual debate concerns attempts to construct theoretical explanations for corporate criminal liability. A lively debate between Donald Cressey, for whom such explanations are impossible, and John Braithwaite and Brent Fisee, for whom an explanation is quite possible, ended in what many observers considered a draw. For a brief summary of the arguments made by each side, see Geis, "Corporate Criminal Liability," in *Encyclopedia of WCC*, pp. 212–213.

[39] *N.Y. Central & Hudson R.R. Co. v. U.S.*, 212 U.S. 481 (1908).

[40] *Mousell Brothers v. London and North Western R.R.*, 2 K.B. 836 (1917).

[41] Gilbert Geis and Joseph DiMento, "Empirical Evidence and the Legal Doctrine of Corporate Criminal Liability," *American Journal of Criminal Law* 29 (Summer 2002), pp. 1, 4.

[42] Kathleen Brickey, "Rethinking Corporate Criminal Liability Under the Model Penal Code," *Rutgers Law Journal* 19 (1988), p. 593. Cited in Geis and DiMento, "Empirical Evidence," pp. 632–633.

[43] *Vaughn & Sons, Inc. v. State*, 737 S.W.2d 805 (Texas Crim. App. 1987). See Evan Kramer, "This 'Old Corporation Dog' Can Hunt: The Realized Doctrine of Corporate and Association Criminal Liability in Texas," *Texas Tech Law Review* 20 (1989), and Robert Hamilton, "Corporate Criminal Liability in Texas," *Texas Law Review* 47 (1968). Cited in Geis and DiMento, "Empirical Evidence," p. 14.

[44] Geis and DiMento, "Empirical Evidence," p. 9. One of the earliest and most vocal critics of corporate criminal liability under the Model Penal Code declared that "a substantial portion of the world rejects corporate criminal liability after more thought and contemplation than has ever been given to the subject in this country." Gerhard O.W. Mueller, "Mens Rea and the Corporation: A Study of the Model Penal Code Position on Corporate Criminal Liability," *University of Pittsburgh Law Review* 19 (1957), p. 35.

[45] John C. Coffee, "Foreword" to Richard Gruner, *Corporate Crime and Sentences*, (1994), p. ix. The early European shift toward the imposition of corporate criminal liability is documented briefly in The Law Commission, "General Principles: Criminal Liability of Corporations," [Working Paper No. 44, 1972], pp. 12–14. A more recent and comprehensive review of this development is The Law Commission, *Le Criminalisation Du Comportement Collective: Criminal Liability of Corporations* (Hans de Doelder and Klaus Tiedemann, eds., 1996). Cited in Geis and DiMento, "Empirical Evidence," p. 11, footnote 122.

[46] Geis and DiMento, "Empirical Evidence, " p. 14. Geis and DiMento make two additional points. First, in Japan a corporate conviction cannot be obtained without proving criminality on the part of at least one individual employee. Second, there is a paradox here: whereas Japanese culture tends to emphasize collective

responsibility for wrongdoing, the United States is far more individualistic. For further international perspectives, see generally John Braithwaite and Brent Fisse, "Varieties of Responsibility and Organizational Crime," *Law & Policy* 7 (1985).

[47]   An excellent discussion of the manslaughter prosecution under English law that arose following the Herald of Free Enterprise ferry disaster at Zeebrugge, Belgium, can be found in Celia Wells, *Corporations and Criminal Responsibility*. New York: Oxford University Press, 1993, pp. 44–48, 69–72. William Maakested, one of the authors of this book, served as a consultant to the prosecution in the ferry disaster case.

[48]   See, for example, Joanne Harris, "Wheels of Injustice," available at http://www.thelawyer.com (September 13, 2004), pp. 1–2. Though the legislation has been the subject of much debate since it was first proposed in 2000, it has not yet become law. For a timeline of recent cases and other events pertaining to this legislation, see also Norton Rose, "Insight Into Corporate Killing," available at http://www.nortonrose.com (June 2004), pp. 1–2

[49]   Geis and DiMento, "Empirical Evidence," p. 11.

[50]   See Geis and DiMento, "Emplirical Evidence," especially pp. 368–374. See also Sally Simpson, "Strategy, Structure and Corporate Crime," *Advances in Criminological Theory* 4 (1993). Even Kathleen Brickey, an ardent supporter of corporate criminal liability, has observed that "through the feat of anthropomorphic sleight of hand, the common law subtly transformed the inanimate 'corporation' into a 'person' capable of committing criminal delicts and harboring criminal intent." Brickey, "Rethinking Corporate Criminal Liability Under the Model Penal Code," *Rutgers Law Journal* 19 (1988), p. 593.

[51]   An extensive and thoughtful agenda for further empirical research on corporate criminal liability is presented in Geis and DiMento, "Empirical Evidence," pp. 13–16.

[52]   A few state criminal codes, and the Federal Sentencing Guidelines (Sec. 8C1.1), authorize a "corporate death penalty. The federal provision was used for the first time against a government defense contractor who supplied substandard screws, bolts, nuts and O-rings for space projects, misrepresenting them as highly tested products. The company, American Precision Components, Inc., had had a history of similar problems and admitted the fraud. See Brickey, *Corporate and White Collar Crime*, pp. 912–913.

[53]   Green, "Sentencing Guidelines," in *Encyclopedia of WCC*, p. 732.

[54]   *Ibid*, pp. 732–37, and Webb, Molo, and Hurst, "Understanding . . . Criminal Liability," p. 69.

[55]   Green, "Sentencing Guidelines, " p. 735. See also Department of Justice, *Department of Justice Manual*, Sec. 9-27.230.

[56]   Brickey, "Enron's Legacy," pp. 233–234, including footnotes 59–62.

[57]   Green, "Sentencing Guidelines," p. 736. Commission research has also concluded that the two most important environmental factors in an organization contributing to noncompliance are [1] renumeration incentives for unethical behavior and [2] employees' perceived threats of reprisal for reporting violations.

[58]   Brickey, "Enron's Legacy," p. 234. For a more detailed discussion see generally Vikramaditya S. Khanna, "Corporate Crime Legislation: A Political Economy Analysis," Michigan Law & Economics web site, and John C. Coffee, Jr., "Does

Unlawful Mean Criminal? Reflections on the Disappearing Tort/Crime Distinction in American Law," *Boston University Law Review* 71, especially pp. 216–219.

59   Green, "Sentencing Guidelines, " *Encyclopedia of WCC*, p. 733.

60   See generally Khanna, "Corporate Crime Legislation." Khanna presents three reasons why corporate interests may actually prefer legislative expansion of corporate criminal liability to expanded civil liability: (1) corporate criminal liability is generally less costly than civil liability; (2) corporate criminal liability is enforced by the DOJ only, whereas civil liability cases may be brought by private litigants and agencies like the SEC as well; and (3) corporate criminal liability may deflect attention from third parties, such as officers, directors, accountants, and underwriters.

61   See generally Geis and DiMento, "Empirical Evidence." For an abbreviated discussion, see Gilbert Geis, "Corporate Criminal Liability," in *Encyclopedia of WCC*, pp. 211–213. For a scathing parody of how government enforcement policies allow corporations to escape criminal prosecution see R. Mokhiber, "Playbook," *Corporate Crime Reporter*, vol. 19, no. 11 (March 14, 2005), pp. 5–6.

62   2004 Brickey interview with author.

63   Kathleen F. Brickey, "Enron's Legacy," *Buffalo Criminal Law Review* 8 (2004), pp. 235–237.

64   *Ibid.*, p. 235, footnote 67.

65   *Ibid.*, p. 240, footnote 84.

66   Webb, Molo, and Hurst, "Understanding . . . Criminal Liability," p. 625.

67   821 F.2d 844 (1st Cir. 1987).

68   *Ibid*, p. 856.

69   2004 Brickey interview with author.

70   This criticism is not new. For example, a Maine court in the mid-nineteenth-century declared: "[W]hen a crime or misdemeanor is committed under color of corporate authority, the individuals acting in the business, and not the corporation should be indicted." *State v. Great Works Milling & Mfg. Co.*, 20 Me. 41, 44 (1841). For a brief summary of the arguments for and against corporate criminal liability, see, for example, Brian Becker, "Corporate Successor Criminal Liability: The Real Crime," *American Journal of Criminal Law* 16, especially pp. 462–463. Both cited in Geis and DiMento, "Empirical Evidence," p. 342–343, footnotes 2, 7.

71   See generally, for example, V.S. Khanna, "Corporate Criminal Liability: What Purpose Does It Serve?" *Harvard Law Review* 109 (1996).

72   See generally, for example, Daniel Fischel and Alan Sykes, "Corporate Crime," *Journal of Legal Studies* 25 (1996).

73   John S. Martin, "Corporate Criminals or Criminal Corporations?," *Wall Street Journal* (June 19, 1985), sec. 1, p. 30.

74   Peter T. Jones, "Sanctions, Incentives and Corporate Behavior, " *California Management Review* 27 (Spring 1985), pp. 126–127.

75   One of the earliest and clearest arguments in favor of this position is found in Richard Posner, *Economic Analysis of Law*, 2nd ed. Boston: Little, Brown, 1977. For a response to the Chicago school of law and economic thought, see John C.

Coffee, "Corporate Crime and Punishment: A Non-Chicago of the Economics of Criminal Sanctions," *American Criminal Law Review* 17 (Spring 1980), pp. 419–476.

[76]   Stephen Yoder, "Criminal Sanctions for Corporate Illegality," *Journal of Criminal Law and Criminology* 69 (1978), p. 55. Note also that if publicity is used as a substitute for (or supplement to) a fine, the collective "sanctioning power" held by consumers is even more direct.

[77]   Lawrence Friedman, "In Defense of Corporate Criminal Liability," *Harvard Journal of Law & Public Policy* 23 (Summer 2000), especially pp. 4, 9–10, including footnote 103.

[78]   *Ibid.*, p. 10, footnote 94.

[79]   Arthur Miller, *All My Sons*. New York: Penguin Classics, 2000. In an interesting "life imitates art" scenario, the very first use of the corporate death penalty provision under the Federal Sentencing Guidelines involved a government defense contractor who supplied substandard screws, bolts, nuts, and O-rings for space projects. Brickey, *Corporate and White Collar Crime*, pp. 912–913.

[80]   E.A. Ross, *Sin and Society: An Analysis of Latter-Day Iniquity*. New York: Harper and Row, 1907.

[81]   Edwin H. Sutherland, *White Collar Crime*. New York: Holt, Rinehart and Winston, 1949. Sutherland reportedly first publicly used the term 10 years before the publication of his groundbreaking book at an academic conference of sociologists.

[82]   Upton Sinclair, *The Jungle*. Urbana, IL: University of Illinois Press, 1988, annotated edition.

[83]   For a fascinating history of the development of tort law in the United States during the nineteenth century, see Chapter 7 in Lawrence Friedman, *A History of American Law*, 3rd ed. New York: Touchstone, 2005.

[84]   A number of books on the Triangle Fire have appeared over the years. One of the best social history accounts can be found in David Von Drehle, *Triangle: The Fire That Changed America*. New York: Touchstone, 2003.

[85]   William Greider, *One World, Ready or Not*. New York: Touchstone, 1998, pp. 337–339.

[86]   See Simison, "Job Deaths and Injuries Seem to be Increasing After Years of Decline," *The Wall Street Journal* (March 18, 1986), sec. 1, p. 1.

[87]   See Debra Ross, "Film Recovery Systems," in *Encyclopedia of WCC*, pp. 319–320. While the guilty verdicts in the jury trial were reversed on appeal, the court refused to dismiss the charges in the indictment and cleared the case for retrial. Ultimately all three individuals entered guilty pleas and received sentences ranging from 30 months probation to three years in prison.

[88]   See Debra Ross, "Imperial Food Products," in *Encyclopedia of WCC*, pp. 415–417. Though the owner of IFP pleaded guilty to involuntary manslaughter and received a 20-year sentence, the plea bargain allowed his son, a senior manager in the operation, to escape prosecution.

[89]   Coffee, "Does Unlawful Mean Criminal?," pp. 216–219.

[90]   Friedman, "In Defense of Corporate Criminal Liability," p. 11.

Index